Literature of Consciousness

Cross-Roads.
Polish Studies in Culture, Literary Theory, and History

Edited by Ryszard Nycz
and Teresa Walas

Volume 8

Jakub Momro

Literature of Consciousness

Samuel Beckett – Subject – Negativity

Translated by Jan Pytalski and Cain Elliott

PL ACADEMIC RESEARCH

Bibliographic Information published by the Deutsche Nationalbibliothek
The Deutsche Nationalbibliothek lists this publication in the Deutsche
Nationalbibliografie; detailed bibliographic data is available in the internet at
http://dnb.d-nb.de.

Library of Congress Cataloging-in-Publication Data
Momro, Jakub, 1979-
  [Literatura swiadomosci. English]
  Literature of Consciousness : Samuel Beckett - subject-negativity / Jakub Momro ;
translated by Jan Pytalski and Cain Elliott.
      pages cm. — (Cross-Roads ; Volume 8)
  Includes bibliographical references.
  ISBN 978-3-631-62727-3
  1. Beckett, Samuel, 1906-1989—Criticism and interpretation. I. Pytalski, Jan,
translator. II. Elliott, Cain, 1983- translator. III. Title.
  PR6003.E282Z78147 2015
  848'.91409—dc23
                            2015008432

The Publication is funded by Ministry of Science and Higher Education of the
Republic of Poland as a part of the National Program for the Development of the
Humanities in 2012-2015.
This publication reflects the views only of the authors, and the Ministry cannot be held
responsible for any use which may be made of the information contained therein.

NARODOWY PROGRAM
ROZWOJU HUMANISTYKI

Cover Design:
© Olaf Gloeckler, Atelier Platen, Friedberg

ISSN 2191-6179
ISBN 978-3-631-62727-3 (Print)
E-ISBN 978-3-653-02590-3 (E-Book)
DOI 10.3726/978-3-653-02590-3

© Peter Lang GmbH
Internationaler Verlag der Wissenschaften
Frankfurt am Main 2015
All rights reserved.
PL Academic Research is an Imprint of Peter Lang GmbH.

Peter Lang – Frankfurt am Main · Bern · Bruxelles · New York ·
Oxford · Warszawa · Wien

This publication has been peer reviewed.
www.peterlang.com

Table of Contents

Preface

… To be an artist is to fail, as no other dare fail, that failure is his world and the shrink from it desertion, art and craft, good housekeeping, living.[1]
– Samuel Beckett

Art has no universal laws, though in each of its phases there certainly are objectively binding taboos. They radiate from canonical works. Their very existence defines what forthwith is no longer possible.[2]
– Theodor W. Adorno

The enigmaticalness of artworks remains bound up with history. It was through history that they became an enigma; it is history that ever and again makes them as such, and conversely, it is history alone – which gave them their authority – that holds at a distance the embarrassing question of their raison d'être.[3]
– Theodor W. Adorno

What is bad in artworks is a reflection that directs them externally, that forces them; where, however, they immanently want to go can only be followed by reflection, and the possibility to do this is spontaneous.[4]
– Theodor W. Adorno

In all likelihood, most of the readers and spectators of Beckett's plays sentence themselves, perhaps willingly, to a permanent fascination with author's face. In photographs, the author of *Endgame* seems to resemble one of the characters inhabiting his many works – with a sharp, penetrating look, his face is permanently furrowed with creases and with the passing of years, as Polish writer Andrzej Stasiuk observed, it increasingly resembled the inhuman shape of a rare mineral.[5] It is a sign of presence that announces yet another form – transformed, a victim of the merciless passage of degrading time. Beckett's face seems to be an emblem of his entire project as a writer, one that successfully led literary modernity to its conclusion. This point is made absolutely clear by his precise construction and conscious provision of space for what is chaotic, dark, unspeakable, and random.

---

1   Beckett, S. *Three Dialogues*, in *CE*, vol. 4, p. 563.
2   Adorno, T. *Aesthetic Theory*, translated by Robert Hullot-Kentor, Minneapolis 1997, p. 308.
3   Ibid., p. 120.
4   Ibid., p. 174.
5   See Stasiuk, A. "Twarz Samuela Becketta," *Kwartalnik Artystyczny*, 1996 no. 4, p. 157.

His face is what brings disillusionment to men who would like to treat themselves as self-aware subjects. At the same time, it preserves the force of sceptical powers, which are constituted by a willingness to save reason and its singularity. Finally, it forces language to undergo definite destruction – a process that is the agent for the revival of the poetic power of the word.

Wolfgang Iser meticulously noted all those troubles, fascinations and contradictions converging in the singular place where we ought to start our reading. Our goal would be to find sense in this text and interpret the world deposited within its boundaries. First, I would like to provide an extensive citation of Iser, which grasps the precise stakes of an encounter with Beckett for any reader:

> In some modern texts, this fact can be studied under almost experimental conditions. The works of Beckett are among those whose indeterminacy content is so high that they are often equated with a massive allegorization. The tendency to regard them as allegories is in itself a kind of exasperated form of meaning projection. What causes this exasperation, which can clearly only be pacified by imposing some meaning on the text? Beckett's works, with their extreme indeterminacy, cause a total mobilization of the reader's imagination; the effect of this, however, is that the totally mobilized world of imagination finds itself to be powerless when called upon to explain. And yet this impotence on the part of one's own imagination seems to be necessary if one is to accept Beckett's work at all, for the individuality of his text only becomes apparent when the world of our imagination is left behind. It is not surprising therefore, that one's first reaction is to mount a massive operation of meaning-projection in order to haul the texts back within the limits of normal thinking.
>
> If fiction stubbornly refuses to reveal the sought-after meaning, then the reader will decide what it has to mean. But then one realizes that by imposing an allegorical or unequivocal meaning onto the text, one's approach tends to be superficial or even trivial. Should not this allegorization be seen as an indication of the nature of our current conceptions and preconceptions rather than as a means of explaining the text? If so, then such texts will show us the fundamental lack of freedom resulting from our self-imposed confinement within the world of our own ideas. In making his reader experience the embarrassing predicament of the failure of his understanding, Beckett opens up a road to freedom which can be embarked on whenever we are prepared to shed the preconceived notion that so far have dominated our outlook.
>
> The works of Beckett provoke a desire for understanding, which can only be satisfied if we apply our own ideas to the text, to have them duly rejected as redundant. It is precisely this process that both stimulates and exasperates us, for who likes to learn that his own ideas have to be subjected to a fundamental revision if they are to grasp phenomena that seem to lie beyond their scope?[6]

---

6   Iser, W. "Indeterminacy and the Reader's Response in Prose Literature," in *Prospecting: From Reader Response to Literary Anthropology*, Baltimore 1993, pp. 27-28. See also, *Der implizite Leser. Kommunikationsformen des Romans von Bunyan bis Beckett*, München 1972. In English, *The Implied Reader: Patterns of Communication in Prose Fiction from Bunyan to Beckett*, Baltimore 1978.

All the fundamental questions concerning the exceptional status of Beckett's artistic project are present in the passage cited above: imagination, cognition and the understanding of crisis, or the invention and innovation that accompany the act of reading. Iser noticed a fundamental difficulty that surfaces during the reading of Beckett's works. It resides in the simultaneous presence of two contradictory tendencies and desires: the necessity to leave the writer's idiom intact in its autonomy, while establishing, along with every new act of reading, an equally necessary and different context that yields an understanding of the work. The logic that holds both in place is exceptionally demanding. The text is both an open invitation to experience a different world and a simultaneous announcement of the impossibility of arriving at this very destination. In this sense, the work seduces the reader precisely through an interpretive mechanism of exclusion. These two contradictory devices meet as parts of the interpretive experiment and experience of Beckett's work.[7] It is true that Beckett's works are a peculiar kind of trial, focused on probing the range of consciousness and capabilities of language, which allow for the pronouncement of the most basic and the most difficult intuitions about the human condition. It is also true that Beckett's work allows readers to experience, or live through, all of these contradictions as an important existential trials, rather than purely textual, philosophical or anthropological exercises.

Iser identifies an additional characteristic of Beckett's work that is perhaps the most intriguing. The author of *Endgame* constructs a critical apparatus through texts that are structurally closed, even hermetic. It is in this critical juncture that signs of the writer's originality are transformed into challenges for his readers, who must attempt to ascribe meaning to the traces of authorial inventiveness, which are dispersed over the surface of the text. Through this procedure, the effect of the crises purposefully evoked by the writer (concerning reference, the ontology of the literary work, and the category of the subject) become opportunities for the reader – chances for communication with the world by means of the text, raising questions about the character of these relations. In my opinion, it is from this simultaneous crisis and tipping point that one should commence a relationship with works of Beckett.

---

7   My intention is to introduce a vague category of experience that appears often in this
     study. Depending on the context, I will be interested in "experience" understood as a
     literary, linguistic or thought "experiment," as well as "familiarity" [*Erlebnis*], process
     and experience [*Erfharung*]. I will also use the term in relation to "happening," which is
     sometimes identical in meaning with experience understood as familiarity [*Erlebnis*], and
     which sometimes breaks apart its structure (in the sense of *Erfharung*). For the history
     of the term in contemporary philosophical discourse, see Jay, M. *Songs of Experience:
     Modern American and European Variations on a Universal Theme*, London 2005.

At this point, I ought to indicate main lines of my own interpretive procedure. Beckett is a central figure in this book, but its pages are not entirely occupied by his work. His plays, prose and poetry allowed me to understand that the questions posed in the language of his own creations – which are difficult to translate into other or "external" languages – confer with the central questions tackled by the most prominent thinkers of modernity. If we define the modernist debate as a discussion over the possibilities of existence, the status and shape of the subject, and individual consciousness that attempts to find its place in a world of radical alienation, in which art remains the last surviving method for restoring lost time and experience, then Beckett is one of the most important discussants. It is in this space that these two complex and ambiguous notions appear in different forms throughout this book (happening, experiment, experience, etc.). My interest was more often drawn to tracing and conceptualizing various transformations of forms of subjectivity, rather than strictly literary analysis. More than the universal character of different problems, I was interested in the multiple tensions born from the clash between consciousness and the world. These tensions constitute the building blocks of the history of the struggle of the modern subject with what is negative: death, the void, and the absence of sense and life's pretensions.

The second half of the book examines the following questions and lines of thought. First, I attempt to take a closer look at strategies employed by Beckett in constructing the subject, with its transformations and dependencies negotiated by figures of voice and death. In the third part, devoted entirely to reading the play *Not I*, my reflections work at understanding the relation between the happening (occurrence), the conditions of its possibility, and the range of expression and suffering which constitute the proof confirming the veracity of existence. In the chapter entitled "Dreams of Stability," I try to make out the unwieldy concept of constructing subjectivity that ranges from the early literary works of Beckett to the late works that occupy this first section. Looking at works from the late period of Beckett's activity, this first section begins from the perspective of Cartesian principles, which were already prominent early in his career. I also discuss an essay about Proust, whose work is juxtaposed with that of Schopenhauer (while still following and commenting on Beckett).

Are we therefore dealing with Beckett as a philosopher? Personally, I would struggle with providing a definite or final answer to this question. As Iser observed, Beckett puts questions of meta-language on a razor's edge. In order to talk about his texts we need to find new means of description, and continually establish new contexts. But this need is constantly thwarted by the impossibility of going beyond the horizon of the crisis of "perception and understanding." Beckett is a philosopher only insofar as the term is meant to designate not a systematic thinker and presenter of problems exclusively, but also a writer testifying to literature as a domain of thought. In other words, he is a philosopher inasmuch as I have attempted to read his texts as such, bearing in mind the impossibility of capitalizing on any economic exchange between his work and general theoretical discourses, notions and conceptualizations. The more Beckett's works "stay evanescent in their own immanence" – following Paul Klee – the more they demand to be read as an extremely coherent literary project. And as it seems, the process of reading might very well be endless.

Introduction

Beckett – Critical Literature

What sprouts out of the ashes of / Samuel Beckett?/ somewhere in this space is/ his fading breath/ and then a motionless utterance/ in the beginning was the word/ in the end the body.[8]

– Tadeusz Różewicz

The expression that there is nothing to express, nothing with which to express, nothing which to express, no power to express, no desire to express, together with no obligation to express.[9]

– Samuel Beckett

Samuel Beckett's writings occupy a mythical status in contemporary literature. Perhaps, we might take this claim further by saying that they are taken as signals of the maturation of modernity as a cultural formation. His œuvre is finite, complete, and closed. It resists interpretative efforts[10] and functions as one of the most important references for modernist research.[11] It therefore remains stable in its structure, while at the same time revealing itself as a tale of recurring themes undertaken over and over again – right from the author's lyrical beginnings to the minimalism of his mature and late period. The themes at work are absence, silence, consciousness, and inexpressibility. That is why the condensed and minimalistic language of Beckett, self-cleansing of any redundancies, either pushes readers away or serves as a magnet for drawing others into his unprecedented literary realities. Those taken in are offered unique opportunities to follow the intensity of the formation of an idiom, as he grants access not simply to a complete work, but to the very practice of writing that inseparably ties emotion, thought and language. It is in this sense that Beckett is both a figure of modernity fulfilled, with the unanimous myth of writing as an infinite work of consciousness or consciousness, and the producer of writings marked by skilfully hidden, extraordinary but

---

8   Różewicz, T. "Love Toward the Ashes," in *Sobbing Superpower*, translated by Joanna Trzeciak New York 2011, pp. 152-153.
9   Beckett, S. *Three Dialogues*, in CE, vol. 4, p. 556.
10   See the brilliant monograph written from this particular perspective, Cronin, A. *Samuel Beckett. The Last Modernist*, London 1996.
11   See Began, R. *Samuel Beckett and the End of Modernity*, Stanford 1996.

capricious erudition. This is a work in which a plethora of forces and desires collide: attempting to record the entirety of individual experiences in the text and expressing precisely what is inexpressible through language, always guided by the ambition of forsaking one's own voice and creating a space for total silence within language. In those terms, the practice of writing becomes an attempt at realizing an impossible project, cracking at its very foundations and inhibiting its interpretation. Martin Esslin accurately captured this precise confusion:

> In the end, Becket was a simple author – in a sense, because he was likewise extremely complex, somebody who dominated most of the so-called scholars intellectually. It is a simple fact that his entire œuvre is a monolith because it is nothing other than a constant and everlasting internal monologue. He was someone who undertook the challenge (in my opinion, the shared product of his ethical beliefs) of presenting his own existence with a conviction that everything that a man is capable of as a thinking and feeling being – he was Cartesian in this regard – is to speak about what is happening inside.[12]

Jacques Derrida expressed himself in a similar vein:

> No doubt that's true. A certain nihilism is both interior to metaphysics (the final fulfilment of metaphysics, Heidegger would say) and then, already, beyond. With Beckett in particular, the two possibilities are in the greatest possible proximity and competition. He is nihilist and he is not nihilist. Above all, this question should not be treated as a philosophical problem outside or above the texts. When I found myself, with students, reading some Beckett texts, I would take up three lines, I would spend two hours on them, then I would give up because it would not have been possible, or honest, or even interesting, to extract a few "significant" lines from a Beckett text. The composition, the rhetoric, the construction and the rhythm of his works, even the ones that seem the most "decomposed," that's what "remains" finally the most "interesting," that's the work, that's the signature, this remainder which remains when the thematics is exhausted (and also exhausted, by others, for a long time now, in other modes).[13]

Derrida's remarks are not only connected with a deconstructive reading of Beckett's texts, but also seem to touch upon the very core of their legitimation and general problem of their interpretation. Derrida rightfully points to the pursuit of an elusive sense, which is treated as the goal and a rule of writing, as well as the border that serves as the rule of ontology inhabiting the text. The reading of Beckett's works becomes a constant search for the justification of the attempt to analyze them, with the texts constantly pushing back through a simultaneous refusing and demanding of commentary. This antinomy cannot be weakened by any form of external discourse, as is well known by anyone who has tried to

---

12   "Głosy i glosy," translated by Marek Kędzierski, in *Kwartalnik Artystyczny* 1996 no. 4, p. 152. English translation Cain Elliott and Jan Pytalski.

13   Derrida J., "This Strange Institution Called Literature": An Interview with Jacques Derrida, in *Acts of Literature*, edited by Derek Attridge, New York 1992, p. 61.

write about Beckett's works. Interpreters are forced to search for some form of theoretical equivalency for the glimmering, borderline status of Beckett's texts, finding a way to break the monopoly of language's immanence that sustains the works. The commentator should seek for a way to speak about them without committing to a complete trust in a concrete, technical meta-language, as well as avoid believing in the possibility of arriving at a definite, final meaning of the work, revealed and explained through critical analysis.

This is how two fundamental interpretative traditions appear. On the one hand, Beckett's œuvre has many distinguished exegetes, both from the first "heroic period" of research on his works, as well as faithful translators and guardians of his heritage. Although this kind of critique is important, or even necessary, it can be problematic from the standpoint of textual criticism and philosophy. This is particularly true since these approaches tend to rely on the protection of orthodox interpretations and remain faithful to established exegetical methods, which are rarely free from hidden assumptions. In this way, interpretation becomes an unending paraphrase of the writer's own words or a meticulous, strictly philological, effort. On the other hand, since it has become the object of intense research by critics, Beckett's work has been a mirror in which most of twentieth century philosophy and theory has observed its own reflection. Hence, we encounter Beckett in his phenomenological, psychoanalytic, thematic, or deconstructive representations. Obviously, one might claim that these are observations that have already been made and that they illustrate typical hermeneutical problems for all scholars willing to confront the grand texts of contemporary literature. However, I believe that Beckett's work is far more radical than other modernistic projects. That is the source of problems, mentioned from different perspectives by both Esslin and Derrida, which seem to be headed in the direction of ceasing to ask how we might interpret and read Beckett, and instead asking how such reading might begin and if interpretation is even possible. In this analytical impasse mentioned by Derrida, there is, paradoxically, the chance for traversing the binary opposition of two interpretive traditions of Beckett's works. This is about the attempt to design a pattern of interpretation that would almost rest "in between" these two traditions. Along these lines, while following the imagination and explanations proposed by the author, our efforts should be focused on a reading that would be open to an inventiveness allowing us to set figures appearing in the text in different contexts and notice their intriguing "otherness" against the contrasting autonomy of the work.

This book is devoted to figures of subjectivity in works of Samuel Beckett. However, it is important to note that it does not pretend to be a description or a catalogue of all the protagonists in which the subject surfaces. This is not to suggest that the text lacks a general interpretive rationale. On the contrary, by reading certain texts through the prism of philosophy, I attempt to retain a variety of possible actualizations of the subject and propose my more concrete vision. I try to read Beckett's texts through different discourses, at the same time keeping in mind that, as Derrida stated, the power of the "remnant" will eventually win over even the most elaborate, multi-lingual commentaries.[14] While the principle references of this work are the discourses of philosophy and general theory, it would be hard to imagine an analysis that disregarded certain assessments delivered by "Beckettian" literature. This is why there are various references to dictionaries made throughout the book, which provided interesting points of clarification and diversion. Amongst the many thinkers appearing in the pages that follow, certain pairs of names rose to prominence: Deleuze and Derrida, Foucault and Nancy, Hegel and de Man, and Heidegger and Levinas. That having been said, I have found Theodor W. Adorno and Maurice Blanchot to be the most important guides in my own attempt to develop an operating manual of the subject in Beckett's works. Their philosophical works on Beckett are perhaps the most significant in this overcrowded field. The first of the two thinkers in question allows us to see Beckett's works from the intriguing perspective of the dialectic process of extracting contradictions from the relation between consciousness and literature as work of art, as well as through the primacy of epistemologically oriented critical rule. The latter helps us to discover an unorthodox ontology within Beckett's writings. Both thinkers touch upon the theme of negativity that brings them closer to Beckett. Providing a modal framework for my own text, these two perspectives likewise offered an opportunity to examine how fundamental categories of consciousness and negativity "operate" in Beckett's works. Most importantly, they seem to provide a form of philosophical interpretation that allowed the actual voice of the texts themselves to be heard better, while allowing the project of Beckett's writing, in which consciousness and negativity are paramount, to be more comprehensively understood.

Subject as Dilemma

The "*Il faut continuer*," the conclusion of Beckett's *The Unnamable*, condenses this antinomy to its essence: that externally art appears impossible while immanently it must be pursued. What is new is that art must incorporate its own decline; as the critique of the spirit of domination it is the spirit that is able to turn against itself.[15]

– Theodor W. Adorno

---

14   See Derrida, J. *Monolingualism of the Other; or, The Prosthesis of Origin*, translated by Patrick Mensah, Stanford 1998.

15   Adorno, T. *Aesthetic Theory*, Op. cit., p. 320.

What is the common denominator between authors like Adorno and Blanchot? In all honesty, answering such a question would require a separate volume, but we can preliminarily state that both thinkers, although coming from differing traditions, attempted to grasp the specificity of Beckett's writing through the category of the subject, as problematised by the writer himself.[16]

Let us begin with Adorno. My intention is to not focus solely on his texts devoted to Beckett, but to examine his general vision of modern subjectivity that is formulated in relation to the works of Beckett. In *Aesthetic Theory*, a work that was posthumously put together by Adorno's students and dedicated to Beckett, Adorno presents a multi-dimensional critique of the category of the modern subject. By his measure, the subject remains entangled in Kantian-Fichtean idealism, while likewise being caught up in the project of the individual's total emancipation within the Hegelian dialectics of the spirit. Both options enclose reflection on the question of subject within the framework of a system: either in the Kantian subduing of differences or the Hegelian annihilation of difference with the gesture of overcoming (sublimating). Both approaches assume the impossibility of placing the subject beyond strictly demarcated territories of discipline (Kantian authorities) or method (Hegelian dialectical speculation).[17] While drawing on both of these models of modern subjectivity, Adorno reveals the falsity of their basic assumptions – that the subject can become a purely heuristic fiction that justifies the work of consciousness through the primacy of controlling reality or the actualization of what is singular in what is common. Each of these ways of formulating a thesis about subjectivity (transcendental and/or positive and teleological dialectic), in leading to a complete rationalization of reality, makes it impossible for the individual that gradually disappears without a trace to appear in the radically affirmative process of disenchanting the world.[18] According to Adorno, it is the dictate of what is general and systemically empty that poses a central threat to this existence, and only aesthetic experience can sustain the

---

16 Demonstrating interest in the subject, here is an interpretation comparing both projects: Ravel E., *Maurice Blanchot et l'art. au XXème siècle: une esthétique du désœuvrement*, Amsterdam – New York 2007. In particular, see the chapter: "T. W. Adorno et M. Blanchot, avant-gardisme, post- modernisme, et question éthique de la creation."

17 Stefan Morawski wrote on this subject extensively in the article "Czytanie Adorna" in his *Na zakręcie: Od sztuki do po-sztuki*, Kraków 1985. See also Jay, M. *Adorno*, Cambridge 1984 (in particular, the chapter entitled "Atonal Philosophy").

18 It is best seen in Hegel, who in the introduction to *Phenomenology of Spirit* states that the subject realizes itself in the spiritual substance. It means that freeing of the subject is constituted by the movement of "spiritual reanimation of what is general." According to dialectic, the experience of awareness is a possibility of making it the subject of experience. Thanks to this cancelation, subject acquires a level of general rationality. See Hegel, G. W. F., *Phenomenology of Spirit*, translated by A.V. Miller, Oxford 1976.

separation of an individual being. This experience is itself a remnant of resistance against the rule of identity and the reality of the project that assumes – even the most distant – synthesis of sense:

> The reality and unreality of artworks are not layers superimposed on each other; rather, they interpenetrate everything in art to an equal degree. An artwork is real only to the extent that, as an artwork, it is unreal, self-sufficient, and differentiated from the empirical world, of which it nevertheless remains a part. But its unreality – its determination as spirit – only exists to the extent that it has become real; nothing in an artwork a count that is not there in an individuated form.[19]

As a result, a work of art is dependent on both sensual reality and a purely rational world of full presence, even if it is held together by an authoritarian decree. However, it is run by its own set of rules. Amongst these, it is not the question of ontological status that is most important, but the sphere of mediation that is no longer (as in Hegel) an announcement of the reconciliation of contradictions. It is also not a cancelation or sublation [*Aufhebung*], but rather a support of the impossibility of working through antinomy. Adorno remains attached to the opposition between what is real and what is unreal, because he is searching for the language of a different reality by means of aesthetic experience. Access to this alternate reality would be granted to both the creator and recipient. The described mediation [*Vermittlung*] is not mediation between fundamental oppositions (transcendental vs. empirical, subject vs. object), but within the very disposition of an artwork, its potential and inexhaustibility through the sense-creating energy of interpretation. Hence, when talking about literature we could state the following: the text is unreal, because from the perspective of the possibility of the appearance of sense, it (the text) is an attempt to contradict any possible representation. On the other hand, it is precisely in this radical resistance to any kind of representation that the work of art separates itself from the empirical sphere where its realness would be located. Let us notice that Adorno is not attempting to petrify the work of art.[20] He does not build his reflection around a conviction about its absolute immanence. His interpretation is much more subtle. It assumes that the modern language of the work of art travels between the two poles of transcendentalism and empiricism and avoids being dominated by either of them. In that way, Adorno establishes the relational character of the language in question and reveals its irreducibly dialectical negative moment, in which, with all its force, the singularity of the work of art is revealed. This work is impossible to overcome or subsequently be redone in any other form of presence and permanent sense.

---

19   Adorno, T. *Aesthetic Theory*, p. 279.
20   See Bürger, P. *The Decline of Modernism*, translated by Nicholas Walker, Cambridge 1992.

Author of *Negative Dialectics* proposes an original path for the modern subject. However, it would be a mistake to assume that he is interested solely in stabilizing the primacy of an aesthetic experience. He is equally interested in the question of consciousness that allows for the introduction of a critical sanction into aesthetic thinking, as with a feeling of autonomy (and not simplistically understood complete separateness) of a work of art. The sense of literature will be placed outside of the rule of generality, which means outside of the scope of the abstractness of the notion (crossing it, but never being subordinate), and has to remain anchored in the task of recognizing what is negative (what cannot be enclosed within homogenous and complete sense). As stated by Adorno in one of the seminal passages in his work:

> The literal is barbaric. Totally objectified, by virtue of its rigorous legality, the artwork becomes a mere fact and is annulled as art. The alternative that opens up in this crisis is: Either to leave art behind or to transform its very concept.[21]

There are a few important questions touched upon by Adorno in this short excerpt. Firstly, "barbaric literalness" needs to be referred to the process of reification, behind which we can find metaphysical separation of object and subject. Consciousness, while attempting to control the world through its disenchantment, turns it into a thing, and object to which it loses access, but over which it can extend its power. Secondly, the alternative mentioned by Adorno seems to not be definite, but rather permanent and constitutes a camouflaged definition of art. The work of art can remain so as long as it remains submitted to the law of a continuous reworking of its own language – language that is protected by the consciousness (of both creator and recipient). It is not, however, only about sustaining the category of intention in power (Adorno's category is situated as far from essentialism as possible), but also about aesthetic experience, which will be possible only for the price of enabling one's consciousness in the critical phase, that is right before its own entropy, but in the state of full tension. The critical state of subjectivity is also its crisis, and the other way around: crisis turns out to be a chance for returning to the focused work of consciousness. The negativity of the dialectics of the work of art is based around the fact that the moment of transition from crisis to critique turns out to be this precise double movement of profits, and the only possible guarantee at the same time. In other words, only rational legitimization of the crisis that is embedded in the history and frailty of every individuality can become an "adequate reason" for the work of art. In a skilful way, Adorno turns around Hegel's aesthetic equation, which states that art

---

21   Adorno, T. *Aesthetic Theory*, p. 61.

is based on link between sensual content and idea[22] and concentrates only on the moment in which language capable of enriching the idea is exhausted. That way, the subject becomes a function of its own displacement, endlessly situated against the necessity of finding new definitions, suiting the ever-changing character of the work of art. But also critique becomes a form of total distrust toward every form of identity (against the abstract notion, idea, or definition) possessing a potential charge of power and violence. In relation to literature one could ask: how to speak about literary experience and not fall victim to irrationality released by the affirmation of autonomous "elements of speech" and at the same time avoid the conviction of critical sanction fleeting away from language?

Adorno proposes two possible solutions. The first involves keeping one's focus on the relation between the consciousness and mediation in the work of art's space. The second opens the possibility of embracing the modern subject as a subject of aesthetic experience.

> When artworks are viewed under the closest scrutiny, the most objectivated paintings metamorphose into a swarming mass and texts splinter into words. As soon as one imagines having a firm grasp on the details of an artwork, it dissolves into the indeterminate and undifferentiated, so mediated as is it. This is the manifestation of aesthetic semblance in the structure of artworks. Under micrological study, the particular – the artwork's vital element – is volatized; its concretion vanishes.[23]

In the above passage, Adorno makes some assumptions that will hold for his entire concept of the work of art, but also refers directly and with full strength, which will be obvious to any reader of his essay on *Endgame*, to Beckett's works. According to Adorno, the pair of objectivity and subjectivity should not be understood as a stabilized, binary opposition, but as dialectic terms, which actualize themselves in the act of aesthetic experience. Consciousness can never achieve its full presence within the work of art – a work which perception could create and justify by its own means. Instead, it reveals itself in the very moment of experience, which questions the autonomy of the work. It is not, however, only about the work being dependent on various relations with external reality (social, ideological, economic, etc.), but also about the most basic dependency, which is its relation to the empirical sphere. The recognition of this sphere – as long as it exists, learns about reality and proposes rulings on the world – cannot be reduced by consciousness to chaos or undifferentiated materiality. That is why mediation is ultimately an ambivalent process. It could represent an opportunity for consciousness, an effort to save itself and to retain cognitive power, as well as the power to differentiate itself from its own interior. It desires upholding the sanction of its own name.

---

22   See Hegel G. W. F., *Hegel's Aesthetics: Lectures on Fine Art, 2 vols.,* translated by T. M. Knox , Oxford 1998.

23   Adorno, T. W., *Aesthetic Theory*, Op. cit. p. 101.

However, this is only one side of the dialectical relation that accompanies aesthetic experience. It is the side, which holds negativity as heroic, and is based fundamentally on a scheme of loftiness, an elevated model of the subject. From this perspective, the subject is clenched within the complete autonomy of a progressive and distinctive mind, as well as fear of the abstraction attached to the notion. It is a notion that, from the promise of cognition, becomes a sign of the potential annihilation of existence. Adorno complicates the picture by adding that aesthetic experience, as such, is as risky for consciousness as it is for the autonomy of the work of art. On the one hand, any work of art is completely enclosed within its own immanence, because every interference of individual consciousness into its order illustrates the work's anchoring in fabrication. This fabrication is not merely a mimetic illusion, but a certain type of necessary resistance against the epistemological claims of the individual. On the other hand, however, the work itself – or its language rather – turns against consciousness by recognizing its unclear motives and the displacement of its foundation.

Where is the space for saving one's own name, if aesthetic experience poses either a threat or becomes a moment of loftiness that the subject experiences in the face of what presents itself – by forcing itself through "the web of language"[24] – as fully negative and completely absent? An opportunity for saving subjectivity can be found in the very reflection of mediation and the cognitive and rhetorical effects it causes. These opportunities appear in moments disturbing the metaphysical relation between subjectivity and objectivity. Finally, they are found in reflection over the distance between consciousness and the language of the work of art. In *Dialectic of Enlightenment*, co-written with Max Horkheimer, Adorno included a concept to which he remained loyal for the rest of his philosophical career. It is a relation full of tension, between myth and emancipation, which renders disintegration a fundamental characteristic of the modern subject. An individual trapped between opposite poles – both magic and the direct influence of art and Enlightenment in the work of the mind, in which consciousness operates not for its own existentially understood fullness, but for a technically understood mastering of reality – thereby becoming hostage to the process of the disenchantment of the world. As a result, the pursuit of complete rationality (of the world or the subject) eliminates the possibility of emancipation, because – following the lawgiver of Enlightenment – "exiting immaturity" becomes a space for the complete illusion of autonomy and self-transparency of the conscious individual, fixed by a restrictive mind. The authors demonstrate that modernity should be viewed from a slightly

---

24   Adorno used this metaphor in the relation to the structure of the text, which –according to his project – should constitute a kind of constellation of mediations, recordings of relations between subject and object. See Adorno, T. *Minima Moralia. Reflections on a Damaged Life*, translated by Edmund Jephcott, New York 2005.

different perspective than one based purely on the strong disjuncture between myth and enlightenment. The way to exit this impasse is fidelity to critical rule, which cannot attain the form of a "regulative Idea," but becomes a means of salvation in thinking as a fundamental, existential disposition of an individual. However, thinking does not constitute – as in Heidegger's[25] work – an extrapolated state of primary directness and the possibility of access to the source of being as such. It is rather a fundamental neurosis of the modern subject in the form of a "dialectics of meaning." Wandering Odysseus – the raconteur relaying stories of these very wanderings – is the figure of this varied entanglement. His narration is a matrix of relations between consciousness and the language of modernity for the authors of *Dialectics of Enlightenment*:

> The speech which gets the better of physical strength is unable to curb itself. Its spate accompanies the stream of consciousness, thought itself, like a parody: thought's unwavering autonomy takes on a moment of manic folly when it enters reality as speech, as if thought and reality were synonymous, whereas the former has power over the latter only through distance. Such distance, however, is also suffering.[26]

From the excerpt above one could draw, in a way that is essential for understanding Adorno's vision of the subject, a negative dialectic of individuality and generality. On the side of what is general, we will find not only the autonomous notion, which – similarly to Hegel's concept – achieved its substantiality in the course of its development to be become the highest form of subjectivity[27], but also language *tout court*. Speech becomes a causative factor for the disenchantment process, because it allows one to learn more about reality, speech allows for its recognition and through recognition – control. However, at the same time, it undermines its well-grounded, ontological status or mythological structure. Consciousness becomes gated from the world by the veil of language, which creates a completely new reality of pretense and autonomous fantasy. What is more, it is language's system, the creative and inertial force of speech, which causes the subject to be unable to stop the process of rationalization or expressing the mute world. There is no way of counteracting the power of discourse that would allow for dialectical balancing or reworking of the potential of inertia trapped in language. How can an individual save himself as a subject? While preserving the epistemological primacy of consciousness, how can a subject simultaneously refuse the temptation of complete submission to the merciless rigor of progressive disenchantment?

---

25 On this subject, see Quattara, B. *Adorno et Heidegger: une controverse philosophique*, Paris-Montreal 1999.

26 Horkheimer M., Adorno T. W., *Dialectic of Enlightenment: Philosophical Fragments*, translated by Edmund Jephcott. Stanford 2002, p. 54.

27 See Siemek, M.J. "Heglowskie pojęcie podmiotowości" in *Hegel i filozofia*, Warszawa 1998.

In his own works along with his writings with Horkheimer, Adorno proposes radical solutions, which includes his critical notion of mediation. This change in the understanding of the subject could be briefly, however not simplistically in my mind, explained as follows: speech is an agent of emancipation, a means for achieving complete knowledge or a full realization of consciousness. On the other hand, it erases the possibility of an independent existence for subjectivity, this fragile, unstable position in the world, constantly exposed to hostile actions of the alien external world. The solution lies in attempts to restore – by means of critique – autonomy to what is singular. These means of critique, respectively, will be a recognition of what is non-identifiable[28] in every examined form of identity. This means that thanks to language and through language (and so, by the same means that allowed for an exit from myth, a movement toward the autonomy of the mind and the emancipation of consciousness) one is able to verify the status of every term aspiring to be a description of the world. However, the authors of *Dialectics of Enlightenment* state that this is something more than merely noticing a "blind spot" within symbolic systems, with which we describe the world and through which we try to recognize it and gain control over it. The separation of thinking from language is not a kind of "epistemological cut," taking place outside of the subject in the space of cognitive discourse's autonomy. This distance is, at the same time, real and inaccessible to language, a moment in which consciousness stops not at the level of self-knowledge, but in the face of, understood existentially, the experience of suffering. This experience cannot be reworked through the "cunning" of speech – a coherent narration about oneself – or a final sanction of consciousness, which can materialize itself.

The possibility of thinking or even further: thinking as an existential act, when presented from this perspective, connects with the critical condition (in a twofold sense of the word, which was explained at the beginning of this introduction). Only a vision of the subject based on the gap between speech and thinking, language and reality, or consciousness and reality, could attain the rank of objectivity and thereby constitute an impossible to reduce signature or trace of suffering. By giving hope for liberation of an individual from what is contingent, Enlightenment reveals its opposite or negative side. Consciousness that is fully present and ready to recognize and subdue the entirety of reality to itself moves to the position of a myth that was born out of the same language initially delegated to cancel this very myth. In other words, complete presence and pure cognition – immobilized within identity – become fantasies thanks to which an individual can construct him or herself as a subject and through which he/she can create the

---

28   It is a formulation that very often appears in *Dialectics of Enlightenment*, as well as in Adorno's other works. One could say that the ideal of "disabling" every identity is a shortcut, but an accurate description of the critical ideal in this particular incarnation.

mythical narration of autonomy. The identity of the subject and its myth constitute an inseparable pair of oppositions endlessly entering into dialectical relation, which cannot be cancelled by any of the elements of synthesis. What is more, identity presents itself solely in the form of a function of what is changeable and unidentifiable.[29] One might assume that subjectivity is not only connected with what is negative from the perspective of the possibilities of the presence of sense (and, by extension, language), but also reveals a negative element in the supposedly stable identity of knowledge. It is knowledge that should be the result of the proper use of notions by the subject. One could say that this particular dilemma (Hegelian *Zerrissenheit*) – both as an element of the unidentifiable and as a break between thinking and reality – is the right place for subjectivity, which finally gains access to what is real only through suffering and conflict. Language in this arrangement is not only on the side of speculative narration (in the sense of the history of self-liberating consciousness), but creates the possibility of storytelling (understood as an aesthetic pretense). These two possibilities, as suggested by the aforementioned excerpt, enter into unending conflict, which brings effects in the form of a "nexus of myth and enlightenment."[30] This is precisely what Adorno indicated about individuality as a dilemma in *Negative Dialectics*:The power of the status quo puts up the facades into which our consciousness crashes. It must seek to crash through them. This alone would free the postulate of depth from ideology. [...] Where thought transcends the bonds it tied in resistance – there is its freedom. Freedom follows the subject's urge to express itself. The need to lend a voice to suffering is a condition of all truth. For suffering is objectivity that weighs upon the subject; its most subjective experience, its expression, is objectively conveyed.[31]

But what does the statement, heavy with poetic emphasis, mean in suggesting that "suffering is objectivity that weighs upon the subject"? Is it really what Agata Bielik-Robson calls in her commentary a praise of the philosophy of surface, in which, employing an organic metaphor, the surface in question is an "epidermis" of the individual? According to which it is the first and most sensitive area of contact with what, according to subjectivity, is other and alien?[32] I believe that the situation looks slightly different. Contact between consciousness and reality seems to be tainted from the very beginning with a mark of mediation (that is

29 M. Horkheimer, T. W. Adorno, Op. cit. p. 103.
30 I refer here to the exceedingly accurate formulation of Habermas, briefly describing the character of *Dialectics of Enlightenment* and used in *The Philosophical Discourse of Modernity* (1985).
31 Adorno, T W., *Negative Dialectics*, translated by E. B. Ashton. New York 1973, pp. 17-18.
32 See Bielik-Robson A., *Duch powierzchni. Rewizja romantyczna i filozofia*, Kraków 2004, pp. 457-459.

how I interpret the metaphor of the "facade" or surface). This stain successfully blocks access to what is real, or what truly escapes the authority of subjectivity.[33] Can we then think of another reality, from the perspective of the subject, than one disguising itself as an ideologised[34] (identity-based) illusion? It seems that contact with the surface is merely an introductory step to a deeper critical act – the only act that is capable of saving the position of the consciousness. As a result, consciousness cannot constitute a perfectly constructed theoretical subject that is any longer separated from experience. The rule of critique transforms the very act of thinking into experience, which will make both the work of the consciousness and hope for experiencing what is actually reliable (and what Adorno describes simply as true). Speculative or theoretical thinking can no longer legitimize the singular trace of existence, because it makes suffering, born from the primal loss of access to what is genuinely real, a necessary element in the process of mutual cancelations and substitutions. At the end of this process a goal emerges taking the form of ultimate identity. Adorno turns a positive dialectical equation around by saying that the gap between thinking and reality is a primal lack that is impossible to fill. This is a lack embedded into the constitution of the modern subject.

Is the dilemma, which constitutes the subject, a final sanction of reality? If so, what would a hypothetical breaking through of the facade created by the forces of reality mean? It seems that there are two possible answers to this question. First (previously mentioned), the decisive moment of "objectivity" is the moment of a critical reaction of consciousness to what is identical. Behind this identity there is hidden violence of abstraction that erases the individuality of concrete existence. Subjectivity finds itself in the gesture of revealing the potential negativity and mediation that is rooted in every certain contestation of reality. Our second answer complements the first by revealing an irreducible element of the empirical character of suffering, a testimony of physical pain. The consequences of such a displacement seem to be radical: pain cannot be extrapolated and made into a metaphor, or a handy idea,[35] and there is an inherent inability to foresee or design it. In that way, an epistemological act becomes an act of consciousness directed toward real suffering that always strikes the body too soon, ahead of consciousness. What then is expression? An attempt to break the stubborn truth

---

33 Or, otherwise, the authority of self-determination stemming from subjectival self-knowledge [*Setzung*]. See Hegel G. W. F., *Encyclopaedia of the Philosophical Sciences* in 3 vols, translated by A. V. Miller, J. N. Findlay, Oxford, 1971/1974/2004[§ 425].

34 I will add here that ideology should be understood in broad sense as a resistance against fetishism of cultural economy on the one hand, and instrumental use of mind on the other.

35 Adorno was probably right when he claimed that pain expressed, or locked within a framework of any symbolic order (regardless from its postulated range) stops being pain and becomes an element of social economy and a building block of ideology.

about suffering nestled before consciousness? Or maybe it is the other way around and expression is a recognition and an act of giving voice to suffering? It seems that only the attempt to combine these two presents an opportunity to save what is individual. Let us listen to Adorno once more:

> Conscious unhappiness is not a delusion of the mind's vanity but something inherent in the mind, the one authentic dignity it has received in its separation from the body. The dignity is the mind's negative reminder of its physical aspect; its capability of that aspect is the only source of whatever hope the mind can have. The smallest trace of senseless suffering in the empirical world belies all the identitarian philosophy that would talk us out of that suffering: "While there is a beggar, there is a myth," as Benjamin put it. This is why the philosophy of identity is the mythological form of thought. The physical moment tells our knowledge that suffering ought not to be, that things should be different "Woe speaks: 'Go.'"[36]

Suffering can surface most fully in the work of art, which through its tension created at the junction of what is empirical and what is consciousness-bound, that is impossible to unload (impossible to be reworked into a positive sense). It reveals the most basic impossibility of not only representation, but also of experiencing what is real. But it is precisely this affirmation of impossibility, a utopian attempt to express what is completely absent from our consciousness that can become an opportunity for the authentication of the existence of the subject. Through this gesture of confrontation the subject would gain unquestionable existential weight, or in other words – consciousness of its own suffering, which this very consciousness is impossible to defeat. Of course, the work of art is not only a pretense, but also a space in which an individual can deposit the dream of absolute uniqueness.

This fantasy, a utopian faith in an event potentially buried within the work of art, is the only form of self-realization available for an individual. It is about the moment of experience, in which critical consciousness and existence in deep crisis meet and confront each other. The subject subdued to such a dream would be at the same time impossible, since it would not be able to resist the force of the event, and possible due to the event revealing its primary heteronomy. When describing the subject juxtaposed with the event, Adorno points to the necessity of its situating, a displacement between two extremities: silence, complete wordless absence, and an epiphanic accessibility of complete presence. Such a vision of the subject locates itself – although in a radically reformulated way – on the side of the critical philosophical tradition. The subject as a dilemma [*Zerrissenheit*], realizing itself to the fullest in an aesthetic experience, is marked by deep scepticism. It is devoid of faith in the possibility of finding a path of thought leading to "things in themselves." At the same time, it remains embedded in the project of saving

---

36   Adorno, T. *Negative Dialectics*, Op. cit., p. 203.

an individuality that can be completed only by the subject itself in allowing for an approach to what is negative. A vision of the subject based on the dilemma between epistemological scepticism and metaphysical dogmatism turns out to be an existential possibility. However, there is one condition to this possibility – the individual must choose the path of critique, which is the path of crisis at the same time. Adorno's description of this negative dialectic is as follows:

> Melancholy is the shadow of what in all form is heterogeneous, which form strives to banish: mere existence. In happy artworks, melancholy anticipates the negation of meaning in those that are undermined, the reverse image of longing. What radiates wordlessly from artworks is that *it is*, thrown into relief by *it* – the unlocatable grammatical subject – *is not*; it cannot be referred demonstratively to anything in the world that previously exists. In the utopia of its form, art bends under the burdensome weight of the empirical world from which, as art, it steps away. Otherwise, art's consummateness is hollow. The semblance of artworks is bound up with the progress of their integration, which they had to demand of themselves and through which their content seems immediately present. The theological heritage of art is the secularization of revelation, which defines the ideal and limit of every work. The contamination of art with revelation would amount to the unreflective repetition of its fetish character on the level of theory. The eradication of every trace of revelation from art would, however, degrade it to the undifferentiated repetition of the status quo.[37]

But how does this particular vision of the subject help us to better understand the works of Beckett? I believe that Adorno's philosophy in some aspects – also discussed in this work – seems to be perfectly attuned with the texts of Beckett and highlights his practice of writing as a form of thinking. At this point, I would like to note only the most important of these similarities. It has become customary to say that from the point of view of philosophical influences, Beckett's works are reliant on Descartes and Schopenhauer.[38] Unquestionable philological facts point to such conclusion. The first text published by Beckett was an erudite poem *Whoroscope*, full of ironic footnotes and dedicated to Descartes. As many researchers[39] have

---

37 Adorno, T. *Aesthetic Theory*, pp. 105-106. Emphasis in the original.

38 Probably the most important work on the subject is the study of Hugh Kenner entitled *Samuel Beckett. A Critical Study*, New York 1962. In the work one can find a figure of a "Cartesian centaur" that in a briefed way envelops the vision of subjectivity in Beckett's texts. Also Harold Bloom makes an interesting comment on the margins of his theory of poetry: "The protests against Cartesian reductiveness never cease, in constant involuntary tribute to him. Beckett's fine handful of poems in English are too subtle to protest overtly, but they are strong prayers for discontinuity." Bloom, H. *The Anxiety of Influence*, Oxford 1997, p. 40.

39 See Harvey, L. *Samuel Beckett: Poet and Critic*, pp.3-66, Princeton 1970., Trezise, T. *Into the Breach: Samuel Beckett and the Ends of Literature*, Princeton 1990., Katz, D. *Saying I No More. Subjectivity and Consciousness in the Prose of Samuel Beckett*, Evanston 1999 (particularly the chapter "Will in Overplus: A Graphic Look at Beckett's Whoroscope")

previously shown, these original influences deeply shaped Beckett's emerging
vision of the subject. This was a vision of the subject marked by a deeply
ambivalent approach toward the body and constantly redirected to the imperative
of the search for certain knowledge. This also exposes a concrete problem with
the possibility of justifying the fact of consciousness' existence. A second major
influence, clearly visible in the early essay devoted to works of Proust, reveals
a more subtle face of the young writer, who knowingly employs the philosophy
of representation from Schopenhauer's *The World as Will and Representation* in
order to analyze the experience of time. This is how one could read, in short, the
legacies which are close to Beckett: from one he drew a conviction about the
deep separation of the self from the material world, and from the other he picked
formulations that brought him closer to encompassing relations between the will
to exist projected by the individual and the consciousness of its fragile historicity.

This patronage, thoroughly described in numerous works of international
"Beckettology," allows to talk about the works of the writer as if in his own words,
and as a consequence, forcing any commentator into paraphrase. At the same time,
the philosophy of Adorno, who matched his indebtedness to this tradition with the
rigor of his critique, assists us in identifying a slightly different, more complicated
and more accurate, position of subjectivity in Beckett's works. Firstly, Beckett's
writings remain one of the most vivid literary projects of modernism, because
they revolve around a critical take on the category of the individual as a subject
and issues of writing, with the questionable primacy of the epistemological
perspective, at their centre. Writing, in the practice of Beckett, is a permanent
search for access to what is real. This is accomplished through the work of
consciousness and language. This search takes place at the price of the destruction
of all possible modes of realizing singularity through language and therefore, it is
conducted through the demolition of a mimetic and expressive model. Secondly,
the critical relation described above takes place between various dimensions of
experience: between the sphere of consciousness and the empirical, and between
consciousness and language as a represented form. Thirdly, the aspect of strong
negativity is inscribed into the research project that can be realized through the
construction of its own literary idiom. The pre-stable impossibility of negativity's
guarantee. Lastly, the epistemological sanction stands in relation to an existential
domain that stems from the impossibility of rational, aesthetic, or the metaphysical
justification of the primal suffering of an individual.[40]

---

as well as the collection: *Beckett avant Beckett. Essai sur les premières œuvres*, edited by
J.-M. Rabaté, Paris 1984.

40   The question of unending suffering resulting from the possibility of an eliminated
consciousness of existence is one of the most important of Beckett's obsessions. This
entire theme is most comprehensively summarized by the quote taken from Calderon

Metaphysical Experience

One can therefore see that Adorno's interpretation oscillates around the problem of the subject, which needs to perpetually legitimize its own existence in face of the absence of any constant points of reference. Individual existence, embedded in the world of contemporary disenchantment, cannot justify, permanent or otherwise, any form of position that supposes any kind of reality – a position as a being that is self-aware. At the same time, it does not stop asking questions about itself, about the place it speaks from, about the network of dependencies it enters into with other discourses and powers of authority. It is in concurrent alienation and involvement in "that, which is different" where a reformulation shifted into radically negative context surfaces – a metaphysical question, which reaches out toward the issue of conditions necessary for consciousness to come into existence, as well as those in which it is being questioned. Adorno points to Beckett as an ally in this negativism. As he indicates, Beckett's work is something different than an iconoclastic method of reworking through the trauma of the Holocaust:[41]

> Beckett has given us the only fitting reaction to the situation of the concentration camps – a situation he never calls by name, as if it were subject to an image ban. What is, he says, is like a concentration camp. At one time he speaks of a lifelong death penalty. The only dawning hope is that there will be nothing any more. This, too, he rejects. From the fissure of inconsistency that comes about in this fashion, the image world of nothingness as something emerges to stabilize poetry. [...] As long as the world is as it is, all pictures of reconciliation, peace, and quiet resemble the picture of death. The slightest difference between nothingness and coming to rest would be the haven of hope, the no man's land between the border posts of being and nothingness. Rather than overcome that zone, consciousness would have to extricate from it what is not in the power of the alternative. The true nihilists are the ones who oppose nihilism with their more and more faded positivities, the ones who are thus conspiring with all extant malice, and eventually with the destructive principle itself. Thought honors itself by defending what is damned as nihilism.[42]

The way in which the works of Beckett exist is not simply aesthetic, symbolic or tragic. They do not constitute a "direct" diagnosis of the existential status of the individual, but rather speak to the infinite labour of thinking, which is founded on the negativity of being. This cannot be neutralized by means of literary language or philosophical speculation. That which is negative is always outside of the

---

(and later repeated by Schopenhauer in *The World as Will and Representation*): "To desire immortality for the individual is to perpetuate an error for ever."

41   See Philips, J. "Catastrophe, Autonomy and Spirit of Adorno: Trying to Understand Adorno's Reading," in *Samuel Beckett Today/Aujourd'hui (After Beckett/D'après Beckett)*.

42   Adorno, T. *Negative Dialectics*, pp. 380-381.

reach of images and concepts. This paradoxical affirmation of what is negative is supposed to bring visible results, or the defence of consciousness' sanction of singular existence. The battle for the survival of a subject does not involve seizing what is external in relation to its interior structure, but on saving the movement of thought itself. Thanks to this movement, an individual singularity can confront what is real – an enigmatic element of reality – that exists and demands recognition through presence, but will never be able to become an element of representation.

What is negative, does not fit within the economy of being and nothingness, within a notion and direct presence[43], but situates itself "in between." Understanding the question of subjectivity requires a fundamental reformulation – consciousness does not have any pre-programmed warranty of sense, but development cannot stop at the level of the ascertainment of the absurdity of existence. This nihilistic moment is reworked in the practice of comprehension through writing as the possibility of analyzing the critical situation of a subject clashing with what is negative. Metaphysical experience, after which Adorno strove, has nothing of the conciliatory, stabilizing and generalizing power of the language of philosophy. It transfers the entire burden onto the practice of writing, where what is heteronomous and ambiguous can find its voice, by extension giving voice to what is singular. Hence, metaphysical experience enables the search for an idiom, which transcends the opposition between the abstract, idealistic world of notions and mythical reality of what is immanent – what exists locked in silence.

In conclusion, metaphysics cannot be transgressed, nor painlessly discarded. It remains in the form of necessary distance, which does not allow for the simple gesture of identification serving the purpose of mastering reality. This essential dilemma gives birth to the modern subject, heroically struggling between the two extremes of the modernistic project – reification and myth – between which it is eternally trapped. Both forms constitute a type of not only social but also existential alienation, as philosophically diagnosed. This alienation forces the subject into a false existence, one that is a mere pretense subdued to external instances of power. Adorno writes:

> Pure immediacy and fetishism are equally untrue. [...] Yet the surplus over the subject, which a subjective metaphysical experience will not be talked out of, and the element of truth in reity – these two extremes touch in the idea of truth. For there could no

---

43   Contrary to Sartre's version of existentialism, Beckett (and Adorno following) would not feel the urge to frame the question of nihilism within the clear order of an idea, created by an uncritical acquisition of terms without content (absurdity, for example). Such ideas and terms do not change the economic and hierarchical order of conflicts, hence they do not stop the process of the alienation of what is singular.

more be truth without a subject freeing itself from delusions than there could be truth without that which is not the subject, that in which truth has its archetype.[44]

The category of the subject is still binding, because it is only due to this category that we are capable of analyzing the question of what is real. Adorno's suggestion is quite clear on this point: the subject cannot exist as an empty, arbitrary epistemological construct, which claims every external space for itself, but it also cannot become one of the many building blocks of the network of relations which become real within the notion. However, Adorno's remarks point toward more positive conclusions as well. A basic securing of sense in the form of up keeping consciousness warrants a persistent search for what is real and excuses "freeing itself from delusions." Against the anti-essentialist and dialectical approach of Adorno, it functions not only as an irrefutable method of truth seeking, but also as a manner of thinking and existing. This way, reflection over the contradiction emerging at the meeting point of what is subjective and what is subject to the laws of subjectival internalization becomes a definition of contradiction, due to which conscious existence becomes plausible. "The transcendent is, and is not,"[45] says Adorno, pointing to a force which does not allow reflection to finally settle in the realm of idealism, keeping subjectivity in the abstract, or the space of a silent world, where that which is other reigns.

The work of negation conditions a different kind of "metaphysical experience," which, at the same time, does not annihilate the category of the subject, but gives it a mark of concreteness. However, the price for this "revival" is high: consciousness ceases to function as merely a source of well-founded assertions, which organize reality for an individual and transform into an instance of critical vigilance. The subject will exist to the extent of its ability to observe cracks in its relations with the world, certain breaks in continuity and ambivalence, which cannot ultimately be eliminated through the work of the notion. However, one can attempt to allow them to speak. Only within this gesture of opening consciousness and language can the reality of singularity truly surface. Adorno claimed that under the all-subjugating identity principle, whatever does not enter into identity, whatever eludes rational planning in the realm of means, turns into freighting retribution for the calamity which identity brings upon the non-identical.[46] This critique of a centralized and unified mind, conducted by Adorno, leads us once more to Beckett. The sense of his works gravitates endlessly around the previously mentioned notion of un-identity, taken (so to speak) by the figures of a subject, realized in multiple configurations and dimensions. The fundamental position of

---

44   Adorno, T. W., Op. cit., pp. 374-375
45   Ibid., p. 375
46   Ibid., p. 320.

consciousness does not allow for releasing oneself from the necessity of searching for a proper language to describe this experience, and thereby elevating itself to the rank of the objective. At the same time, the concept of un-identity suggests a different, far more radical possibility for understanding Beckett's project.

In his lectures devoted to the "concepts and problems" of metaphysics, Adorno expresses in the form of a strong thesis his former subtle divagations over Beckett's project. This thesis could be formulated as follows: Beckett remains within the orbit of metaphysics' influence, however it is a kind of metaphysics filtered through the necessity of the expression of a fundamental and unlikely quality of all the modes of explication and the appearance of all possible experiences. Thanks to such a radical approach, Beckett is able to save the opportunity of experiencing what, in the words of Adorno, "transcends life." Positioning literature's task in the place of absence, from which suffering subjectivity attempts to speak, paradoxically, opens a path for a search of what is irrefutably real. Beckett's work constitutes a topography of emptiness," and an "attempt to portray nothingness as it is." Yet, it is not about grasping "nothingness as such," but about working "within complete negativity."[47]

The Rhetoric of Impossibility

Maurice Blanchot, right after the publication of the final novel of the "trilogy," dedicated an enthusiastic text to *The Unnamable,* which, even though received as a dense interpretation of the work, seems to be impossible to understand outside of the context of Blanchot's own philosophy. Since I develop the interpretation in the second part of this book I will only point here to the crucial points of Blanchot's ontology of literature – particularly with respect to a certain version of the literary language that emerges from Beckett's texts and his overall project.

For Blanchot, the concept of neutrality (or the neutrality of language) plays a key role. This concept could be described as a contradiction of the possibility of making sense present in a traditionally understood and metaphysically structured presentation. Neutral language cannot be metaphorical, but it progresses in the direction of the uttering of silence, or the experience of "the silence of the sense."[48] According to Blanchot, this is precisely what enables the understanding

---

47   Adorno T. W., *Metaphysics. Concept and Problems*, edited by R. Tiedemann, translated by
      Edmund Jephcott, Standford 2001, pp. 135-136. As the editors of Adorno's writing point
      out, the philosopher wanted to devote a separate book to Beckett, in which – following
      the example of *The Unnamable* – he would attempt to describe this "nothing," which "is
      not" conceptually understood "nothingness."

48   Poulet, G., "Mallarmé", translated by Donata Eska, in, *Metamorfozy czasu. Szkice
      krytyczne*, edited by J. Błoński i M. Głowiński, Warsaw 1977, pp. 271-272.

of literature. That is why literature can speak only before any possible presence and outside of any of its forms. In the end, it is about searching for the source of language, which is not something primal and indivisible, but becomes a mythical "starting point." This starting point simultaneous reveals the ability and inability of authorial expression. This search, or the very movement of writing, is in principle – as claimed in the title of one of Blanchot's most important works – an "infinite conversation" unable to stabilize the subject involved in the process of writing/ reading and the anonymous external sphere. The subject remains completely alone in this conversation, not in the regular sense of the word, but in relation to the complete separateness of every individual imagination, which has to struggle with the mystery of language on its own. This language appears as a sign of alien anonymity and, most of all, a sign of death. In order for the writing to become trustworthy, one must open to the voice of the absolute event. In case of works by Kafka and Rilke, Blanchot observes that the movement of the event forces itself upon the language used by the subject within "literary space" in a double direction. On the one hand, it orders the subject to tell the story of the death of its own name – a destruction of its own signature given away to the anonymous voice of the exterior. On the other, it forces a continuation in this gesture of separation – a disconnect – understood as a condition for conversation. It is all enclosed within a gesture, which could be the only means of saving the randomness of existence through literature. Death serves as an absolute logic of time, as a necessity, which triggers the imagination and death as a chance for saving the historicity of the subject constituting two different versions of *écriture* attempted by Blanchot in his project:

> I write to die, to give death its essential possibility, through which it is essentially death, source of invisibility; but at the same time, I cannot write unless death writes in me, makes of me the void where the impersonal is affirmed.[49]

Death is reflected in language. It takes the form of an infinite process of celebrating the act of distancing and disconnection, differentiating separation and figurative distortion of language. In order to capture this mechanism of speech and writing (writing as conversation), Blanchot uses the term *"désœuvrement,"* which suggests passiveness, immobility, and deactivation. However, it is also a result of disinheriting, or rather an exiting of the subject beyond its own language. This gesture of stepping out, which in theory was supposed to bring one closer to the reality of experience, simultaneously establishes absence as a primal moment of every act of writing. How is this at all possible? It seems that the logic of the conversation proposed by Blanchot, who exposes the radical absence (developed

---

49   Blanchot, M. *L'espace littéraire*, Paris: 1955, p. 193. In English, see *The Space of Literature*, translated by Ann Smock, Lincoln 1989, p. 149.

in "other night") as a source of all writing, reveals how radically this "other night" is dependent on time. Language, as an independent sphere with which consciousness enters into a dialogue, becomes a warranty of disagreement. In particular, it constitutes a deferral and delay of the moment of the confrontation of subjectivity with death. In this case, death is announced by the event, which is an embodiment of the absolute "now" – it is an event, which cannot be neutralized. This logic of deferral was clearly explained in Blanchot's commentary on Marcel Proust's writings:

> Proust's work is a complete-incomplete work. When one read *Jean Santeuil* and the innumerable intermediate versions in which he tried out the themes to which he wanted to give form, one is amazed by the help he received from destructive time, which, in him and against him, was the accomplice of his work. This work was above all threatened by an over-hasty completion. The longer it takes, the closer it gets to itself. In the movement of the book, we discern this postponement that withholds it, as if, foretelling the death that is at its end, it were trying, in order to avoid death, to run back on its own course.[50]

In conclusion, what is necessary is to keep language in a state of constant movement. It keeps pronouncing its own inefficiency and its own finite character. Language will pronounce its inability to perform a synthesis, as well as an inability for a return to the most basic level of the identity of the word and object. Time is impossible to disregard, not only because it determines narration and makes writing possible, but also because experiencing it is the only form of a defence against death. But time, appearing in Proust's works as if in epiphanic flashes, simultaneously portrays a radical discontinuity, which determines a subject searching for safe haven in the language of existential narration. The time of telling is unavoidably tainted with fragile *innoportunité* and leaves subjectivity helpless in the face of the inability, as well as the necessity, of writing to end. From this perspective, Proust was incredibly close to Beckett. That is why, in the case of his works, Blanchot talked about "the dissolving of literature," or its glimmering existence on the border of language and silence. Beckett discussed a nearly identical experience in his early study devoted to *In Search of Lost Time*:

> The old ego dies hard. Such as it was, a minister of dullness, it was also an agent of security. When it ceases to perform that second function, when it is opposed by a phenomenon that it cannot reduce to the condition of a comfortable and familiar concept, when, in a word, it betrays its trust as a screen to spare its victim the spectacle of reality, it disappears, and the victim, now an ex-victim, for a moment free, is exposed to that reality – an exposure that has its advantages and disadvantages. It disappears – with wailing and gnashing of teeth. [...] The narrator cannot sleep in a strange room,

---

50   Blanchot, M. *Le livre à venir*, Paris: 1959, p. 36. In English, see *The Book to Come*, translated by Charlotte Mandell, Stanford 2003, p. 24.

is tortured by a high ceiling, being used to a low ceiling. What is taking place? The old pact is out of date. It contained no clause treating of high ceilings. The habit of friendship for the low ceiling is ineffectual, must die in order that a habit of friendship for the high ceiling may be born. Between this death and that birth, reality, intolerable, absorbed feverishly by his consciousness at the extreme limit of its intensity, by his total consciousness organized to avert the disaster, to create the new habit that will empty the mystery of its threat – and also of its beauty. [P, p. 517]

From the perspective of Beckett's later writing, elements that are brought to the forefront of attention include: dialogue, in which the writer involves himself with Proust's work – by means of a "transcribed" language taken from Schopenhauer's writings – and an analysis of the impossibility of actualization within language of the experience of time.[51] Obviously, the other element is far more important. Beckett likewise raises his most prominent themes, including unnamable time, empty vastness, and pure difference – this unspecified "in between" one "habit" and another, enabling the stabilization of the space of consciousness and helping to preserve language in its referential mode. In the meantime, the epiphany of time, already successfully stripped of its entire metaphysical aura by Beckett, becomes simultaneously "unbearable" and fascinating. Consciousness does not stand the test of time, meaning that it cannot grasp it (time) and enclose it within the field of presence, as well as transform it into a linguistic representation. An isolated moment is deadly and beautiful, unspeakable and impossible to experience. Subjectivity is exposed to the workings of time and the only profit emerging from this experience on the side of writer is a continuous approaching of the moment of exclamation, in which the consciousness confronts what is most real. Time will never let itself be forgotten, just as it will never let consciousness rest from attempting to meet its challenge.

Blanchot was right when he wrote that the primary issue of Beckett's writing is the relation between consciousness – desiring to come into existence in the world through a cognitive act – and the sphere of a completely negative emptiness, which is unable to permanently retain any kind of sense. Blanchot pointed – in accord with his general idea of literature – to radical passivity as a way out. This would be a passivity in which consciousness surrenders, but gains an anchoring in the network of natural language. It seems that this is precisely the point where the path of Beckett and his critic (and, to a certain extent, his rival in this radical, literary and existential experiment) diverge. Blanchot seemed to miss (as many other readers), that Beckett's language is fully transparent and subject-free only at first sight.

Bruno Clément[52] grasped this substantial divergence in his exceptional and monumental study devoted to the rhetorical character of Beckett's works. In order

---

51   See Pilling, J. "Beckett's Proust" in *Journal of Beckett Studies*, Winter 1976.
52   See Clément, B. *L'œuvre sans qualités. Rhétorique de Samuel Beckett*, Paris 1994.

to describe the phenomenon in which we are interested, he introduced the figure of "epanorthosis," which could be explained as: self-correction, retraction, or in most simple terms, as "referencing."[53] The act of writing can be neutral only under one condition, which is its complete "submersion in otherness" and complete loss of the possibility of becoming. The very movement of passivity itself is not supported solely by the gesture of free submission to the forces of neutrality. In fact, it is an effect of consciousness at work, however slight. Clément, when arguing for the existence of the impossible to ease the multi-directional tension between subjectivity and time, language and reality reconstructs in great detail the trope – so vivid in Beckett's works – of an obsessively self-controlling individual, struggling to save its subjectivity. As Clément demonstrates, Beckett's writing is based on impossibility, but it remains connected to the function of language, which wants to actualize its existence. But the act of speech merely initiates a series of corrections and negations. It seems that Clément managed to grasp the essence of the issue. Beckett's language is, on the one hand, progressive, directed at determining and thereby gathering reality. On the other hand, it is critical and it forces consciousness to be constantly moving – substituting and verifying the positions it occupies. However, his most prominent, and surfacing as if by accident, feature is the strength of negativity, which by the act of ontological cancellation of the external world changes possible representations of what is real in a form that is "hollowed of sense."[54] The progression of speech and writing in Beckett's work seems to go beyond the discovery and affirmation of what is absent. By marking itself as a paradoxical trace, which does not direct itself toward any dimension of previously present reality, language merely suggests what is negative. It keeps reordering everything and exposes consciousness to what is different, alien and external.

From this perspective, I believe, one can more clearly grasp the attempt to reformulate the ontology of literature undertaken in regard to Beckett's works by Maurice Blanchot. Epanorthosis, along with catachresis,[55] constitute two main

---

53   The theme of "referencing" also appears in an inspiring book about the subject in the works of Beckett analysed from the perspective of the reworking of myth, which is most significant for the writer – that of Narcissus and Echo. See Hunkeler, T., *Echos de l'ego dans l'œuvre de Samuel Beckett*, Paris-Montreal 1997.

54   I use Adorno's formulation from his text entitled "Parataxis: On Hölderlins Late Poetry," in Theodor W. Adorno, *Notes To Literature: Volume 2*, translated by Shierry Weber Nicholsen, New York 1992, pp. 109–49.

55   Catachresis is a double trace. On the one hand it prolongs hope for finding a new word, which could describe the state, emotions, or the take on reality in question. On the other, it reminds us mercilessly about the unoriginality of language, which could potentially constitute a space of inventiveness. In this way, of course, catachresis connects with *epanorthosis*. Daniel Katz, mentioned above, uses Blanchot's interpretation when

figures of the rhetoric of impossibility, realized by Beckett in his writerly project. First one keeps language in the state of perpetual mobility, and the second one is a sign of radicalization of a fundamental element of literature's program mentioned by the Beckett in his early age and cited in motto. In conclusion, it is all about the attempt to describe, over and over again, the fact that there is nothing new to be said, but also: to try and express what is impossible to express differently every time.

Hearing Subject

> Here form is content, content is form. [...] It is not to be read – or rather it is not only to be read. It is looked at and listened to. His writing is not about something; it is that something itself [...] When the sense is sleep, the words go to sleep. [...] When the sense is dancing, the words dance.[56]
>
> – Samuel Beckett
>
> Entendre, seulement entendre.[57]
>
> – Maurice Blanchot

Blanchot's thought is valuable for a different reason. The author of *The Space of Literature* grasped the problem of the status of the voice in Beckett's works with remarkable acuity. In his text devoted to *Comment c'est*, later included in his monumental *The Infinite Conversation*, the same question keeps reappearing, as if transcribing Beckett's central theme: "what is this voice like," who speaks with this voice, who and under what conditions can it be controlled, and what is its genesis?[58] In a certain sense, he attempts to "rewrite" this question about the rule into his own language, which commands a peculiar form of presence, and remains only within the logic of exclusions and differences. The voice – as understood by Blanchot, himself following Beckett – is neither a substance, nor a substance of sense. It is not a sign pointing to a given designation or a piece of empirical data. It is impossible to grasp, but at the same time it is perceptibly

---

describing relations between the subject and the voice. He also uses the conclusions of Blanchot's faithful reader, Paul de Man, pertaining to autobiography. Katz, as his primary figures, chooses catachresis and *epanorthosis* understood according to de Man. See Katz, D. Op. cit., pp. 11-16.

56 Beckett, S., Dante...Bruno. Vico...Joyce, in *CE*, vol. 4, p. 503.

57 Blanchot M., "Les paroles doivent cheminer longtemps" p. 482, in *L'Entretien infini*, Paris 1969. "Words Must Travel Far," translated by Susan Hanson in *The Infinite Conversation*, Minneapolis 1993.

58 See Clément, B. "Mais quelle est cette voix?," *Samuel Beckett Today/Aujourd'hui* (*Borderless Beckett/Beckett sans frontièrs*), Tokyo 2006.

present. The voice is likewise not a confirmation of the realness of the subject's interior (understood as an "interior voice"), nor does it exist as a vocal trace of what is inside and what could be perceived. It cannot confirm identity (e.g. of the speaker) and does not belong to the intimate sphere. Accepted as a figure embodying those contradictions, the voice uncovers the sources of the idiom that fills the works of Beckett.

> At the end there is a kind of hypothesis: it is perhaps the voice of all of us, the impersonal, errant, continuous, simultaneous and alternating speech […] Not something to hear, perhaps the last written cry, what is inscribed in the future outside books, outside language.[59]

As the author of *The Infinite Conversation* correctly observes, the question of the voice cannot be summed up in a comprehensive definition. It is also extremely difficult to point to functions that this voice could perform in the literary project of Beckett. However, by situating itself in the centre of the unsolvable mystery of the project, it reveals something else – a feature from which Blanchot would like to escape: the structure of the subject. One could say that the voice exists only under the condition of a functioning consciousness. It does not become a pure sphere, released from the subjectival will of existence or automatised act of writing. It is the unobvious object of a struggle for consciousness with a simultaneous necessity and impossibility of establishing itself as subjectivity.

By skilfully observing and describing the category of the voice in Beckett's work, Blanchot turns him into a witness of a particularly important debate within late modernity focused on the ability/inability to think about the subject in a way different than that proposed by the most prominent discourses of modernity (particularly in the Cartesian-Kantian discourse, or the positive dialectic discourse of Hegel). While admitting that Blanchot is right, it is important to specify and correct a few of his interpretative suggestions. There are references to texts by Roland Barthes and Jacques Derrida in later parts of the text, but here I would like to point to one more possible take on this complex question.

In one of his essays, Jean-Luc Nancy describes the figure of an individuality that one could describe as "a hearing subject." In the case of this particular issue, what is important is the shifting of interpretative stress from the level of the autonomous, anonymous and mythical voice beyond the control of consciousness, to the plain of various dependencies by which it involves itself with consciousness. Also, his distinction between two different modes of "hearing" is particularly noteworthy. The first – *écouter* – is an act, which depends as much on the passivity of the subject, as it does on subject's intentional attitude. It is comprised of both hearing and vigilant listening. The second – *entendre* – is also translated as an act

59 Blanchot M., "Words Must Travel Far," Op. cit., pp. 330, 331.

of careful listening, but in everyday French the term relates mainly to the act of understanding, or if we were to take it literally, "grasping," harnessing something that was initially indeterminate into a system of meanings. The first mode seems to be more significant, since it contains the entire ambivalence of the ontological status of voice, as well as epistemological restrictions of the subject, which tries to deal with its enigmatic character of presence. Nancy rightfully observes that the presence of the sound, which is heard, is not equivalent to the being's presence. Rather, it is a different kind of presence, one that is based on the phenomena of coming, passing, extending, and penetrating.[60]

> For this reason, listening – the opening stretched toward the register of the sonorous, then to its musical amplification and composition – can and must appear to us not as a metaphor for access to self, but as the reality of this access, a reality consequently indissociably "mine" and "other," "singular" and "plural," as much as it is "material" and "spiritual" and "signifying" and "a-signifying."[61]

After all, the concept of the "hearing subject" should not be perceived through the perspective of the phenomenological potentiality of pure insight into the nature of things, but rather as a kind of destabilizing factor of the very same possibility of a fundamental marker of the consciousness – a reflection. At this point, certain decisions are made. What is an alternative way to think about the question of subject? The voice's central position as a sign of contradiction allows us to treat it differently. The issue revolves around the following:

> The subject of the listening or the subject who is listening (but also the one who is "subject to listening" in the sense that one can be "subject to" unease, an ailment, or a crisis) [...].[62]

There is one more reason why Blanchot and Nancy's opinion is of such great importance. In relation to Beckett's works, where one is fully entitled to look for close kinship with the poetic rule of minutely planned repetitions creating the "rhythm" of an idiom, any strict differentiation between writing and the voice is undermined. Both forms of the desire to actualize sense through literature engage each other in a subtle dialectical relationship, from which it is impossible to disengage, as long as the process of writing is taking place. That is how one can understand Beckett's obsessive attachment to the precise form of molding linguistic material from a different perspective. If there is common agreement on Beckett's texts being the equivalent of a musical score (regardless of their genre, for the stage or purely in written form), it seems that this attachment is not about

---

60   Nancy, J-L. À l'écoute, p. 31, Paris: 2002. In English, see Listening, translated by Charlotte Mandell, New York 2007, p. 13.

61   Ibid., p. 31. In English, see p. 12.

62   Ibid., p. 45. In English, see p. 21.

(at least not entirely) a neat metaphor describing the writer's technique. Rather, it revolves around the writer's efforts to rethink (over and again, after the lesson of Joyce) the aporia between the materiality of the sign and etherealness of the voice of literature.

Blanchot was right when he added one more element to Beckett's tightly sealed literary program – the reader. Communication takes place in the form of an intimate hidden relationship that has to display and utter the respective consciousness of both the author and reader.

> Behind the words that are read, as before the words written, there is a voice already inscribed, not heard, not speaking; and the author, close to this voice, is on an equal footing with the reader – each nearly merged with the other, seeking to recognize it.[63]

Blanchot's intuition seems correct. In coupling with Beckett's work, the reader is stimulated to interpret and demand a constructed meaning from him, all while witnessing the sabotage of this very request. By revealing the emptiness of language that sustains his works, he simultaneously opens his work up to an infinite field of interpretations and surrounds it with confounding inaccessibility. Blanchot's intuition leans toward the conclusion that there is no way out of this bind. The only possible and trustworthy access to Beckett's idiom seems to be a form of critical reflection and affirmation of the aforementioned contradictions, along with "listening, only listening" to the voices of texts themselves. It is an attempt on the part of the consciousness of readers to reach an enigmatic place – around which it gathers – the "unspeakable home."[64]

---

63   Blanchot, M., "The Absence of the Book," in *The Infinite Conversation* ," translated by
       Susan Hansons, Minneapolis 1993, p. 329.
64   These are the last words from the work *neither* – "unspeakable home." Beckett, in *CE*,
       vol.4, 425.

PART ONE
DEMONS OF DESCARTES

Chapter One
Mistaken Consciousness / Consciousness in Distress

Fallor, ergo sum.[65]
– Samuel Beckett

The eye will return to the scene of its betrayals.[66]
– Samuel Beckett

It all started with Descartes. Vico and Schopenhauer appear later. A young man, the twenty-four-year-old author, sends his more than hundred-verse-long[67] poem, devoted to Descartes, to an ephemeral competition. The poem is strange. On the one hand, it is a clear display of erudition, containing detailed information from the realm of the history of philosophy. On the other hand, it proposes a formula combining the modernism of T. S. Eliot, old poetic traditions, and an almost scholastic mode of thinking.[68] Descartes is the main protagonist, but also a figure in whom Beckett attempts to unite his own obsessions and his untamed literary knowledge.[69] First and foremost, the text reveals a certain kind of authorial attachment to the heritage of rationalism. However, it is not a statement of blind devotion. Beckett emerges as a follower of Descartes, and he will remain one for the rest of his days. However, this access to a certain intellectual tradition is accompanied by a particular, creative betrayal.[70]

---

65   Beckett, *Whoroscope*, in *CE*, vol. 4, p. 6. These are the changed words of Descartes, from the *Meditations*, woven into poetic form by Beckett.
66   MVMD, French ed., p. 32, English ed., p. 458. See also S. Beckett`s *Mal vu mal dit/Ill seen lll said. A Bilingual, Evolutionary, and Synoptic Edition*, edited by Ch. Krance, New York 1996.
67   Extended footnotes, an integral part of the poem, are not included.
68   See a detailed interpretation of his text: Harvey, L. *Samuel Beckett: Poet and Critic*, Op. cit.
69   See Hunkeler, T. *Echos de l`ego dans l`œuvre de Samuel Beckett*, pp. 127-130, Op cit.
70   See Coetzee, J. M. "Eight ways of looking at Samuel Beckett" in *Samuel Beckett Today/ Aujourd`hui (Bordless Beckett/Beckett sans frontièrs)*, Op. cit.

The title itself speaks volumes about this dance. *Whoroscope* is a horoscope written together with a vulgar name for a prostitute – indicating, at the very least, the contaminated character of the name. In almost the entirety of the text, Cartesian rational certainty is limited to a parody of scholarly conversations, tributes to one's own aberrations, and to loathing and fear mixed with awe constituting his own approach toward the body. In the end, it seems that the body is the centre around which Beckett organizes the work. But it is a degenerated body, one that has been thrown aside and taken over by the dominating mind and, at the same time, the dominating, impossible to tame, random and deadly force of instincts.

The dualism of body and the spirit remains in Beckett's works, but the central position of consciousness in his project as a writer seems to be far more important. It is a consciousness that is revealed in a gradual and methodical destruction of all pretenses, possibly obscuring the foundations of cognition and being. Beckett rips off the cloak of sensuality, but also questions the supposed legibility of all possible representations of the mind. He sees the opportunity to save an individual within the sceptical gesture itself, which he later completes with a hint of irony, or even sarcasm in relation to the idea of autonomous subject. From Descartes' teachings, Beckett chooses to retain the structural rule of testing the epistemological conditions of the capabilities of the human mind. He compares and contrasts this rule with the language of imagination, which, along with the experience of physicality, sabotages the possibility of anchoring an individual's knowledge about itself and the world. The ambivalent position of the body should also be treated as the "heritage" of rationalism. Beckett sees it as responsible for the falsity of empirical sensations, which do not respond to the commands of subjectivity. The body presents itself to the individual as the only proof for its own and reality's existence. Finally, the third crucial element is language as a form enabling mediation between the individual and the world. It is not difficult to observe that this is the point where Beckett moves furthest away from the Cartesian model, undermining the representational power of language, its semantic transparency and obviousness. He points to language as not only an obstacle for individual expression, but also – and most prominently – as a sign of consciousness in crisis. It cannot be resolved, because it is this particular crisis that becomes a marker of the human condition.

In many of Beckett's works, it is this complicated Cartesian approach to the question of consciousness that is highlighted in an astonishing way. The more advanced his minimalistic approach in writing becomes, the more we observe this philosophical stance expressed through madness and silence. *Ill seen Ill said* is one of the texts in which the main theme will be the effort to establish the position of consciousness and its relation to the sphere of sensuality and the external world.

Necessity to Look, Necessity to Speak

Before we move to reading the text itself, let us stop for a minute to consider Descartes himself. He will bring us closer to the rule and structure of thought assumed by Beckett. His famous proclamation on the method of cognition is presented in the *Meditations*. This cognition constitutes the unreachable point of total self-knowledge for the subject:

> I shall now close my eyes, I shall block up my ears, I shall divert all my sense, and I shall even delete all bodily images from my thought or, since this is virtually impossible to achieve, at least count them as empty and worthless; and I shall try, by conversing only with myself and looking deep within myself, to make myself gradually better known and more familiar to myself. I am a thinking thing, that is, one that doubts, affirms, denies, understands a few things, is ignorant of many others, will this and not that, and also imagines and perceives by the senses. [...] And therefore I seem already able to lay down, as a general rule, that everything I very clearly and distinctly perceive is true.[71]

In this well-known catalogue of the features of *res cogitans*, the question of being a subject and the will to mark the thinking self as the very sense of reality is revealed, one could say, by chance. As Descartes correctly foresaw, the rational and sceptical method, which has the certainty and inviolability of cognition as its goal, cannot be purged of what is random, accidental and physical. The command of senses is suspended, losing the contest with the rule of mind, behind which stand not only the "clarity" and "sharpness" of representation, but also the will itself, as expressed by Descartes at the beginning of the third meditation. This initial aspect of the will, commencing the work of consciousness, cannot be detached from the ability of intellectual distinction. However, this is the will of a sovereign kind of consciousness, which allows for the questioning, not the ruin, of the reality of the thinking individual's existence. As Husserl writes:

> The world is for me absolutely nothing else but the world existing for and accepted by me in such a conscious *cogito*. It gets its whole sense, universal and specific, and its acceptance as existing from such *cogitations*. [...] By my living, by my experiencing, thinking, valuing, and acting, I can enter no world other than the one that gets its sense and acceptance or status [*Sinn und Geltung*] in and from me, myself.[72]

Absolute certainty – explained by Descartes later in the work – is guaranteed by the presence of God, who legitimizes sense and all possible mistakes committed by an individual and removes doubts, which become a vehicle for arriving at the

---

71   Descartes, R. *Meditations on First Philosophy*, translated by Michael Moriarty, Oxford, 2008, p. 25.

72   Husserl E., *Cartesian Meditations*, translated by Dorion Cairns, The Hague 1982. p. 21

truth. The concept of the infinite,[73] which cannot be created by man himself, is a proof of the mind's limits, as well as the impetus for a fundamental desire for grounded knowledge.[74] In this way, searching for the foundations of knowledge and the conditions in which the "I" can become insusceptible to any kind of questioning is not something natural and given, but the practiced result of the will to reach the essence of things.[75] The sphere of the senses remains defined as a hurtful pretense, a fiction which obscures reality *in crudo*, but one that – thanks to the inferior character of existence – can be treated as an epistemological obstacle and not a valid form or path to cognition. Descartes goal is clear: to locate a primal, metaphysical sanction for every act of the mind, with every effort of striving for reflection becoming significant only to the extent that it is anchored by the certain self-knowledge of a subject. After all, it will be the subject that achieves priority over the sensual, trying to seduce with pretense, the random sphere of physicality. This priority will be the result of the subject's ability to dominate the sphere completely, rather than exclude it.

Beckett's loyalty to the domination of rationalism should be understood through the prism of his texts proving the impossibility of exiting categories of thought through sceptical reduction. The author of the *Endgame* will add his own ironic and anti-essentialist vision of a man as a thinking being to the optimistic and metaphysical vision of Descartes. Faced with the disintegration of a stable foundation of for being and cognition, he shifts the borders of individual consciousness toward madness and silence. He likewise replaces progressively emergent doubt, allowing for an opening of the horizon of stabilized knowledge and recognizing the relations between a subject and the world, with an absence and pure ability to simply doubt and ask questions. The necessity to look, listen and speak constitutes three versions of the same kind of desire of an individual, which remain in Beckett's texts as *ad hoc* sanctions, legitimizing experiments conducted by the author on consciousness. This ambiguous imperative, resulting in multiple effects, is an attempt to test the reality of the world that appears to the subject.

The sensation of affinity between consciousness and madness is connected with two distinct scenarios: absolute identification and death. In both cases, consciousness attempts to verify its own position and enclose itself in an irrevocable sign or gesture. It wants to exclaim its appurtenance to itself, to discover or invent a language allowing the individual to speak, without leaving the sphere of immanence. This is the impossibility, which Beckett kept alive in his writings. It is impossibility, both created and made credible through writing

---

73   Descartes R., *Meditations*, pp. 32-33.
74   See Poulet G., "The Dreams of Descartes" in *Studies in Human Time*, translated by Elliot Coleman, New York, 1959.
75   See Descartes R., *Meditations*, Op. cit., p. 46.

as a process, a practical and thought experiment. Beckett's last text seems to be the most significant testament to this point. In his *"Comment dire* / what is the word,"* we find the clash between the hermetic world of immanence and external reality reaching its climax. In the text, the subject undermines not only the possibility of exclaiming the experience of watching and speaking, but also questions any kind of form of reality that the senses can experience. The madness of perception is connected with madness of the external world that attempts express itself. The text's structure suggests that such a strong relation cannot be disbanded and ended as long as the subject is capable of extracting another word from itself – one that will describe the unreality of both empirical and transcendental guarantees.

Madness, silence and absence – these are all descriptions of the same ontological hypostasis (and only hypostasis), which Beckett attempts to bring to life by means of his literature. Jacques Derrida, writing on the margins of Foucault's text, observes that the Cartesian order cannot account for exclamation, because the speech it evokes tends to systematize even the gravest excess. At the same time, however, every single serious act of reflection situates itself at the very edge of madness. This inseparable closeness of the cogito and of what remains impossible to grasp forces one to look differently at the possibility of the act of thinking as a way of establishing a subject. Every form of language, even the simplest phrase reduced to the bare ellipsis, which will later become Beckett's standard building block, carries meaning that cannot be eradicated in the later phase of purifying consciousness to turn it into the external ground of language. The wish to actualize silence within language becomes fanatical. At the same time, the wish for absolute identity heads toward the representation of complete madness. In Beckett's works, what it is possible to express and what is inexpressible is presented from the perspective of consciousness, which in turn attempts to envelop everything that is presented in a "clear and distinct" form of presence. Derrida describes this issue in the form of alternative:

> Either do not mention a certain silence (a certain silence which, again, can be determined only within a language and an order that will preserve this silence from contamination by any given muteness), or follow the madman down the road of his exile.[76]

In the case of Descartes, the situation looks as follows:

> In its most impoverished syntax, logos is reason and, indeed, a historical reason. And if madness in general, beyond any factitious and determined historical structure, is the

---

76   Derrida J., "Cogito and the History of Madness," in *Writing and Difference*, translated by Alan Bass, Chicago 1978, p. 36.

absence of work, then madness is indeed, essentially and generally, silence, stultified speech, within a caesura and a wound that *open up* life as *historicity in general*.[77]

The logocentric order mentioned by Derrida is based on a necessary gesture of exclusion and an act of establishing ontological hierarchy according to which, that which would be defined as madness will not be able to be expressed. Hence, it will not exist at all. How then should we understand this close relationship of madness, silence and language?

As Derrida suggests, we are facing the necessity of a choice between alternative. On the one hand silence and madness function as foreseen elements of language as a system, which structurally do not differ from other meanings. On the other hand, however, they force the infinite inventiveness of speech, which attempts to follow what is special, beyond the confines of logos: order, sense, mind and presence. In the case of Beckett, we are dealing with the dramatization of this alternative. By not taking sides, Beckett simultaneously discovers sources of his own idiom. Keeping the question of the relation between speech as a necessary aspect of describing the experience of consciousness and silence as a sign of madness unsolved, he attempts to give voice to both modalities of existence. The emerging chiasmic relation of the silence of madness and the madness of silence lies at the base of a radically negative vision of subjectivity, which remains torn between two extremes. These extremes will involve the inability of describing the experience of one's own self-knowledge and existential identity (the silence of madness) and helplessness toward the gap, which emerges between consciousness and the external world. In this world, the role of a connecting factor will be played by a symbolic representation (the madness of silence). As a result, in Beckett's works, only the bare structure of Cartesian method is left in place. There is no longer a metaphysical foundation for the mind's search. Lonely consciousness, while searching for any kind of form of "sufficient reason," finds itself in stubborn defence of pure negativity, which – paradoxically – conditions its liveliness. Right where we find this negativity is where *Ill seen Ill said* begins.

Se voir

The title itself points to the rule guiding relations between consciousness and the world. The main protagonist is a female subject attempting to move around and find herself in space composed of only a few elements (a wall, stone circles, plants and a "safe-haven," which, depending on perspective, might turn out to be a grave). Above all else, she desperately tries to recognize her own position,

---

77   Ibid., p.54

while looking and verifying this very position. The narration is conducted by an impersonal voice that describes the actions of the heroine, but at the same time guides them becoming an agent objectivising her existence through and within language. One could claim that by taking away the ability to speak in the first person from the protagonist, Beckett made her fully dependent on the anonymous voice – one, which can seem to be, in the final instance, not prone to any critical reduction. Beckett complicates the work of scholars by distorting the referential power of language and never deciding finally, whether one can find the "master of discourse." What we read could be understood as projection of an enigmatic source of subjectivity, hidden behind neutral language, but also as a complex, yet still mimetic, description of an "external" situation.

Beckett managed to create tension, upheld throughout the course of an entire text. Both dimensions of language overlap in a way which makes it impossible to decide on what side one should place the burden of being and meaning, presented in the text. As a result, we witness a subtly written history of consciousness, which struggles with the will of self-determination, with language capable of describing the effort, and finally with the Other, placed as the point of reference for the objectivity of the subject. The imperative of seeing, source-less, determines the protagonist's actions, but is also a necessity, forcing movement toward imagination:

> To the imaginary stranger the dwelling appears deserted. Under constant watch it betrays no sign of life. The eye glued to one or the other window has nothing but black drapes for its pains. Motionless against the door he listens long. No sound. Knocks. No answer. Watches all night in vain for the least glimmer. Returns at last to his own and avows, No one. She shows herself only to her own. But she has no own. Yes yes she has one. And who has her. [ISIS, s.453]

Within this description, both layers of experience seem to overlap: the sphere of visible sensuality and the sphere of speculation, examining singular identity. Consciousness approaches itself, as well as the external world, as a subject of an experiment. It keeps asking, checking, questioning and nagging. The experiment displays a constant, but inexhaustible movement directed from within to the outside and back again.At the same time, however, Beckett remains extremely mistrustful, as far as the possibility of consciousness exiting the sphere of its own immanence goes. This pendulum-like movement is in reality a safety measure, protecting the signs of subjectivity's existence from erasure. The final sentences from the quoted passage indicate one more possible reading. A possible interpretation is one of imploding consciousness, which, when confronted with an impossible to establish relation between itself and the world, retreats almost entirely to its own intelligible world. In this very world it will try to conduct a kind of intimate dialog with itself. However, this insignificant distance (coming into existence by virtue of the act of consciousness itself) makes the emergence of language possible. In return, it creates an environment for a dialogue, but at the same time sabotages the very sense of such an exchange. To brand subjectivity as consciousness, which is capable of defining itself and the conditions of self-cognition imply the necessity of projecting this reflection to the other: the "other, whom I could become myself." The existence of this otherness is necessary. Without it, subjectivity sentences itself to an obsessive and barren circulation of thought, which cannot be revealed in a form of permanent meaning. Madness corners the subject in Beckett's work from two sides, changing its topology. It is before the language of consciousness (it anchors itself as an abysmal sphere of what precedes the act of thinking), as well as that, which is outside of it (in a sense in which absolute identity does not need any kind of language). The subject confronted with two kinds of madness cannot perceive itself, as long as it will use language as a form of actualizing itself within a tedious process of establishing its own position. Yet, whenever it stops speaking and allows the irrational to take the lead, it does not slump into incoherent ramble, but brings "silence, rattling silence of thinking that does not think its own words" closer to itself.

The sphere of sensuality is not revealed in Beckett's work in an obvious way either. The supposedly neutral description of a situation displays its own incoherence: the gaze does not touch objects, but stops at a seemingly transparent cover, beyond which one's sight is incapable of reaching. The physical boundary of a glass window, which evolves into a border denoted by dark shades gives an idea of how strongly this apparently neutral mediation is in reality blocking direct access to any kind of externality. Empirical reality brings nothing beyond alienation. By disinheriting an individual from the world of matter it forces it to attune its identity through an initiation to the murderous movement of language. The game of direct contact and separation results in consciousness' inability to recognize itself as a permanent, coherent being, but legitimizes its own existence solely within finding and exclaiming moments and places of incoherence, gaps and fiction. That is when the knowledge of the narrator is allowed to take the stage and stop efforts at a precise appropriation of the current state of the subject. It also makes actions unifying events and observations into a stream of narration more reliable:

> There was a time when she did not appear in the zone of stones. A long time. Was not therefore to be seen going out or coming in. When she appeared only in the pastures. Was not therefore to be seen leaving them. Save as though by enchantment. But little by little she began to appear. In the zone of stones. First darkly. Then more and more plain. Till in detail she could be seen crossing the threshold both ways and closing the door behind her. Then a time when within her wall she did not appear. A long time. But little by little she began to appear. Within her walls. Darkly. Time truth to tell still current. Though she within the no more. This long time. [ISIS, pp. 453-454]

It is precisely the distanced language of narration and description that marks the borders of reality, within which the heroine can appear. The conditions presented as necessary for the appearance of the heroine are precise and methodical. This is so precisely because of external events establishing and pulling consciousness from its own world – one to which no other form of language has access. To "see oneself" – similarly to getting to know oneself – is an impossible task. The only description available is the one created by someone else. It is a description, which retains its power at the edge of singular immanence. It brands the existence of consciousness with a mark of mystery.

The sight of a "final sparkle" for which the heroine is waiting could be treated as an incarnation of the enigmatic form of an anonymous, abstract presence that remains on the dividing line between existence and non-existence. It suggests an ambiguity of the word used by the author. The ambiguity of sparkle is well understood, but in French "la lueur" has one more possible meaning: a subtle hazy light or a flickering flame. This "final sparkle" could signify the arrival of a weak light, which will not be able to fully lighten the darkness of the external world and the internal reality of the self. It could also protect her from getting lost in the dawning of negativity. By searching for the most reliable foundations of reality, Beckett becomes one of the most radical critics of faith in the "view from nowhere." Still, however, one can find this travesty of longing for obvious presence, or patient work of negative reflection allowing for the ascertainment that what is "visible" is "wrongly seen," hence "wrongly exclaimed."

Illusion of Autonomy

In one section, the narrator observes a slightly different situation (and in this particular scene the protagonist is not present). The event alters not only the rhythm of narration set by patient descriptions of observations and movements of the heroine, as well as changes in the set-up of the narrational voice, but also shifts the entire interpretation in the direction of space where no kind of subjectivity is possible.

> But she can be gone at any time. From one moment of the year to the next suddenly no longer there. No longer anywhere to be seen. Nor by the eye of flesh nor by the other. Then as suddenly there again. Long after. So on. Any other would renounce. Avow, No one. No one more. Any other than this other. In wait for her to reappear. In order to resume. Resume the – what is the word? What the wrong word? [ISIS, s. 455]

Let us observe how far Beckett decides to progress in terms of reduction. He questions not only reality presented sensually, but also undermines the possibility of establishing any kind of ontological instance which would be capable of confirming the heroin's existence. The narrator's voice is unable to stabilize itself completely and transform itself into a language of obvious sense – a language able to make all dimensions of reality unquestionable. The rule of limitations touches directly upon the narrator's structure, but at the same time does not allow him to stop him from speaking. The heroin's departure does not connote the loss of the subject of description for the narrator, but shows the border of his own language. He cannot cross this border, which is, paradoxically, supplying momentum to rhetorical invention. It is not about a particular way of celebrating the aesthetic opportunity to speak, but rather about the ironic gesture pertaining to the possibility of a conceptual, as well as symbolic, take on reality. The finale of the quoted passage sounds almost like a parody of speculative jargon, which allows the horrific simultaneity of speech and sudden silence to explode.

He confirms the irony of language trapped in a solipsistic dance around negation and the very notion of otherness, which repeated enough times, shifted and devalued by repetition's inertia, stops meaning anything. Language immobilizes what can be seen, while not being able to follow changes in reality. Gradually and with increasing force it alienates the one who is actually speaking. The "other" is an unchanging point of reference, against which the appearing figure must define itself, in order to adopt any actual form. The unspeakable and unfocused becomes a condition of ability for the possibility of presence. The subject is not a figure of ascetic consciousness attempting to free itself from an eerie empiricism (the female protagonist – heroine), nor does it contain itself within the gesture of a continually undertaken restitution of the act of reflection (the narrator's voice). In the first instance, the individual's actions are limited to – so common in Beckett's late and mature period – a process of observing and staging of the sensual sphere of experience. In the second, actions are limited to acknowledging the final consequences of interiorizing the process of establishing one's consciousness.

The entire dilemma pertains to the fundamental inability to grasp this empty space/place within the act of representation (after the subject's departure and the other's fall into silence, ascribing sense to the heroine's existence). It is a space/place, which Beckett attempts to reach through procured figures from his text. At the same time, however, this empty space/place, this sphere of non-existence, of pure nothingness, cannot be revealed as long as perceiving, thinking and functioning consciousness remains in existence.

The object of a thought process is precisely what does not exist, that which is not a sphere of objectival empiricism, or what constitutes the subject's structure. For Beckett, the self-definition (or self-localization) of consciousness (which barricades itself with what is different, at the same time falling into a trap of what is external, and which appears at the peak of identity's narration performed by subjectivity) becomes the fundamental gesture. Thanks to this gesture, speech and language – perceived in this radical manner – create a situation in which everything that is other, "non-native," questions the foundations of the ability for self-definition.[78] In this vital moment, the self-transparency of the subject seems to momentarily turn into the chaos of the inability to differentiate.

Finally, after such a deep act of reduction, there is a desire to rethink the beginning. Or rather, there emerges a desire to grasp consciousness in its initial movement – a movement that brings hope, born out of a new beginning. The desire to reach the "beginning" is undermined by the forces of the initial question about the ability to express (in speech) this initial movement. The same question, however reformulated, goes even further. Double negation does not bring about any synthesis, any reconciliatory sense, but rather emphasizes painful silence, which emerges instead of any kind of answer in a positive form. The complete autonomy of the subject turns out to be fiction and a mistaken meaning. However, these are fictions and mistake necessity for the persistence of consciousness and ascribing its acts with an existential weight.

Necessity of Telling

To become silent in a singular way means to kill oneself as a subject. To remain silent and prolong the meaning imbedded in the system of language is to keep telling, to keep speaking, but in a different kind of language. The power of the senses, which bring chaos and uncertainty, constitute the backdrop for this scene in Beckett:

> Already all confusion. Things and imaginings. As of always. Confusion amounting to nothing. Despite precautions. If only she could be pure figment. Unalloyed. This old so dying woman. So dead. In the madhouse of the skull and nowhere else. Where no more precautions to be taken. No precautions possible. [ISIS, s. 456]

The final consequence of the desire for the self-determination of subjectivity is not absolute identity, in the end, but complete chaos. It renders any kind of distinction impossible. As a result, all that could emerge on the horizon of consciousness is "revoked," because it is impossible to distinguish. Once again, absolute identity is equalized with lethal immobility, out of which no form of will can be extracted; a will, which sought to be the "caution of the mind." Beckett phenomenally shows

---

78   Nancy observes that the "Cartesian point of The Same" or the "point" of awareness' identity in which the rule of subjectivity finds its realization, does not focus within itself what is singular, or what is different. Ability to self-define by the subject is conditioned by the ability to treat language as a medium used for actualizing the existing, hence thinking, "me." See Nancy, J-L, *Ego sum*, Paris 1979.

the mechanism of internalizing the act of consciousness, behind which there is nothing except an empty thought structure faithfully guarded by subjectivity. The madness "inside the skull" resonates with a voice that does not make any sense and which cannot receive any meaning from the outside. At the same time, this madness can be conditioned only by consciousness. It is a madness that undermines not only the realness of the female protagonist (changing into purely functional product of fantasy, not even of the author himself, but rather his voice), and also the rationale behind the gesture of reflection made by the individual (the case of the impersonal narrator). This proclaimed, but in reality impossible – completely internal, fully merged and individual – existence (the existence "inside the skull") possesses a quality of fantasy, encircled by Beckett's description. The thought experiment proposed by Beckett attempts to incorporate two extremities: the work of consciousness, trying to recognize itself and guard itself from reality, as well as a dream of existence in a pure state; an existence which is freed from internal and external boundaries, of being in a sphere of complete chaos and a lack of differentiation.

The desire for undisturbed existence, a *de facto* dream of achieving a position of impersonal lasting, is confronted with the work of consciousness, which is also a work of memory. This effort of extracting the speech of the primal contamination of existence, which is unable to justify its own presence, happens without referring to this source negativity. In this way, the fantasy of neutrality is turned into that of an individual freed from all ethical responsibilities. It is a state in which no form of "certain knowledge" remains necessary. The imperative of posing questions and the obligation of uttering words, which could fill tormenting emptiness, become of the utmost importance:

> The long white hair stares in a fan. Above and about the impassive face. Stares as if shocked still by some ancient horror. Or by its continuance. Or by another. That leaves the face stone cold. Silence at the eye of the scream. Which say? Ill say. Both. All three. Question answered. [ISIS, s. 459]

This is both a beautiful and surprising vision and an excellent explanation of Beckett's concept. It is a description of a situation where sight is the achievement of control over that which is outside, the external world. The observed heroine becomes locked in a frame of the gaze, which grants it the access to the past and thereby experience. However, this very experience, even though acutely present and determining the location of a speaking subject and the heroine, remains unnamed. In one image, the entirety of an unspecified "horror" is concentrated. The figure of synaesthesia: "silence at the eye of the scream" is a juxtaposition of all registers of existence: all the possibilities and unreliability of speech, sight, consciousness and the body. Melding all in one, dense and composed of contaminated orders of the image – the figure becomes, in a way, a "final" figure of the subject; a figure which, in theory, would eliminate the need to look and talk. This extreme, however, is not final in the works of Beckett. It transforms into a different starting point, from which a concrete practice, even if rudimentary, can begin – a practice of telling stories about the fate of consciousness. Tearing through the creations of its own imagination, through the resistance of the materiality of language, breaking through its inadequacy, and finally foreseeing its own death – lonely subjectivity attempts to continue its narration on all of those dependencies, and about itself; about its own internal world to which it has already lost access.

Contemplating Emptiness

In its movement toward self-determination, consciousness is fully autonomous. It is, however, lonely. The unmanageable entanglement of necessity and impossibility (looking, thinking and speaking) forces it to perpetually correct its own position, as well as its movement toward emptiness. The phenomenon of emptiness, functioning as a form, which cannot be filled with any sense-producing act of consciousness, becomes the paradoxical foundation of reality. The drive to capture the "zero level" of perception and cognition is certainly one the Beckett's obsessions, but it also explains why everything that is of any importance for the subject is perceived as "ill seen and ill said":

> Such – such fiasco that folly takes a hand. Such bits and scraps. Seen no matter how and said as seen. Dread of black. Of white. Of void. Let her vanish. And the rest. For good. And the sun. Last rays. And the moon. And Venus. Nothing left but black sky. White earth. Or inversely. No more sky or earth. Finished high and low. Nothing but black and white. Everywhere no matter where. But black. Void. Nothing else. Contemplate that. Not another word. Home at last. Gently gently. [ISIS, s. 460]

Existence is perceived not as a perpetual catastrophe, but as a conscious reworking of the "fallen" character of individuality. That is the reason for such strong desire, on the part of the consciousness, to find and confront a pure, unmediated source of what is negative. As a result, consciousness could achieve an irrefutable legitimization of its own existence. But the outcome of such an experiment is doubly tragic. On the one hand, death produces only fear, but on the other – the symptoms of the subject's actions bring alienation. The subject is left with the scraps of language, which do not match any kind of wholeness of sense and cannot be made precise in any form of act on behalf of consciousness, or fear, which allows the subject to know that it still exists.

However, as is usually the case with Beckett, despair is a situation and a state that occurs "after the end." It is thanks to despair that the subject is able to try and grasp, "with clarity," different forms of absence in which that which is real presents itself without any linguistic cloaking. However, we are again confronted with a situation where the structure of the thought process and the system of language force the subject into hypostasis, establishing the thinnest possible boundary between individual consciousness and negativity. It is this very establishing of a boundary, which creates a distance between subjectivity and what is real, allowing the understanding of literature as a form of expressing the existence of an unbearable gap. The clash of incompatible spheres of consciousness and the world presents an opportunity for a game. After the previous assertion of the impossibility of a certain subject, the looking and speaking subject concerns the game with unending change of perspective.

Consciousness saves itself only when, as its initial condition, it accepts its own mistake, confirming consciousness' finite character, and when, in a lethal gesture of approaching the boundary of madness and death, it tries to fight it. The possibility of a pure, unbiased gaze is just one more, sarcastically noted, illusion of representation. This possibility becomes incorporated into the chain of an indifferent language, which, as long as it can anchor itself as a trace and resound as a voice, will prolong the deadly game of subjectivity. Changing points of view or changing the optics of a gaze, consciousness celebrates its own fictionality, but at the same time tries to handle the randomness of the body, the arbitrariness of language and its own lack of transparency and helplessness when facing what is absent and without sense. This is how Beckett is tied to the Cartesian dualism of the soul and body, consciousness and senses, subject and object – although there is no sign of epistemological optimism, characteristic of the founder of modern rationalism present in this reference. Standing firmly by what is negative, Beckett offers the readers faithful company in the adventures of the figures of consciousness he presents. In other words, he offers the patient awaiting of the arrival of sense, which might be the only profit from literature as a form of thought. He proposes standing on the lookout for "silence at the eye of the scream."

Chapter Two
The Invention of Time or the Trap of Consciousness

Not the least of the torments which plague our existence is the constant pressure of time, which never lets us so much as draw breath but pursues us all like a taskmaster with a whip. It ceases to persecute only him it has delivered over to boredom.[79]
– Arthur Schopenhauer

But already will, the will to live, the will not to suffer [...].[80]
– Samuel Beckett

Aside from Descartes, the most important philosophical reference for Beckett was the figure of Schopenhauer. Although Beckett, in his early twenties and making plans about his own work, did not treat the thinker with a speculative solemnity, his ingenious use of the philosopher's treaties was clearly visible in his future, strictly artistic, practice. In particular, reading Schopenhauer assisted Beckett in his interpretation of *In Search of Lost Time*. There are those who claim that the essay on Proust is a recording of Beckett's literary program rather than a thorough analysis, as well as those who see the text as an original commentary on the novel. Both are likely right. One way or another, almost all the important figures for Beckett's project appear in a crystalised form in the pages of the essay: consciousness, suffering, time, possibility and the boundaries of cognition and speech. Let us see the constellations in which these issues assemble themselves.

The Illness of Time

Beckett begins his analyses with a strong statement, throwing the reader right in the middle of his concern:

But the poisonous ingenuity of *Time* in the science of affliction is not limited to its action on the subject, that action, as has been shown, resulting in an unceasing modification of his personality, whose permanent reality, if any, can only be apprehended as a retrospective hypothesis. The individual is the seat of a constant process of decantation, decantation from the vessel containing the fluid of future time,

---

79   Schopenhauer A., Schopenhauer, A. "Additional Remarks on the Doctrine of the Vanity of Existence," In Philosophical Writings, edited by Wolfgang Schirmacher, New York 1998, p. 260.
80   Beckett S., *Proust*, in CE, vol. 4, p. 528.

sluggish, pale and monochrome, to the vessel containing the fluid of past time, agitated and multi-coloured by the phenomena of its hours. [P, pp. 513-514]

The subject is established in the necessary appearance of consciousness and existential adjustment. It lacks stability, which comes "too late" and is more of an effect of the forced conceptualization and fictionalisation of life happening, rather than any concrete form of unquestionable presence. Already here one can spot a strong echo of Schopenhauer's ideas, or rather a certain notion that, beginning with "Proust," will be perpetually present in Beckett's works. I am thinking about the positioning of individual consciousness against reality and time, or rather: reality, which emerges from time. In Beckett's description, the subject is forced into discontinuity, involved in a fight with its own fragile condition of temporality. However, the determination Beckett shows with respect to the disillusion of the autonomy of the subject is somewhat surprising. Similarly to Schopenhauer's main work, the question of representation becomes a central issue and a point of departure. It focuses within itself both the subject and the object, engaging an interplay between the two categories. As a result, time is not a mythical unconditional and undefined duration, but a way of actualizing experience, thanks to which the rudiments of subjectivity can finally crystalise; subjectivity which attempts to give itself the objective rank of a centre of meanings. When Beckett describes the subject as a place in which different aspects of temporality find a common place, it is a topological schema that is almost an exact repetition of the conclusions of Schopenhauer on the "nothingness of existence":

Time and the fleeting nature of all things therein, and by means thereof, are merely the form wherein is revealed to the will-to-live, which as the thing-in-itself is imperishable, the vanity of that striving. Time is that by virtue whereof at every moment all things in our hands come to naught and thereby lose all true value. What has been, no longer is; it as little exists as that which has never been. But everything that is, is the next moment already regarded as having been. And so the most insignificant present has over the most significant past the advantage of reality, whereby the former is related to the latter as something to nothing.[81]

Time as a power degrading the possibility of individual existence is not, after all, final, but merely informs one about the helplessness of human striving. At the same time, however, it brings to life a thinking individual, who can attempt to face what Beckett, along with Schopenhauer, mysteriously calls reality. The rule of the will is subjected to the rule of conscious existence, thanks to which nothingness, proclaimed by both authors, can be rendered observable. The will to live, however – this is where we observe a shift of stress in Beckett's work as opposed to Schopenhauer's – is possible only as a correction of the state of discontinuity, a

---

81   Schopenhauer, A. "Additional Remarks on the Doctrine of the Vanity of Existence", in *Parerga and Paralipomena*, translated by E. F. J. Payne, Oxford 2000, p. 283.

change made from the perspective of time. Only cohesiveness as a form imposed ex post facto conditions the stability of the subject, at the same time making it dependent on the fiction of representation, separating from the experience of what is real, which cannot be captured or held in any form of symbolic mediation. From the perspective of the possibility of linguistic legitimation, the present identified as an event becomes a complete catastrophe of sense and existence:

> The future event cannot be focused, its implications cannot be seized, until it is definitely situated and a date assigned to it. When Albertine was his prisoner, the possibility of her escape did not seriously disturb him, because it was indistinct and abstract, like the possibility of death. Whatever opinion we may be pleased to hold on the subject of death, we may be sure that it is meaningless and valueless. Death has not required us to keep a day free. [P, p. 514]

Let us compare this with Schopenhauer's statement:

> In such a world where there is no stability of any kind, no lasting state is possible but everything is involved in restless rotation and change, where everyone hurries along and keeps erect on a tightrope by always advancing and moving, happiness is not even conceivable. [...] In the first place, no one is happy, but everyone throughout his life strives for an alleged happiness that is rarely attained, and even then only to disappoint him. As a rule, everyone ultimately reaches port with masts and rigging gone; but then it is immaterial whether he was happy or unhappy in a life that consisted merely of a fleeting vanishing present and is now over and finished.[82]

The power of the present is also a power that reveals and anchors reality but which has to remain hidden and unspoken to retain its force. However, this does not concern the impossibility of stating the event, but rather addresses the merciless logic of catastrophe that is connected to the principals of consciousness, unable to be tamed by time. According to Beckett, the subject is a site of passivity, a place marked by the "flow" of the dark matter of different forms of time, which does not yield to the subject as a realization of the will's rule. This uncontrollable movement, in which the individual is subject to the law of merciless disillusionment and alienation is completed by the ironically presented rule of establishing individuality, disappearing under the weight of unnecessary actions and words. Once again, Beckett, following his philosophical mentor, attempts to outbid him when it comes to pessimism, describing a state in which the subject has no hope for fulfilment in a state of blissful ataraxy, revealing its own existence with the distance of irony. Schopenhauer presents an individual, bouncing off the threshold marked by the finality of death and re-enacting his/her own individuality as a role, solely through ephemeral, completely unreal appearances. Beckett attempts to drag the diagnosis over to his side of the argument and interpretation, in which disillusionment, although important, becomes merely a primary condition for

---

82   Ibid., pp. 20-21.

constituting subjectivity. Disillusioned consciousness is a preparatory stage for negative dialectics, in which the unclear, dark and mumbling part of a singular life will gain a more mature shape.

This relation between time and death could be described in a different way. At the centre one would find the present, around which Beckett's interpretation is circling. At the very beginning of the essay on Proust, Beckett, trying to sketch the general framework in which we could understand the concept of time, smuggles in his own concept of the subject:

> Yesterday is not a milestone that has been passed, but a daystone on the beaten track of the years, and irremediably part of us, within us, heavy and dangerous. We are not merely more weary because of yesterday, we are other, no longer what we were before the calamity of yesterday. A calamitous day, but calamitous not necessarily in content. The good or evil disposition of the object has neither reality nor significance. The immediate joys and sorrows of the body and the intelligence are so many superfoetations. Such as it was, it has been assimilated to the only world that has reality and significance, the world of our own latent consciousness, and its cosmography has suffered a dislocation. [P, pp. 512-513]

The double conditioning of Beckett's ideas is crucial. On the one hand, he remains the heir of idealistic philosophy in which it is the subject that conditions the existence of the object and where indispositions are a kind of empirical residue, covering the very essence of the act of cognition. On the other hand, however, this is a stream of time that is not empirical or transcendental, which distracts and degenerates the realness of the subject, locked in the sphere of potentiality. The paradox, which Beckett continually deepens, leads him toward a radical rethinking of human nature – the individual exists as far as he/she realizes his/her own temporal dependence. At the same, however, in this very movement of gaining consciousness, the individual excludes the possibility of taming time, enclosing it within a notion and, as a consequence, annihilating itself. There is no way out of this situation and the only "real" effect it has is a return to the subject, to the "empty" place in which everything again becomes fluid. Consciousness is asleep but attempting to gain control over itself, the external world and guide the rule of time, thereby bringing upon itself the "catastrophe" of madness and solipsism. Schopenhauer correctly observed that only a subject understood not substantially, but as "incorporeal spectre," a pure, autonomic appearance, which cannot be experienced, known, or grasped in any form of language that brings it closer to realness, can be a result of such desire:

> Every individual is on the one hand the cognitive subject, i.e. the complementary condition for the possibility of the whole objective world, and on the other hand a single appearance of the will, which is precisely what objectifies itself in everything. But this duality of our essence does not remain in a self-subsisting unity: otherwise we would be able to be aware of ourselves in ourselves and independent of the objects

of cognition and willing: but this is absolutely impossible. Rather, as soon as we try for once to understand ourselves, and to do so by turning in on ourselves and directing our cognition inwardly, we lose ourselves, in a bottomless void and find ourselves like hollow, transparent spheres from whose void a voice is speaking, which the cause of it is not to be found within, and in wanting to grasp ourselves we shudder as we catching nothing but an insubstantial phantom.[83]

Is this not what Beckett meant, when he spoke about the helpless "latent" situation, the most internalized dimension of individuality? The subject may stabilize itself, which turns it into a hollow space filled with nonsensical events coming from the outside, or becomes a pure fiction, evolving into a kind of oppression of madness, born out of the desire for the absolute identity of individual consciousness. This heritage of idealism, for which the focal positioning of the subject as a ruler of external reality was so important, remains intact in Beckett's work. However, as was said before in the context of the writer's relation to Descartes' philosophy, he purposefully turns around the direction of the thought impulse, keeping its time, general structure and rule in power – it is not a resignation from the category of consciousness, nor from the rule of sceptical reduction, but rather an exercise in its critical re-evaluation. What reaches consciousness, in other words: what happens to it, demystifies the idealistic fiction of the subject as consciousness' model of adequate representation of objects, hence cognition. But, as Beckett remarks himself, the consciousness operates even when it recognizes its own powerlessness and its downfall, even when it confronts its own will of survival with the will understood as an independent power – time, that by passing destabilizes the wish for survival of the subjectivity. Even more, it completely degenerates the subjectivity as a permanent instance of cognition and existence – "cosmography destroys the inner world."

The existence of consciousness is an autonomic existential proof – it makes it impossible for the final stabilization of the individual as a being having the ability of a limited cognition, as well as protecting subjectivity against the nihilistic surrender to the rule of time. Consciousness does not exercise full power over death, but is merely an attempt at a notional, abstract and hence objective grasp of it. The absence of consciousness, however, is the most fundamental of lacks, the loss of access to the rule of the will to live. The possibility of consciousness, the possibility of representing the world by the subject does not release it from the fear of death, but allows one to understand that he/she is experiencing it. In Beckett's works, the negative reduction leads to an eradication of this vital element and constitutes a kind of blemish on every emerging sensation that is, eventually, deprived of the privilege of hope. As a result, time can be perceived

---

83   Schopenhauer, A. *The World as Will and Representation*, Vol. 1, translated by Judith Norman, Alistar Welhman, Cambridge 2010, p. 304.

only as a syndrome of the "sickness" of the subject, which cannot and does not wish to retrieve itself in full presence. Beckett arrives at an extremity at this point, but skilfully stops right at its edge. In this interpretative strategy, the subject which is not only a theoretical construct that is outside of time, but a desperate act of consciousness struggling with death, its representation and attempt to mark its own position. The subject reveals its own longing for a form of existence different from the human. According to Schopenhauer, the world deprived of hope is a world of animals, a world of what is pure and unmediated in any representation or movement, consciousness and the energy of persistence, focused in a single point:

> Animals are much more satisfied than we by mere existence; the plant is wholly satisfied, man according to the degree of his dullness. Consequently, the animal's life contains less suffering, but also less pleasure, than man's. This is due primarily to the fact that it remains free from *care and anxiety* together with their torment, on the one hand, but is also without real *hope*, on the other. And so it does not participate in that anticipation of a joyful future through ideas together with the delightful phantasmagoria, that source of most of our joys and pleasures, which accompanies those ideas and is given in addition by the imagination; consequently in this sense it is without hope. It is both these because its consciousness is restricted to what is intuitively perceived and so to the present moment. Thus only in reference to objects that already exist at this moment in intuitive perception, does the animal have an extremely short fear and hope; whereas man's consciousness has an intellectual horizon that embraces the whole of life and even goes beyond this. [...] The animal is the embodiment of the present; the obvious peace of mind that it thus shares frequently puts us to shame with our often restless and dissatisfied state that comes from thoughts and cares. [...] It is just this *complete absorption in the present moment*, peculiar to animals, that contributes so much to the pleasure we derive from our domestic pets. They are the present moment personified and, to a certain extent, make us feel the value of every unburdened and unclouded hour, whereas with our thoughts we usually pass it over and leave it unheeded.[84]

The animal present, paradoxically, provides an existence outside of time, but also outside of the possibility to reconcile mind and experience. Pure, isolated persistence, enclosed in one moment, lacks the mystical revelation of the essence of world to itself, but rather constitutes a movement toward anonymity and an affect-less structure of life. The existence of animals, however, does not constitute the reverse of human existence. Animals are not figures of a condensed, alternative anthropological model, but show the possible central point of life itself. Despite the obvious, immanent character of this philosophy (attachment to the "Eastern" idea of individual "resignment"), one could claim that Schopenhauer returns to the tormenting problem of what is real and what cannot be experienced by the subject

---

84   Schopenhauer, A. "Additional Remarks on the Doctrine of the Suffering of the World", Op. cit., pp. 32-33. Emphasis in the original.

when basing epistemological belief on the truthful capacity of representation. The young Beckett expands this initial trajectory of doubt by adding an additional uncertainty, concerned with the critical status of consciousness. Since the event, which is the aim of a reliable cognition, remains forever ungraspable, the only way for a subject willing to fight for its own position (as real as time focused in the present) will be to suffer through "the illness of time," or confronting consciousness with what perpetually escapes it. According to Beckett, the subject can save itself only by remaining faithfully tied to the rule of verifying its own position against what is real, or impossible to represent. Time is not essential, but it demarcates the range of what is real and accumulates in an event, which helplessly, but perpetually, demands its equivalent in language. Subjectivity, as presented by Beckett, belongs to an empty space, outside of essence, which creates the possibility of interpretation of both its own "immanent dynamism" [P, p. 515], as well as the infinite flow of events happening in the external world.

Painful Habit

Beckett also describes the transition of the subject to a different, higher level. He does not seal it permanently within the nihilistic diagnosis of life as a downfall and a void, but rather seeks the salvation of the subject in the very gesture of self-consciousness. A single being takes concrete shape once it is ascribed to a dynamic system of boredom and suffers opposition. By situating itself between the two and being revealed in ever changing form it attempts to gain a level of realism. It is an escape from the lethal power of pure temporality – of what is "real." This power takes away the ability to speak and returns the individual to the sphere of fictional identity, one granted by the subject to itself from the perspective of past events and experiences. This is the kind of memory rejected by Proust and Beckett – memory built on a slow and fundamentally false reconstruction of what is past. The truly important element of memory is spread between moments, when the complete "catastrophe" of confident subjectivity takes place and the boundaries marking its topology (or "cartography," following the author's terminology) is completely erased and finally, when the internal world of sensual experiences and reflections of an individual are cancelled and exposed to the workings of the evil power of unmarked temporality. Subjectivity exposed to boredom is doomed to engage in a barren act of the repetition of "the same." However, when it opens up to the event, it invites pain:

> The laws of memory are subject to the more general laws of habit. Habit is a compromise effected between the individual and his environment, or between the individual and his own organic eccentricities, the guarantee of a dull inviolability,

the lighting-conductor of his existence. Habit is the ballast that chains the dog to his vomit. Breathing is habit. Life is habit. [P, s. 515]

By using his predilection for merciless sarcasm and dark humour, Beckett transcends both Schopenhauer's pessimism, as well as the nihilistically ironic dandyism of Proust. He announces that in the deepest sense there is no hope for the individual. It is enough to look at the way in which Beckett describes "the compromise" between the individual and the world, or life. There is no kind of soothing confirmation within the chain of awkward mediations that the subject needs to perform in order to survive, sentencing itself to the endless boredom of passive repetition. Habit has nothing to do with reconciliation between man and reality, it rather resembles the reign of the embodied pretense, or in the radical instances, and it can stand for a relationship with the only form of being a subject, which is bearable. Despite this forgetting of primal pain or erasing consciousness of its irreducible source, suffering is still considered to be an act of will. Hence, it still withholds the individual from surrendering him or herself to the void. What does that mean? Beckett explains himself directly and refers to a strong metaphysical concept of indelible blame, which could be the only "profit" of existence:

> Habit then is the generic term for the countless treaties concluded between the countless subjects that constitute the individual and their countless correlative objects. The periods of transition that separate consecutive adaptations [...] represent the perilous zones in the life of the individual, dangerous, precarious, painful, mysterious and fertile, when for a moment the boredom of living is replaced by the suffering of being. [...] The suffering of being: that is, the free play of every faculty. Because the pernicious devotion of habit paralyses our attention, drugs those handmaidens of perception whose co-operation is not absolutely essential. Habit is like François, the immortal cook of the Proust household, who knows what has to be done, and will slave all day and all night rather than tolerate any redundant activity in the kitchen. But our current habit of living is as incapable of dealing with the mystery of a strange sky or a strange room, with any circumstance unforeseen in her curriculum, as Francoise of conceiving or realizing the full horror of a Duval omelette. Then the atrophied faculties come to the rescue, and the maximum value of our being is restored. But less drastic circumstances may produce this tense and provisional lucidity in the nervous system. Habit may not be dead (or as good as dead, doomed to die) but sleeping. [P, s. 516]

Within this descriptive analysis of the creation of metaphysical pain and the birth of unfulfilled dialectical boredom and existential suffering, the definition of the latter seems to be the most interesting. Would it not be a kind of paradoxical freedom, dictated by the desire to cross the boundaries of an individual's abilities and overpowered by an unimaginable, unpredictable presence, which accompanies the persistence of a moment? With all certainty, but one should certainly answer that in this "game" man is bound to fail from the very beginning, the day of birth.

Becket introduces the category of a game, but does not get attached to it as to a metaphor describing the universal faith in all of existence. Rather, he treats it as a kind of structure of individual existence, from which there is no exit, but which multiplies the names of impossibility, which describe a singular existence. From that perspective, Beckett discovers a focal point of his most distinguished works, from *Watt*, through *Endgame* to his final works. This point will become the enigmatic place of every creative act of speech. It will be a game between individual consciousness, representation and what is real and lasting as long as the idiom resounds; an idiom capable of expressing the complexity of relations that take place between those instances.

At the same time, within the approach toward pain perceived as an ultimate proof for individual existence, there still resides the influential echo of a deeply implicit metaphysics of suffering. This metaphysics combines biblical reflection with Schopenhauer's concepts. The Cartesian equation is supplemented and transformed from "I think, therefore I am" to "I suffer, therefore I am." But opportunities for explication of the position of consciousness in Beckett's works become interrelated and turn into epistemological and existential pillars of the subject's structure.

> That human existence must be a kind of error is sufficiently clear from the simple observation that man is a concretion of needs and wants. Their satisfaction is hard to attain and yet affords him nothing but a painless state in which he is still abandoned to boredom. This, then, is a positive proof that, in itself, existence has no value; for boredom is just that feeling of emptiness.[85]

Boredom is not only a state of unreflective persistence, a passive dissolution of a conscious individual in a uniform pattern of repetition, which disables the experience of time. In the space of boredom, existence becomes not only a mere pretense. It also aligns with the external world, with the monotonous nature of objects' transformation. Existence attempts to model its own cycle of life on this very monotonous nature. Beckett goes one step further. Suffering is not only a tool for recognizing the condition of an individual, but also a factor in the process of existential alienation. Pain can appear only as a singular event and as long as it lasts, it remains unspeakable. On the one hand, there is boredom reclaiming the originality of what is singular (the boredom of language, literature, art and philosophy understood as a system of representations), on the other, suffering which, although it makes the sphere of the real accessible, blocks the possibility of singular articulation, enclosing subjectivity in the immanence of the very experience of pain. The subject cannot escape from between these two alienating

---

85   Schopenhauer, A. "Additional Remarks on the Doctrine of the Vanity of Existence," Op. cit., p. 23.

extremes and eventually prolongs its own existence through diagnosing and describing this tension:

> The pendulum oscillates between these two terms: Suffering – that opens a window on the real and is the main condition of the artistic experience, and Boredom – with its host of top-hatted and hygienic ministers, Boredom that must be considered as the most tolerable because the most durable of human evils. [P, s. 520]

Subjectivity and Falsehood

The natural consequence of Beckett's conclusions about Proust is an interpretation of the category of "involuntary memory," not only as its only true form, but also as something outside of psychology and beyond representational attempts to grasp what is past. Longing after the objectivity of the automatism of memory is seen as a framework of reality that is undermined by the peculiar structure of consciousness which, torn by two contradicting powers of boredom and pain, cannot establish its own position as indisputable. On the contrary, the more it requests certainty, the more the subject remains powerless against the current representation of the world of events and senses.

The epiphany that accompanies memory seems to be the apparent solution. Beckett describes this mechanism with the vivid example of the failure of love for the Proustian narrator. Meeting with Albertine on the coast, or rather the protagonist's contact with her lazy gaze, not only changes him, but also triggers the endless workings of memory. At the beginning, Albertine is merely an idealized event anchored in the protagonist's memories, "cocooned by imagination" only to be excused by the workings of consciousness, which the narrator puts in place ex post facto. The following levels of initiation – following encounters with his lover – turn out to be further levels of disappointment to which the narrator has to remain loyal in order to upkeep his own identity. Toward a person that changes according to his altered perspective, he turns out to be powerless. That way the falsehood of hibernating memory (the fictitious status of an imagined Albertine) is supplemented with the inescapable mistake of subjectivism, in which opposing tendencies happen to collide. Faith in mythical representation confronts the rigorous pursuit of determining precisely what is happening right here and right now. The logic of imbalance between these two orders is merciless in Proust's work:

> And then, since memory begins at once to record photographs independent of one another, eliminates every link, any kind of sequence between the scenes portrayed in the collection which it exposes to our view, the most recent does not necessarily destroy or cancel those that came before. Confronted with the commonplace and

touching Albertine to whom I had spoken that afternoon, I still saw the other mysterious Albertine outlined against the sea. These were now memories, that is to say pictures neither of which now seemed to me any truer than the other.[86]

According to Beckett, this lack of a definite choice between one of the forms of the presence of the beloved is concerned with the more general nature of reality and its relation to the subject. It becomes focused in a moment in which it is impossible to recognize what is real:

> Thus is established the pictorial multiplicity of Albertine that will duly evolve into a plastic and moral multiplicity, no longer a mere shifting superficies and an effect of the observer's angle of approach rather than the expression of an inward and active variety, but a multiplicity in depth, a turmoil of objective and immanent contradictions over which the subject has no control. [P, s. 530]

Once again, the problem of the subject as a deserted space after certain (epistemological) and complete (ontological) consciousness that recognizes the reality and itself, due to the representation, comes back to the forefront. This time around, however, Beckett observes a kind of "cold" radicalism within the Proust's critique of the consciousness' foundations. The reduction of consciousness has been pushed very far, as far as the borderline of biological reflexes, which then become the base of a laboriously constructed, contemporary and existentially unstable vision of the reality. Beckett notices the mechanism of disenchantment with the double force: Firstly, because of the demystification of subjectival stability, and secondly as an impossibility of resistance against the merciless logic of reduction. Bodily impulses, the ability to sense the world through intuition, all of the "organic" or sensual and empirical ways of not only observing but also learning of the reality, all of these serve to build his own worldview.

From that perspective, the body serves as a synecdoche of what is accidental, and hence hostile toward abstraction, becoming a paradoxical confirmation of a singular existence. This is paradoxical because it does not allow subjectivity to achieve any kind of permanent or mature form (experience stops at the "internal" level of sensations and feelings which are impossible to express). However, at the same time, within this limitation, it allows for the achievement of a certain kind of self-knowledge (the reduction of existence to the level of a body is a result of consciousness at work). As a result, the world of perception and affects remains in the service of a reductive mind that attempts to confirm the importance of an individual. Any kind of perception can be upheld in its original condition because it immediately becomes interwoven in the chain of linguistic borrowings and mediations. In Beckett's reading, Proust takes the author's "side" – as a

---

86   Proust M., *In Search of Lost Time*, Vol. II, translated by S. K. Scott Moncrieff, New York 2000, p. 322.

critical writer, who constantly monitors the actions of the imagination, the body and language and of all these instances of human activity, which consciousness strives to control.

From that perspective, it is easier to understand Beckett's "strong" interpretation. In the seven volumes by Proust, he sees, first and foremost, a sign of the drama of disenchanted consciousness. It cannot anchor itself in the mythical space of memory (since it cannot be subdued to the will, hence it is independent from the laws and authority of subjectivity), nor in the representational form of presence (this, on the other hand, flees too fast, not allowing the linguistic sign to leave its mark). Finally, it cannot base itself on a kind of impression or impulse (one that inevitably becomes inscribed in the system of linguistic symbolism and becomes unable to achieve the status of an independent being). Writing becomes a sphere of an experiment understood as the possibility for designing the experience of "I," which surfaces in many forms. However, the gesture of design is accompanied by the inability to know and describe the relations between the subject and reality. As a result, literature as a form of consciousness is a search for a language register that would allow for the simultaneous description of existence and utterances about singular existence, designating an epistemological certainty and impossibility where that which is "endangered, dangerous, risky, troublesome, mysterious and fertile" is revealed.

With what is the abandoned consciousness left? In order to answer this question, let us go back again to the relation between the main protagonist and Albertine. According to Beckett, in the character of the narrator we see two features of the subject: the inability of achieving romantic satisfaction, which would be an opportunity for literature and a failure of the well-grounded and forceful position of the subject. Albertine, on the contrary, is a "Goddess of Time." Her elusive character does not belong to the order of sensual pretense, but refers to the sphere of instability and fluidity, which degenerates the subject's position and blocks its representation of reality. Time and love are the two powers that, according to Beckett, establish the necessary relationship between subjectivity and falsehood:

> No object prolonged in this temporal dimension tolerates possession, meaning by possession total possession, only to be achieved by the complete identification of object and subject. Thee impenetrability of the most vulgar and insignificant human creature is not merely an illusion of the subject's jealousy […]. All that is active, all that is enveloped in time and space is endowed with what might be described as an abstract, ideal and absolute impermeability. [P, s. 535]

Subjectivity's condition is based on its collision with the kind of being which cannot be revealed through representation. Confrontation with the immanence results in the question of the subject being outside of the abstract order and spreading over existential sphere. Describing the desire to possess could be explained, in accordance with the spirit of Proust's work, as a kind of technique of desire, but it could also be treated as a combination of a closed world that presents itself to the subject in its empirical and hermetically sealed traces, as a history of the subject's continuation. In that case, the meanderings of subjectivity are not merely a "technical" error with a cognitive procedure determined in advance, but an error of much greater range, one that at the same time establishes and implodes the possibility of the subject's presence. This metaphysical stain returns in the form of an epiphany and the experience of time. It saturates existence in a form of relations with the material world from which the individual cannot escape. However, it can bring a vague and difficult confirmation of its own reality:

> He only truly exists in the present, and the unchecked flight of the present into the past is a continuous passage into death, a constant dying; this is because his past life, aside from its eventual consequences for the present and the testimony it provides about the individual's will, is already completely dead, killed off, it is no more [...]. Every breath we take wards off the perpetual onslaught of death; in this way, we struggle against death at every moment, and again at greater intervals, with every meal, every sleep, every time we warm ourselves, etc. Death has to win in the end: because we have been cast into death ever since birth, and it is only playing with its prey for a while before devouring it.[87]

Beckett resituates this pessimistic diagnosis in the context of the conditions of critical subjectivity. Upholding the central points of Schopenhauer's ideas – time and representation – he shifts the weight of the possibility of subject's existence onto the fascination with the immanence of the object, which is unattainable for the power of consciousness. No representation is able to subdue it. At the same time, it conditions the "jealous," impossible to fulfil, condition of the subject built on unstable, historical foundations.

The most profound proof of this "temporalized" gap between the subject and the object is the experience, or rather the impossibility of the experience, of the death of someone close. When Albertine dies, the narrator not only cannot fully grasp the reality of this event, but also remains helpless against the growing distance between himself and external reality. The fiction of his interior is never verified in any external form of objectivity. Finally, the death of his beloved turns out to be the furthest point, one that the narrator will never reach. And consciousness of this impossibility is the end result of love. This is how Beckett describes the experience:

> Her death, her emancipation from Time, does not calm his jealousy nor accelerate the extinction of an obsession whose rack and wheel were the days and the hours. They and their love were amphibious, plunged in the past and the present. [P, pp. 536-537]

---

87   Schopenhauer A., *World as Will and Representation,* vol. 1, Op. cit., pp. 337-338.

Hence, the incomplete constitution of the subject that allows the desire of fusion with what is external remains resistant to the influence of time. Being immersed in time, consciousness cannot free itself from fascination with the immanence of desired objects and, as a result, cannot identify with them and diminish the distance between itself, as striving for the stability of the individual, and the sphere of objects that disappear in the stream of passing time. Time is the ultimate victor in Proust's cycle. It wins by not allowing the subject to forget about this difference and forces the subject into a vicious circle of despairing contradictions:

> Thus, at the end as in the body of his work, Proust respects the dual significance of every condition and circumstance of life. The most ideal tautology presupposes a relation and the affirmation of equality involves only an approximate identification, and by asserting unity denies unity. [...] Consequently the Proustian solution consists, in so far as it has been examined, in the negation of Time and Death, the negation of Death because the negation of Time. Death is dead because Time is dead. [P, pp. 542, 544]

Now, it is easier to observe Beckett's attachment to Proust, whose work he reads as a long history of the subject. The "ambiguity" mentioned by the author is conditioned by the existence of consciousness that desires to finally establish itself as an epicentre of sense. However, this is precisely what would make it mortal and completely surrendered to time. Meanwhile, thematising the impossibility of agreement about its own fusion and describing the distance between "I" and the perceived and experienced reality; distance, which with every attempt at description opens one to the experience of pain, becomes the only way to save subjectivity. Individual identity is inescapably relational in the most fundamental sense – it is immersed in time and cannot become real in the form of an absolute present. Negation should not be understood as a linguistic check or an intellectual method guaranteeing reconciliation between projecting consciousness and the world; a world, which destabilizes the order of consciousness by invading its interiority. It should be understood as a general form of consciousness workings, as an attempt to anchor it in what is real.

The last sentence of the quoted excerpt is almost a pure artistic manifesto of Beckett. It is a manifesto, which is impossible to realize. The totality of "death" cannot bring anything but even more acute self-knowledge, otherwise known as impossibility and negativity. When analysing Proust's work, Beckett announces his own faithfulness to the principals of consciousness, which, when unable to create any form of synthesis, any positivity or sense, begins to prolong the desire for subjectivity in order to break through the veil of falsehood. It does all of this in order to become a real subject, a ruler of time, and thereby a ruler of... death.

Assisting in One's Own Absence

In Beckett's commentary one comes across a particularly important theme, which deserves to be discussed separately, mostly because at one point it will become a central issue in Beckett's works. The theme in question appears in an excerpt devoted to the telephone conversation between Marcel and his grandmother. This time the key category is a voice that performs a double function: it enables the presence of the Other, as well as suspends the possibility of any form of reality. Let us see what Proust's narrator says:

> A real presence, perhaps, that voice that seemed so near – in actual separation! But a premonition also of an eternal separation! Many are the times, as I listened thus without seeing her who spoke to me from so far away, when it has seemed to me that the voice was crying to me from the depths out of which one does not rise again, and I have felt the anxiety that was one day to wring my heart when a voice would thus return (alone and attached no longer to a body which I was never to see again), to murmur in my ear words I longed to kiss as they issued from lips forever turned to dues.[88]

This is about the real form of presence, the realization of present time that cannot be contained in an immobile representation and implodes it from within – the "real presence" is after all an announcement of lasting, lethal separation, as well as the result of the former split, founded by the true act of hearing that special voice. It was a voice – and this is an extremely important point – increasingly more autonomous and outside of time (as if the writer tried to hold in its figure the fundamental dream of final conjunction of the opposites). Through its "appearance" it recalls the lethal temporality of all being. It is a sign of death, but also a figure of dispersion, elusiveness and the disappearance of what assumes, even briefly, the perpetual shape of presence.

Beckett seems to make a final point: the presence of the voice is the most paradoxical proof of reality, of what is the present moment. This follows the logic of exclusion completely. The voice is not essential, nor formless. It delineates the range of presence and remains fully ephemeral and invisible. On the other hand, it is not fully immaterial because by resounding, it addresses the empirical order. The end of the story of the relationship between the narrator and his grandmother turns out to be a decisive factor in his fate. The transition from conversation – which was fundamentally impossible, negative and created a kind of salutary distance allowing for Marcel's existence – to meeting with his grandmother as a real person becomes a final act of disillusionment and a deadly confirmation of his own identity. According to Beckett, this is so because:

---

88   Proust M., *In Search of Lost Time,* vol. 3, translated by S. K. Scott Moncrieff, New York 2000, p. 278.

> He is present at his own absence. And in consequence of his journey and anxiety, his habit is in abeyance, the habit of his tenderness for his grandmother. His gaze is no longer the necromancy that see in each precious object a mirror of the past. The notion of what he should see has not had time to interfere its prism between the eye and its object. His eye functions with the cruel precision of a camera; it photographs the reality of his grandmother. And he realizes with horror that his grandmother is dead, long since and many times, that the cherished familiar of his mind, mercifully composed all along the years by the solicitude of habitual memory, exists no longer, that this mad old woman, drowsing over her book, overburdened with years, flushed and coarse and vulgar, is a stranger whom he has never seen. [P, p. 520]

Predictably, Beckett's diagnosis turns out to be radical in the end. For the boredom of memory and forgetting, for the routine of consciousness that cannot and does not want to exit the world of false identifications, the only counterbalance turns out to be the flash of negativity exposing the pain that accompanies the separation of the subject from the external, unreachable world. That is what happens to the narrator of Proust's novel. The voice announced its own loneliness and dilemma stemming from the impossibility of the true being of the grandmother. However, the force of the gaze that fully exposed the drama of the incommensurability of the imagination and visible reality became a mark of tragic silence, a final act of helpless consciousness that cannot find its place (either in memory, or its own representations, or in the space of sensual data).

Beckett's interpretation of the narrator's attitude toward his grandmother reveals this irreducible and negative side of what takes place in the absolute identity of time. Marcel lead by the longing for "real presence" hastily heads for Paris in order to meet his grandmother, but the moment he sees her, he experiences complete and full disappointment, which gradually grows into fear. However, this cannot be driven away by the sheer force of will, or anchored in a sign. The protagonist sees his grandmother, but his gaze does not grant any form of affection and instead of removing the sensation of being distant – which was the original intention – it makes it worse. As a result, the true meeting with the grandmother turns out to be a failure in two ways. It exposes the gap between consciousness and the world even more vividly. The gap emerges at the moment of the emergence of a naked, pristine form of presence and degrades subjectivity, which is unable to precisely identify its condition and no longer hears any voice "from the other side" (which was still possible during the conversation on the phone). According to Beckett, the price for desire and for attempting to capture the experience of what is real persists in a moment of complete negativity. Just like the narrator of *In Search of Lost Time*, who cannot approach his grandmother while watching her, that is to say that he cannot truly meet her (even in such proximity), the subject reveals the emptiness of its own interior. At the same time, he/she wishes for final reconciliation with the external world. As a consequence, the subject is forced to "assist its own absence." [P, p. 520]

It seems that it is from this very point of silence and absence that Beckett commences his own writing and thinking. Taking up the effort that conditions the method he seems to be unable to construct; a method that would guarantee a peaceful return to an initial point of departure. He is unable to discover the formula for subjectivity, which would allow for the simultaneous experience and description of the original state of existence. However, the process of writing excuses this critical helplessness.

PART TWO
VOICE AND DEATH

d'où
la voix qui dit
vis
d'une autre vie[89]
– Samuel Beckett

The short text of Maurice Blanchot dedicated to the prose work of Samuel Beckett – seen from the distance of several decades – has created a path for a number of scholars, particularly within France.[90] The interpretative suggestion of Blanchot still holds out an incredible clash of coinciding of languages and the sensibility of the author and critic, as well as intriguing intuition of how to read Beckett. All of these elements should be treated as expressions of the intellectual and artistic similarity of both authors. One could directly say that on the pages of Blanchot's essay, the two giants of twentieth century literature have met; authors exploring themes of absence, lack, void and non-existence. There is no way one would not take up the themes taken up by Blanchot and left, in a way characteristic for his work, in a state of dynamic incompletion. Who knows, however, if this incomplete statement is not one of the most impressive moments in the history of the reception of Beckett?

The categories of the voice and death mark a symptomatic sphere of Beckett's imagination in my research. The sphere of voice is more a space of sounds with an uncertain status, around which the senses in different texts are focused, rather than a stable structure of meanings, a sphere of a variety of sounds actualized during the reading of the work, a question of his famous musicality,[91] that begins from the

---

89   Mi, p. 42.
90   It is hard to list all those "intellectually indebted" to Blachot among the scholars of Beckett. However, a significant number of the scholars admitting to being inspired by Blanchot appear in the pages of this work. See M. Blanchot, "Où maintenant?" Qui maintenant?", in *Le livre à venir* [*The Book to Come*] Paris 1951. Beyond this text, inspirations are drawn from several other texts: M. Blanchot, *L`espace littéraire*, [*The Space of Literature*] Paris 1955 ; *L`écriture du désastre* [*Writing of the Disaster*], Paris 1980; *L`Entretien inifini* [*The Infinite Conversation*] Paris 1972; *Le Pas au-delà* [*The Step Not Beyond*], Paris 1973; *La Part du feu* [*The Work of Fire*], Paris 1949; *L`Amitié* [*Friendship*], Paris 1971.
91   On this subject, see the collection *Samuel Beckett and Music*, edited by M. Bryden, Oxford 1976.

literal level of the text, treated as a musical score and ending with the inexpressible problems of silence and enigmatic voices coming from the outside. All of that is true, but one particular and intractable problem presented by the entire body of Beckett's work is even more important. When we attempt to examine the character of the "internal music of the word" in particular texts, when we attempt to specify the ungraspable essence of the connection between the image and the melody of language through which this image is being summarized, it turns out that as readers – despite being equipped with various analytic tools – we remain indefinitely helpless. In this way, however, going back to the interpretative starting point in which the impossibility of speech was ascertained, writing and reading are in general real and trustworthy: from the depths of the crisis and from the inside of the pre-established impossibility of expression and existence, the impossibility meets us – similar to Beckett's Winnie in *Happy Days* – before we opened our mouth.

The metaphorical notion of the sound of the text does not refer solely to a paradoxical order of speech, with the help of which the author attempts to record the impossible to express, although accessible and sensed experience of a complete otherness, alienness, which transgresses the rigor of language as a system of meaning. The space of language is not only a sphere of the fullness of sense, or, at least, it does not reveal itself in the text that is written down in the form of a complete presence in the meaning granted by traditional metaphysics. Language constitutes not only the extension of experience. It does not represent, but rather, through various effects (euphonic, rhetorical, syntactic, etc.) creates a space of experience. In other words, in Beckett's work language itself, in its entire complexity, becomes an experience of a particular kind.

Blanchot's intuition seems rich and inspiring after the passing of many years because it allows readers to grasp Beckett's work in the form of a constellation of problems grouped around the category of the voice and death, and not in the form of a coherent thesis. It remained interesting because it allowed for an observation of the price of that the artist had to pay for following a dream of completing one's project. He answers the complicated and difficult idiom of the writer with his own, inventive language of interpretation. One should take a critical look at this confrontation of languages. The attempt to reconstruct Blanchot's stance[92] will be accompanied by a reflection over the correspondence between his thought and Beckett's practice, as well as ideas of Adorno, Derrida and Foucault. In the first chapter of this section, the category of the voice will be filtered through the onto-theological critique and in the chapter that follows I will attempt to describe the possible systems of meanings, grouped around the notion of the "unnamable" in the context of a modern conflict over the status of the authorial subject.

---

92   For an excellent introduction to the thought of Blanchot, see Hill L., *Blanchot: Extreme contemporary*, London–New York 1997.

Chapter One
A Persistent Trace Inside of Silence

It is necessary to think originary-being from the trace and not the trace from originary-being.[93]

– Jacques Derrida

You complain about the stillness, about the hopelessness of the stillness, the wall of the Good.

– Franz Kafka[94]

Introducing the concept of "neutrality," Blanchot was intending to describe a broader phenomenon of modern literature and philosophy, one that – appearing in various systems of organizing discourse – is not based on totality and identity, but on dispersion and a purposefully introduced incoherence. Blanchot states:

> But the fact is that at that point it would be not only a bland, absent, and neutral writing, it would be the very experience of "neutrality," which one never hears, for when neutrality speaks, only one who imposes silence on it prepares the conditions for its hearing, and yet what there is to hear is this neutral speech; what has always been said cannot stop being said and cannot be heard, a torment we get a presentiment of in the pages of Samuel Beckett.[95]

On the other hand, the category of expectation or waiting is designated as a synonym of not only a certain more general state of literature, or more precisely: "literary space," but also constitutes a diagnosis of the category of the subject in late modernity. We mean a subject that is guided by the rule of "waiting," but also one that is guided by the necessity of "speaking." The author of the *Aminadab* was not interested in a simple erasure of the very notion, but in its fundamental rethinking and separation from essentialist roots. In such an interpretation, the subject would not be a sign of conscious presence, but it would also not disappear completely: its concept would be transported and stripped of the illusion of substantial certainty. In Blanchot's reflection one can notice a paradoxical longing after the impossible subject, one that simultaneously keeps sending one back to the principal of consciousness, and at the same time resigns from it. Let us try to take a closer look at those contradictions and the possible consequences stemming from them.

---

93 Derrida J., *Voice and Phenomenon: Introduction to the Problem of Sign in Husserl's Phenomenology*, translated by Leonard Lawlor, Evanston 2010, p. 73.

94 Kafka F., *Blue Octavo Notebooks*, translated by Ernst Kaiser, Eithne Wilkins Cambridge 2004, p. 23.

95 Blanchot M., *The Book to Come*, Op. cit., p. 209.

In *Le livre à venir* [*The Book to Come*], Blanchot begins with an interpretation of the mythological figures of the sirens, which tried to lure Odysseus with their singing. For our purposes, however, an additional, almost symbolic, aspect of the interpretation remains important. Blanchot treats the singing of the mythical creatures as a representation of the category of the voice, not ontologically, but outside the essence of the exterior. In his critical project there is a clear tendency for the cancelation of traditional metaphysical differentiation. The same applies to the internal/external opposition – if not entirely negated, then at least strongly distorted and contaminated with different pairs of classic contrasts (to the ones mentioned before we should add essence – the illusion, the source – and epiphenomenon). The suspension of these dichotomies is connected with the possibility of changing the location of the category of the exterior that is incredibly meaningful because it problematizes the experience of the act of reading. The primary encounter with the text is the starting point and the finishing point, which is the discovery of the impossibility of reading. That is the general meaning of the figure of Odysseus in Blanchot's reflections. Even though the initiatory moment is seemingly clear (the original surprise accompanying contact with the work), the highest point of the reading process remains ungraspable at first sight. Indeed, within the process of reading/writing there is no element finalizing analytical and interpretative work, and the fullness of sense is not revealed through decoding the meaning of textual figures and literary methods. In such a radical temporal perspective on reading, both entering and exiting the text is equally fantastical and in the end constitutes an interpretative hypostasis of the beginning of reading. When beginning the process of reading we enter the space of a fundamental disagreement between the time of the novel and the time of the reader that is external to the text. Hence, reading will not be anything else in this case but an act of following that irremovable temporal split between the reading "I" and the flow of the novel – a split that will determine the ontology of the writing space, actualized every time by an interpretative interference. Reading should be treated as a disproportionate participation in the dialogue with the work. What does it mean?

Nothing more than the perpetual following of traces of the text with the consciousness of inevitable cognitive failure. Reading does not open any epistemological horizon and cannot be designed in any way, meaning it cannot be subdued to the markers of reception. In other words, for Blanchot, proper reading begins when the available interpretative and grammatical references are exhausted. That way the essence of the experience of literature, on the one hand, becomes a confrontation with what is completely alien to language (or impossible to represent) but possible to be sensed. On the other hand, it becomes an actualization of the infinite, a secret process of the dislocation of the borders of the interior and the exterior of the text. Let us begin with the question of the exterior. The process of reading can be described as a deciphering of the "other" that is completely external to the reader's timeline of the plot, and as translation of the immanent order of work into a language of commentary. However, as we well know, that external temporal organization covers only the inaccessible world of the metamorphosis of a different time constituting an *iunctim* between the reader and the text. In particular, we are concerned with the time of the imagination, thanks to which it is possible to create a new topology of work every single time: a creation of continuous shifts, building up distance between the sign and its referent, between meaning and sense, speech and silence. The time of imagination allows for the creation of a space in which the reader is moving around, helplessly trying to understand and absorb what is alien. From that perspective, externality cannot be understood as an effect of interpretative work, a point of reference for the imagination in the process of reading. It is rather a metaphysical "winding down," a sign of the cancelation of all the strict differentiations enabling the event that accompanies encounters with a text that is being read. For Blanchot, that which is external becomes a lack that is inscribed into the immanent order of the work – a lack understood as a challenge for the reader who demands a linguistic invention.

It seems that Blanchot is concerned with sustaining certain convictions on the subject of the ontology of the text. According to Blanchot, literature is considered to be literature so long as it is capable of exciting and sustaining its own intransitiveness and so long as its language enables a sphere of experience that goes beyond "literary space." Blanchot presented this situation under the guise of Odysseus's journey that is in essence a story about the interpretative condition of the individual. It is a narration to which the mythical hero is, in a way, sentenced. That necessity of interpretation, or of explaining the signs of the revealed world leads the protagonist to a place where the siren's call stops being elusive: it takes on presence, although it remains incomprehensible and untamed. This fairly straight forward metaphor could be interpreted as follows: reading cannot have a beginning or an end because the voice exists in an enigmatic space "between" dichotomies, the division between the interior and exterior, and reveals itself in the form of textual figures. It clashes with the immanent logic of the work. On the level of poetics, one would be concerned only with the fit of the timing of the phrase, the melody of language, and syntactical complications which, by removing divisions of genres and sub-genres, would allow for the creation of a specific effect described by Blanchot as an ungraspable tone or metaphorically as the sirens' call.

Beckett is simultaneously near and distant from the image presented by Blanchot. His correction of that particular interpretation of the voice is significant in this case. The facticity of the event upon which this entire philosophical reading is based remains essential. I believe it is also one of the pillars of Beckett's thought:

awaiting the voice that will never appear or can never be heard; one that, while constantly present through its inclusion in the net of language, is never physically present. It reveals itself in the work of art but the legitimacy of its existence is cancelled by the arbitrariness of language. If we were to take the subject (that of the reader, the author, or the textual itself) as the principal theme of reflection, then the category of voice would stand as one of the fundamental ontological determinants. Subjectivity exists solely to hear the sound of the voice, to bring the sphere of the hermetic deterioration of language closer. It is a space that is no longer perceivable as exteriority, but as a sphere of unnameable alienness. A difference appears when Blanchot desires to completely surrender the experience of the voice to the power of neutrality, while Beckett insists on the rule of consciousness. According to Blanchot, the truly real, desired voice is a fantasy of literature imagined as a discourse about the impossible (distorted, tainted, or blurred) standing at the beginning of all possible narration and metaphor, as well as accompanying existential sense. Neutrality is for Blanchot an idealized, imaginary site of emptiness in which language is disinherited from its conventional meaning – it becomes a site of the radical absence of sense within the text. This kind of absence, however, is meaningful in some unclear way because it restrains the dialectic of interior and exterior, of the existence and non-existence.

The negation of sense constitutes an attempt to break through to the inaccessible sphere of pure experience – an experience without the subject. In that way literary space remains open to all that does not fall under the ultimate project – death. The "rule of waiting" (for example *Waiting for Godot*) is simultaneously a rule of heroic failure – it enables the logic of disproportionality of a singular existence against the necessity of death, which is a warranty of literature's sense as a form of experience. Blanchot's reflection is headed toward the cancelation of theoretical (which is to say distanced) attempts to understand and tame death. It should not be understood or imposed in some hermeneutical order but accepted as the unpronounceable "touch" of the exterior. Under those conditions the need for any kind of literature finally disappears: the experience of writing will never be unchallenged and trustworthy against what is radically different. The hope for writing lies not with attempts to control or enclose it within a term or an image. The question of the conditions of the possibility of writing discourse that is not willing to subordinate itself to speech but by its silent, mute and severe existence dramatically demands a voice remains valid. In other words, the posing of a question about the void, the transcription of language from the sphere of the absolute exterior to the plane of representation, of describing that which through a particular form of vocality mimics silence, becomes an opportunity to allow literature to become real.

One could say that the paths of Blanchot's critique and philosophy and Beckett's literary practice diverge at a certain point. Although both authors arrive at the description of the same experience of the voice it is not the same experience for each of them respectively. While they both recognize the identical tension that accompanies a working consciousness that confronts the world, it is only Beckett who, understanding writing as a process, stubbornly stands by the rule of subjectivity to the very end. They both meticulously reconstruct all the signs of the voice as a signal of being, it is Blanchot himself who becomes an avid listener. Beckett is marked by far more scepticism in this regard. The difference of their opinions is based on a divergence on the level of solutions for two fundamental issues. The first is concerned with the primacy of epistemology in Beckett's works. The dominance of cognition does not allow for a resignation from the sanctions of consciousness in writing and determines language and imagination (which would differentiate it from Blanchot's writing project, fundamentally anchored an ontological mode of thought). Second, as a result of the first issue, both need to address the problem of the source and status of language as medium for the actualization or the representation of sense. In the case of Blanchot, resistance to the Cartesian-Kantian and Hegelian matrix of reflection, a resistance that is aimed at trust in the ability of description by means of the terms (but also experience) of reality remains the foundation for his work.

But the result of that rejection is not obvious or convincing. Blanchot does not fully resign, because he cannot, from using available conceptual tools for the description of the ungraspable matter of the voice, but at the same time he stops searching for his own idiom that would narrow his idea of the "ontology outside of ontology" at the level of its neutralization. Language reveals itself as a purely negative sphere. However, it is a negativity that stems from an all-encompassing, and proclaimed in advance, passivity, behind which stands the basic gesture of an unconditional fascination with death, as well as the acceptance of the rule establishing the relation between the subject and writing. Blanchot remains faithful to Heidegger in that regard.[96] In Beckett, however, neutrality is never a final state assumed by being or the last stage of language's progression but functions on the rights of a vague, unreachable goal that consciousness chooses within its necessarily incomplete project.[97] Before we move to reading a particular work of Beckett, it is wise to consider the problems and issues that he chooses to approach.

---

96   From Tsushima M., *The Space of Vacillation: The Experience of Language in Beckett, Blanchot and Heidegger*, Bern 2003.

97   See. Willits C. G., "Le lecteur blanchotien. L`écrivain in situ", *Europe* 2007 no. 940-941.

The Voice and Non-Speech

As is already obvious, the question of voice is not clear at all. It has a certain
priority within Blanchot's thought, but it does not constitute a permanent figure
or full presence. On the contrary, it situates the subject within the boundaries of
literature and philosophy, in the context of chiasm and aporia – the two figures of
insolvable contradictions that likewise correspond to the boundaries of an infinite
negotiation of the conditions of sense and the possibility of communication.
Hence, the voice is no longer an unshakable attitude of existence but a sign of
oscillation between what is internal and external. We have already talked about
a desire that Blanchot has inserted into his writings, the full submission to the
neutrality of writing as a kind of disinheritance from subjectivity. He who writes
confronts the indivisible exterior and remains in the enigmatic sphere of the image.
Ontology dominates in this view, and – as I have already observed and will further
indicate – should be traced back to the Heideggerian monological language of the
authenticity of being.

In one of the chapters of *L'Entretien infini* [*The Infinite Conversation*],
Blanchot comprehensively describes the character and structure of the category of
the voice: it's a description that – in many regards – can be treated as a summary of
his analysis of Beckett. Treating Beckett's works as the true arrival of modernist
literature, Blanchot observes that from the very emergence of philosophical and
artistic modernity, it was the voice that held priority over speech. What is the
difference between them? Here is one of his attempts at an answer:

> The voice that is not simply the organ of subjective interiority but, on the contrary, the
> reverberation of a space opening onto the outside. […] The voice frees not only from
> representation, but also, in advance, from meaning, without, however, succeeding in
> doing more than committing itself to the ideal madness of delirium. The voice that
> speaks without a word, silently – in the silence of a cry – tends to be, no matter how
> interior, the voice of no one. What speaks when the voice speaks? It situates itself
> nowhere, neither in nature nor in culture, but manifests itself in a space of redoubling,
> of echo and resonance where it is not someone, but rather this unknown space – its
> discordant accord, its vibration – that speaks without speaking.[98]

In this excerpt, one can observe the switch that Blanchot is attempting to perform
in order to justify his own vision of the relations between writing and subjectivity
based on abandoning the expressive model for the sake of an impersonal literature.
One should interpret this attempt in a kind of dual subjective-subjectival as well as
passive and neutral ontological frame. On the one hand, the voice appears almost

---

98   M. Blanchot, "L'athéisme et l'écriture. L'humanisme et le cri," in, *L'Entretien infini*,
      Op. cit. p. 386. In English, see *The Infinite Conversation*, translated by Susan Hanon,
      Minneapolis 1992, p. 258.

as a primal, innate and natural function of presence created by a consciousness that comes to life. On the other hand, it constitutes a sphere of the paradoxical, inexpressible, potentiality of being. The voice simultaneously is and is not dependent on the will of the subject and coming out of the interior it directs itself toward the absolute exterior (that is why Blanchot talks about its variable or "temporary" character).

Blanchot distances himself from attachment to the sanctions of the individual will but – or so it seems – he is unable to definitely release himself from it. The question "who is speaking?" is placed in the ontological context that by definition is supposed to relocate notions of traditional metaphysics. That work of relocation suggests that the search for a permanent source of linguo-phonetic presence that could conceivably be articulated. The goal therefore seems to be straightforward: to highlight the gesture of certain autonomy of the voice that creates a space of a different sense, or allows for the construction of a different meaning. Hence, we are not dealing with a dialectics between the word and the voice, or between writing and the voice but with a radical turn toward the most fundamentally implicit and at the same time most enigmatic rule of all presence. However, any certain and coherent vision of the conditions and possibilities of what could become truly present is never proposed. Blanchot suggests another kind of relation, one that is created between immanence, which is described through an internal voice, which is possible to sense but impossible to articulate, and the totality of what is external. Immanence remains individual. It is a kind of the implosion of sense that is impossible to be uttered by anyone under any conditions. It is a kind of voice that, speaking more vividly, cannot be brought to the surface, even though one knows perfectly well that it exists. That is how we arrive at certain contradictory formulations in Blanchot's work that can be understood precisely in the order of a radical inability to express the experience of a separate existence, but also – which seems even more interesting – formulations that could be treated as an attempt to express a particular, negative and critical form of subjective existence. The paradoxical terms seem to serve this unstoppable highlighting of the infinite character of subjectivity that cannot undergo– in a gesture of passivity – the process of emancipation itself and, at the same time, control it. The totality of internal experience, while being inexpressible and moreover impossible to pass on would become proof of a singular existence. However, it would serve only as a negative proof, emerging only, so to speak, on the surface of language. It would be a gesture of an utterance, a rhythm and a sound that does not carry with itself a defined meaning – it would be the "voice that speaks silently."

This negative phase of establishing the voice as a superior ontological category is used by Blanchot to stabilize the aporetic vision of depersonalized writing. Both definitions of "vision" and "writing" are extremely important in this case. "Stabilizing" means that Blanchot is not willing to transgress the boundary set by simultaneously actualizing contradiction or aporia. "Impersonality," on the other hand, reveals a strong assumption of the necessity for going beyond the negative state of subjectivity, or a potential, incomplete and intelligible voice. It also assumes entering, through unconditional affirmation, into the sphere of the total exterior. Blanchot already utilizes this strong ontological assumption at the beginning of the aforementioned fragment. In reality, the voice is not an absence, an impossible testimony to pure emptiness, but a sign with an opposite vector – it contains the potentiality of all utterances but also all kinds of silence. It is a similar situation with the category of sense that can appear disguised only as a fantasy, pure pretense, hence … a desire for a pure sound. This quasi-transcendental starting point, one in which the critic points to the pre-arranged form of the possibility of every utterance as the autonomy of the voice meeting with its own reversal at the end point, in which the reality of sound is feigned or stopped in the pure potentiality noted earlier by Blanchot.

The unclear complication of assumptions and rhetorically subtle strategy of Beckett allows us to observe the fundamental question of the conditions of possibility for subjectivity from a slightly different perspective. This time, however, the question of the authorial-subjectival sources of language, concerning the status of subjectivity itself, is attuned to the question of the position of the voice as a primary figure in the process of writing, as well as of the structure and the position of the existence. It doesn't seem however, that there is a possibility for an unambiguous answer. Blanchot – as we ought to recall – connects both issues: the subjectival status of the utterance and the separation of the voice itself. In doing so, he transfers both questions to the very centre of the passive aporia (simultaneous speech and silence) and chiasm of extra-representational, non-metaphysical form of presence. By making this step, he resigns – quite consciously – from the first segment of that coupling. The result of that work was supposed to be a language scene only, or the separated space of a neutral, indifferent vibration of the voice that, in turn, is an "answer" to the calling of the exterior, or – to put it more simply – it constitutes its function. "Resonance" and "echo" are treated here as figures of that strange "presence outside of presence" and are completely deprived of a source. As a result, Blanchot diagnoses the situation in which sense has evaporated from language and previously constructed meanings have collapsed. Speech has lost its communicative function and its power to actualize. And the voice itself, carrying unwanted traces of subjectivity, is reduced to the enigmatic gesture of spatialising[99] the sounds. Again, vibration and doubling (which are also kinds of

---

99   See Derrida J., "The Theater of Cruelty and the Closure of Representation," in *Writing and Difference*, translated by Alan Bass, Chicago 1978. Derrida's comments on Artaud seem to belong to the same "family" of thought as Blanchot's reflection on the subject

strengthening[100]) are merely secondary features of the same act of separation, but they do not provide a strong definition of the category of the voice, the description of which, in the end, stops at exclusionary terms and becomes a figure of false autonomy. Jean-Luc Nancy claimed that when thinking about that kind of subject – the subject of listening/subject in listening – one should treat "pure resonance" not only as a condition for rethinking the category of presence, but as the very "beginning and opening up of sense, as beyond-sense or sense that goes beyond signification."[101] In that case, the subject would present itself as a function of the ability to feel "acoustics," it would occupy a place in which the very fluctuation of sounds resides, one that accompanies the act of listening. It would melt into one with the echo of sense that is not fully present but always comes from elsewhere.

But it is this falsity, the irreducible mistake in the positioning of consciousness (which, while it exists, cannot become ideally neutral and at peace with what is external to it) that decides about the status of the voice understood as an unmarked, unique and temporary vibration. This last, temporal aspect turns out to be the most difficult to grasp and serves as proof for Blanchot of the almost natural, or physiological, necessity of falling silent:

> Finally, the voice has the characteristic of speaking in a way that does not last. Fleeting and destined to the forgetting in which it finds its end without either trace or future, what it prefers thereby breaks with the book's perpetuity, its closure, its proud stability: its pretension to enclose and to transmit the true by making into its possessor the very one who will not have found it. A speech that has vanished when it has scarcely been said always already destined to the silence it bears and from which it comes; a speech in becoming that does not keep to the present but commits itself and the literature it animates to its essence, which is disappearance. The voice is also perhaps always, at least apparently, outside or to the side of the rules, as it is beyond mastery, always to be won back, always once again mute.[102]

Disregarding the specific tone characteristic to the style of Blanchot, almost all of the issues that are interesting from our perspective are present in this passage: the disappearance of the category of intention (the authorial subject retracts from the space of literature and thereby loses control over it), questioning the stable and intersubjective character of meaning and the transfer to the affirmation of the voice event that collapses the representational order of literature. This last point, which also constitutes a turn in the author's thinking, makes us aware of how important the problem of the invincible antinomies between the closely

---

of the dialectics of impossibility and the necessity of thinking about representation ("the scene of meaning") as the source of all writing.

100 Le rédoublement means both "doubling" and "strengthening."
101 Nancy J.-L., Listening, Op. cit., p. 31
102 Blanchot M., Op. cit., pp. 258-259.

understood space of writing and the sphere of presence that becomes freed from the necessity of meaning really is. This brings us back to the question from which Blanchot, when proposing literature as a form of the alternate presence, wanted to extricate himself – the dialectics of writing and the voice.

However, in Beckett's vision this is a dialectic that has been radically reformulated because it is consciously left unfinished and situated within – an almost mythical – sphere of the "resonance" of the exterior. This is a form of pre-deconstruction. The voice of an individual is only one of the elements in the systemic network of substitutions of the meaningful. On the other hand, the voice constitutes not so much a vessel for meaning but a physical veil that annihilates any possibility of the appearance of an individual. In order to remain faithful to his fundamental and incredibly forceful act of siding with the isolated, "vibrating" voice with which the subject lost access, Blanchot proposes creating a more precise definition of the category of writing as a developing process of opening to the exterior; an action that constitutes an attempt to free itself from any form of a stable sense motivated by the force of a conscious act[103]. Literature, as a consequence, becomes a medium of impersonal, but in a way profound, poetic vocality that does not reveal a clear sense but – through rhythm and pure sound – presents a different dimension of presence that brings closer that which is a source:

> [...] The impersonality of the voice is a silent appeal to a presence-absence to the hither side of every subject and even every form; anterior to beginning, it indicates itself only as anteriority, always in relation to what is anterior.[104]

Writing, on the other hand, is a fossil of "old" senses, a continuity of traces of death that immobilize the gesture of the writer. The refusal of metaphysical, subjectival-objectival assumptions leads to a dynamically understood process of writing:

> Writing ceases to be a mirror. It will constitute itself, strangely, as an absolute of writing and of voice. A "mute written orchestration," Mallarmé will say: time and space united, as successive simultaneity, an energy and a work wherein energy gathers (*energeia* and *ergon*); a tracing wherein writing breaks always in advance with what is written. Born of this pressure, beyond the book, is the project of the Work, in its very realization always yet to come; a Work without content since always going beyond what it seems to contain and affirming nothing but its own outside, that is to say, affirming itself – not as full presence but, in relation to its absence, the absence of (a) work, worklessness.[105]

There are statements in the above passage concerning Blanchot's ontology of literature that must be considered to be the effect of a negative reaction of the

---

103   See Dolar M., *A Voice and Nothing More*, Cambridge-London 2006.
104   Blanchot M., Op. cit., p. 259.
105   Ibid.

philosopher to the metaphysical concept of presence and a phenomenological belief in the possibility of direct insight. The site of a dialectical negotiation between writing and the voice is taken by writing, understood as an inexhaustible energy. Blanchot cognizes this in a specific way. Writing evolves in a rhythm of a purely imaginative boundary model and glimmering existence of the text and sense, a consciousness and mythical text (a work). This is how one of the most important notions introduced by Blanchot – le désœuvrement – can be understood. It combines otherwise impossible to reconcile orders of literature as forms of thinking about the indeterminacy between presence and absence, as well as literature as a "place" of a staged separation, or conversation. On the one hand, the "work" remains a closed totality and is never fragmented. On the other hand, its autonomy is dependent on the gesture of separation, disconnection and distinction. The ideal proposed by Blanchot: literature as a pure sound outside of oppositions, a pure rhythm of being transgressing metaphysical extremities and, finally, as a form allowing for the confrontation of the language of the text with, so to speak, the ethereal nature of sense; all of these come together in one point of impossibility – a complete passivity and undertaking of the individual effort to differentiate, or even express the very difference between consciousness and the neutrality of language. These two contradicting aspects are as focused in literature as in the echo of being, sources of which cannot be found but which have to be constantly sought out. By destabilizing the permanent position of the cognitive subject, Blanchot does not stop asking: "Who is really speaking?"[106] But also, it seems that when facing the annihilation of subjectival sources he has nothing left but to multiply new versions of the same question.

Lethal Beginnings

Postponing and distorting the question constitutes Blanchot's strategy. He wishes to show countless possibilities of different constellations that the subjectivity, sentenced to the aporetic condition, can assemble itself. However, he is not entirely successful. As a gesture of upholding the motion of contradictions Blanchot loses the unique quality of his own idiom and turns out to be the successor of the onto-theological critique of the version of metaphysics conducted by Heidegger. Let us take a look at those dependencies, this time, however, from the Blanchot's

---

106   That way the literature understood as an institution that guarantees a discursive possibility of "recognizing" that rhythm can become not only an "echo of being," but also an "echo of the subject." See Lacoue-Labarthe Ph, L`Echo du sujet, in Le sujet de la philosophie. Typographies 1, Paris 1979. In English, see The Subject of Philosophy, edited by Thomas Trezise, translated by Thomas Trezise et al., Minneapolis 1993.

perspective. In *On the Road to Language*, Heidegger analyzes, among other works, two poems by Stefan George. When summarizing his analysis he states:

> Word, language, belongs within the domain of this mysterious landscape in which poetic saying borders on the fateful source of speech. At first, and for long, it seems as though the poet needed only to bring the wonders that enthrall and the dreams that enrapture him to the well-spring of language, and there in unclouded confidence let the words come forth to him that fit all the wonderful and dreamlike things whose images have come to him.[107]

He directs his attention to the specific kind of intensity of poetic language that, by its own presence, comes closer to revealing the origins of language in general. The character of poetry is unique, but this is not due to the fact that it grants one insight into the true nature of reality. Rather, poetic language is a signal of absolute primality. The verse (*oratio vincta*) reveals the nature of the source that does not fall under the laws of a technical language of terms. Such instructions are burdened with two serious consequences. Firstly, poetic language, as the quintessence of all possible speech, has to remain beyond the sphere of representation in order to be able to communicate (or "inform" according to Heideggerian jargon) sense. Secondly, sense cannot present itself solely in its direct form without entering into relations between the subject and the object but removing the need for any kind of mediation. At the same time, however, the announced necessity of direct access to the sources of speech, hence to the sources of the sense, transforms into a mythical tale of opening out of pure possibility – through a proper, meaning poetic, use of language: the dimension of the primality of existence. Only "action" such as a fictional form of presence that is guaranteed not by any means of objectifying but by "undisturbed trust" in the isolated strength of language itself can serve as the genesis of language-sense and its sources.

This is one of the larger difficulties connected with understanding the Heideggerian concept of poetry, which is almost entirely aligned with what Blanchot proposes in his own works. We should not be misled by minor differences. Both authors talk about sources, originality (understood as primality and singularity) as well as, which seems to be the most important for us, another form of presence that cannot be assigned to metaphysical schemes and hierarchies of pretense and essence.

That is why the voice is so important, along with its multiple dependencies on what is different and external; the voice that points not only to the sole credible "essence of language" but also to the status of a unique kind of borderline function of speech that reveals and simultaneously hides the abyss of being. In the works

---

107   M. Heidegger, *On the Way to Language*, translated by Peter D. Hertz, Joan Stambaugh, New York 1982, p. 67.

of both authors, the voice becomes so important precisely because it delineates the smallest possible range of action of the representative veil. The voice exists but it is a mediated existence, shifting and condemned to disappearance. It is an existence that allows for the maintenance of hope for proximity with the source. Similarly to Blanchot, Heidegger admired literature (poetry) because it allowed him to circumvent the consciousness confrontation with what is negative. The rule of the subject in this case is purely a kindling of the oppressive attempts to "mute" the primary speech of being, fragments of which remain outside any possible form of presence graspable for the subject.

In the same text, Heidegger comments on the comparison of words and flowers by Hölderlin. The approach of language to the undetermined and completely primal matrix of being can be real only thanks to freeing speech from the yoke of consciousness and leaving it at the mercy of anonymous "uttering":

> When the word is called the mouth's flower and its blossom, we hear the sound of language rising like the earth. From whence? From Saying in which it comes to pass that World is made to appear. The sound rings out in the resounding assembly call which, open to the Open, makes World appear in all things. The sounding of the voice is then no longer only of the order of physical organs. It is released now from the perspective of the physiological-physical explanation in terms of purely phonetic data. The sound of language, its earthiness, is held with the harmony that attunes the regions of the world's structure, playing them in chorus. This indication of the sound speaking and of its source in Saying must at first sound obscure and strange. And yet it points to simple phenomena. We can see them once we pay heed again to the way in which we are everywhere under way within the neighbourhood of the modes of Saying.[108]

This difficult passage suggests a very specific thesis that allows for the presentation of the consequences of the "source" relationship between external notions of thought about being and language that was supposed to adhere to being as such. Heidegger's enigmatic formulation of the "Open,"[109] referring to a revelation undisturbed by any representation of existence, seems to be close to Blanchot's desire for a completely external sphere. This gesture is meant to render or present objects in a direct manner. At the same time, their uniqueness dissolves into a homogenous shimmering of the speech of being, and language itself becomes another object. Paradoxically, the realized desire of an absolute opening can end in only one way – with a deadly indifference that was supposed to be the realization of the desire for a complete dissolution into the sphere of non-differentiation that remains ungraspable with the language of notions. The second consequence seems to be more disturbing. If poetic language is a meeting place; a place of contact, of touching the real world (or "World," as Heidegger puts it), then ultimately poetic

---

108 Ibid., p. 101.
109 Which is, of course, linked with Rilkean concept of „Open".

speech does not contain a special mark of distinction but functions solely as a convenient instrument in an endless monologue of unmarked Being. In that sense, the appreciation of Blanchot and Heidegger addressed to the voice, as well as an attempt to erase from that category all the signs of conscious and representational force, brings a result reverse to the one intended: the voice never becomes a freed stream of sounds that announce "closeness," it does not become a completely anonymous "resonance" but the sign of the perfect indifference of being within a deadly enframement.

For Heidegger, nothingness is treated as the base of every important act of speech. On the other hand, language constitutes a kind of foundation of a real and unquestionable presence – it is a sphere for the "attunement" of being. This is further clarified if we recall that Heidegger was driven by a critique of the philosophy of consciousness, which covered the oppression of technical, calculative reason. With reason occupying a central position, consciousness feigns its own independence while establishing its position in the form of a domineering and timely subject. Its true verification, in the end, is the gesture of opening followed by the revelation of nothingness as that which is most primal and most mysterious:

> Uncanniness reveals itself authentically in the fundamental attunement of anxiety, and, as the most elemental disclosedness of thrown Dasein, it confronts being-in-the-world with the nothingness of the world about which it is anxious in the anxiety about its ownmost potentiality-of-being. What if Dasein, finding itself in the ground of its uncanniness, were the caller of the call of conscience? [...] The caller is unfamiliar to the everyday they-self; it is something like an alien voice. What could be more alien to the they, lost in the manifold "world" of its heedfulness, that the self individualized to itself in uncanniness thrown into nothingness? "It" calls, and yet gives the heedfully curious ears nothing to hear that could be passed along and publically spoken about. [...] The call does not report any facts; it calls without uttering anything. The call speaks in the uncanny mode of silence.[110]

Heidegger's conclusions about the nature of nothingness' appearance seem to be crucial at this point. He makes a clear gesture of transferring the source of voice and places it within the framework of negativity that remains outside of the rule of meaning, communication and representation. This unobvious presence of nothingness is dependent on two features: the imperative of "opening" and the preservation of distance. This second aspect raises questions: How should we understand this peculiar kind of presence, this silence that does not constitute a fulfilment or counterbalance to speech but reveals a completely different order of the world? How should one interpret this special kind of relationship between absolute distance, an unreachable exterior and the presence appearing in the form of language, one in which nothingness has been given a voice?

---

110   Heidegger M., *Being and Time,* translated by Joan Stambaough, Albany 2010, p. 266.

One could say: the speech is an "echo of Being," or a non-representational reflection of the primal, indivisible voice of existence that – even though it resounds – means nothing and does not create a space for communication. Poetic language, revealing its fundamental "mood," is possibly the most complete sign of indeterminacy of that primal voice. And the analysis of its position, an attempt to break through to its beginnings, allows for the excavation and rethinking of an aspect of its radical negativity. The beginnings of language remain bound with death, the mood [*Stimmung*] of literature's language is "attuned" to death. In consequence, the poetic voice resounds as a pathos of the call for understanding that is simultaneously ethical. In insightful comments on Heidegger's thought, Giorgio Agamben observed the following:

> The experience of the Voice – conceived as pure and silent meaning and as pure wanting-to-have-a-conscience – once again reveals its fundamental ontological duty. Being is the dimension of meaning of Voice as the taking place of language, that is, of pure meaning without speech and of pure wanting-to-have-a-conscience without a conscience. The thought of Being is the thought of the Voice.[111]

Consciousness and the "Destruction of the Voice"

Blanchot and Heidegger treated the voice as a figure of "interiority" and "being," absolute spaces against which consciousness could acquire legitimacy for itself. But the gesture of turning toward what is external, or that which is its source, unleashes a possible annihilation of subjectivity. Within the views of both authors, singular consciousness loses its autonomy and is surrendered to the mercy of the anonymous and indifferent speech of being or the exterior and neutrality. Paradoxically, the authenticity of singularity is legitimized only within the boundaries of total negativity – of death, with which the subject should not confront itself and which it should not attempt to overcome but experience and commence the act of writing or speaking from its perspective.

When pondering the question from the perspective of Beckett's work, both diagnoses seem important but incomplete. Total neutrality as well as the actualization of the speech of Being cannot constitute the final point of retraction. Without forsaking the sanctions of consciousness, Beckett cannot establish subjects that speak in their own texts as figures of an ultimate anonymity or as signs of the "echoes of Being" that stop at the doorstep of the potentiality of meaning. At the same time, he is interested in an effect of a slightly different kind. By upholding

---

111 Agamben G., *Language and Death: The Place of Negativity*, translated by K. E. Pinkus, M. Hardt, Minnesota-Oxford 2006, p. 61.

this passive or almost nihilistic moment in power, he attempts to keep fighting and to "loose on his own terms" during his confrontation with the force of death.

The stubbornness with which Beckett undertakes this effort seems to suggest an immediate affinity with writings of Kafka. In order to prove this, let us take a look at one short work of Kafka in which the ambivalent position of consciousness in relation to death and the voice is explore. I am specifically interested in "The Silence of the Sirens," in which Kafka introduces a theme that was – as we well remember – so important for Blanchot. While Blanchot interpreted the mythological situation as a testimony exposing the subject to the influence of externality and that which is alien, for Kafka the meeting between Odysseus and the sirens is the symbol of the ambiguous status of consciousness. In his interpretation, the mythical hero remains faithful to his own resolution to the very end and it is because of this and not due to any practical efficacy of his own actions that he is able to prevail. The fidelity to one's own cunningness that Kafka articulates brings about results that are more interesting than the description of a pragmatically understood victory over mythical powers. The author suggests that it is not the singing but the silence of the sirens that was their most powerful weapon. The sirens "created" silence that has been lethal to travellers but over which they had total control. Odysseus enters a peculiar relation that nevertheless stabilizes his reality in relation to the sirens: by plugging his ears not only does he not hear their singing but is also unable to recognize their silence. His entire shrewdness – as Kafka states ironically – is achieved with the help of "childish strategies." At a slightly different level, this might also be construed as the outline of a particular modality of subjectivity.

No sound reaches Odysseus ears, but his internal silence is also artificially created – it is the result of an artful gesture of defence against the seductive and deadly voice of the sirens. For that reason, the hero is able to survive his confrontation with them. But the entire encounter becomes almost entirely imaginary, turning into a kind of mute masquerade or pantomime[112]:

> But Ulysses, if one may so express it, did not hear their silence; he thought they were singing and that he alone did not hear them. For a fleeting moment he saw their throats rising and falling, their breasts lifting, their eyes filled with tears, their lips half-parted, but believed that these were accompaniments to the airs which died unheard around him. Soon, however, all this faded from his sight as he fixed his gaze on the distance, the Sirens literally vanished before his resolution, and at the very moment when they were nearest to him he knew of them no longer. But they – lovlier than ever – stretched their necks and turned, let their awesome hair flutter free in the wind, and freely stretched their claws on the rocks. They no longer had any desire to

---

112   See Geier M., *Gra językowa filozofów*, translated by Janusz Sidorek, Warszawa 2000, pp. 36-37 [German: *Das Sprachspiel der Philosophen*, Hamburg, 1989].

allure; all that they wanted was to hold as long as they could the radiance that fell from Ulysses' great eyes.[113]

This mixture of orders affects both "sides" of the conflict. Odysseus can recognize neither external reality nor himself immersed in his own interior. He purposefully deafens himself in a defensive gesture and his powers of perception become limited to an imperfect sense of sight. He stops, seduced by the very motions and gesture of the sirens. The sirens, on the other hand, being purely fantastical, disperse in the air under the weight of the indifferent gaze of Odysseus. As a result, in comparison with the mythological matrix, the relationship between figures has been reversed: the hero of antiquity was triumphant at the price of losing his hearing that kept him safe from the voice of the sirens. At the same time, however, this left Odysseus with a gaze that had only one ability, that of establishing a phenomenal, illusive reality. That which is visible functions as a pure illusion and does not possess any positive ontological value. It is a fiction simulating the materiality of the world. But the very gaze seduces and kills... That is why the sirens are stuck to the rocks hunting for the long gaze of Odysseus.[114]

Kafka's negative rearrangement of the mythical template is extremely powerful. The voice dies down. It no longer carries the fullness of presence and it does not seduce, nor is it marked with the stigma of death. In order to stay alive, consciousness, personified in this case by Odysseus, has to perform what might be its last available maneuverer – to take back its own voice. It must annihilate its own language in order to survive. Dispersing and anonymous, the external voice that is symbolized by the sirens that can never be heard by consciousness because its real presence means death. The sheer force of the gaze no longer establishes consciousness, the power of which becomes limited to the misleading reign of simulacrum that never penetrates reality *in crudo*.

What is most interesting is the ending of Kafka's apocryphal tale. Consciousness and death, the voice and reality, power and pretense create a thick tangle:

> If the Sirens had possessed consciousness they would have been annihilated at that moment. But they remained as they had been; all that had happened was that Ulysses had escaped them. A codicil to the foregoing has also been handed down. Ulysses, it is said, was so full of guile, was such a fox, that not even the goddess of fate could pierce his armor. Perhaps he had really noticed, although here the human understanding is beyond its depths, that the Sirens were silent, and held up to them and to the gods the aforementioned pretense merely as a sort of shield.[115]

---

113 Kafka F., "The Silence of the Sirens," *in The Complete Stories,* edited by Nahum. N. Glatzer, New York 2012, p. 431.

114 Politzer H., "Milczenie syren," in *Milczenie syren. Studia z literatury niemieckiej i austriackiej,* translated by J. Hummel, Warsaw 1973, pp. 21-22.

115 Kafka, F., "The Silence of the Sirens," Op. cit., 432.

Kafka is clearly standing on the side of consciousness, even if it were to be reduced to the gesture alone, only a power over total pretense and even if it were founded on an almost complete reduction of individuality. The temporary deafness of Odysseus makes possible a kind of control over reality, but this power remains limited to the sphere of the fantastical. At the very end, Kafka introduces a fundamental correction that allows us to better understand the weight of Odysseus's move. Consciousness, even though it remains helpless against the external world, can defend itself according to the same rule that isolates it from that very world, or the attempt to reign over illusion. The hero lives as long as the efforts of his mind bring results in the form of a defence against the seductive powers of the voice that are simultaneously the forces of death. This fantastical being – Blanchot's "image" – possesses a double nature. It both hides true reality and simultaneously constitutes the only proper defence against the totalizing force of death. The work of the mind and the efforts of consciousness that create new mediations are always used for the same purposes – to survive. In the case of the sirens, however, the situation is reversed. As the messengers of death they constituted a kind of representation that was supposed to mislead with its inevitability of a triumphing presence. The sirens would be executed only if they were able to recognize themselves by means of a confrontation with the gazing and silent Odysseus.

Kafka presents the same problem of radical negativity which consciousness must confront, but contrary to Blanchot or Heidegger he continues to defend the possibility of its existence in the presence of the stability and fullness of the voice of externality or being; a voice that in the end always turns out to be that of death. In Kafka's version, Odysseus is a synecdoche of consciousness that is not so much a gesture of indisputable self-determination but an attempt to save the same reductionist movement of the mind confronted by time and faith in itself. The deafness of consciousness and its internal silence are the results of the work of cleansing, a reduction to the minimum. Thanks to that work, consciousness is capable of taking back the remains of sense from the ultimate and lethal silence of death.[116]

The Ontology of Sound

Beckett's position could be described as being in conflict with the first option sketched (Blanchot on Heidegger) and much closer to the second option (that of Kafka). Beckett remains faithful to the rule of negativity, but this is not a negativity

---

116   See Moses S., *Ulysse chez Kafka*, in *Exégèse d'une légende. Lectures de Kafka*, Paris 2006.

that comes from the affirmation of passivity but rather from the reduction of establishing the subject as an instance of cognition. With respect to Beckett's vision of individuality conscious of itself, one could say that epistemology takes precedence over ontology. The more the subject is becomes capable of questioning itself the more it exists. What seems particularly interesting is what the possible outcome of such questioning might be. Let us take a look at this problem from the perspective of a central category of the voice. The voice does not simply appear as a form of the endlessness of externality or an undefined and impersonal persistence but as a sign of concrete presence that cannot be recognized or described. That particular character of existence can be observed in the short work entitled *Bing*.[117]

The circumstances of that text are extremely similar to those from Beckett's later works,[118] characterized by small, enclosed spaces and a precise, emotionless and almost "technical" description of the anonymous figure and a small number of components that undergo constant relocations and permutations. The work is likewise characterized by a particular euphonic intensity and rhythm that holds the text together with a peculiar "musical" coherence.[119] This is how things look from a strictly formal side. From the outset, the tension is clearly visible between the concreteness of the body residing in a clearly delineated, limited sphere and the world of sounds:

> White walls one yard by two white ceiling one square yard never seen. Bare white body fixed only the eyes only just. Traces blurs light grey almost white on white. Hands hanging palms front white feet heels together right angle. Light heat white planes shining white bare white body fixed ping pixed elsewhere. Traces blurs signs no meaning light grey almost white. Bare white body fixed white on white invisible. Only the eyes only just light blue almost white. [B, p. 371]

In this passage, we are confronted with the aporia of a complete recognition of reality and the "transparent" mystery of the world. The work of consciousness hidden beneath ascetic language is headed toward dynamism – the sphere in which the described body is present is known and unknown at the same time. Between these two possibilities of perfect knowledge and a definite conclusion there is a tension that comes to life and upholds the rhythm of the entire work. All possible

---

117 It can be seen on the example of differences between specific textual solutions used in versions in both languages. See Fitch B.T., *"The Status of the Second Version of Beckettian Text: The Evidence of the Bing/Ping manuscripts,"* Journal of Beckett Studies, (Special Double Issue), no. 11-12, 1989.

118 This particular work was written after the most "geometrical" works of Beckett – *Le Dépeulpeur /The Lost Ones*. From that point on, Beckett moved toward radical minimalism. See Knowlson J., *Damned to fame*, Op. cit., pp. 542-543.

119 See Libera A., "Jak zbudowane jest 'Dzyń' Becketta?," in *Literatura na Świecie* 1975 no. 5.

descriptions point to a peculiar kind of half-existence – an unfulfilled existence, captured in the enigmatic dimension between the fullness of the presence and nothingness. It is a space that is both chaotic and disappears among the identities of other colours that move to the overexposed white, all the way to – in an expression so often used by the author – shades of grey. The body is almost entirely described, frozen in waiting. But this motionlessness itself belongs to some unspecified order. Additionally, we encounter signs held in the middle of their decomposition. They do not form meanings anymore and become arbitrary elements of the actualized world. These are traces that dissolve any clear constellation of sense. That which exists reveals itself in an incomplete, imperfect form. However, the presence of all the elements of the world represented in the text cannot be reduced to some finally stabilized foundation. What is immobile becomes identified finally as a fiction created by the mind and sustained by the veil of language. We are confronted simultaneously with dislocation and fulfilment.

It is pointless to look for any form of synthesis. A strongly expressed desire for directness does not bring any relief in the form of an arrival at the foundation of presence undisturbed by any conscious filter. It brings one to the edge of immanence. "In front of silence" is the point of access for this desire for impersonal persistence that can reveal itself only in language and through language, hence in an impossible to overcome difference between the speaking subjects (even if the instance of singularity was pushed into an impersonal form) and the hermetically closed sphere of what is singular. A seemingly anonymous voice pointing to the initial circumstances ("all is known") only hides the nameless character of the entire world – the workings of language serve to depersonalize but do not erase the activity of consciousness that holds on by means of the smallest instinctual reactions which it wants to control and to which it wants to grant some sense. Internal silence can be understood both literally as a state inside of a precisely sketched space as well as a state of the most profound immanence to which consciousness has no access because it is located always "on the outside."

Consciousness both exists and at the same time attempts to describe this existence. This double coding is upheld throughout the entire text where, in effect, the empirical order becomes overlaid with the order of consciousness. In that way, the work of the autonomisation and establishment ("immobilizing") of the subject speaking through the natural language becomes possible. By constantly correcting its own position, it shows, however, that this particular state is local or impossible to be achieved ("the immobile is somewhere else"). As long as consciousness keeps speaking it creates distance, thanks to which we can see the "screen" of total silence. When it finally becomes silent, it will resound with the noise that is not the voice of an individual or a meaning, but a final trace of a clash between subjectivity and what is exterior. The work of all subjectival "tropisms" seems to serve that particular arrival in the final sounds of the remnants of form, creating a space for a contradictory form of presence – a voice reduced to onomatopoeia; one that does not belong to either the external world or consciousness or to external reality, but instead splits the uncertain stability of a singular being into these two possibilities. The smallest movement in that space forces the subject to make a correction of its position that is subsequently complemented by the event of sound:

> Bare white body fixed ping fixed elsewhere. Only the eyes only just light blue almost white fixed front. Ping murmur only just almost never one second perhaps a way out. Head haught eyes light blue almost white fixed front ping murmur ping silence. Eyes holes light blue almost white mouth white seam like sewn invisible. Ping murmur perhaps a nature one second almost never that much memory almost never. [B, pp. 371-372]

The signals of an external voice, the mysterious "murmurs" constitute a kind of presence that is not complete and cannot be entirely counteracted. The neutralizing function of language serves in this case only as means of highlighting the unspecified status of particular kind of sounds. They last based on the rule of half-life, "almost" and "barely," without suggesting any stable or possibly externalized form. This goes in the other direction as well: there are various modes of indeterminacy and speculation, organizing into varying configurations of sound understood as pure possibilities free from definitions. The power of memory is radically limited and brought to an incomplete, mnemonic-technical ability to recreate. Finally, the purely physiological genesis of those murmurs is also unclear. The lips of the protagonist are tightly sealed, barely visible, almost invisible.

The dislocation (the "hop"), which is created in this space, is an event of difference that is created as a result of a collision of these two kinds of sounds, of an empty frequency "between" a murmur and the "ping." However, both forms remain linguistic, even though the rule of total reductionism would be headed toward establishing a level on which the voice, cleared to a-semantic sound was to exist outside of the form of representation. In the meantime, Beckett clearly describes the problem of that sound difference using a poetic register, through the free verse character of the entire text, locating final presence within the matrix of relations between four orders: language as an arbitrary system of word conventions, an external voice, isolated sound and silence. This complex relationship superimposes itself over the dependencies of yet another kind that have been mentioned before – a relationship between what is sensual and what is transcendental; between what is transcendental and what is immanent.

Reactions of the body inscribed into the linguistic system, even if they exist in a radically minimalistic form, instantaneously become marks of knowledge about the world and create a distance impossible to diminish; one that blocks access to formless directness. The rudimentary voice vibrates as something unspecified.

On the one hand, it is an empirical element that is impossible to control and, on the other hand, it is a kind of presence that still and/or already is not bound to a final implosion or an enclosure "inside the silence." These multiple entanglements result not only in a reality sketched by the author becoming relational and escaping the permanent metaphysical distinctions. But, most importantly, it appears as impermanent and temporal. Consciousness and language are not able to catch up with the "work" of the event that remains inevitably disproportionate to the kind of presence it creates. The subject whose desire would settle in an abstract, closed and completely transparent language is released from the force of fantasy of "being immobile." This is likewise a staged confrontation with resounding noise.

> Planes meeting invisible one only shining white infinite but that known not. Nose ears white holes mouth white seam like sewn invisible. Ping murmurs only just almost never one second always the same all known without within. Ping perhaps a nature one second with image same time a little less blue and white in the wind. White ceiling shining white one square yard never seen ping perhaps way out there one second ping silence. [B, p. 372]

The progression of language suggests varying possibilities of connecting phrases into meaningful units but in this rhythmical speech-text, in its breaking of syntax, something meaningful happens. We are dealing with an oscillation between deadly immobilization that cannot bring any grounded presence and the world of movement in which all is dispersed through an endless metamorphosis. Awaiting the arrival of the right moment in which all the frequencies of the voice, all the sounds, will be in *unison* seems like a false goal. Language deceives with its mimetic and methodical consistency and serves to highlight a gap which is impossible to breach; a gap that is exposed and experienced every time there is a need to describe the subject's status. That is why the most radical anonymity is a form that is granted to the unformed, wordless world of immanence as a gesture of the last opportunity given to the subject and literature as a form of expressing its situation. But this "tension effect" or this spread between the absence of formal markers of singularity and the attempt to grasp the universal rule that guides subjectivity could be read as an effort to fulfil one of the leading slogans of Beckett's program he has established at the beginning of his work – finding the right dimension of language for the chaos of reality.

However, this uncertainty between chaos and order is reduced in *Ping* to a minimal form, as if sense could only be a kind of permanent, although not belonging in the end to any particular sphere of reality, sediment of sense. The entire process of ambiguity, the entire movement of dialectics does not allow for the reworking of the extremities described here but stops at the edge of what is truly negative and lacking a resolution. The building blocks of the represented world are the tools used for that task. They reappear in constantly changing configurations: sound and silence, and the body and space that surround both. Their existence is crystalised in the paradoxical image of a mystery that is recognized at the right moment or in a border that persists between the interior and exterior. The possibility of escaping the trap of the world shrinking to its minimal form becomes an extension of the power of the persistence of consciousness and representational fiction. What remains serves as proof of the importance of a singular being as the irremovable presence of transition – a passage from sound to silence.

In this way, Beckett attempts to yet again arrive at the edge of consciousness and language. This epistemological peregrination is accompanied by the experience of existential unreliability. The fiction of reality receives a supplement in the form of the phenomenal illusion of a singular merger. Individual life submerged in an abstract system of speech becomes indifferent for only a moment. It does so in order to be reborn in a critical gesture that proclaims its own impossibility, thereby killing itself:

White ceiling never seen ping of old only just almost never one second light time white floor never seen ping of old perhaps there. Ping of old only just perhaps a meaning a nature of one second almost never blue and white in the wind that much memory henceforth never. White planes no trace shining white one only shining white infinite but that known not. Light heat all known all white heart breath no sound. Head haught eyes white fixed front old ping last murmur one second perhaps not alone eye unlustrous black and white half closed long lashes imploring ping silence over. [B, p. 373]

The temporal descriptions serve as not only highlights of the reverberating sound but also are a modal frame of what could possibly the space of consciousness and what could be excavated from the abyss of memory. The rigorous process of its purification, removing what is accidental and physical (this is what traces are, after all) is condemned to failure. Full control over the body, even though it has been reduced to the most basic of affects, is not possible. The same is true with respect to control over the external space from which the enigmatic voice emerged.

The last phrase of the text confirms the logic of the entirety of Beckett's work. The consciousness has to create an imaginational space using language; one in which all the contradictions can be temporarily removed and in which all that lays at the bottom of that reality appears simultaneously. All the elements of the world are identified according to the same order but only for a brief moment. After its passing, this created reality arrives at a state of primal disintegration. The moment of integration is accompanied by a moment of chaos and destruction. Subjectivity searching for the source of its own personality and attempting to control the body can exist while being absent. It can speak of itself, and thereby establish itself as a subjectivity "in the name of the other" – through language understood as a convention of meaning. As a result, consciousness in Beckett's writing can become silent (although it loses its own uniqueness when it attempts to express itself) but can also be identified with a completely alien, unexamined silence. Finally, it remains stuck in the place where it is torn and the place of non-identity. It experiences them, but cannot express in words this very experience. It searches for its idiom in the description of the state whose fullest phenomenon, theme and problem is the voice reduced to the homeless sound. This sound does not allow it to die or live, constantly delaying the experience of reality. Feeding on the existential power of this aporia, consciousness can never finally retract and surrender to the anonymous truth of "Being." It has to keep searching for the confirmation of its own language register thanks to which its existence could become totally unquestionable.

The Stage of Life, the Stage of Consciousness

What a theatre, breath![120]

– Émile M. Cioran

The problem of the ontological status of the subject and consciousness is equally vivid in drama. In a short text entitled *Breath*,[121] Beckett provides what is perhaps his most radical take on these conjoined subjects. At the most basic level, his attempt to reconstruct the dramaturgic situation on the least developed level stumbles into extreme difficulties. The text constitutes a score, in the strict sense of the word – there is not a single word uttered in it that is meant to be spoken off the stage. The entire play is limited to rudimentary stage directions. According to the author it was the sound, light and subtly organized space that were supposed to pay the only and significant role in the play. This shift is obviously meaningful because imagining the actual production of the play is replaced by a function of negating the presence and accessibility of the word in the text. In this intermediary space the human dimension becomes limited to the breath we find in the title as well as to screaming and wailing. Reality remains almost entirely contained within the author's technical and – as is often in the case of Beckett – extremely pedantic commentary; the creation of a dramaturgical space but also hides it in a gesture of a rigorous limitation. The possible stage world becomes revealed through the authorial signs and gestures that highlight its peculiar, ungraspable and fleeting character. The stage directions of the author that constitute a recording of the entire work do not determine the textual reality *tout court* but provoke the effect of the voice's presence. This is not only an experiment with the potentiality of a

---

120   Cioran É. M., *Drawn and Quartered,* translated by Richard Howard, New York 2012.
121   Beckett, S., *Breath*, in *CE*, vol. 3, p. 401.

mute work that constitutes a script for the director and performers, but a staging of the paradox of its existence. In other words, the works could be treated as a collection of guidelines for a theatrical production, or they could be read in an immanent order as a text in the form of practical instructions and calculations. Finally, the work might represent an attempt to record the author's obsessions.

From that perspective, *Breath* appears as a narration that clearly divides itself into two parts. The first begins and ends with darkness from which a faint, grey light emerges suggesting a twilight that is not only real but also metaphorical, stretched over the sphere of the entirety of being that is available in the space of a dramaturgical world. In such surroundings, there is a quiet scream coming from an unknown source. Right after that, one can hear the "sound of breathing in." Simultaneously, the brightness of light changes and it goes from twilight to maximum brightness, as designated by the author. The coupling of light and sound is repeated in the same manner on the occasion of exhaling. After that, there is a cooling of movement, quieting down and finally becoming darkness. In the second act, similar to the beginning, after raising the curtain one can see garbage that lies flat on the stage. A scream, that in reality is a "strip of a recorded squealing," similar to the first act, becomes synchronized with a breath and a proper light setup that is strengthened in comparison with what has come before. The whole thing ends in a fadeout, although the lack of authorial commentary describing the closing of the play once again suspends the elements of the world in the space of twilight and the sphere denoted by an echo fading away sounds and still vibrates as the breath dies out.

In the most obvious but also the most fundamental interpretative dimension, breath constitutes a modus of existence. The title can be merely metonymy (and not a symbol or a metaphor) because all the other symptoms of existence (screaming and shrieking) can be read as adjacent signs of the same, incomprehensible, participation of the individual in the world. By suggesting an unambiguous trace, the author introduces a mysterious multi-dimensionality of separate symptoms of existence, emerging one after another in the course of the dramaturgical action. It is precisely the rule of metonymy that causes, despite substantial differences, all the elements of a staged reality to remain versions of "the same." They are revealed as signs of life, signs of existence on the borders of sense. They are ungraspable in their articulation and remain before the word and its concreteness. The conflict between independently controlled revelations of indisputable presence and tormenting materiality, as well as the infinite boredom of carnal persistence, is revealed in Beckett's *Breath*. Darkness is not only a goal of the stage action but also a natural environment surrounding a singular being that has been elucidated with a flash and filled by an organic sound of screams and breath. Repetition and the temporality of these revelations points simultaneously to the momentariness of experience and to the impossibility of stopping and taming the moment that is instinctually perceived as filled with presence. As a result the moment remains monstrous and impenetrable, unstoppable for the net of language and description of darkness.

While darkness and the flash of light in Beckett's work coexist on the basis of the negative dialectic[122] that does not allow to work through the contradictions but in which every assemblage of extremities opens the space of yet another cognitive and existential impossibility, the voice remains completely enclosed within its own autonomy. Breath is the most primal sign of life and the most fundamental external representation and actualization of impossible to understand sounds, deposited within the organism. Yet, it remains barely audible. That is why the text is an affirmation of a focused, intense listening to one's own body and the rhythm set by the signs of its presence as well as a manifestation of the fundamental terror of a fleeting character of such signs after appearance of which nothing more can ever happen again. But that way of treating physicality results in vivisection, being the fundamental and only reliable action, the power to establish a subject. All of that happens in an act of cleansing, as a fundamentally passive contemplation of the body's reflexes, through which the foundations of existence are exposed. There is no way of localizing their sources because – even though they are repeatedly experienced – they cannot be known. The breaths, screams and shrieking in Beckett's work come back as different versions of the same authorial obsession: the namelessness impacting the world and humans.

A short intermedium also constitutes an ascetic history of existence in the sense of fulfilling human fate. As is usually the case in the works of Beckett, the sense of existence becomes inscribed into the cycle of "coming into existence and dying," or a cyclical time between birth and death. In terms of the way the play is written down, limitations are extended as far as possible – life is reduced to a quieted and amplified breath; reduced to a moment in which one can hear every scream as well as the short cries of an infant. This last sound is played from a recording and can be interpreted as an additional (although provoked by – of course – technical and scenic necessity) mediation that makes the direct experience of the world impossible.[123] The effect of mechanical repetition, also used by Beckett in *Krapp's Last Tape*, results in the concreteness of a stage sign to be replaced by

---

122 See the classical interpretation in which the problem is formulated in a slightly different manner: Knowlson J., *Light and Darkness in the Theatre of Samuel Beckett*, London 1972.

123 Małgorzata Sugiera interprets the work similarly. For her, it constitutes an example of the fundamental isolation of the world of the stage that is purposefully walled from the world outside of the theatre. "*Breath* is not the end point of the entirety Beckett's theatre. Exhausting the possibilities for minimizing traditional stage fiction, as well as the representational world serving it as physical support, Beckett began his *via positiva*."

a logic of repetition and temporality. The recreated voice only feigns presence through its automatic repetition which, in turn, makes the perceived sounds less real. An additional effect of identity is supposed to be evoked by the identity of both screams (from the first and second acts). In reality, however, they allow one to realize the fantastical character of a physical sign. The identity of both voices is also only a deceiving fiction born out of the difference in time between them. Their similarity cannot be substantial, hence it constitutes the impossibility of an expression of the existential truth of experience that is composed of an irreversibly lost individual past of which a significant remnant is the voice on tape, as well as singular presence, as illusory as the broken screams that takes place between the inhaling and exhaling of breath.

That is why the figure of voice – let us repeat – is not functionally different from the figure of breath, because they both remain bonded with body and externality. The voice, although physical at its source, is also purely acoustic. Even though it falls under the rule of stage autonomy, simultaneously and constantly directing us back to its own personal source. However, in this case we are not talking about a stable subject that would intentionally decide about the choice of a moment in which one should speak up. In place of punctual identity, there is breath, as a sign of the body, constantly recalling its hidden existence. The voice, reduced to articulating the minimum of a breath, constantly sends one back to its organic source, even though it simultaneously points to this genesis without any effect, because it's located "between," or... on stage. Personal expression is purely illusory because the voice, which belongs to a concrete actor in a theatrical production, will always send one back to the sphere of anonymous externality. What happens on stage is contaminated with fictionality, hence possible as a stage experiment. Simultaneously, however, it appears as a sign of the desire to go outside of any form of a symbolic representation.[124]

The order that is set by the category of voice of breath is based on an insurmountable contradiction. On the one hand, Beckett presents this category as an allegory of pure presence deposited in sound, in the potentiality of the isolated persistence outside of human reality that is expressed solely as a boundary, impossible to represent, between existence and non-existence, as an almost wordless whisper, an a-semantical scream or a pure contamination of sounds. On the other hand, this category might belong to the directness of experience, the

Sugiera M., *Beckett: kondensowanie świata*, in *Potomkowie Króla Ubu. Szkice o teatrze francuskim XX wieku*, Kraków 2002, p. 142.

124 One could treat *Breath* as a kind of peculiar, unfulfilled, "performative creation of materiality." See Fischer-Lichte E., *Estetyka performatywności*, translated by M. Borowski, M. Sugiera, Kraków 2008, p. 210 [German: *Ästhetik des Performativen*, Frankfurt am Main 2004].

irremovable physicality of existence that appears through short, muffled screams or a half-hysterical, half-methodical confirmation of life through listening intently to breath. From the perspective of those conflicting orders, the voice is not entirely a mark of physicality, nor does it remain fully transcendent. It exists in an unshakeable order of ideas beyond specific time and space, even though it simultaneously determines the empirical status of a single being (on stage) and is seen as a trace in the form of concrete signs, images and figures of language (in the text). The tension between these two characteristics of the voice constitutes a fundamental dramaturgical axis of *Breath* but also refers to almost all the mature works of Beckett.

The voice and "literary space" are the two names of the same involvement required for writing and reading the work. Hence, if the reading that is freed from a desire for passivity and realized in a perpetual resignation from the possibility of a final interpretation is impossible, then the experience of intellectual hopelessness when facing the text will turn into an existential powerlessness. The need for expression, despite the recognized failure of the explication of the signs of the world, situates the speaking subject in the enigmatic place of the disintegration of language. In that "unknown silence," as the often repeated phrase from *The Unnamable* suggests, this necessity forces the reader and the spectator to look at the empty and dark stage on which, similarly to *Breath*, the long awaited voice has to be heard at the right moment; a voice that does not belong to anyone anymore. It is a voice as a symptom of a radical deprivation of the being of man. The gesture of cleansing takes place on stage and – as an element of representation – it reveals the fundamental impossibility of touching the life itself.

In that sense, Jacques Derrida was right when – commenting on the phenomenology of Husserl – he claimed that the source of sense remains fundamentally unmatched with the experience of consciousness being contaminated with a semiotic heteronomy and difference that allows a representation in general at the dawn of consciousness. He was also right when he claimed that from the perspective of the subject (understood as self-verifying consciousness) life always and inevitably exists as a concept, hence it can be expressed both through the form of mediation as well as actualization. From that point of view, life can only be a "life." One cannot remove a trace of physicality that inevitably accompanies the process of subject creation through, however broadly understood, the gesture of reduction. Only through the power of language can self-conscious individuality constitute itself. However, it will never have complete power, as it is given to fall with every act of expression into the chaos of unmarked, perfect generality or by risking falling into a complete silence. According to Derrida:

> The subject does not have to pass outside of himself in order to be immediately affected by its activity of expression. My words are "alive" because they seem not to leave me,

seem not to fall outside of me, outside of my breath, into a visible distance; they do not stop belonging to me, to be at my disposal, "without anything accessory." [...][125]

An objective "mundane" science can surely teach us nothing about the essence of the voice. But the unity of the sound and the voice, which allows the voice to produce itself in the world as pure auto-affection, is the unique instance that escapes from the distinction between intramundanity and transcendentality; and by the same token, it makes this distinction possible.

It is this universality that results in the fact that, structurally and in principle, no consciousness is possible without the voice. The voice is being close to itself in the form of universality, as consciousness. The voice is consciousness. [...] Ideally, in the teleological essence of speech, it would then be possible for the signifier to be in absolute proximity to the signified aimed at an intuition and governing the meaning. The signifier would become perfectly diaphanous due to the absolute proximity to the signified. This proximity is broken when, instead of hearing myself speak, I see myself write or gesture.[126]

Derrida makes a valid point here. It is not – obviously – about speech as a directly understood presence of the unquestionable sense but about understanding the voice as the deepest and irreducible way of actualizing of what is coming from a source and making it possible for consciousness to self-determine. Without going into great details concerning the phenomenological terminology[127] one could say that the instance of the personal voice becomes, by necessity, an *a priori* of a true and real presence and what follows – sense. Derrida protests against omitting this presupposition which, from that point of view, turns out to be fundamental for understanding the project of phenomenology as an objective description of both what appears within the field of consciousness and of means of that appearance. The critique, however, is not aimed directly at the very possibility of insight into the nature of things but at the unbreakable bond between the voice, sense and presence. The voice never reveals itself as a complete presence but is ultimately contaminated by the presence of physicality that contains the presence and sense within the frame of absence and death. All of seemingly dwarfed firms of voice proposed by Beckett have nothing of the totality of Being or Exterior in them and are more of testimonies of the impossibility of fulfilling the phenomenological project of the total actualization of "now" that has within itself all the potentialities of time[128]. But these reduced dimensions of the voice do not constitute a singular

---

125 Derrida J., *Voice and Phenomenon,* Op. cit., p. 65.
126 Ibid., pp. 68-69.
127 It is important to mention that this is about the difference between "expressing" and "pointing" and between "sound" and *phone*.
128 "Every experience of consciousness is surrounded by a temporal horizon and sensed through its flowing, arriving and passing. Both retention and protention are bonded with perception and constitute three aspects, or time phases proper to every act of consciousness

epiphany and turn out to be an effect of a critical work of consciousness. It can recognize itself only through a difficult gesture of the affirmation of the impossibility of the consciousness-driven unification of the individual as a part of "thinking over" the disintegration of the orders of "closeness" described by Derrida: language and sense, interior and exterior.

Both in the ideas and practices of Beckett one can find a kind of incarnated critique that is full of the presence that is assumed by the voice. Reduced to a physiological, organic and mechanical necessity, consciousness is stripped into the pure possibility of a non-mediated access to reality. It also takes away its bearing capacity from its conviction about the sensibility of efforts aimed at marking universal, external to history, conditions of the possibility of establishing a subject,[129] and leaves only a critical, "timed" movement of questioning that is simultaneously affirmative. The "drama of breath" that takes place on stage (potentially in the text's score) is also a paradoxical sign that, by situating itself outside of language understood as a system of inter-subjective meanings, sends one back to this system during that very moment in which it lasts. It is a sung – leftover remaining after the personal voice, a song that lonely consciousness attempts to leave "inside silence," in the sphere of the anonymity of death; a death that does not answer to consciousness, the image or notional language. It attempts to mark its own fragile and temporal presence.

Breath is a theatrical exercise of consciousness, an experiment through which reality beyond of the stage (external to representation) is suspended. This critical-deconstructive *epoché* leads to revealing the most fundamental of facts: for subjectivity attempting to establish itself as autonomous, life can only be a consciousness of life and not pure – uncontaminated with a linguistic mediation – physiological and silent persistence, a fullness of sense or a well-grounded presence that in an obvious way could be treated as a form of individuality's existence.

---

together. The present is a 'fleeting present,' being at the same time the 'arriving present,' or in other words: it always appears as a fleeting moment. The present [...] is not a statistical point, self-reliant and an isolated 'now.' It is intertwined with what 'is not yet' and with that which 'is gone already.' It cannot be separated from them in an absolute way. Every act is a complete entity of what is 'now,' 'not anymore' and 'not yet'." Buczyńska-Garewicz H., *Metafizyczne rozważania o czasie*, Krakow 2003, p. 31.

129   As Krzysztof Michalski stated: "The question about the consciousness of time – a question that seemed to be a local problem (or just one of many questions) – turns out to be a universal problem. It is a question that encompasses everything. It is the one question that philosophy always is." Michalski K., *Logika i czas. Próba analizy Husserlowskiej teorii sensu*, Warszawa 1988, p. 204.

Chapter Two
Between Nameless and Unnamable

All human errors are impatience, a premature breaking off of methodical procedure, an apparent fencing-in of what is apparently at issue[130]

– Franz Kafka

One of the first signs of beginnings of understanding is the wish to die. This life appears unbearable, another unattainable. One is no longer ashamed of wanting to die; one asks to be moved from the old cell, which one hates, to a new one, which one will only in time come to hate. In this there is also a residue of belief that during the move the master will chance to come along the corridor, look at the prisoner and say: "This man is not to be locked up again. He is to come with me." [131]

– Franz Kafka

Our salvation is death, but not this one. [132]

– Franz Kafka

The perspective imposed on Beckett by Blanchot is – of course – a strong, conscious and meticulously constructed interpretation, and from it emerges a changed work. But the philosophy and practice of Beckett are also presented in a different light. It seems that there is no escaping from that double bond but it also forces the readers of both authors to remain cautious. Blanchot appears to be accompanying Beckett in his work of reduction only to a certain degree. In particular, to a point where Blanchot decides to stand by "relieving" consciousness, neutralizing one's own idiom and falling back under the rule of untamable exterior. In Beckett's work, the transparency of consciousness and language has been a seemingly overpowering myth, one that has stifled all the movements of the will. The reverse is true with Blanchot: the primacy of the absolute exterior, the reign of death and the power of neutrality result in the power of will never being able to establish a form of subjectivity. In place of the subtle and negative dialectic of Beckett, in which individuality, struggling for its own respect, clashed with what is negative, one finds an equally subtle force of chiasm, a rhetorical structure in which traces of subjectivity remain truly dispersed in neutrality, depriving it of the mechanics of

---

130 Kafka F., "Reflections on Sin, Suffering, Hope, and the True Way," in *The Great Wall of China: Stories and Reflections*, translated by translated by Willa and Edwin Muir, New York 1946.
131 Kafka K., *Blue Octavo Notebooks*, translated by Ernst Kaiser, Eithne Wilkins, Cambridge 2004.
132 Ibid.

a linguistic structure.[133] The difference between the two projects is fundamental. Wherever Beckett looks for a chance to save his own idiom (in the persistent work of reduction and tearing apart), Blanchot notices only another stage in the anonymous work of writing or the dispersing of the sense, its dislocation in an infinite series of aporias and chiasms.

Even though Blanchot, most clearly among Beckett's commentators, poses a question about who really speaks in the author's texts, he cleverly traffics elements of his own ideas that substantially weaken the question. Attempting to do justice to Beckett, one should state the following: in Beckett's texts it is the voice itself speaking. It is a final and irreducibly contradictory instance of subjectivity; contradictory because belonging to the one speaking (it is a signal, a sketch of its personality) but at the same time circulating in the communication space. It is contradictory because the voice is a sign of the deepest presence of individuality and this presence, simultaneously, carries something of the nothing of its essence. Blanchot shifts the weight of Beckett's struggle, justifying subjectivity and recognizing its existence among other languages, to the abstract, or even purely potential, level of crossing idiomatic expression with the common, peculiarity of voice (timbre, vibration[134]) and the anonymous system of speech – this impossible to verify, quasi-transcendental difference and totality of the rule of the "postmortem sphere." Finally, he shifts to the plane of a pure relation between presence and absence.

Both the critique and practice of Blanchot are headed toward the annihilation of the subject. This happens in different ways. Subjectivity does not gain its legitimacy in a gesture of establishment, in a movement separating the *cogito* from the external world, a screen of anonymity from which the voice of an individual is reflected. The gesture of attaining autonomy is illusory, somewhat destabilized in a residuum of consciousness already in the moment in which the decision about establishing the "I" as a subject could be made. Blanchot reads in Beckett this pre-established and mistaken step (*faux pas*) and similar to a transcendental order, uncovers an aspect of passivity and desperate resignation from the will to conscious existence.

However, the relation between subjectivity and language in Beckett's work is rather different. The desire to free oneself from the shackles of working consciousness is accompanied by the necessity to describe every movement of reflection. Due to this duality, Beckett's texts constitute a kind of staging of tension between the necessity of making a decision and the ficitionality of such a movement that is impossible to deescalate. This "theatrical" motif, thanks to which the consciousness of a separate being is not exhausted in the act of a

---

133   See Derrida J., "La loi du genre," in *Parages*, Paris 1986.
134   See Derrida J., "*Désistance*," in *Psyché: Inventions de l'autre*, Paris 1987.

negative reduction but opens up for the unforeseen event (one cannot fully plan what will become on the "stage of language" or "stage of consciousness"), is consciously omitted and placed within the space of torture by Beckett. Its source is no longer individuality fighting for the right to subjectivity but the inertia of language that speaks somewhat "from behind the grave" of the subject. Blanchot cannot recognize the game based on making and avoiding decisions that takes place in *Endgame*, after the end of the world, because the effect of any action has been already foreseen. This is a dissolution of the neutrality of statements in the third person and the myth of transparency and withdrawal, about which Georges Poulet wrote that it is a myth of constant failure[135]. One could formulate things in yet another way: Blanchot interprets Beckett's work by inscribing the power of the writer's idiom[136] into his own para-logic of a "step," "mistake" and "negation"[137] – a movement that is a synonym of work and life. This turns out to be impossible because it proves to be contaminated by its own deadly reversibility: rigidity and passivity. There is no exit from that very impasse and the only thing that is left is to describe this entire elaborate construction in which not only the realness of existence is being questioned by fictionality of language but also one in which the depriving force of conventional and arbitrary speech is marked by the stigma of death. This unquestionable silence is a pre-established condition for autonomous language to come into being; one that becomes a meditation over its own falsity. On the other hand, the delaying of death in the works of Beckett that confirms an individual's right to existence – this Kafkaesque waiting for the arrival of "proper death" – is connected with the question of the individual. Beckett's figures of the

---

135 See Poulet G., *Myśl nieokreślona*, translated by Tomasz Swoboda, Warsaw 2004, p. 256.

136 With regard to Beckett, the concept of force that we will be coming back to in the third part of this book can seem paradoxical, since the protagonists created by the author, subjects and different kinds of reality are characterized by a radical "weakness" – they are described in categories of failure and catastrophe and exist, so to speak, in a state of absence. However, this ruination is fulfilled by will to being nonetheless. The work of Beckett is an exercise, an experiment with passivity, but it is not just passivity itself that is the fundamental foundation. See Connor S., *Samuel Beckett. Repetition, Theory and Text*, Aurora Colorado 2006, p. 187. It is significant that the entire chapter was devoted to this exact question of the interdependence between power, repetition and the construction of the idiom of the works of Beckett.

137 It is the logic of exclusion and a relocation of the subject "tertium datur." Blanchot's "step beyond" [*le pas au-delà*] is simultaneously a negation (homonym of the word "pas") of its possibilities and a "false step," a "mistake" and "blunder" (*faux pas*). That is why, as Derrida has observed, the entire category of neutrality is "a proof of a singular place of passion beyond the opposition of passive and active." See Derrida J., *Demeure. Maurice Blanchot*, Paris, 1998, p. 33. In English, see *Demeure: Fiction and Testimony*, translated by Elizabeth Rottenber Stanford 2000.

subject clash with the powers of anonymity and fight with fear of a deadly, final silence that does not allow for the erasure of traces of subjectivity understood as indestructible marks of consciousness that present themselves – in acts of reflection – in reality. In Blanchot's project writing is a passive acceptance of the reign of death against which the philosopher, but also the writer, can only set out a totalizing rhetoric of absence[138] and a fossilized language of abstraction – cyphers of dying out existence – that finally remove any credibility of any language of subjectivity.

The Subject that Disappears

We may now return to the question that appeared at the very beginning of this set of our reflections. It is true that both Beckett and Blanchot ask about the same relationship between the possibility and impossibility of situating subjectivity enclosed in a question: Who is speaking? However, only Beckett consistently formalizes and solidifies his own idiom, while Blanchot radically relocates that question into the "postmortem sphere," dispersing with sense within the boundaries marked by the rhetoric of impossibility that he is consciously unwilling to cross. As a witness to these modernist struggles with the question of subjectivity, we must add the name of another philosopher – Michel Foucault.

In his famous essay "What is an Author?" Foucault seems to be repeating the doubts of Beckett, Blanchot and the entire cast of authors, theorists and philosophers who struggled with the question of legitimizing the speaking subject from at least the middle of the past century. It is important to note that Foucault placed a phrase taken from Beckett in the middle of his own reflection; a phrase around which the two most important strands of his deliberations circle.[139] Let us take the closer look:

> Beckett nicely formulates the theme with which I would like to begin: "What does it matter who is speaking, someone said, 'what does it matter who is speaking.'" In this indifference appears one of the fundamental ethical principles of contemporary writing. I say "ethical" because this indifference is really not a trait characterizing the manner in which one speaks and writes but, rather, a kind of immanent rule, taken

---

138   In a gesture of reduction, Blanchot, who interestingly limits himself to a kind of visual-phonetic contraction, proposes a greatly unspecified *absens* in place of the category of absence (*l'absence*) See Blanchot M., *L'attente l'oubli*, Paris 1962. In English, see *Awaiting Oblivion*, translated by John Gregg, Omaha 1999.

139   Yet another excerpt from the ending of *The Unnamable* opens the inaugural lecture at Collège de France from 1970. See M. Foucault, "The Order of Discourse," in *Untying the Text*, edited by Robert J. C. Young, Boston 1981.

up over and over again, never fully applied, not designating writing as something completed, but dominating it as a practice. [...] Writing unfolds like a game that invariably goes beyond its own rules and transgresses its limits. In writing, the point is not to manifest or exalt the act of writing, nor is it to pin a subject within language; it is, rather, a question of creating a space into which the writing subject constantly disappears.[140]

In the works of Foucault, the description of the borderline conditions of subjectivity is conducted in the negative mode and is closely connected with the act of writing. What is an act of writing not? Firstly, it does not produce an autotelic aesthetic order and does not contain itself within it or create a stable sense that is separated from other spaces of experience. It does not create a fully separate linguistic-representational reality independent from life itself. It is a game but situates itself outside the sphere of text constantly and inevitably entering the exterior. It shapes the existence of the one who writes and of the one who reads and enters into different relationships with institutional and social orders. The autotelic character of literature does not go well with the practice of writing, in which one is interested neither in practicing defensive strategies against approaching multi-dimensional reality, nor in treating "literary space" as a place dedicated solely to a linguistic experiment. All those activities, by aiming at delineating an essential and permanent range and definition of the term "literary," merely illustrate the alienating force of literature as an institution sanctioning the order of expression. The gesture of exposing oneself to what transgresses literature is precisely a moment of granting the writing process an existential weight. The moment of moving toward the exterior is, at the same time, a moment of confrontation with what is different from language, writing and literature. It is a moment in which writing moves to the side of an unexpected revelation of experience. The gesture of opening to what is different constitutes – as Foucault states at the very beginning – an "ethical principal" of literature.

Secondly, if it is not about "pinning down the subject within language" then – as one could assume – it must be about the reverse movement: breaking the "I" free from the rule of conventional linguistic characteristics and opening it to a reality that is neither simply empirical nor transcendental. The practice of writing cannot be understood as part of an exercise of the mind or through the logic of a spiritual task. It must be grasped according to an order that transgresses the very notion of language as a system. This is the paradox that Foucault attempts to develop while commenting on the words of Beckett: one can speak only when language is absent and practicing writing means resigning from the presence of speech. One must recall what idea of language Foucault has in mind. He is interested

---

140 Foucault M., "What is an Author?" in *Aesthetics, Method and Epistemology,* edited by James D. Faubion, New York 1999, pp. 205-206.

in an arbitrary system of differences, in which "I" can exist as an element that explodes the cohesive whole, or – as Jakobson and Lacan claimed[141] – as an empty sign, a cipher that communicates both the presence of subject as well as its fictionality and the deprivation of individuality resulting from the pressures of the normative system of meaning. The search for the space for individuality cannot take place under the auspices of establishing a homology between language and the subject as a function of a general system or structure. This is made possible by tracing the remnants of its various incoherencies, cracks and insolvability. From that perspective, the speaking subject would be exactly that – a trace of its own absence.

What does this description possibly mean? Foucault states that what marks modern literature is the "opening of the space in which the writing subject constantly disappears." This observation could lead us into a historical approach in which the development of modernity is focused in the prism of literature that increasingly adopted an impersonal form of language, alongside an anonymous form of the presence of the being. Beyond that incredibly important context,[142] Foucault proposes an additional, conceivably more interesting, possibility – the ambivalence that accompanies the process of writing.

The subject disappears in *écriture*, but who first "opens the space" proper to this practice? It is a critical point[143] through which Foucault reasserts the role of impersonality belonging to the subject attempting to speak, in defence of itself, within the framework of the institution of literature (not about the language of literature itself, freed from authorial power). We thereby arrive in the middle of Beckett's paradox – even in its humblest form, there is no escape from the event pointing to the subjectivity of writing/speaking. There is a performative contradiction in asserting that the disappearance of the subject is both necessary and impossible. To be clear, this discussion is not concerned with literally making words form or about the transcendental administration of rules,[144] or about individuality understood within a solipsistic structure[145] but about the very act of writing that Foucault has discussed as a part of logical consequences of his own

---

141   The problem of "I" as an empty sign of individual identity was one of the crucial issues touched upon by structuralists (Jakobson and Beneveniste) as well as Lacan, who borrowed heavily from their research.

142   This context is, of course, the line of modernist literature from Flaubert to *nouveau roman* [new novel].

143   As the Polish monographist of Foucault describes it, it is a "linguistic trap." See Komendant T., *Władze dyskursu. Michel Foucault w poszukiwaniu siebie*, Warszawa 1994, pp. 166-178.

144   Hence, it is also not about the structure that, according to the famous slogan by Paul Ricœur, has replaced the Kantian transcendental subject in structuralism.

145   See Nycz R., "Tropy 'ja'. Koncepcje podmiotowości w literaturze polskiej ostatniego stulecia," in *Język modernizmu. Prolegomena historycznoliterackie*, Wrocław 1997.

discourse. Although the ideal of impersonal language remains, this is extremely hard to realize in artistic practice. This "impossible necessity" or the removal of the subject by means of the same methods it used to establish itself seems to be both an ironic commentary on the modernist rule of subjectivity in general, as well as a description of the situation in which writing as a process of subjectifying can take its strength from the realized and reworked circumstances of the author's death. Not so much from his final disappearance (let us repeat: not empirically nor transcendentally) but in the sense of his radical displacement and situation within the framework of other discursive practices. Foucault states:

> The second theme, writing's relationship with death, is even more familiar. This link subverts an old tradition exemplified by the Greek epic, which was intended to perpetuate the immortality of the hero: if he was willing to die young, it was so that his life, consecrated and magnified by death. [...] Our culture has metamorphosed this idea of narrative, or writing, as something designed to ward off death. Writing has become linked to sacrifice, even to the sacrifice of life: it is now a voluntary effacement that does not need to be represented in books, since it is brought about in the writer's very existence. The work, which once had the duty of providing immortality, now possesses the right to kill, to be its author's murderer, as in the cases of Flaubert, Proust, and Kafka. That is not all, however: this relationship between writing and death is also manifested in the effacement of the writing subject's characteristics. Using all the contrivances that he sets up between himself and what he writes, the writing subject cancels out the signs of his particular individuality. As a result, the mark of the writer is reduced to nothing more than the singularity of his absence; he must assume the role of the dead man in the game of writing.[146]

And yet the dislocation of the subject itself does not seem to solve the problem. This paradox of the author is concerned simultaneously with a different kind of thinking about literature. It shifts the entire question from the plane of a critical verification of the subject's status to the level of both existential and epistemological metaphors that speak strictly about the interdependence of writing and death; writing that is no longer a form of expression but a signal, a sign or a trace of its own, planned disappearance. From that perspective, the death of the author and the subject is an incarnation of the same paradox of modern disenchantment. On the one hand, modernist writers since Flaubert have dreamt about complete impersonality in literature, a desire to cut loose from any form of authority (a pre-established metaphysical sense, a material history of the epoch, psychological truth, or the reliability of representation) and on the other – a description of "death" that never stops solely at the level of a metaphor that corresponds with certain external, institutional functions with which the subject or author used to be burdened. They accomplish the same goals as the subject but in completely different conditions – a

---

146   Foucault M., Op. cit., pp. 206-207.

dead author comes alive in linguistic figures and in the power of a strong idiom that is imposed on the "external" world of intersubjectivity and communication. In that sense, the conscious annihilation of the authorial signature does not result in its complete erasure but is merely a confirmation of its variable, double status.[147] Also, the very gesture of the erasure of what is individual and singular[148] constitutes a strategy that confirms the necessity of subjective existence that experiences its own mortality and situates itself in relation to that mortality. Writing is a kind of dual activity. It appears in a somewhat unobvious affirmation of what is negative, but it is that very movement that demonstrates the inability of crossing the horizon of negativity. Beckett, who Foucault failed to remember, did not desire to surrender himself to an "indifferently murmuring voice" but wanted to persist by a deadly and unending series of ambivalences. We are permanently dealing with a "technical" version of authorial death in the form of a questioned intention, a mimetic model of representation, and relations between the interior and exterior in Beckett's text. However, this is merely an initial condition for the work of consciousness that, in a way, cleanses itself in order to again stand up to the challenge of itself and reality. From that perspective, more reasonable seems to be the modal meta-reflective framework of almost all mature works of Beckett, starting with *Watt*, in which the madness of the logical syntax of language is accompanied by a constant reflection on the direction in which this particular language is headed and ends with his last text – *comment dire/what is the word* – in which the principle of repetition serves as a constant correction of the what and how of speech.

Death and disappearance are the elements of the conflict, the clash between the world and the one who is speaking, who "inhabits" language, and thereby passes one's own existence through the filter of structured and arbitrary speech. The loss of individuality does not cause the trace or voice of a singular absence to be stated indifferently in Beckett's work. On the contrary, the lack of easily graspable subjectival intention is not the final indication of the counterbalance of deadly writing,[149] nor does it become a madness of meaning. In diagnosing[150] the problem, Beckett does not fetishise it and does not free himself from it carelessly.

---

147 See Derrida J., "Signature Event Context," in *Margins of Philosophy,* translated by Alan Bass, Chicago 1982.

148 The figure of "erasure," taken from the title of Thomas Bernhard's novel, is one of the short-hand interpretations of the modernist tradition symbolized by Beckett.

149 According to Beckett, it is an attempt at a naïve and critical return to the poetic sources of all forms of the "experience of literature."

150 At this point, one might mention that while borrowing heavily from Joyce's project, Beckett caused to its reversal, or to the change of the model of literature as total, scholastically ordered and autonomous reality to the model of literature as the work of language for the sake of its own cleansing.

Foucault does so, however, when speaking about the "nameless murmur" that easily resolves the complex question of the relationship between consciousness and literature.

The Gesture of Death

All that Foucault consciously moved to the level of an all-encompassing network of relationships between power, sovereignty and dependencies being established within a network of discourses have been discreetly brought back to life by his contemporary commentator Giorgio Agamben. While reading Foucault, Agamben keeps in mind the critique of the category of the author understood as an instance of sense, a warrant of the coherence of the text but simultaneously shows a different – seemingly more important – aspect of that category, or the understanding of the author as a specific function of the general structure of the subject:

> From this perspective, the author-function appears as a process of subjectivation through which an individual is identified and constituted as the author of a certain corpus of texts. It thus seems that every inquiry into the subject as an individual must give way to the archival record that defines the conditions and forms under which the subject can appear in the order of discourse.[151]

Agamben highlights the fact that the text is not concerned with establishing the subject as a stable centre of meanings. The vision of subjectivity understood as the authorial function is not based on self-determination and autonomy. Such a subject is sentenced to existence as an element of a discursive chain on which it remains almost entirely dependent. According to Agamben, for Foucault the Cartesian-Kantian act of reflection and its significance survives only in its reduction to a gesture. One could say that the true and final reduction never takes place because its only real goal is a discovery of mediation, recognition of the conditions and of the field of forces in which the speaking "I" (speaking about itself, about others and to others) situates itself. What is left is not the principle of a phenomenologically strict search for the foundations of all cognition but the general structure of the practices of writing and thinking (one that discovers a double epistemological-semiotic entanglement) in which the subject finds itself. The uncovering of that general structure has a somewhat ethereal nature because it cannot be anchored in the directness of experience or defined as one of the building blocks of the structure of language. But is the gesture of the absent author

---

151 Agamben G., "The Author as Gesture," in *Profanations,* translated by Jeff Fort, New York 2007, p. 64.

a sign of a practice that brings the subject back to life? This question brings doubts
of yet another kind:

> The author is not dead, but to position oneself as an author means occupying the place
> of a "dead man." An author-subject does exist, and yet he is attested to only through
> the traces of his absence. But in what way can an absence be singular? And what does
> it mean for an individual to occupy the place of a dead man, to leave his own traces
> in an empty place?[152]

The subject cannot employ reality but at the same time it is not able to escape
from the necessity of existence within the game of its own becoming. The shift
of accents with regard to a classic dualism or transcendentalism is extremely
clear here – the subject is not something stable (in a sense that it is not a result,
an effect of some permanently marked cognitive process) but on the contrary: it
discovers itself solely in the confrontation with an indifferent system of language
with which it plays a game for its own recognition. It makes gestures that, on the
one hand, simulate its own stability and autonomy from language but on the other
keep colliding with it and confirm the inevitably alienating power of speech. This
duality cannot undergo a further process of reduction. At the same time, however,
the affirmation of that doubling seems to be the only reliable confirmation of
subjectival singularity; it is the only and paradoxical confirmation because the
gesture in which these two spaces of the subject intertwine – one depriving the
subject of a language and one enclosing the subject within language – become, in
the end, a stigma of death.

In Foucault's interpretation, later on complemented by the work of Agamben,
the author is sanctioned as a dead hermeneutic deity that leaves behind it
dispositions, rules, structures of understanding but most importantly clearly
marked borders of sense. Traces of consciousness reveal themselves on contact
with language that, in turn, force the subject to write as a practice of its own death.
Hence, presence is contaminated by the necessity of the celebration of its own
impossibility:

> The author marks the point at which a life is offered up and played out in the work.
> Offered up and played out, not expressed or fulfilled. For this reason, the author can
> only remain unsatisfied and unsaid in the work. He is the illegible someone who makes
> reading possible, the legendary emptiness from which writing and discourse issue.
> [...] The author's gesture guarantees the life of the work only through the irreducible
> presence of an inexpressive outer edge.[153]

This impossibility should be understood only in a certain order of expression,
full presence and clarity. Agamben proposes yet another option, one that is more

---

152   Ibid., pp. 64-65.
153   Ibid., 69-70.

subtle but at the same time much more enigmatic. The presence of the author-subject mentioned by Agamben suggests a hidden, "weak" ontology in which reasonableness and communicative potential of the statement are not the object but the alternation between the possibility and impossibility of speaking. This hesitation does not bring any reconciliation of the contradictions that would allow for the emergence of not even sense but the very conditions of the possibility for sense.

In the meantime, the *arché* of speech can appear as pure absence, it can appear in an empty gesture made by a subject and feigning permanence of ontological and cognitive appearances and interpreted as a modal frame of any possible statement. Negativity is the source of language as long as one will approach it as an impossibility of closing the reduction to the state in which "I" achieves unquestionable realness. It is exactly that impossibility that warrants the practicality of the process of writing. Negativity should be understood here as a source of writing that does not allow itself to be instrumentalized. Language remains an obstacle, indifferent to the workings of the mind, but points to the trace of individuality that cannot be erased with any kind of action that wants to grant it a final function (aesthetic, cognitive, ontological, or theological, etc.). Such interpretation of the gesture of writing results – as Agamben rightfully observes – not only in resignation but in driving the subject onto the playground where it is unstable, founded on the experience of negativity; it is a game – one has to say, going beyond the thought of Foucault and Agamben – for life and death:

> And just as the author must remain unexpressed in the work while still attesting, in precisely this way, to his own irreducible presence, so must subjectivity show itself and increase its resistance at the point where its apparatuses capture it and put it into play. A subjectivity is produced where the living being, encountering language and putting itself into play in language without reserve exhibits in a gesture the impossibility of its being reduced to this gesture.[154].

When summarizing his reflections, Agamben finally reveals his cards and points to the two most important consequences resulting from the question posed by Foucault. Firstly, the subject can establish itself only in a linguistic (more broadly: symbolic) mediation. Secondly, the existence of the subject can be described with categories of a game, lack of formulation, unreadiness, becoming and not through stable ontological notions. This is also how one could understand the ethical recommendation that Agamben mentions at the end of his essay. The subject exists during its own absence which can only mean that it exists within the effort of the will, in the gesture of exciting desire in order to speak in one's own voice and according to one's own rules.

---

154   Ibid., p. 72.

Trapped in Language

A picture held us captive. And we could not get outside it, for it lay in our language and language seemed to repeat it to us inexorably. [155]

– Ludwig Wittgenstein

That is how we return to Beckett (although I do not think we have gone too far). Negativity, a game with the language as the will for individuality to survive absence and death – these are all questions clearly and strongly posed by Beckett in his writing. It seems that he is much more radical than both philosophers we have summoned as witnesses – Foucault and Agamben. Let us try and take a closer look at that bundle of issues, using as an example the ending of the most complex and least interpretable works of prose by Beckett – *The Unnamable*. The problem with the process of becoming a subject is revealed in the form of monologue that constitutes a principle of cohesiveness for the text. Before we attempt to analyze separate phrases, it is important to look at an extended excerpt:

[…] I don't hear everything, that must be it, the important things escape me, it's not my turn, the topographical ad anatomical information in particular is lost on me, no I hear everything, what difference does it make, the moment its not my turn, my turn to understand, my turn to live, my turn of the lifescrew, it calls that living, the space of the way from here to the door, it's all there, in what I hear, somewhere, if all has been said, all this long time, all must have been said, but it's not my turn to know what, to know what I am, where I am, and what I should do to stop being it, to stop being there, that's coherent, so as to be another, no, the same, I don't know, depart into life, travel the road, find the door, find the axe, perhaps it's a cord, for the neck for the throat, for the cords, or fingers, I'll have eyes, I'll see fingers, it will be the silence, perhaps it's a drop, find the door, open the door, drop, into the silence, it won't be I, I'll stay here, or there, more likely there, it will never be I, that's all I know, it's already been done already, said and said again, the departure, the body that rises, the way, in colour, the arrival, the door that opens, closes again, it was never I, I've never stirred, I've listened, I must have spoken, why deny it, why not admit it, after all, I deny nothing, I admit nothing, I say what I hear, I hear what I say, I don't know, one or the other, or both, that makes three possibilities, pick your fancy, all these stories about travellers, these stories about paralytics, all are mine, I must be extremely old, or it's memory playing tricks, if only I knew if I've lived, if I live, if I'll live, that would simplify everything, impossible to find out, that's where you're buggered, I haven't stirred, that's all I know, no, I know something else, it's not I, I always forget that, I resume, you must resume, never stirred from here, never stopped telling stories, to myself, hardly hearing them, hearing something else, listening for something else, wondering now and then where I got them from, was I in the land of the living, were they in mine, and where, where do I store them, in my head, I don't feel a head on me, and what do I tell them with, with my mouth, same remark, and what do I hear them with, and so

---

155   Wittgenstein L., *Philosophical Investigations,* London 2009, § 115.

on, the old rigmarole, it can't be I, or it's because I pay no heed, it's such an old habit, I do it without heeding, or as if I were somewhere else, there I am far again, there I am the absentee again, it's his turn again now, he who neither speaks nor listens, who has neither body nor soul, it's something else he has, he must have something, he must be somewhere, he is made of silence, there's a pretty analysis, he's in the silence, he's the one to be sought, the one to be, the one to be spoken of, the one to speak, but he can't speak, then I could stop, I'd be he, I'd be the silence, I'd be back in the silence, we'd be reunited, his story the story to be told, but he has no story, he hasn't been in story, it's not certain, he's in his own story, unimaginable, unspeakable, that doesn't matter, the attempt must be made, in the old stories incomprehensibly mine, to find his, it must be there somewhere, it must have been mine, before being his, I'll recognize it, in the end I'll recognize it, the story of the silence that he never left, that I should never have left, that I may never find again, that I may find again, then it will be he, it will be I, it will be the place, the silence, the end, the beginning, the beginning again, how can I say it, that's all words, they're all I have, and not many of them, the words fail, the voice fails, so be it, I know that well, it will be the silence, full of murmurs, distant cries, the usual silence, spent listening, spent waiting, waiting for the voice, the cries abate, like all cries, that is to say they stop, the murmurs cease, they give up, the voice begins again, it begins trying again, quick now before there is none left, no voice left, nothing left but the core of murmurs, distant cries, quick now and try again, with the words that remain, try what, I don't know, I've forgotten, it doesn't matter, I never knew, to have them carry me into my story, the words that remain, my old story, which I've forgotten, far from here, through the noise, through the door, into the silence, that must be it, it's too late, perhaps it's too late, perhaps they have, how would I know, in the silence you don't know, perhaps it's the door, perhaps I'm at the door, that would surprise me, perhaps it's I, perhaps somewhere or other it was I, I can depart, all this time I've journeyed without knowing it, it's I now at the door, what door, what's a door doing here, it's the last words, the true last, or it's the murmurs, the murmurs are coming, I know that well, no, not even that, you talk of murmurs, distant cries, as long as you can talk, you talk of them before and you talk of them after, more lies, it will be the silence, the one that doesn't last, spent listening, spent waiting, for it to be broken, for the voice to break it, perhaps there's no other, I don't know, it's not worth having, that's all I know, it's not I, that's all I know, it's not mine, it's the only one I ever had, that's a lie, I must have had the other, the one that lasts, but it didn't last, I don't understand, that is to say it did, it still lasts, I'm still in it, I left myself behind in it, I'm waiting for me there, no, there you don't wait, you don't listen, I don't know, perhaps it's a dream, all a dream, that would surprise me, I'll wake, in the silence, and never sleep again, it will be I, or dream, dream again, dream of a silence, a dream silence, full of murmurs, I don't know, that's all words, never wake, all words, there's nothing else, you must go on, that's all I know, they're going to stop, I know that well, I can feel it, they're going to abandon me, it will be the silence, for a moment, a good few moments, or it will be mine, the lasting one, that didn't last, that still lasts, it will be I, you must go on, I can't go on, you must go on, I'll go on, you must say words, as long as there are any, until they find me, until they say me, strange pain, strange sin, you must go on, perhaps it's done already, perhaps they have said me already, perhaps

they have carried me to the threshold of my story, before the door that opens on my
story, that would surprise me, if it opens, it will be I, it will be the silence, where I am,
I don't know, I'll never know, in the silence you don't know, you must go on, I can't
go on, I'll go on. [U, pp. 405-407]

The question of subjectivity in *The Unnamable* is posed more clearly than in all
the other works of Beckett. But "more clearly" is not meant to imply that the text
is straightforward. On the contrary, in the last part of the "trilogy" Beckett's own
idiom reaches a state of particular intensity, as if every single word – beginning
with the initial questions and ending on the final imperative – were sentenced to an
iridescent, borderline status between presence and meaning, void and nonsense.

Paradoxically enough, the only axiom present is the "I" which – of course –
does not constitute a permanent and stable cognition, being, or ethical instance
but is also not entirely dispersed among the traces of writing: it constitutes an
element that points to the continuous work of an individual consciousness that
exists stretched between the sphere of mythical, absolute silence and the sphere
of language. Consciousness attempts to gain access to itself, a definite and
unquestionable admission, even though its every movement turns out to be an act
of questioning the conditions of that certainty. That is why language has a double
role to play. On the one hand, it is a veil that separates us from an important,
irreducible and true reality of silence. On the other hand, it appears as an unnecessary
force mediating subjectivity in reality, making its recognition possible. Hence, if
we accept the same guiding principles of epistemology and consciousness then
the textual strategy of Beckett becomes much more understandable. Linguistic
practice realizes itself in various registers (from the lyrical to discursive) in order
to catch up with the efforts of the mind. We should also add that the Cartesian
tradition we have mentioned earlier turns out to be an inheritance as blessed as
it is cursed. The *ego* that is trapped in language cannot become a complete, self-
determining presence because it is the very structural principle of speech that
results in the primal presence being a fantasy of the mind and an entrapment inside
of representation. Beckett remains faithful to the Cartesian certainty that refers to
res cogitans but it is a faithfulness toward an empty structure of subjectivity that
cannot be filled with any positive experience. The act of thinking cannot designate
a sphere of unquestionable primality (or more modestly, it is not synonymous with
it) but it shows its topological character, its structural principal is the presence of
what is negative. In short, this means that it is painfully present for the subject but
reveals itself, its accessibility and recognisability, only in a mode of negation and
exclusion, in a mode that does not bring any dialectical synthesis of sense.

This peculiar form of presence that cannot be definitively verified through
a differentiating force of language accompanies the reader from the very
beginning of *The Unnamable*. The subject, an ironic-neurotic "I," desires its

own self-determination, which means it wants to grasp itself in a thetic moment. It struggles without success to free itself from the world of happanstance and randomness through an effort of self-analysis. The reality of consciousness is not an unquestionable warranty of conscious existence because its fetishisation displays its fictional, illusory character. The subject that is split into several parts in *The Unnamable*,[156] cannot piece itself together and separate itself from the outside world. It exists in a different way, in fragments, and inhabits the cracks and unspecified places, or moments in which language stops and announces a closure of the expressed story by catching the enlightened consciousness. But it is that meta-reflective gesture that seems to be the only possible confirmation of the existence of subjectivity. The end of narration is identified with the end of the subject, but that true, real end will never take place within the boundaries of literature. The more the protagonists of Beckett will attest to the inevitability of the closure of their own representation,[157] the more this representation will be necessary.

This necessity has its source in the foreground placement of consciousness but is also a condition posed language. Subjectivity holds tight to that borderline, a diminished form of establishing and up keeping the operations of consciousness in a critical-reductive movement. Let us observe that this is what the speaking (not transcendental or empirical) "I" is based upon. Beckett searches for certainty but establishes an extremely narrow passage through which one can reach it. It is not about direct insight into the nature of things or a critique based on unshakeable cognitive foundations, nor about the dialectic that cancels contradictions in a positive sense, but about existing in the state of a dynamic passage between the system of language and the order of complete immanence. Beckett's figures speak of that distance with a deadly irony:

> [...] what difference does it make, the moment it's not my turn, my turn to understand, my turn to live, my turn of the lifescrew, it calls that living, the space of the way from here to the door, it's all there, in what I hear, somewhere, if all has been said, all this long time, all must have been said, but it's not my turn to know what, to know what I am, where I am, and what I should do to stop being it, to stop being there, that coherent, so as to be another, no, the same, I don't know, depart into life, travel the road, find the door, find the axe, perhaps it's a cord, for the neck, for the throat, for the cords, or fingers, I'll have eyes, I'll see fingers, it will be the silence, perhaps it's a

---

156 Apart from the thoroughly analyzed dimension of the disintegrating "I" that attempts to establish itself through the act of speech, all the forms of its doubles, or the protagonists inhabiting works before *the Unnamable*, are important.

157 I refer here to Derrida's formulation from his previously mentioned work on Artaud. See Derrida J., "The Theatre of Cruelty and the Closure of Representation," in *Writing and Difference*, translated by Alan Bass, Chicago 1978.

drop, find the door, open the door, drop, into the silence, it won't be I, I'll stay here, or there, more likely there, it will never be I, that's all I know [...] [U, p. 405]

The subject exists only as much as it speaks, but existence within the sphere of speech is fictional because it disappears in the abstract, arbitrary and ahistorical space created by language in *The Unnamable*. Hence, the "I" is never able to fully exist because it sometimes becomes an empty element in the network of language and on other occasions it is completely quiet and surrenders to the mythical, totalizing and deprived space of silence. That is why faithfulness to the epistemological principle of minimization is so important. But the order of immanence does not provide an opportunity for full emancipation – the critical force of consciousness is stopped in advance and is only fully realized in the radical (and maybe the most progressive within contemporary literature) act of disenchantment. This can be observed at the beginning of the quoted excerpt from *The Unnamable*: entering the sphere in which "all has had to be said" is a final but also the first and only possible gesture of subjectivity which – in order to sustain its life – has to postpone the moment of its self-identification. The critical action of the mind is somewhat paralyzed because the moment of the ultimate reconciliation of the individual consciousness with itself is also a moment of fundamental linguistic powerlessness. It is a moment in which the speaking "I" can enable another string of contradictions ("but it's not my turn") and corrections of its position that keep it alive. At the end of that path of questioning there is the only possible certainty, the certainty of doubt ("but it's not my turn to know what, to know what I am, where I am, and what I should do to stop being it, to stop being there, that coherent, so as to be another, no, the same, I don't know.")

Specific registers remain incompatible with one another: language, the voice and the will of individual existence overlap and cast light on each other but do not allow for a merger into a coherent and permanent centre of the self. But it is that dispersement of subjectivity into several separate instances that grants power to writing. This begins with a statement about a fundamental discrepancy, an impossibility of uniting all the powers of the subject. Spread across the surface of the text, markers of separate instances of the subject create a set of signs of the impossibility of the full existence of the individual, the signs that at the same time propel with that same impossibility the act of storytelling. The neurotic force of narration about the impossibility of any narration allows subjectivity, if only to a small degree, to realize itself. The voice points to the presence of the one who speaks but also illustrates one's dependence on several other centres of speech (the imagination that "creates" the Other as well as language that is a material veil that separates us from external, empirical reality). The statement itself is at the edge of the existence of consciousness, attempting to ground itself thanks to language that disinherits it at the same time.

This is one of the key moments in Beckett's project of the literature of consciousness. In *The Unnamable*, the critical force of the mind is directed in two opposing directions that cannot be reconciled but that simultaneously allow for writing as such. From the certainty of Cartesian epistemology, Beckett is only left with a kind of attachment to the process of a continuous purging of consciousness, of reducing the subject to a primal state. That level of absolute primality is a postulate, a desire that once spoken becomes transformed into an element that is arbitrary and deadly for the individuality of language. On the one hand, the subject from Beckett's prose desires to realize its own individuality within the framework of literature.[158] On the other hand, it attempts to break free from its power entirely.

In *The Unnamable*, this double gesture becomes more serious and pronounced. Subjectivity strives to identify itself with the hard, immovable core of silence that could become a definite proof of its existence. However, consciousness is not reduced to pure being and remains within the realm of naming and determination. Complete silence turns out to be a myth of complete and epistemologically reliable reduction that not so much liberates (the process of thinking, hence of writing) but limits through its own oppression (that immobilizes the subject in the obsession of destruction and its own disappearance). The ego, creating its narrative, is not capable of speaking directly about silence. It merely suggests traces thanks to which its otherwise complete otherness is drawn closer to the moment of becoming a more concrete form of presence. That is how silence becomes somebody, not something, different, an irony-filled double of the speaking subject that in the process of the mind's work turns from pure abstraction into the witness of individual struggles. This image of doubling situates itself close to the figure of madness, as if the desire for total identity that places the subject in the close vicinity of the world of absolute silence had to be completed with an equally strong, but more sensual and closer to the human sensitivity, image of that madness that is based on the splitting of consciousness that recognizes both itself and the world. An absolute and finally inhuman silence is coupled with the narcissistic madness of reflection, seeing itself reflected in the Other that functions according to the rules of the projection of the imagination.

These two figures (mythical silence and the imagined double), by appearing together, clarify the stakes of Beckett's game. Even though he realizes that

---

158 Here, one should provide an explanation of the differences between theatre and writing as a medium. From the perspective that interests me, facing the primacy of the question of consciousness, the scene is one more element that mediates the subject and complicates its status. The whole issue is, of course, going in many directions. I wish to point here to a question that could be summarized as a tension between an understanding of the works of Beckett as a project and an understanding strictly within the genre. Opting for the first possibility, I try not to ignore the latter.

"impersonal writing" is possible, he cannot at the same time (and does not want to) resign from the primacy of consciousness that, in turn, points to the primacy of the name: an individual fighting for the right to a unique, even if rudimentary, presence. The impersonality of literature, its "zero level," constitutes a way of speaking about the split of consciousness that, even though infected with death, does not want to surrender permanently to its laws. The subject cannot disappear completely and, in way slightly different to that envisioned by Agamben and Foucault, it does not reveal itself exclusively in the traces of its own existence but stages its own conflict with negativity, death and absence. It fights for life, even if the price for the confrontation is the collision with madness and the risk of approaching a silence that could not be called off with any symbolic gesture.

It seems that this is where we arrive at the core of the question of authorial absence and the author's entrapment in language. Beckett wants to constantly remain at the border, shifting position but never definitively crossing. Death, madness and silence are vague points of the real, around which consciousness keeps circling in search of its own idiom. It circles but never reaches them. It becomes a part of the process and the rhetoric of questioning but never undermines it, because – despite its lacking – it is thought and language that support the individual will to live and delineate its borders. A shapeless territory, to which no form of consciousness has access, stretches. However, there is no exhaustion of the ways of speaking present in Beckett's works. Instead, we encounter the opening of another, richer speech, driven by the particular experience of language and consciousness' resistance, a story that will make finding different forms of existence possible. That is the focus of the next excerpt from *The Unnamable*:

> [...] there I am far again, there I am the absentee again, it's his turn again now, he who neither speaks nor listens, who has neither body nor soul, it's something else he has, he must have something, he must be somewhere, he is made of silence, there's a pretty analysis, he's in the silence, he's the one to be sought, the one to be, the one to be spoken of, the one to speak, but he can't speak, then I could stop, I'd be he, I'd be the silence, I'd be back in the silence, we'd be reunited, his story the story to be told, but he has no story, he hasn't been in story[...][U, p. 406]

Silence becomes another sign, this time of the depriving power of language that transforms the desire of individuality into an overwhelming power of abstraction but also, while being a myth, allows one to get accustomed to the impossibility of access to what is real. Hence, this not a permanence or final immobilization, so desired by Beckett's protagonists, but a sign of the split of the subject which – in order to mark its presence – has to continuously question the foundations of its existence. There is no escaping that impasse. The sustaining and celebrating of that aporia is the most extreme point in Beckett's "epic of consciousness." One can also understand why the characters speaking in Beckett's works push for that last (one could say "always last"), final effort of will to speak about the fate of thinking that inevitably becomes self- and meta-reflection. The stakes of telling a story (a story about oneself) is a confrontation with both mythical and purely abstract spheres of silence and language. They simultaneously establish the boundaries of individual consciousness, as well as block its full articulation, after which no word used by consciousness would be necessary to describe its own position. Beckett presents us with an "impossible tale" in which the narration transforms into a reflection on the structural conditions of both the possibility and impossibility of all statements.

Il faut continuer

There is a goal, but no way; what we call a way is hesitation.
There is no having, only a being, only a state of being that craves the last breath, craves suffocation. [159]

– Franz Kafka

This clash between subjectivity, language and silence is radical for a different reason. Self-determining and self-describing subjectivity is aware that by engaging in the clash with both of those powers – silence and language – it is doomed to fail. Despite that, or maybe thanks to that, the fight for the voice of individuality becomes a central issue in writing. On the one hand, the permanence of subjectivity in the literary space of Beckett is impossible, because without any mediation, any connecting element between itself and the world, it becomes a degraded form of "I" – a purely subjective or solipsistic "I." On the other hand, this drive to authenticate absolute individuality is a kind of imperative of persistence in the face of the world, a final necessity of the will for life, an affirmation of negativity that appears at the moment of recognition of the radical separation of the subject from its inaccessible external world. Let us observe that it is that precise announcement that situates consciousness in a different place; it is no longer stranded between language and what is real, between a notion (almost always mythologized in Beckett's works) and the physical sensation of existence, pure presence that is not contaminated by language but existing in its borders. It is focused in the moment in which these oppositions become invalidated.

This is a result of the sceptical and ironic attitude of the speaking subject that, while searching for its essence, knows perfectly well it will not find it. Consciousness, searching for its own foundations, attempts to tear down all the

---

159 Kafka F., "Reflections on Sin, Suffering, Hope, and the True Way," *in The Great Wall of China: Stories and Reflections,* Op. cit.

veils of mediation, although in order to accomplish that it has to employ them. The moment of the experience of negativity is not something like resignation and exhaustion, but, possibly, it could provide definite proof legitimizing efforts of standing by the rule of the will-speaking subject that, thanks to language, could stay alive. Activating all of the cognitive faculties (memory, language, and imagination represented as "fantasy") brings the same results over and over again – the realization of the deadly and incomplete search for of a concrete "sufficient right" for the consciousness that examines itself. The mumbling forms of language that appear in *The Unnamable* are the final stages of its degradation as much as they are the result of an opposition to the forces of alienation. The final result of that effort of thinking through one's own non-identity undertaken by a lonely individual could be the ambivalent, "cold" sign of negating the realness of every dimension of "I":

> [...] pick your fancy, all these stories about travellers, these stories about paralytics, all are mine, I must be extremely old, or it's memory playing tricks, if only I knew if I've lived, if I live, if I'll live, that would simplify everything, impossible to find out, that's where you're buggered, I haven't stirred, that's all I know, no, I know something else, it's not I, I always forget that, I resume, you must resume, never stirred from here, never stopped telling stories to myself, hardly hearing them, hearing something else, listening for something else, wondering now and then where I got them from, was I in the land of the living, were they in mine, and where, where do I store them, in my head, I don't feel a head on me, and what do I tell them with, with my mouth, same remark, and what do I hear them with, and so on, the old rigmarole, it can't be I [...] [U, pp. 405-406]

The tale, even though impossible, or held up in its potentiality, is a guaranty of the existence of not only the subject but also reality. The force of the experience of negativity weakens the stiff boundaries between the fictional sphere of speaking consciousness and the inevitable sphere of what is real and – as a consequence – that which marks a peculiar, indefinite place in which Beckett's subject resides. Adorno provides a great description of that relationship:

> Art's processual character has been overtaken by the critique of semblance, and not merely as the critique of aesthetic universality but rather as that of progress in the midst of what is ever-the-same. Process has been unmasked as repetition and has thus become an embarrassment to art. [...] Beckett, indifferent to the ruling cliché of development, views his task as that of moving in an infinitely small space toward what is effectively a dimensionless point. This aesthetic principle of construction, as the principle of *Il faut continuer*, goes beyond stasis; and it goes beyond the dynamic that it is at the same time a principle of treading water and, as such, a confession of the uselessness of the dynamic. In keeping with this, all constructivistic techniques tend

toward stasis. The *telos* of the dynamic of the ever-same is disaster; Beckett's writings look this in the eye.[160]

The experience of negativity belongs to the order of time and – paradoxically – deprives consciousness of the hypnotic power of the gaze of "disaster" of which Adorno spoke. One is concerned with up keeping and transmitting this peculiar experience into language and retaining it within the frame of a linguistic system. The moments of experiencing what is negative anchor themselves in language, constituting a kind of remnant that suggests a completely different order of reality, a sphere of being that is impossible to be described within the categories used by the metaphysics of presence. That is because the remnants in question are "that which last" but simultaneously "that, which did not remain." Once again, it seems that Adorno was right when he stated that:

> In that artworks relentlessly chip away at the nexus in which meaning is founded, they turn against this nexus and against meaning altogether. […] Beckett's œuvre already presupposes this experience of the destruction of meaning as self-evident, yet also pushes it beyond meaning's abstract negation in that his plays force the traditional categories of art to undergo this experience, concretely suspend them, and extrapolate others out of the nothingness. […] Beckett's plays are absurd not because of the absence of any meaning, for then they would be simply irrelevant, but because they put meaning on trial; they unfold its history. His work is ruled as much by an obsession with positive nothingness as by the obsession with a meaninglessness that has developed historically and is thus in a sense merited, though this meritedness in no way allows any positive meaning to be reclaimed. […] Artworks that divest themselves of any semblance of meaning do not thereby forfeit their similitude to language. They enunciate their meaninglessness with the same determinacy as traditional artworks enunciate their positive meaning.[161]

From that point of view, the strategy of constructing the subjectivity employed by Beckett seems far more understandable – the subject must find itself but not in the movement of a merger, but in a moment of the experience of one's own discontinuity and untimeliness. At the same time, as Adorno rightfully observes, that very act of questioning is not focused on undermining the sense of all events, words and objects (if that was the case, the work of art would be merely a sign of pure reactive nihilism), but a vigilant questioning of the form of mediation through which sense revealed itself in an obvious way. One can see clearly that Adorno's interpretation is headed in a critical direction – the rule of negation does not serve the construction of a coherent vision of the world and does not allow for building a synthesis in the form of clear meaning but is a point of resistance against that which is abstract, notional and general.

---

160   Adorno, T. *Aesthetic Theory*, Op. cit., p. 224.
161   Ibid., p. 153.

If one were to attempt to refer these statements to the analyzed excerpt from *The Unnamable*, one could say that the speaking consciousness becomes torn between two forces. On the one side, it is confronted with the sphere of what is inexpressible. That is how the story of the "unnamable" could be read; a story that is being told by an ironic "I." It is a story that "does not exist" in the sense of the ontological calculation of being and nothingness. That is why the proclaimed "existence in silence" is a mythical screen from which, patiently, the voice of consciousness repeatedly reflected. On the other side, consciousness is still surrounded, pierced and reached by the incomprehensible sparkle of language and not fully articulated speech that does not name anything but which likewise cannot be left behind. This murmuring of nameless language constitutes an unspecified form of presence through which the speaking "I" becomes defined as a mistake and a danger to its own autonomy. However, this is also a form of language that destabilizes the division between internal consciousness and the external world and brings all the dimensions of the statement to that one simple, neutral and completely alien and impossible to tame, unformed intensity.[162]

This tension could be described in yet another way. The French title of the last part of the "trilogy" suggests two equivalent possibilities for explication. *L`Innommable* could be both the "unnamable" as well as "nameless." Both possibilities are also a shortcut of definitions of the two extreme points between which the figures of consciousness in Beckett's works keep oscillating continuously. On the one hand, consciousness remains exposed to the mercy of the impersonal, neutral speech; of that unspecified and deprived of subjectival voice[163] that cannot be trapped between frames of a linguistic system. On the other hand – by continuously correcting its own position, by searching for the foundation of its own existence and a proof for the existence of the world, consciousness builds its own identity based on the circumstances of the impossibility to express itself. But the inexpressible is not the unreachable, the mystical sphere in Beckett's work is an inseparable element of the work of consciousness, which time and again, reaches a critical moment in its process of self-determination. The final part of the "trilogy" is special in that respect. For the first time with such determination, Beckett used his own version of negative dialectics, to which he remained faithful until the very end of his career, to the point in which the cleansed figure of consciousness will not be able to stop asking the question: *comment dire, what is the word,* – how to say that?

---

162 See Ackerley Ch., "The Uncertainty of Self: Samuel Beckett and Location of the Voice," *Samuel Beckett Today/Aujourd`hui (After Beckett/D`après Beckett)*, pp. 39-52.

163 See Ackerley Ch., "The Unnamable`s First Voice?," *Journal of Beckett Studies* 1993, no. 2.

The Unnamable leaves the reader with a particular feeling – the history of consciousness telling a story about itself that seems to be without end because it is the imperative of ending that could be the only reliable principle of writing and thinking, as well as – which complicates this already complex rhetorical-existential strategy of the author – becoming an actual annihilation of his own idiom. The description of the experience of the limits of consciousness and language becomes for Beckett both a defence against a simplistic surrender of his own imagination and his own literary project without even putting up a fight. That could be proven by the closing (but are they truly the "last?") lines of the novel:

> […] it will be I, you must go on, I can't go on, you must go on, I'll go on, you must say words, as long as there are any, until they find me, until they say me, strange pain, strange sin, you must go on, perhaps it's done already, perhaps they have said me already, perhaps they have carried me to the threshold of my story, before the door that opens on my story, that would surprise me, if it opens, it will be I, it will be the silence, where I am, I don't know, I'll never know, in the silence you don't know, you must go on, I can't go on, I'll go on. [U, p. 407]

This is probably one of the most famous fragments of Beckett's writing, even though it is also one of the most mysterious ones. Both registers of language – namelessness and the impossibility of expression – become contaminated with one another and to the very end of language's persistence they sustain a tension that cannot be neutralized. That which is anonymous brings the power of rhetorical inertia to the door of consciousness, to which the former has no real access. In an almost pure form, one can observe the primary aporia of Beckett that sustains the paradoxical "weak strength" of his idiom. The passage of the subject inside the story it develops is impossible. It either pushes it back into the abyss of the myth of silence or puts it under the depriving principle of abstract language that excludes privacy. That very moment of a critical deconstruction[164] sentences consciousness to the effort of an unending process of postponing entry inside its own story, but also it is fundamentally unreliable and purely fantastical. In effect it is a speech that remains the last bastion of reality, these are the words, or rather remnants of connoted meanings that turn out to be a final points of resistance against the dispersement of individuality inside the darkness of silence. They grant – according to Adorno – sense to the senseless effort of consciousness and

---

164 Figures of doors and doorsteps point to the impossibility of passage and the stabilization of the subject that – according to Freud's formula – "is no longer a master in his own house." Just like in Kafka, for whom "entering into the law" was unreal but at the same time sustained the very structure of dependency, in Beckett the aporia of a critical mind remains in place; a mind that knows that it cannot access a finalized identity but at the same time has to persist on the work of consciousness. See Derrida J., "Before the Law," in *Acts of Literature,* edited by Derek Attridge, New York 1992.

the work of yet another kind, based on the perpetual linguistic reconstruction of those efforts. That is where the rhetoric of a delay and the ironic counter-punctuation of one's own position ("I'd be surprised") which is one of the more clear ways of sustaining consciousness in motion, does not constitute a point of access but is an opening to what is more troubling and enigmatic, what needs to be developed in the movement of thought but what remains mandated with a ban on the "continuation" of the reflection.[165]

However, this crucial point for understanding Beckett's project in which that which is inexpressible crosses with that which is nameless does not seem to be its fulfilment. Consciousness and language, the subject and its ideas about the world seem to be acquiring signs of real exhaustion of their own possibilities in one more area. Beckett brings his own version of a logical syntax to a peculiar state of sensitivity in which the imperative of preserving the subjectival position of consciousness is supplemented with the deepest existential experience that confirms the irreducible loneliness of those who attempts to speak. This experience, an attempt to almost touch negativity, which in Beckett is not left disguised in a costume of some *a priori* category is a pure, uncontaminated with any randomness, pain; a final pain that does not undergo any demands of exchange nor any economy. It is a proof of a singular existence. In a radical gesture of reduction, Beckett upholds the structure of a dynamic aporia in power. It is based on the simultaneous impossibility and necessity of exclaiming individual suffering. On the side of refusal there is a working mind thanks to which the search for a grounded basis for existence and the world is legitimized. On the side of the imperative and affirmation there is a necessity for a verification of the subjective feeling of being in the world and a mediation with symbolic forms.

Pain, according to Beckett, constitutes an inseparable pair with sin that could be understood as a figure of a peculiar, paralyzing sensation of an inability to go beyond the closed condition of the individual. The experience of pain that accompanies consciousness' gesture reveals "sin" as innate, inexplicable and escaping both the logic of notions and power of the literary image of the sickness of the individual being. Only within the boundaries of the staging of that dramatic tension, in a movement of insolubility, thanks to which these mutually exclusive modalities of consciousness and existence can appear, does literature becomes a space in which the voice of a subject can resound. Let us refer back to Adorno's conclusions, in which he described this situation using classic categories of presence and essence, *mimesis* and mediation:

---

165 That is how one can understand the key aporia of *The Unnamable* which is: "I can`t go on. I'll go on."

Dissonance is effectively expression; the consonant and harmonious want to soften and eliminate it. Expression and semblance are fundamentally antithetical. If expression is scarcely to be conceived except as the expression of suffering – joy has proven inimical to expression, perhaps because it has yet to exist, and bliss would be beyond expression – expression is the element immanent to art through which, as one of its constituents, art defends itself against the immanence that it develops by its law of form. Artistic expression comports itself mimetically, just as the expression of living creatures is that of pain. The lineaments of expression inscribed in artworks, if they are not to be mute, are demarcation lines against semblance. [...] Through expression art closes itself off to being-for-another, which always threatens to engulf it, and becomes eloquent in itself: This is art's mimetic consummation. Its expression is the antithesis of expressing something.[166]

Adorno, similar to Beckett, is interested in delineating a field for a different kind of expression that would not be contaminated with faith in the directness of language but, simultaneously, would not force a resignation from the sanctions of subjectivity in general. He points to sources of that new model of expression, located at the very heart of the principal of the experience of the work of art, or the principal of *mimesis*. The term still holds its power but no longer as an autonomous sphere of a pretense, separated from sensual experience and the sphere of the mind, but as a mediation between these particular spheres and the world of aesthetic representation. The experience of suffering coded in the signs of a work of art seems to be the fullest example of such a position – it is not an act of simple mimicry, nor does it contain itself within the idea, a notion, but constitutes a "demarcation line" that separates a mute, impossible to pass on to the reality of immanence (of the suffering subject that desires to discover the proper register of speech for its own pain) and intersubjective space of meaning.

The practice of Beckett and the philosophical reflections of Adorno become parallel at this point. Speaking and writing become legitimate only as forms of their refusal and as dramatizations of that impossibility. The force of aporia constitutes in *The Unnamable* a principle upholding thinking that, although it surrenders itself to the rules of the impossible to share experience of a singular immanence, attempts continuously to express this experience verbally. Beckett's speaking subject is sentenced to be wavering in the pathos of a hermetically sealed and unrecognized pain, thanks to which the effort of thinking followed by the expression of the process of that thinking results not so much in a disabled, absolutized mistake of language but a warranty of existential failure. That very failure is experienced, however, according to its own singular rules and constitutes a precisely designed project of the definite "closure of representation." Finally, and paradoxically, it revives literature understood as a process of shaping consciousness.

---

166   Adorno T. W., Op. cit., pp. 110, 112.

PART THREE
LONG HOURS OF DARKNESS.
THE SUBJECT IN CRISIS

The non-I is for the I, appears as non-I for an I and on the basis of an I. Everything: which is to say that the I, the exception to and condition for everything that appears, does not appear.[167]

– Jacques Derrida

There is no act I know of that will liberate me into the world. There is no act I know of that will bring the world into me. I am a torrent of sound streaming into the universe, thousands upon thousands of corpuscles, groaning, gnashing their teeth.[168]

– John Maxwell Coetzee

In *Not I* the question about the source of speech has a particularly strong manifestation, starting with the title itself. It is a question that, even though it forces itself with such force, questions itself with equal strength. This mechanism of self-negation is hinted at by the very structure and content of the work. On stage, there is only a Mouth present, from which flows a stream of chanted words, all uttered almost in one breath but at the same time precisely planned and developing according to the progression of associative language as well as the story that is being told. The Listener remains the silent witness of the monologue; a Listener that has been placed by Beckett on the side of the stage so that he can remain almost invisible to the audience. The story that is being told (or rather: attempted to be constructed) by the Mouth is concentrated on the faith of an unhappy woman who attempts to recover pieces of her own experiences from her memory, thus chaotically and strenuously piecing together a biography of her own intimacy.[169]

---

167   Derrida J., "Qual Quelle: Valéry's Sources," in *Margins of Philosophy,* Op. cit., It is important to mention here Blanchot's tendency to play around with the word "pas" that delivers different meanings depending on the context it was placed in by the author. In Beckett's works "pas" referred to both the negation of the obvious pronoun "I" (just like in the title of the French version, "pas moi") as well as to steps (according to yet another title of a different play).

168   Coetzee J. M., *In the Heart of the Country,* New York 1982, p. 4.

169   A direct impulse for the creation of *Not I* was double. Beckett mentioned that he was inspired by Caravaggio's painting representing the head of St. John the Baptist that he saw on Malta and a situation he remembered from Algeria, where he was watching a

But the message of the text cannot be reduced to a question of existence's tragedy because such a description is basically suggested in the title by the subversive element directed toward subjectivity in which moving force is located – as the text progresses – within autonomous speech.

Not I is a text in which the signs of the existence of subjectivity are visible over and over again and the technique of "erasing" their traces through poetic ordering of the text that is based on the permutation of repetitions and rhythm constitutes a dialectic supplementing these forms of presence.

This unsolvable and dense entanglement of signals of presence and the disappearance of different versions of the subjectivity can be seen most acutely when observed in the drama from the perspective of a structure of the event[170] that is concerned in an obvious way with the staging possibilities[171] but most importantly is inscribed in the structure of the work.[172] It is revealed in three dimensions: genealogical one, ontological and anthropological. Firstly, one should ask about the possibilities, range and character of the event itself but also about whether truly – as Kierkegaard claims – that which happens only once, does not happen at all in reality.[173]

---

mother picking up her child from school. As he used to say: "t'was about the idea of watching the one watching." See M. Gussow, *Conversations with and about Beckett*, New York 1996, p. 34, J. Knowslon, *Damned to fame*, Op. cit. pp. 588-599.

170 According to Bruno Clément the axis of the drama is located somewhere else. He claims that "the Mouth in *Not I*, having to justify the title and crown the experience of the 'impossibility to name' or more strictly of the 'impossibility of individuality,' violently refuses to abandon the third person that makes the lips slip over only the words of the title but also the space and the act of speaking in its entirety. In effect they confirm some of the more unwanted and banned, rather than inexpressible 'I.' [...] To say 'Not I' means not only to forbid oneself to use the first person singular but also to forbid the last word (is this not the final and elliptic expression of prohibition when formulated that way?)." Clément B., *L'œuvre sans qualités*, Op. cit. p. 219.

171 This cannot be forgotten when interpreting works by Beckett. The individual, actor's performance of extremely precise stage directions is incredibly important. Every time – despite the mathematical precision of the author – it looks different. In that sense, one should talk about an event in a primal, theatrical and stage sense. In order to prove my point, I will provide two radically different examples that have influenced my reading of *Not I*: the canonical interpretation of Billie Whitelaw and a performance by Julianne Moore. It seems that the concrete performance embodies the philosophy of an event, or – in order to fully express the matter – it becomes an event. Hence, when interpreting the text I always refer back to particular stage productions.

172 In an inspiring study dedicated to figures of subjectivity in Beckett's works, Daniel Katz proposes a similar thesis. See Katz D., Op. cit., pp. 182-183. He attempts to prove that the "character" of the Mouth constitutes, in fact, a certain model of subjectivity which – similarly to mature prose – has to find its place in order to be articulated. It is all about the vocal effect of consciousness and not a metaphor of the internal world of an individual.

173 See Kierkeggard S., *Fear and Trembling / Repetition*, translated by Edna H. Hong, Howard V. Hong, Princeton 2013.

Chapter One
Against the Event

Genesis of the Event. Between Repetition and Difference

The progression of language in *Not I* shows the uselessness of the dictionary of traditional metaphysics for describing this text (and other works of Beckett),[174] relating being in categories of permanent oppositions between which there is no passage. While exploding the stability of being, the energy of speech heads toward expressing the event. Thinking the event will be possible once one assumes that the event situates itself between repetition and difference. Such an attitude reveals the classic binary division between what is essential and that which is accidental, what is spiritual and material; they show a reality in which there has to be a sanction that warrants and upkeeps the hierarchy of those opposing pairs. In the meantime, the philosophy of the event reverses this order and marks a return to reflection on the conditions of what is empirical, posing a question about the origins of that which reveals itself in the world and conditions the possibility of subjectivity appearing in the form a subject that expresses itself. The attempt to reveal the source of the empirical does not release one from reflecting on the transcendental order. Omitting that sphere pushes reflection into a naïve reductionism or a radical solipsism and, as a consequence, makes it impossible to legitimize the event. On the one hand, the transcendental order that appears in the figures of repetition constitutes a barricade against surrendering subjectivity to the pure sensuality that would ultimately silence it. On the other hand, it is that sphere of empirical reality that escapes meaning, that forces the repeating subject to open to that which is other and that explodes the arbitrary structure of language. The question of the "conditions of possibility" of the event is even more complex.

The radical separation of the two orders does not allow us to see any point of passage that would reveal the strength of the event.[175] But this is also the point

---

174 I am reminded of the general thesis I have proposed in the introduction to this book. *Not I* from among all the possible cases – except for *The Unnamable, Worstward Ho* and *A Piece of Monologue* – seems to be the most complex example of Beckett's writerly practice.

175 The category of strength is important here for several reasons. First of all, strength is considered to be an inseparable element of the event. Secondly, its description comes from a modern philosophical tradition that is significant for me personally, the origins of which can be found in Leibniz's reflections and culminating in the writings of Deleuze. Thirdly, strength constitutes an indefinable, dynamic element of reality's creation. It

at which the chaos of origins reveals itself; origins that cannot be thought of as a source of sense that warrant a permanent hermeneutic and ontological reference. The origins are concerned with what is primal in the sense that they present themselves as a field on which varied forces collide. That is why repetition cannot be understood without difference, but difference also reveals itself only in that repetition. However, that is why thinking about pure difference (as realm of matter that does not undergo distinction) and pure repetition is identical with hypostasis thanks to which it is possible to ask questions about the event. Hypostasis is necessary because it reveals the fundamental extremes of the possibilities of sense between which the speech of the Mouth travels.

The first of these extremes is based on the imperative of striving for silence that is being destroyed from within by the steam of uttered words. Silence, in theory, was supposed to reveal the sphere of pure chaos of the world for which there is no way to invent even a single word. Impossible to understand speech that comes from a text or from the stage and is based on approaching the silence reveals the sphere of that which is inhuman. But that precise, autonomous speech over which one cannot have control creates conditions for silence to become a significant state. Silence as such – from the perspective of the origins of the event – is one of the many incarnations of indefiniteness that does not allow itself to be represented. Approaching it is not a simple gesture of negating the power of language but opening its space to that which is mute, hence untamed. Deleuze writes:

> Indifference has two aspects: the undifferentiated abyss, the black nothingness, the indeterminate animal in which everything is dissolved – but also the white nothingness,

---

is a difference in movement; it constitutes the very energy of differentiation. Fourth, belonging to the logic of an event, strength belongs simultaneously to the logic of sense and not to the logic of stating or truth. Fifth, the final sanction of the event could be a theological sanction (Leibniz) which means that all possible events are contained within the framework of the "event above all events." Also, an event can achieve a sanction of complete immanence (Deleuze) becoming, as its own perfection, a pure nameless peculiarity, or neutrality. Sixth, strength is concerned with language, or rather it works for its sake through expressing (or making it expressible) the event as a movement and metamorphosis. Seventh, strength is a link between two possibilities of legitimizing the event: the theory of sense, based on logical origins and ontological theory. The category of strength appears repeatedly in those reflections in numerous configurations and establishes all those meanings that allow us to see the radical character of Beckett's project. Here, I would like to refer anyone interested to works that I found extremely instructive on the subject: See. Deleuze G., *Logique du sens*, Paris 1968, along with *Le pli. Leibniz et le baroque*, Paris 1988; Cichowicz S., *Wyraz, zdarzenie, siła* [introduction to] G. W. Leibniz, *Korespondencja z Antoine'em Arnauldem*, translated by S. Cichowicz and J. Kopania, Warsaw 1998; Cichowicz S., *Siła. Zarys pojęcia*, "Twórczość" 2001 no 8.

the once more calm surface upon which float unconnected determinations like scattered members: a head without a neck, an arm without a shoulder, eyes without brows. The indeterminate is completely indifferent, but such floating determinations are no less indifferent to each other. […] It is as if the ground rose to the surface, without ceasing to be ground. There is cruelty, even monstrosity, on both sides of this struggle against an elusive adversary, in which the distinguished opposes something which cannot distinguish itself from it but continues to espouse that which divorces it.[176].

If one were to accept the division into two metaphorical versions of the spheres of non-differentiation proposed by Deleuze, then one soon realizes that both of them find their full realization in Beckett's drama. The abyss in which any form of the subject cannot constitute itself and where everything is turned into shapeless physiological reflexes and is deprived of consciousness and the nothingness of the surface of language. It is on that surface that the psychodrama takes place, in which the leading role is taken by words enclosed in fragments of meanings and scraps of sense dissolving into one inside the figure of the Mouth. Silence could be treated according to the laws of a primal universe that one has no ability to reach, but it is also a universe in which in a fleeting language and moment of sense is born for consciousness. That is what the phrases spit out by the Mouth express. Subjectivity utilizes them to reach layers of memory, attempting to recreate any, even the smallest detail from the past. However, from that point of view the absolute emptiness of consciousness that is created upon contact with the body is also an abyss. From that tension between thought and body it is the body that comes out victorious and transforms all the elements of the world into the awfulness of a "calmed surface." That which seemingly surrenders to the power of consciousness and language and allows itself to be expressed has to transfer in Beckett's drama to a position, which is chaotic and non-differentiated. On the level of text, the abyss or the void do not appear in their pure form but in numerous configurations that illustrate the horror of isolated remains of sense, barely constructed meanings and sentences that cannot come to an end. That which is physical and bodily becomes not so much a singular confirmation of existence but functions as a caricature of degraded consciousness, a positive affirmation of Cartesian certainty and ironically transformed in poetic idiom as a figure of *res extensa.*

Both versions of non-differentiation seem to be uncanny mostly because of their inability to be reduced to any kind of form of representation. The sensation of the abyss (found in the text in the form of a traversing into the depths of memory or a clear desire for final, unquestionable insight into its own condition) and the experience of "white nothingness" (seen in the decomposition of the entire text as well as in the highlighted lack of clarity of the beginning and end) are impossible to express. The attempt by the Mouth to grasp the unending "buzzing" of an

---

176   Deleuze G., *Difference and Repetition,* translated by Paul Patton, New York 1995, p. 28.

unknown origin and destination that rings inside the skull turns into a dramatic gesture of a confirmation of somatic or even anatomical principals: determinism and horror[177]:

> ...then listen again... [*silence*] ... no... spared that... all silent as the grave... no part
> – ... what?... the buzzing?... yes... all silent but for the buzzing... so-called... no part
> of her moving... that she could feel... just the eyelids... presumably... on and off...
> shut out the light...reflex they call it... no feeling of any kind... but the lids... even
> best of times... who feels them?... opening... shutting... all that moisture... but the
> brain still... still sufficiently... oh very much so!... at this stage... in control... under
> control... to question even this... [NI, s. 408].

In this fragment one can observe a different, more fundamental dependency that regulates the relationship between a consciousness that constitutes itself, language, and the sphere of an untamed, hence dangerous biology. As it is with the entirety of Beckett's work, the experience of the body in *Not I* is permanently present, however it appears – to use Deleuze's term – as an "elusive adversary." The working consciousness that allows individuality to form itself as a subject is constantly exposed to that which is undefined, overextended and what not only cannot be enclosed within the structure of a notion but also shines in the poetic phrase of the text. The sphere of physicality creates an effect completely adjacent to the word and the object, but that does not constitute a return to the hermeneutic reconciliation of language and life. Based on the continuous movement from founding to decomposition, it opens the experience of the body to the power of speech. By using language, consciousness attempts to free itself from what is singular and accidental in order not only to express the general truth of experience but also to undertake the effort of examining the rules that guide it. As a result, the movement of thought and language is always invigorated by what is non-discursive, mute and that which is always sneaking into the sphere of speech by taking up different forms of reminiscence and association. It also reveals itself within the inertia of developing the momentum of language itself within the monologue.[178] In

---

177   Of course, one could treat the Mouth as Deleuze's inverted idea of a "body without organs"
– an "organ without a body" – an interpretation to which both Beckett's text and the
commentary of Deleuze seem to encourage. During an incredibly fast speech (especially
in the classic performance by Billie Whitelaw), the Mouth becomes an independent being
in the sense of being granted the autonomy of speech. One could say that from such a
perspective, the Mouth is an empty sign, an empty reference of language. In that way, the
"Mouth of the mouth" becomes a symptom of an impossible identity, which results in a
radical neurosis that, in case of Beckett, cannot be presented using a body (movement,
gesture or a facial expression) but is focused in language that is both progressive and
elliptic.

178   See Louette J-F., *De la littérature en général, et de Beckett en particulier, selon Deleuze*,
in *Deleuze et écrivains. Littérature et philosophie*, éd. B. Gelas et H. Micolet, Paris 2007.

other words, the title "not I" is a recording not so much of the disintegration of a subject, but a diagnosis of speech with an unknown source and an unknown goal that becomes ever more independent. It moves between the arbitrary structure of language and unordered silence, attempting to express the event.

The second hypothesis is constituted by a repetition. The hypostatically treated rigor of repetition leads to a question about the status and the shape of language by which repetition can take place. In order to properly grasp this mechanism, one should look into the beginnings of modern philosophy, hence to the philosophy of Hegel in which the complex relationship between a subject, a sign and pathos are all truly important elements. In his *Lectures on Aesthetics*, Hegel makes a clear statement that the primary function of the symbol is designation. At the same time, by showing the arbitrary character of the sign and preparing the introduction to the dialectical take on the symbol, he establishes the primary axis of interiority and exteriority, on which aesthetic thought is supposed to travel:

> In that case this expression, this sensuous thing or picture, so far from presenting itself, brings before our minds a content foreign to it, with which it does not need to stand in any proper affinity whatever.[179]

Hegel minimalises the symbol, which, in popular understanding serves as the initial phase of art, substantially. It achieves the sanction of importance only after fulfilling itself in the shape of classical art. The classical ideal is, by definition, always a general unity or, speaking more simply, a unity of that which is external, content-related and essential, as well as that which is external, sensual and accidental. In other words, the classical art eliminates the distance created by a symbol understood as a sign, hiding not only the index function but, most importantly, removing the distance created by the conventionality of the sign between what is marked and what is meaningful. The postulated unity constitutes not only the ideal of arts, as an indivisible fullness, but is the result of working through and cancelling the oppositions between the empirical world and the intelligible reality:

> In fact the classical idea is clear because it compasses the true content of art, i.e. substantial subjectivity, and precisely thereby it finds too the true form, which in itself expresses nothing but that genuine content. That is to say, the significance, the meaning, is no other than that which actually lies in the external shape, since both sides correspond perfectly; whereas in the symbol, simile, etc., the image always still presents something other than the meaning alone for which it furnishes the image.[180]

One can clearly see that the destiny of art rests with its expression. According to Hegel, symbolic art merely suggests the art of fullness, or announces the

---

179   Hegel G. W. F, *Aesthetics,* Op. cit., p. 304.
180   Ibid., p. 309.

mechanism of cancelling the necessity of the existence of the signs as ontological certainties and the crowning of art in the theory of art. Between the extremities, which are strictly symbolic art combined with religion and between the ritual and the disappearance of the symbolic character of art and the rule of its self-conscious spirit, there is a symbolic sublimity. Within its structure, it is the inability to express that presents itself most fully, along with the inadequateness of language and the disproportionate character of human and divine orders.

Hegel refers to the Kantian analysis of the sublime form the *Critique of Judgment*, but only in a polemical context. The construction of subjectivity constitutes the point of conflict between the two. Even though, for Kant, the world will exist only when we will be able to impose the notional-interpretational lattice on it, or make it a meaningful reality that would reveal itself only on the territory delineated by the forces of the mind, for Hegel it is impossible to think about subjectivity as an aseptic cognitive structure that excludes everything that is sensual. For Kant, sublimity is created by the effect of the confrontation between the mind and that which is infinite and what does not allow itself to be tamed and absorbed by reason. For Hegel, the relationship and the symbolic character of sublimity are far more complex. Firstly, infinity is defined through a strict, although radically differentiating, attitude toward that which is objective. Examined from that perspective, the Subject locates itself in the sphere created by that which is finished and has at its disposal an arbitrarily ordered language. Using that language it attempts to express that which is infinite:

> Precisely because the infinite is set apart from the entire complex of objectivity as explicitly an invisible meaning devoid of shape and is made inner, it remains, in accordance with its infinity, unutterable and sublime above any expression through the finite.[181]

Sublimity determines the relationship created at the meeting point between the finitude of the subject using language and the infinity of unity and fullness of meaning that cannot be expressed. What is, however, such autonomous and formless meaning? It not only constitutes a radical contrast to the empirically presented world but, above all else, it is the identity of thought, a thought in itself that – according to Hegel – cannot be expressed at all if it is supposed to retain its status. Pure thought or pure consciousness is tautological and total, but it persists. On the one side (that of positivity), it grants the creation of that which is individual, on the other hand – as a self-reflexive unity, it has to "cleanse itself" from what is phenomenal and also what could be treated as particular. Such an understanding is radically dialectical because the vision contained within it is based on its continuous, but not entirely conscious, operation of a boundary; a

---

181   Ibid., 363.

boundary that has to be rethought and what in Hegel's idiom means to be traversed, as well as expressed:

> This outward shaping which is itself annihilated in turn by what it reveals, so that the revelation of the content is at the same time a supersession of the revelation, is the sublime.[182]

In the works dedicated to the "sublime proper" this imbalance between the two orders can be spotted even more easily. God, defined as a being that is unquestionably spiritual and without incarnation or as an absolute substance, remains the final point of reference.[183] In relation to this being there remains that which is earthly and natural. This relationship is of a twofold character. Firstly, one is facing a relationship based on confrontation that establishes an ontological hierarchy. Secondly, the sphere of the absolute creates another relationship of negativity with that which is particular and finite. Sublimity shows itself in the moment of emancipation (transgressing boundaries) of the subject that through confrontation with what is infinite and divine and attempts to escape from the tight corset of the empirical. However, the emergence of that relationship is basically impossible because the attempt to express it transforms, not so much into a movement of decomposition, but into a gesture of "annihilation" that evokes the silence of the subject.

It seems that the most important point from Hegel's divagations is concerned with sublimity. Hegel continuously highlights that sublimity can never appear in the arts because the arts' almost literal, figurative, character makes it impossible to establish a dialectical relationship between infinity and the sphere of that which is worldly. The only space in which the constitution of that relationship could be possible is one delineated by words, because it is only through language that one can attempt to express the truth of meaning that was mentioned before. Most importantly, however, only through language can one undertake such attempts at expression that are nothing other than repetition. One will not find in Hegel any clear confirmation of the repetitive character of language. For him, the distance that can be observed between the subject that establishes itself and infinity is conditioned only by the sublimity that is an intermediate stage or – to be more precise – a borderline stage on the path of subjectivity's development.[184] Precisely on this example, one can see how the element that does not fit the symbolic system and is excluded by the thinker as a symptom of particularity and materiality of the sign comes back under the guise of language's inertia that, ultimately, remains

---

182 Ibid., 363.
183 It can be easily seen even on the level of examples – both mythological and religious – summoned by Hegel that are used to illustrate his research.
184 Put differently, one is dealing with a "cracked subjectivity." See Rouger F., *Existence – Monde – Origine. Essai sur le sens d'être de la finitude*, préface Jean-Luc Nancy, Paris-Montreuil 1994, p. 384.

under the power of repetition. In the deconstructionist reading of Paul de Man, who pushes the idiosyncrasy of the negation of the possibility of articulation, as well as the explication of sense to the extreme, the sublimity of language has to appear solely in its material, written, dimension:

> The idea appears only as written inscription. Only the written word can be sublime, to the precise extent that the written word is neither representation, like as perception, nor imaginative, like a phantasm.[185].

The inscription is an event that is deposited within the materiality of writing. It becomes, out of necessity, an allegory based on the undefeatable negation that cancels all efforts aimed at working out the conditions of the possibility of meeting between the empirical world and the reality of the infinite. The sublime becomes impossible at the moment of meeting between a fragile subjectivity with that which is completely substantial. According to such a position, the epistemological boundary cannot be crossed because consciousness surrenders in the act of expression. The attempt to explicate pure thought transforms into a confirmation of the insoluble, topological character of language. From that perspective, sublimity is a celebration of the impossibility of cognition. The lesson taught by the (mis)interpretation of de Man is extremely interesting given that it illustrates not only the principles of his concept of "aesthetic ideology" but also exemplifies – which is the most important for this study – the importance of negation from the perspective of the philosophy of repetition.

In the key gesture of halting at the very potentiality of expression (and not moving directly to real expression), the concern is not with creating general conditions in which sense could be constructed but about the possibility of negating the division between what is external and internal. In that precise point in the dialectics of the sublime, repetition, as a silently omitted idea in the regulative philosophy of expression, comes to life in full force. Language reveals itself as an arbitrary and dynamically constructed law [Gesetz] as a symbol between the interior and exterior. As a form of mediation, this "law of language" is important in so as far as it shows a deeper arbitrariness, not disclosed by Hegel, of the discursive principle that rules the relationships between the symbolizing and the symbolized, as well as between the subject and the infinite. The figurativeness of a linguistic medium not only wrecks the rhetoric of sublime but, more than anything, makes the true act of explication impossible; one that would lead to the full presence of being – a state in which a division between the exterior and the interior could announce the divine unity of that which is sensual and notional. According to de Man:

---

185   de Man P., "Hegel on the Sublime," in *Aesthetic Ideology,* edited by Andrzej Warminski, Minneapolis 1996, p. 110.

This *Gesetz der Außerlichkeit* implies that the principle of signification is now itself no longer animated by the tensions between its dual poles, but that it is reduced to the preordained motion of its own position. As such, it is no longer a sign-producing function (which is how Hegel valorized the sign in the *Encyclopedia*), but the quotation or repetition of a previously established semiosis. Neither is it a trope, for it cannot be closed off or replaced by the knowledge of its reduced condition. Like a stutter, or a broken record, it makes what it keeps repeating worthless and meaningless.[186]

Repetition cannot be reduced to some secondary mechanism juxtaposed with difference – it exists inseparably with that difference. Additionally, repetition as a stigma of insurmountable arbitrariness and, at the same time, non-transitive character of a linguistic sign (or even a symbol), complicates the problem of a genesis of that which is expressed. The dialectics of sublimity – as de Man announces in somewhat exaggerated manner – is the darkest and the least positive place in the entire Hegelian system. This means that the moment of transition, crossing the border between the worldly reality and the infinite is a pure, epistemological (and not only aesthetic) fiction. The sublime, seemingly reconciling these two contradictory orders, in reality results in the newly liberated consciousness becoming swamped again in an idle repetition of the same; it dies ("annihilates" itself within the structure of language) in the repetition that becomes mechanical and which cannot be stopped by any attempt at an adequate expression. The mechanism of repetition does not base itself on any transcendental order because the sanction that stands behind it is a sanction of a purely idiosyncratic institution or an individual preference. In short, repetition has no source. As a result, a radical treatment, repetition (as "repetition within oneself") does not distance the possibility of an event coming into existence but entirely absorbs this potentiality into a space of language doubling itself. The event remains in a sphere that is impossible to justify or reveal at the surface of language, trapped in the emergence of all acts of expression. Effectively, the inertia of language not only distorts the dialectics of sublimity (devaluing the divine character of the point of reference of the subject) but, most importantly, brings the referential function (constructing meaning) of language to a level of nonsense behind which there is a repetition full of transformations and mechanics.

> In other words, the act by which the event performed by language becomes forgotten and by which meaning and cognition come into life is itself a senseless act. It partakes in the very violence of mindless and absolutely singular positing of the "preceding" linguistic act. Thus, the production of meaning, or figuration, rather than being a beginning is nothing but a repetition of the material and formal linguistic act itself. It remains as punctual, as sterile, as the "first" cause.[187]

---

186   Ibid., 116.
187   Gasché R., *The Wild Card of Reading: On Paul de Man*, Cambridge 1998, p. 84.

This reading points to several qualities of repetition simultaneously. Firstly, it demonstrates the linguistic absence of the source of sense. The word is not only a veil that blocks access to what appears directly and in an obvious way but does not allow for the construction of a meaning, as it gradually loses it referential power and within the progression that guides it is highlighted as having a double and contradictory character: audible and material at the same time.[188] Secondly, by demonstrating the illusory character of the beginning, repetition highlights the paradoxical character of the legitimization of language that was supposed to be both individual and common, idiosyncratic and conventional. Third, the series of repetitions not only allows one to realize the inaccessibility of the centre of sense, but also shows the emptiness of the source that has been – seemingly forever – an inertia of speech itself shifted in time. The speech itself, by suggesting naming of the reality, reveals its own intransitiveness that cannot be reduced, a mechanical and almost arbitrary tropology.

The properties of repetition that focuses itself into a single constitution of subjectivity (as a possibility of the individual consciousness directed at the act of self-determination) and aesthetic experience (considered through changes in the structure of the sign) find their place in *Not I*. Let us take a look at the beginning lines of the text:

> ...out... into this world... this world... tiny little thing... before its time... in a godfor-... what?... girl?... yes... tiny little girl... into this... out into this... before her time... godforsaken hole called... called... no matter... [NI, pp. 405-406]

The beginning turns out to be impossible and the sign of this impossibility takes a form of typography that in an obvious way highlights the segmented, treble manner of expression and simultaneously constitutes a trace of momentary silence, a meaningful lack or suspension of voice that is not enough both in the literal and metaphorical sense. The voice flees before it has a chance to appear, before the sounds spewed out by the Mouth have a chance to acquire any sense and before the words coming together allow for the production of even basic meaning.[189] The remnants of phrases are continuously repeated but never direct us toward some larger whole (a sentence or a narrative). While subdued to the progressive structure of the text, they summon associations while escaping the logic of a sentence. It seems that the only power one can assign to the Mouth, when the mad speech stops for a brief moment, is the repetition of the same words in the motion of language that unintentionally reveals their other side that differentiates the stream of expression.

---

188 Melberg A., *Teorie mimesis. Repetycja*, translated by Jan Balbierz, Kraków 2002, pp. 232-233.

189 In other words, before any form of personal history about the abandoned girl has began to emerge.

What could the triple presence of the word "world" mean? At a very basic level, the words reveal the act of birth in order to confirm the existence of a concrete world that, despite the efforts of the Mouth, cannot gain any stabilizing, substantial definition.[190] This again emphasizes the dual power of repetition. On the one hand, the word appearing several times stops being the same thing and stops meaning the same thing. In that way, the negative aspect of repetition is revealed. A singular word does not the expression of nothing, but becomes an empty sign or a parody of incantation and textual (acoustic on stage) evidence of the semantic defeat of the expression. Examined from that perspective, repetition is an incarnation of the negative force that resides in language itself; language that seemingly names but in reality deprives the name and takes away the signature of individuality.

However, there is another positive aspect of repetition thanks to which speaking in *Not I* is possible. The word, which moves around within the structure of the text that is supposed to constitute the crowning of a utopian combination of the generality of a notion and the energy of an idiom, becomes an embodiment of the impossibility of expression. Language is a physical or material obstacle that renders the work of consciousness impossible. It surrenders every time it is forced to once again repeat the same word, but also when, with full force (in the form of pauses), the most literally understood physicality creeps in and forces the Mouth to stop the stream of continuously less comprehensible expressions. Speech cannot last indefinitely, in so far as there exists an instance that directs the act of speech. That is why there are those moments of a necessary pause, patches of silence, forced by physiological necessity and becoming meaningful, just like the structure of language itself unravelling in the text or on stage. The pause or discontinuity does not reveal itself automatically and in isolation but inevitably in the context of an external mediation in the form of a stream of expression coming from the Mouth.

The written (spoken on stage) word becomes a textual (or dramatic) symptom of the defeat of subjectivity that attempts to form while the Mouth utters words. This failure comes from a striving for a maximized intimacy of the word with

---

190 One encounters a similar problem in *A Piece of Monologue* in which the narrator talks about the experience of the expression of the "first word" which appears with a triple sense: textual (it is a beginning of the story being told), existential (the word summons the individual to life) and epistemological (the meta-reflection pertaining to the act of speech is simultaneously the beginning of the process of self-knowledge). The phrase is: "Parts lips and thrusts tongue forward. Birth." On the subject of the special meaning of that first sentence in the context of the "tasks of the translator" as well as a personal and general metaphysical interpretation of Beckett's work, see Libera A., "Jak przełożyć 'wyrażenie bezpośrednie'? Wokół jednego zdania Samuela Becketta," *Kwartalnik Artystyczny* 2002 no. 4, pp. 24-29.

objects, creating a register of language in which unity would cease functioning as a fantasy or a sign and would turn into a pure thought and a pure presence. At that point, repetition would become a force creating new states of objects (in the positive sense), as well as (in the negative sense) degrading the word to the level of arbitrarily established meanings that do not possess any substance because they are dependent on something completely different. Repetition is not a being but merely its material trace, an externality of language that by repeating "the same" reveals the "emptiness of temporal difference"[191] in the structure of the seeming identity of language. It is exactly repetition that decentralizes a certain, punctual presence of not only a sense but also of the word in the text, as well as of the presence in the form of the sound on stage. Repetition radically disturbs the communication and reference without allowing for a stabilization of the relationship between the word and the described object.

It seems that from this particular perspective *Not I* is more than merely a story about the uselessness of language. It is a subtle work that does not contain any conflicts or drama about its neurotic and inert autonomy. The ability of language to be repetitive strengthens the problem of expression in general and the self-cognition of the speaking self. According to the claims of Hegel, the dialectic relationship between the finiteness of subjectivity and the infinity of a spiritual world is not only defined as sublime but also shows the borderline moment of the constituting of the self which has, as its main goal, the task of recognizing itself. The mouth keeps continuously proclaiming the inefficiency of words that appear, as if the Mouth is satisfied only with word's senseless sounds and were unable to salvage a single one of them from the force of a mechanical repetition that in an equally automatic manner deprives language of the ability to establish any kind of relationship with reality. Within the scheme of the sublime sketched by Hegel, God was a decisive element. In *Not I*, his place is taken by an undiscovered emptiness, which is not so much announced as it is created by arbitrary and conventional language. The emptiness reveals itself on multiple levels: in the abyss of memory from which the Mouth, as indicated in the phrases beginning the work, is not capable of extracting anything; in an aberrational mechanism of repetition, retardation and permutation of the same elements of the whole[192]; in a possessed rhythm of uttering words. After all, the speech itself is an emptiness; a speech that acquires dimensions of a sterile inexpressibility. This would be dialectic of sublimity pushed to the limits[193]; a dialectic that finds its place within the idiom and rhythm of poetry.

---

191 See de Man P., "The Rhetoric of Temporality" in *Blindness and Insight*, New York 1996.

192 We are talking about all kinds of meta-discursive elements describing the phenomenon of speaking (more in a biological, rather than a psychological, sense).

193 Michel Foucault perfectly describes the moment in which the power of speculation behind which the promise of reason and – more broadly speaking – of writing and of

Differently than in Hegel's work, where the theme of negativity has been safely neutralized as a transitive element within the boundaries of the emancipation of the spirit, for Beckett only the power of disintegration and negativity remains, one that never reveals itself in a simple way. Negativity is not similar to, for example, emptiness,[194] but it is experienced as a turning point in which consciousness is no longer capable of controlling the sphere of linguistic mediation. That is why the Mouth does not speak solely about the impossible identity of the subject but constitutes a figure of desire for a kind of experience after which no language would not be able to protect an individual from death, but also: no word would be needed because death could become irrevocably present. This particular patronage of death results in language not naming anything but also – in the process of words uttered by the Mouth – becomes an omnipresent torture without a known beginning and an impossible to foresee ending:

> ... but a moment!... could not make a sound... no sound of any kin... now can't stop... imagine!... can't stop the stream... an the whole brain begging... something beginning in the brain... begging the mouth to stop... pause a moment... if only for a moment... and no response... as if it hadn't heard... or couldn't... couldn't pause a second... like maddened... all that together... straining to hear... piece it together... and the brain... raving away on its own... trying to make sense of it... or make it stop... or in the past... [NI, p. 410]

This is the key section of the work. It reveals with full force the problem of the independence of speech that runs through the body of a speaker whose metonymy is the Mouth. When language becomes autocratic the body turns out to be the only means of relief, but also the worst enemy... Let us observe that the heroine of Beckett's work, while undertaking efforts to stop the stream of words, looks for help in the elementary experiences that confirm her existence in the world. Simultaneously, she trusts consciousness (represented by the figure of "brain") that, while working, evokes the effect of meaning and semiotic driven madness. Both forms of that madness (complete compliance of consciousness with the

---

its capability to materialize that which is absent becomes exhausted and creates only a grotesque image of itself: "Repetition betrays the weakness of the same at the moment when it can no longer negate itself in the other, when it can no longer recapture itself in the other. Repetition, at one time pure exteriority and a pure figure of the origin, has been transformed into an internal weakness, a deficiency of finitude, a sort of stuttering of the negative – the neurosis of dialectics. For it was indeed toward dialectics that the philosophy of representation was headed." Foucault M., "Theatrum Philosophicum" in *The Essential Works of Michel Foucault: Aesthetics, Method, and Epistemology*, edited by James D. Faubion. New York 1998, p. 358.

194 Georges Poulet, using a modified phenomenological language, claimed in his essay about Mallarmé that emptiness, or "empty space in front of the stage," is a place of consciousness that recognizes itself. G. Poulet, *Mallarmé*, Op. cit., p. 275.

language of representation and the dissolution of the subject in an undifferentiated sphere of sensuality) remain inseparable and freely move from one into another. Speech gaining autonomy during the act of expression means less and less and more and more resembles the material, almost physical element of the reality exposed by Beckett. The Mouth is an obvious metaphor of speech, but speech also becomes a separate, embodied being.

All efforts to support the constitution of subjectivity on physiology, on the moment of conceptualization, on the moment of expression, transform into a representation of experience. And all the elements of the body highlight the radically understood failure of expression. The "brain" and "hearing" becomes signs that delineate a significant distance between what is experienced and that, which allows itself to be articulated. Every movement of the body turns out to be fatal because it confirms the lack of any foundation of reality that contains the speaking Mouth. This dual binding of physicality and language is a kind of madness that leads in the direction of a foundation that cannot be marked but would determine the entirety of the text. From that perspective, *Not I* is a story about the absence of the source, but the absence within the drama can be a source of all elements that compose reality born within the borders of the text and the stage. Both the sphere of difference (material and physical elements) and repetition (linguistic inertia and the verbal power of constituting presence) do not enter into any form of contact and force silence on the subject.

The described instances of hypostasis (difference and repetition) show how far Beckett's project went in testing the limits of expression in a situation where there is nothing to single out, or rather nothing is supposed to be stated. But they also illustrate how precisely Beckett constructed his concept, skilfully moving between what situates itself on the side of the sensuality and that which is contained within the rigors of language. Between pure difference and pure repetition an event sneaks in; an event that remains an element outside the rule of repetition and outside of empirical reality:

> The event is not what occurs (an accident), it is rather inside what occurs, the purely expressed. It signals and awaits us. In accordance with the three preceding determinations, it is what must be understood, willed, and represented in that which occurs.[195]

After posing questions about the genesis of an event, it is time to take a look at the conditions under which an event might occur.

---

195 Deleuze G., *Logique du sens*, Op. cit., p. 175. In English, see *The Logic of Sense*, translated by Mark Lester, Charles Stivale, New York 1990, p. 149.

Language – Immaterial Materiality

> So in the end when one is doing philosophy one gets to the point where one would like just to emit an inarticulate sound. – But such a sound is an expression only if it occurs in a particular language-game, which should now be described. [196]
> – Ludwig Wittgenstein

The question about the conditions of an event is a question concerned with the properties of language. In formulating an answer to that question, the event could be described or simply approached. We are thinking about language understood in a specific way, one in which a crucial role is played by the surface of the sign, a mechanism of additive words and "self-constructing" expressions:

> ...tiny little thing... out before its time... godforsaken hole... no love... spared that... speechless all her days... practically speechless... even to herself... never out lout... but not completely... sometimes sudden urge... once or twice a year... always winter some strange reason... the long evenings... hours of darkness... sudden urge to... tell... then rush out stop the first she saw... nearest lavatory... start pouring it out... steady stream... mad stuff... half the vowels wrong... no one could follow... till she saw the stare she was getting... then die of shame... [NI, p. 412]

Describing past life experience is a futile effort because nothing can come outside the "hours of darkness" behind which the entire past lies hidden, as well as everything that could be expressed within the boundaries of imperfect language. Speaking is a process, the sources of which are entirely external and appear as untamed imperatives that force the heroine to change her behaviour and undertake incomprehensible, unmotivated decisions. Beckett makes use of the malleable physiological association between speech and bodily reflexes. This mad run of language results in a semantically empty string of phonemes where random sounds do not provide reference to a stable blueprint of structure and meaning. The act of remembering, while initially recovering the principle governing speech, ultimately reveals the primary and unassailable contradiction of language. On the one hand, a distortion is its source, a deviation from the rule that surely exists, but one which is not be really important for the protagonist speaking through the Mouth. The sound of language is completely incomprehensible because it does not allow itself to be exposed or revealed from the outside. Speaking remains an intimate action, directed at complete closure within the inaccessible sphere of privacy. Dramatic tension appears when the heroine notices or rather keenly experiences a gaze focused on her; a gaze that throws her out of the world of individuality and exposes her to the sight of that which is different (the Other, the Listener). On the other hand – the sound of language acquires an incredibly strong sanction of presence, as if language – after the stage of a split into a sign and its

---

196 Wittgenstein L., *Philosophical Investigations*, London 2009. [§ 261].

referent – inhabited the individual, completely intimate and unable to convey its terrifying empiricality further.

The sensuality of language is demonic, especially when it shows itself in an image of excreting words from the body, but also when "speaking with the body" does not bring any form of satisfaction. Speech becomes bodily, but this passage turns out to be the fantasy of an individual desire with a centre composed of a dream of the perfect expression of presence in the world and, simultaneously, a dream of surrendering to an instantaneous, external imperative of expression. A distorted source and physicality and materiality as contradictory characteristics of language co-exist and cannot be separated.

This complicated status of language is a problem that the Mouth reveals rather directly:

> ... the tongue? ... yes... the tongue in the mouth... all those contortions without which... no speech possible... and yet in the ordinary way... not felt at all... so intent one is... on what one is saying... the whole being... hanging on its words... so that not only she had... had she... not only had she... to give up... admit hers alone... her voice alone... [NI, p. 409.]

On the most basic level, speaking is an action made possible through human physiology. However, it immediately undergoes Beckett's poetic transformation. Expressing words becomes a process of an unending "hammering" words into the body that leads not only to a sensation experienced by individuality as the uniqueness of one's own situation, but, more importantly, it moves almost the entire weight of reflection onto the justification of the importance of being.

The phrase "the whole being ... hanging on its words" shows how important the relationship between aspects of the word is for Beckett: on the one hand, materiality and its fantastical character (in the case of meaning) and on the other – etherealness (in the case of its sound). Existence "clinging to words" does not suggest the possibility of coming back to mythical beginnings where the unity of language remained unshaken. On the contrary, it constitutes an expression of a dramatic search for any kind of point of contact that would allow for the connection of language with personal experience. In Beckett's works – as I have stressed many times before – language is an autonomous energy, but in no way does it resemble a hermeneutic god that constitutes a solid foundation and a warranty of sense that cannot be exhausted in concrete interpretations. Autonomy does not provide any definite confirmation of the stability of the subject; it coerces the subject into an act of expression.

In that same undefined act of coercion, one is able to observe a contradictory movement of an annulment of meanings coming to life, a sense emerging – one that could justify the act of speech. "Clinging to a word" does not constitute any form of protection from the disappearance of the subject but is the last stage of its decomposition leading to the edge of consciousness. The heroine finds it increasingly difficult to justify what she says and the way she says it. That is so because the auto-reflective power of language dissolves with the violence exercised over consciousness by the sphere of an untamed body that is understood more strictly as a movement of face muscles and a set of uncontrollable face contortions. The legitimation of speech does not come from the direction of consciousness and that which is sensual – the word invades the body that in *Not I* is directed at existing within the rhythm of speech outside the oppositions of linguistic structures.

What then is the text that we are reading, if the destruction of language as a representational space has been taken to such extremes? The ultimate answer, but also the most difficult one to justify, is located on the side of the philosophy of the surface and phantasm. In this answer, we find that language is unreal, but only from the perspective in which the subject would want to confirm fully the present character of sense. Hence, one is not concerned with the fact that language loses any ontological credence, but the fact that its presence, or the way it appears is not clear. In turn, that means that it does not undergo the rules of assimilating understanding or structural thinking according to the categories of a stabilizing opposition. Language exists in the text or resounds through the actor's voice on the stage in figures of stubbornly self-sustaining non-transitiveness. At the same time, this materiality does not allow itself to be grasped in any form of persistence or a general notion that would allow for a free assimilation and clear explication. The language of *Not I* has a meaning on the most fundamental level, but that meaning is sabotaged by the progression of language that develops in such a way that it forces a concentration of all attention on itself. Beckett is extremely skilful when introducing the imagery of the organic character of speech, making it only a certain function within the text and not a symbol suggesting the undeniable unity of sense, expression and the body. How should we understand this relationship between the organic and conventional character of language? What is this aporetic tension that is created at the meeting point between materiality and the phantasmal that establishes the speech of the Mouth as well? In order to try and answer these questions, one should return to the thought of Deleuze and Foucault:

> We must articulate a philosophy of the phantasm that cannot be reduced to a primordial fact through the intermediary of perception or an image, but that arises between surfaces, where it assumes meaning, and in the reversal that causes every interior to pass to the outside and ever exterior to the inside, in the temporal oscillation that always makes it precede and follow itself – in short what Deleuze would perhaps not allow us to call its "incorporeal materiality."[197]

---

197   Foucault M., "Theatrum Philosophicum", Op. cit., p. 346.

In Foucault's comments there are three elements of importance that constitute at the same time three stages in the "becoming" of language. The first refers to the independence of the phantasm toward which it is impossible to use any phenomenological, hermeneutic or structural categories. The phantasm – according to the philosophy of difference and repetition – is a surface treated not as an effect, epiphenomenon, or a symbol of existential casualness within the autonomy of the linguistic sign or the sound of an uttered word. The second describes the process of disturbing hierarchical oppositions, the most important of which is the kind that can be observed between the interior and exterior. The phantasm is not a simply understood an "external" surface of representation under which there is a depth hiding (a depth of sense, experience, truth, etc.) but appears as a result of a continuous and mutually complimentary transferring of what is intimate and that which is common. The third element – and the most important of all – makes one aware that the movement of language, or the dislocation of images and figures on the surface of the text is dependent on the workings of time that results in a phantasm emerging as an effect of becoming and transformation. That which will appear in the form of a sign or a voice reveals its own irreducible non-identity and heteronomy that is conditioned by, according to Foucault, "temporal oscillation."

In *Not I*, the movement of language does not allow emerging images to freeze or fully trust summoned histories and facts. The facts that reveal themselves in text immediately disperse in the space created by language developing within the duration of the story. At the same time, however, that which remains unexpressed finds its place within the monologue of the Mouth, as if in passing, even though it decides about the development of the text to an equal extent. The fundamental lack of identity in Beckett's language results in a predatory, fragmentary and seemingly linear narration, which does not die down in a hieratical symbol but develops through the continuous recurrences of the same phrases.

That is what happens, for example, with a figure of speech that in different parts of the work plays different roles. Sometimes the voice comes from inside the brain and exists for a moment, then disappears between nooks and crannies and "dead ends" of narration and sometimes it comes from the outside and penetrates into the internal, dark world of idiosyncrasy and memories.[198]At the crossroads of these two possibilities of the dynamic language we find: the appearance and disappearance of presence, the promise of fullness and ecstasy, as well as the necessity of persistence in the world of repetition, and the coming to life of a language based on an undefeatable contradiction. The aporia of language, framed by Foucault in the formula of "bodiless materiality" is based on questioning the

---

198 See Catanzaro M., "Recontextualizing the Self: The Voice as Subject in Beckett's 'Not I'," *South Central Review: The Journal of the South Central Modern Language Association*, College Station 1990 no. 7, pp. 36-49.

rules of reference and the lasting division between the interior and exterior, and on the other – it is that handicapped, rudimentary speech that becomes a space in which subjectivity can prolong hope for the experience of that, which is real.[199]

The Absolute Event, the Impossible Event

Language constitutes frames for the event, even though it is not a proper event. Does the event, without being the fullest actualization of that which is inexpressible, make space for any kind of symbolic form? In the case of *Not I*, the question of the possibility of the event presents itself radically because it is birth and death that constitutes its matrix. One of Beckett's obsessions returns in the drama and its name could be derived from the words "womb" and "tomb;" words so often appearing in works of Beckett.[200] The "wombtomb" is not only an abbreviated take on the issue of the unbreakable connection between birth and death, but also a metaphor of the entanglement of consciousness in its own birth and its own death. The story told by the Mouth is an attempt to recreate the state of consciousness

---

199 Sandra Wynands sees this question in yet another way and observes that the tension upholding the entire work is of a dual kind. Firstly, it is concerned with the fact that the work is not limited solely to the text but is also destined for a performance on stage and problematizes the relationship between the instances of the text as a source of possible meanings, the receiver and a middleman (the "Other") in the form of a listener. Secondly, the tension in the text is created at the meeting point of what is metonymical (progression of language, logic, association and conceptualization of several recurring issues) as well as that which is metaphorical (references of the order of expression to the off-stage orders that are closely tied with – according to the researcher – with an apocryphal theology). See Wynands S., *Iconic Spaces. The Dark Theology of Samuel Beckett's Drama,* Notre Dame, Indiana 2007.

200 Many great scholars have linked this recurring theme with a personal obsession of the writer. His biographer reminds us that in 1934 in Tavistock clinic, Beckett listened to several lectures delivered by Carl Gustav Jung dedicated to the psychology of depth. Jung was demonstrating his method and his philosophy using the example of a female patient of his that has been plagued by a feeling that she was never really born. Beckett was tormented by a similar sensation (also there is a description of the relationship between Beckett and Wilfred Bion). An evident recollection can be observed in the construction of May, the main heroine of *Footfalls*, in an excerpt written in prose entitled *I gave up before birth* and most importantly in the novel *Malone Dies,* in which the obsession of "wombtomb" is fully realized. One should also observe that the obsession of deadly births was present much earlier, from the moment of his debut – a poem *Whoroscope*. Descartes, the main hero of the text, passionately and with an almost sick curiosity wonders about the origins of life, which is deduced from the young Beckett's presentation of ways in which to prepare eggs by the philosopher, or a phantasm of the dead foetus.

confronted by the ultimate situation that in Beckett's imagination coincides in one inexpressible and nameless experience. Starting with the initial phrases with which the Mouth attempts to extract and preserve the borderline state of birth, all the way to the end in which the theme of light, the meadow and saving loneliness, appears, and the language in the entire work leads toward the expression of these two extreme events. Sometimes, in moments of particular poetic intensity, the simple images of Beckett manage to express this simultaneity:

> ...all went out... all that early April morning light... and she found herself in the – ... what?... who?... no!... she!... [pause and movement 1]... found herself in the dark... and if not exactly... insentient... insentient... for she could still hear the buzzing... so-called... in the ears... and a ray of light came and went... came and went... such as the moon might cast... drifting... in and out of cloud... but so dulled... feeling... feeling so dulled... she did not know... what position she was in... imagine!... what position she was in!... [NI, 406]

Or sometimes more straightforwardly:

> ...all the time the buzzing... dull roar like falls... and the beam... flickering on and off... starting to move around... like moonbeam but not... all part of the same... keep an eye on that too... corner of the eye... all that together... can't go on... God is love... [...] tender mercies... new every morning... back in the field... April morning... face in the grass... nothing but the larks... [NI, pp. 411-412]

The movement of approaching death is incredibly subtle and takes place according to the rules of asymptote: an unending approach of the impersonal language to the sphere of silence, liberated from the necessity of living in words. The heroine disappears in darkness and loses contact with the world only to begin slowly to be reborn. Gradually, she is stimulated back to life by varying impulses; first acoustically and later visually. Still, however, the effect resembling a resounding sound of a church bell,[201] recalling the previous experience of darkness and loss of oneself remains. The body remains numb and exists as if partially, in lack of fulfilment between the reality of a memory about the past sensation and the sphere of existence that has its importance confirmed by experiencing pain, emphasized by the repetition of the phrase ("all numb... all completely numb").

But the world opens itself in an almost ecstatic way. Unspecified light rapidly rips apart the darkness and functions as an obvious metaphor for the beginning of a new life. However, the principle on which this metaphor has been built remains unclear. One could suggest an equally believable interpretation according to which the appearing light hides within several images ("flickering," "ray," or "moon") becomes an impossible to express "light event" that – being unstable – appears and disappears at random. Regardless, in *Not I* birth turns out to be as phantasmal as

---

201   Terminology taken from Derrida. See Derrida J., *Glas*, Paris 1974.

death and through the rhetorical effectiveness of language they become mediated within a trope or a figure.

In the meantime, one can say nothing about the absolute event, except the fact that it inevitably escapes the powers of both the poetic and the commentator's discourses. From the structural point of view, there exists a fundamental homology between the events of birth and death. When we speak about one, we evoke the other. Narrations built around them and based on this fundamental similarity result in a multiplication of the names for impossibility. Events understood in that way are absolute not only because they are impossible events (meaning, they cannot be actualized) but mostly because they allow us to experience what is impossible and constitute events of impossibility as such.[202] One is concerned here with an impossibility of expression (discovering a right register of language), as well as the impossibility of thought:

---

202 Julia Kristeva connects the experience with – according to her – clearly stressed belief of Beckett in the "last myth of modernity," in particular the myth of "femininity." It means that in *Not I* one faces the recognition of an object that is unclosed, sensual and escaping language (which she perceives as "masculine," logocentric language) which is inserted precisely into the monologue by the Mouth that justifies existence through that which is ungraspable: rhythm, tone, a "colour," "happiness inside and across the word," and not, as in the language of presence, where the meaning, resulting and enclosure are all within the structure. In that way, Kristeva seems to be arguing that the value of *Not I* is not so much in the morphology of writing that points to the affirmation of the feminist point of view, but allowing the voices of female desires, structured in a different way than male desires, or desire considered from the male perspective. Seen that way, *Not I* is a story about a search for the language of love after the Father's death (both biological and mythical – God the Father). See Kristeva J., "Le père, l'amour, l'exil," *Cahier de L'Herne*, Op. cit., pp. 256 – 268. Beckett's work has been subject to a number of feminist interpretation to which I refer below: *Women in Beckett: Performance and Critical Perspectives,* ed. L. Ben Zvi, Chicago 1990 (in this collection, Ben Zvi L., „*Not I": Through a Tube Starkly*, pp. 243-248; Diamond L., *Speaking Parisian: Beckett and French Feminism*, s. 208-216; Oppenheim L., *Female Subjectivity in "Not I" and "Rockaby"*, pp. 217-227; Scherzer D., *Portrait of Woman: The Experience of Marginality in "Not I"*, pp. 201-207; A. Wilson, "*Her lips Moving": The Castrated Voice in "Not I"*, pp. 190-200); O'Gorman K., *"But This Other Awful Thought": Aspects of the Female in "Not I"*, "Journal of Beckett Studies" 1992, nr 1, pp. 77-94. One could state things differently, as Slavoj Žižek reminded recalled when commenting an essay by Adorno: "This perception is to be linked to Adorno's famous 'antifeminist' remark, according to which a woman's voice cannot be properly recorded because this demands the presence of her body, in contrast to a man's voice which can exert its full power as disembodied [...]. Adorno's thesis thus effectively asserts feminine hysteria (and not the disembodied male voice) as the original dimension of subjectivity: in a woman's voice, the painful process of disembodiment continues to reverberate, its traces are not yet obliterated." Žižek S., *On Belief,* New York 2003, pp. 44-45.

We should not restrict meaning to the cognitive core that lies at the heart of a knowable object; rather, we should allow it to reestablish its flux at the limit of words and things, as what is said of a thing (not its attribute or the thing in itself) and as something that happens (not its process or its state). Death supplies the best example, being both the event of events and meaning in its purest state. Its domain is the anonymous flow of discourse; it is that of which we speak as always past or about to happen, and yet it occurs at the extreme point of singularity.[203]

Death treated as an unreachable, discursive event is simultaneously a foundation of every language, a paradoxical (because varied and inhomogeneous) source of every expression. As a matrix of all events, it plays the quasi-transcendental role by delineating a horizon of a possible experience of reality. But the source of death understood as a fullness of sense and a blueprint of all events is arbitrary because as purely undefined and an isolated – inaccessible for consciousness – movement of time, it constitutes merely a hypothesis of developing language. Let us observe what Foucault and Beckett are talking about: death in the perspective of the text or a stage production, within the horizon of articulation is never personal and will not happen to an individual consciousness but is always a trace of language, a remaining sign of the work of imagination thanks to which one can dream about connecting words and objects. However, it is only an illusion – which is extremely important – that upholds the process of writing, separating, simultaneously and completely, the subject from the possibility of experience. At the dawn of speech there is not so much as pure presence, revealing in an obvious way, in the form of incarnated word that establishes reality (like in the phrase "out into this world"), but a space that creates a nameless voice and a confusion of different symbolic forms.

At the source, one can observe a slightly different presence understood as an emptiness of language that does not appear within the temporal split in the womb of the sign, but in the vibration of all its modalities. Hence, every linguistic act, if it were to serve expressing the impossible, or to express the event, becomes an act of taming death or exposing oneself to it. Beckett, like other contemporary authors undertaking the theme of death: Adorno, Foucault, Blanchot and Kafka, reverses the dialectical equation of Hegel, which states that only that which is discursive is real and vice versa: that which is real is discursive and points to the fact that the only reality that exists is the space of an event that not only cannot be expressed (because it cannot be repeated) but precisely because it is inexpressible it has to be repeated.[204]

---

203 Foucault M., Op. cit., 350.
204 Here, I'm alluding to Kierkegaard and his reflections on repetition, according to which an opportunity for an individual was in the existential opening that could happen due to a theologically understood repetition. Without that divine warranty the true "repetition" –

That is why language is helpless when confronted with the event of death. However, at the same time, it is only through language that one can attempt to come closer to encircling the understood event. The pinpoint – as Foucault would say – identity of death stems from its uniqueness. It is a closing of the possibility of time. The attempt to introduce it into the order of language results in an event that not only distorts its structure, but also legitimizes its passage. Death, understood as a function or, more radically, as a condition of language determining its structure, finds itself "forever" in the womb of language, but also announces its end, its completion within the act of the final expression. This duality is perfectly visible in *Not I*, in which sentences become stuck in immobile language and through that immobility push the entirety of the plot forward, all the way to its impossible finale that, through the meaning of interpunction, just like the beginning, turns out to be both real and phantasmal. The ellipsis and the hyphen become the agreed borders between which the drama of the tired Mouth will take place. Single words might resound and the rudimentary story of a single life could be told. The story about concrete existence that cannot be formed is accompanied simultaneously by consciousness of the end that is a sign of an unfathomable emptiness, hence that which is outside of words.

But what does it mean to say that a character from the broken narrative of the Mouth, tormented by the necessity to speak, plummets into "long hours of darkness"? Why does he stubbornly and passionately keep coming back to the same fears and even more – as the phrases keep appearing – pale memories and trivial remarks? In other words, why does the Mouth as a narrational instance keep spouting out new scraps of sentences constantly and ever faster? One answer would be that it is all about performing a triply impossible gesture: a return – through speech – to one's own beginnings, expressing the experience of one's own death and representing the existential situation of the experience of the heroine of the narrative. Beckett, by using metaphors of darkness and flash interchangeably, attempts to show the event that constitutes an inescapable distortion of the logic of representation and which, paradoxically enough, is the rule of speech. The rule of the semantic and rhetorical distortion of language results in the inability to escape it because it is language itself that constitutes a form of the oppression

---

one creating that which is real – is only an empty round of language that stops the subject on the level of "aesthetic" stage of the development. A radical affirmation of the event as that, which could happen only once is – from that perspective – completely nonsensical. That, which happens only once and cannot be repeated does not exist – *Einmal ist keinmal*. In the meantime, the project by – as I call them – negative modernists (besides ones mentioned above, also Różewicz, Bernhard or Perec) is based on writing understood as practice thanks to which the maddening hope for an incarnation of aporia of simultaneous impossibilities appears, as well as for the forced expression of the "absolute event."

of the ontological "enigma" by pressing from outside onto existence. At the same time, however, it is language that produces the only accessible space in which one can find a place for that which is entirely singular, cannot be reduced to a scheme of common symbols, and breaks the universal identity of being.

For the subject, speech is a final form of sanctuary against the empirical world, as well as a defence against its own disappearance and the space of meeting death. But Beckett understands this in an unobvious way – for the Mouth, language becomes a sphere in which meanings undergo an implosion of time. The reduction of language is also an attempt at its fundamental metamorphosis aimed at transforming it into an unreachable point of silence:

> Perhaps there exists in speech an essential affinity between death, endless striving, and the self-representation of language. Perhaps the figure of a mirror to infinity erected against the black wall of death is fundamental for any language from the moment it determines to leave a trace of its passage. Not only since the invention of writing has language pretended to pursue itself to infinity; but neither is it because of its fear of death that it decided one day to assume a body in the form of visible and permanent signs. Rather, somewhat before the invention of writing, a change had to occur to open the space in which writing could flow and establish itself, [...] that forms one of the most decisive ontological events of language: its mirrored reflection upon death and the construction, from this reflection, of a virtual space where speech discovers the endless resourcefulness of its own image, and where it can represent itself as already existing behind itself, already active beyond itself, to infinity. The possibility of a work of language finds its original fold in this duplication. In this sense, death is undoubtedly the most essential of the accidents of language (its limit and its centre): from the day that men began to speak toward death and against it, in order to grasp and imprison it, something was born, a murmuring that repeats, recounts, and redoubles itself endlessly, has undergone an uncanny process of amplification and thickening, in which our language is today lodged and hidden.[205]

From the perspective sketched out by Foucault, writing is an action aimed at defending against death and used to immortalize, through preserving in language of an individual experience and one's own name. But it is also something else.

The mythical moment of the confrontation of language with the impenetrability of death (with its "black wall") results in its contradiction, negation within the boundaries of a literary discourse. Death remains the only stable point of reference for the movements of language and the only reliable existential justification. From that perspective, the writer's imperative is based on writing in order to save oneself from death. However, in modern literature – which seems to find its fulfilment in Beckett's work – consciousness of mortality with which every individual is marked is transported from a purely existential level to the level of consciousness

---

205   Foucault M., "Language to Infinity" in *The Essential Works of Michel Foucault: Aesthetics, Method, and Epistemology*, edited by James D. Faubion. New York 1998, pp. 90-91.

that keeps working to bring together contradicting orders of writing and speaking: redemptive and negative. The first one allows access to a form of language that cancels – just like in Hegel – the nihilistic aspect of language in which the abstract character of a notion is purely formal because it is carved from a substantial reality. The form of true, meaning fully rational presence, using the figure employed by Foucault, irons out all imperfections of discourse that could hide what is heteronomic, ambiguous or completely idiosyncratic. Liberation comes through the power of the mind, thanks to which the trace of language is identical with the symptoms of immortality and consciousness, being and an element of the total epic of the spirit, and has a chance to win against death. The second order, proper for the works of Beckett, is based on revealing places that allow for visual representation as the folds of language, as the signs of intransitivity, which are impossible to rework (images or figures based on the cancelation of the generality of the notion). From that impossible to close, semantic and ontological tear, language gets its energy. The mechanisms of Beckett's imagination are the same, reaching irreducible and symmetrical contradictions. The primacy of negativity does not mean a simple, existential reaction to death in the form of fear but points to death as a peculiar centre of sense in which what is most important is the lack one finds at the foundation of every uttered word, both in the sense of its insufficiency in reference to experience and in the sense of its fundamental secondary character against the inexpressible and nameless experience of death.

From the perspective of a difficult relationship between language and the absolute event of death, the most important question remains the problem of repetition that plays such an important role in the surface structure of *Not I*. The Mouth repeats itself continuously, reaching the boundaries of nonsense, not only because that is how the natural consequences of a radically understood logic of language appear, in which sense is contained within an elaborate act of (meta) reflection. This is the case because repetition allows for the realization of the writing program mentioned by Foucault; one that illustrates the problem of the relationship between language and death in Beckett's drama. Speaking and writing produces the effect of shifting words and phrases to new positions and becomes an opportunity for the realization of a final, meaning mortal, identity of the word and body, a sign and a referent. In the end, however, it is not the self-conscious subject speaking anymore, but a speech itself that is announced by the unclear murmuring of death. The concern here is with a meaningful reformulation of the position of the subject that would transform from a self that rationally confirms its own stable presence and cognitive force that would turn into a site of emptiness and a place of waiting for the arrival of the event of death. It would not observe its own reflection in the mirror of language that could reflect the data of his consciousness that organizes external reality, but in the act of reflection it would recognize its own mediation in conventional, symbolic forms. A "strong" subject becomes absorbed by the independent language that not only – on the simplest level – confirms the disintegration of the self speaking through the Mouth, constituting at the same time a medium, as well as the centre of the world. However, repeatedly and according to the rules of an unending series of reflections, it transcends itself. The language in *Not I* constantly transgresses its own structure, beyond a stable meaning thanks to a completely independent force which the speaking Mouth is unable to control, merely surrendering to the mad rhythm of the "stream of words."

Still, however, we remain within the logic of repetition because the rule of transgressing language seems to be naturally connected with it. Repetition results in – as Foucault put it – the effect of "virtual" sense. Language, even though seemingly in excess, in reality loses its semantic binding. The repeated words that are headed toward the incomprehensible, untranslatable semantic chaos reveal the speech of madness, an insane and unstoppable whirlwind of meanings. One of the situations so often described by the Mouth recalls these circumstances:

> ...wandering in a field... looking aimlessly for cowslips... to make a ball... a few steps then stop... stare into space... then on... a few more... stop and stare again... so on... drifting around... when suddenly... gradually... all went out... [NI, p. 406]

But the movement language refers to the very surface of the sign, the material side of language. Within repetition, the word not so much as is inscribed in the chain of symbolic mediatory efforts, which in themselves become the object and focused in one point "immaterial materiality." That is what the fold of repetition is in reality; a fold that hides the possibility of an antinomian interpretation of the position of language. On the one hand, it could perform a function of the sign that, while not possessing an ontological independence, points to that which is beyond it and what is potential, immobile and unshakable. On the other hand, the contradictory movement, based on the multiplication of the initial word that, already at the border of the articulated sound, becomes its own reflection, sabotages the movement of transcendence that establishes the structure of the sign. On the one side, we are witnessing a repetition that highlights the distance of the sign but also the hope for discovering a well-founded and concrete sense that could appear in speech. On the other side, there are an endless series of repetitive phantasms, linguistic "reflections" that point to the fictionality of an uttered word and the arbitrariness and conventionality of its expression in the form of writing.

Both of those positions concerned with the relationship between death and repetition are reformulated by Beckett into a paradoxical formula of hope that does not promise anything and results in a process of experience of that which is totally negative. It is there that the subject finds the makeshift place for its own identity, however, as the Mouth suggests, the process will never be completed:

What she was trying.... what to try... no matter... keep on... [*curtain starts down*]... hit on it in the end... then back... [NI, p. 413]

An intuitively sensed boundary of expressivity becomes dispersed in the end in the experience on negativity for which the Mouth does not find a single word. The only consolation comes in the form of an act of speech – so well-known from the body of work of Beckett – or the motif of beginning of everything anew. Paradoxically, this gesture inevitably brings closer the final confirmation of the power of that which is negative. It announces silence and the coming of death. But it is on that particular contradiction that the enigmatic force making the subject move in the sphere of mythicized unnamable is based. Such force pushes consciousness to undertake efforts to express the absolute event that – stemming from its structure – is as much an impossible event as it is an event of impossibility itself.[206]

---

206   See Kelly K., "The Orphic Mouth in 'Not I' ," *Journal of Beckett Studies*, 1980, no. 6, pp. 73-80.

Chapter Two
Laughter and the Inexpressible

The Reality of the Mouth

Lips, tongue, palate. The entire speech apparatus is mercilessly material. With the use of the same organs we devour a part of the world every day in order to exist. Securing our life is possible due to our mouth and the speech is a wake after the unending funeral of the world, annihilation in the mouth.[207]

– Ryszard Przybylski

When I mentioned before that language in Beckett's work becomes subject to the law of repetition and that it reveals its material aspect, I was talking not only about the broadly understood stage production, or the structural characteristic of the text but also a kind of presence of the body in the most fundamental sense. Words are uttered by the Mouth that, firstly, constitutes an instance of narrative. It seems that they also create a reality of a peculiar kind that cannot be reduced to a psychological sensation. It doesn't seem – paraphrasing Guido Ceronetti's statement about philosophy of the face[208] – that the 'mouth is of the flesh.'[209] On the one hand, the Mouth is fully autonomous in Beckett's text, meticulously separated from the rest of the face and body. They seem to not fulfil any normal physiological function because the speech that is a result of their work successfully disturbs the division between what is normal and pathological. They become an "organ without a body" that functions according to the laws of the machine of desire. On the other hand, however, the Mouth, despite the removed context of the entirety of the body, cannot exist without them and constantly refers back to them. Beckett is a master of showing the tension that appears at the intersection of these two realities: a body aimed and guided by life functions and mute, as a consequence of the Mouth, an organ that is outside of the law of physiology and functionality that reveals through its autonomy that which would otherwise be invisible in the context of bodily wholeness.

---

207   R. Przybylski, *Pustelnicy i demony*, Krakow 1994, p. 88.
208   Ceronetti G., *Milczenie ciała*, translated by M. Ochab, Gdańsk 2004, p. 41.
209   The key concern remains the question whether Beckett means the "Mouth," or the mouth. It seems – and as my analysis progresses, I hope to show – that the writer is perfectly aware of this duality and attempts to foment this effect of insolvability throughout the text. On stage, of course, it becomes much more visible and perceptible (which does not mean it becomes more comprehensible).

One can add two more tensions. The Mouth creates its own reality because that which is bodily and that which discursive meets within it. What is the Mouth? There cannot be a single answer. At this point, we should go back to Foucault's text:

> It is through this mouth, as Zeno recognized, that cartloads of food pass as well as carts of meaning ("If you say cart, a cart passes through your mouth"). The mouth, the orifice, the canal where the child intones the simulacra, the dismembered parts, and bodies without organs; the mouth in which depts. And surfaces are articulated. Also the mouth from which falls the voice of the other giving rise to lofty idols that flutter above the child and from the superego. The mouth where cries are broken into phonemes, morphemes, semantemes: the mouth where the profundity of an oral body separates itself from incorporeal meaning. Through this open mouth, through this alimentary voice, the genesis of language, the formation of meaning, and the flash of thought extend their divergent series.[210]

Foucault does not provide the most important answer directly; instead he disguises his conclusion as a reference to the figure of Zeno. The metaphor of the "chariots of sense" shows at the same time two aspects of the same mouth phenomena. That is because they are simultaneously a borderline that separates that which is physiological from that which is semantic and also points to the dynamic character of that border. Hence, if mouth is a border, it is not in an ontological sense, nor does it establish a permanent division between spheres of being (that which is phenomenal and existent), but it has those properties according to the rules of autonomy and ungraspability. This is about a fundamental shift of where stress falls: thinking about the mouth not in ontological categories (the mouth is not a border) but within the space of metamorphosis (the mouth establishes the border). This is why Foucault managed to contain so many orders in his interpretation of this figure. Each of those interpretations is based on the same premise about change and contamination as a framework, within which one can attempt to understand its enunciations. The Mouth is both a sign of the deepest organic qualities of the body, as well as its surficial decomposition and a place for the creation of sense and its complete annihilation in the world of the acoustic pretense; a space of intimacy to which no form of language has access and an entrance into the public sphere in which the possibility of creating an idiom is reduced.

Beckett places this fundamental contradiction on two separate levels. One of these levels is extremely important from a theatrical point of view – isolation from the rest of the staged reality (and most likely of the rest of the represented world) The Mouth is the articulating instance within and on the surface of which the entire event takes place. The second dimension refers to the level of a laboriously constructed story in which the very fact of speaking is important; a fact thanks to which the entire narration does not become a simple metaphor of human fate

---

210   Foucault M., "Theatrum philosophicum," Op. cit., p. 354.

and the speech is not subjugated to the mute sphere of physicality. The Mouth presents itself in the text as being engaged in perpetual movement, becoming an ambiguous image of the borderline of madness, speech, silence and absence:

> ...whole body like gone... just the mouth... lips... cheeks... jaws... never-... what?... tongue?... yes... lips... cheeks... jaws... tongue... never still a second... mouth on fire... stream of words... in her ear... practically in her ear... not catching the half... not the quarter... no idea what she's saying... imagine! [NI, s. 409-410]

The mouth performs a function of expressing the irreducible secret of speech that orders it to continuously contradict itself. But also its image undermines any kind of possibility of stabilizing clear figures of sense and the transparent orders of the beings. Language becomes an organ that serves to utter words but at the same time it stops being, contradicting its nature, a space for naming the world, communication and reflection. At the same time, however, in the vision of Beckett the Mouth does not become a symbolic form of a lack of understanding and the constrictions of language but allows for the observation of the contradictory character of the very phenomenon of speech: on the one hand, it is stubbornly stuck in a meaningless sphere of physicality and on the other it is surrendered, hence cancelling the uniqueness of the semantic structure of language. The Mouth constitutes a separate reality because it concentrates within itself three simultaneously appearing and impossible to recognize orders: genealogical (the emergence of sense), transcendental (the conditions of the possibility of the sense) and the order of events (pertaining to a modality of the event). None of them can be levelled because that would result in the mouth losing its position of the fundamental poetic figure in the text and being reduced to a clear and mechanically reproduced symbol of the inexpressibility of a single being in different versions. In the meantime, the three orders mentioned allow us to sustain, in a fragile state of equilibrium, the idiomatic weight of the entire text, which means that none of these orders get the upper hand. In other words, at the boundary of the Mouth the word comes into being and sounds, its sense is created and its structure of meaning is developed. It appears, however, along with the crushing force of the silence of the body that reveals the uncertainty of a poetic gesture of naming and illustrates the failure that accompanies the efforts of consciousness, on the one hand attempting to reach the sphere of the unnamable, and on the other – engulfed by the more complete darkness of silence.

Laughter and Death

What is the history told by the Mouth really about? With certainty, it is a thematization of the obsessions of the writer concerned with the memory of his own existence from before his birth, but more importantly – it is a history of fear that is lined with a perverse, impossible to exterminate, fascination. From the perspective of language, death is an absolute event that, even though it endlessly demands an expression, does not allow itself to be expressed. But what is the effect of the efforts aimed at representing individual experience? On the most basic level, it brings about the surrendering of narration, a fall of progressive abilities of language that leans toward silence or forces the Mouth into a burst of laughter. The Mouth, the place of which has been meticulously planned by the author in the fabric of the whole work, on the other hand, does not leave much room for individual interpretation, as it radically suspends, even if only for a brief moment, all forms of existence.

But why does the Mouth stop speaking on four separate occasions and emit a mechanical, inhuman sound instead; a sound that Beckett described as long or short laughter? It seems that it is the only possibility within the space of the text and the scene, in which an event outside of oppositions can occur; an event that – even though it is a memory of mythical simultaneity and the unity of birth and death – creates a unique chance for liberation from these very events. Laughter is an event in so far as it demolishes the horizon of reality and exposes the subject to uncertainty, but also because it stands in extreme proximity to death. The laughter of the Mouth is not a form of the conceptualization of psychological discomfort, or a form of a defensive mechanism against that which is fantastical and untamed, but a figure of nothingness that, even though it escapes representation, has an opportunity to speak within a narrow space of meaning, between what is discursive and what is empirical.

This strict and unbreakable connection between laughter and death accompanies Beckett from the very beginning of his work. It is perfectly visible, almost in pure form, in Beckett's short poetic forms, seemingly resembling haiku and in reality being a testament to the incredible intensity of poetic thought. Beckett writes:

> en face
> le pire
> jusqu`à ce
> qu`il fasse rire[211]

and later:

> samedi répit
> plus rire
> depuis minuit
> jusqu`à minuit
> pas pleurer[212]

---

211   Mi, p. 33.
212   Mi, p. 37.

In case of the first text, we are dealing with an almost classical solution to the question of the existential confrontation with a menacing mystery. It is not hard to observe within this poetic meditation the tradition of a laughing Democritus or Diogenes, who proposed a revolutionary strategy of laughter against the oppressive – in their opinion – philosophy of ideas, full of unjustified pretenses to the absolutization of human reason.[213] But the work of Beckett, even in its distant echoes, does not contain many traces of this clever technique at the margins of philosophy and existence. The situation is just the opposite: that which could be revealed in poetry is a moment of confrontation with what is enigmatic. Let us observe that Beckett doubles the gesture of subversion that accompanies laughter. Firstly, what is unknown and "worst" is given autonomy and it is that unknown that establishes the conditions of reality. Secondly, laughter is not any kind of practice in this case, aimed at freeing the subject and it does not allow for a working of tormenting mystery but reveals only the exterior linguistically in a chain of ambiguous presence, which in the end attains ontological independence. One could say that the four lines of Beckett are a perfect parody of ascetic practices that grant order and simultaneously hint as to how to neutralize the dispersed, demonic and aggressive evil of the world. Perhaps more interesting would be to approach the text as an example of a situation employing an organic subject – on the one hand – through its own condition, and on the other – attacked by what is entirely external and not fully investigated, hence inexpressible.

The primacy of what is individual can be observed from the first word that concludes both the aspect of existence as exposure and a confrontation with externality (*face à face*), as well as it highlights the very ambiguity presence of the face (*en face* additionally suggests a metaphysical aspect). In its depth, as well as on its surface, as in the remarkable photographs portraying Beckett himself, there lies a mystery of the subject that does not remain within the sphere of immanence and instead directs itself toward that which is subjected to the unambiguous evaluation (anonymous "the worst") and remains mysterious. The status of subjectivity is not changed in any way. Beckett leads the subject, the figure of which is the face, to the edge of experience. Contact with what is external is aimed not only at changing the symbolic status of the "screen of language" that produces a changing image (from "the worst" to laughter) that the subject attempts to confront, but it also aims to confront the very mysterious essence of laughter. It is derived from a

---

213 See *Pseudo-Hipokrates, O śmiechu Demokryta. Listy 10-23,* translated by K. Bartol, pp. 86-87. On the subject of Democritus's tradition in works of Beckett see Mével Y., *L`imaginaire mélancolique de Samuel Beckett, de "Murphy" à "Comment c`est,"* Rodophi, Amsterdam-New York 2008. (especially the chapters "Retour à Démocrite", "Humour et mélancolie"). See also Bernard M., *Samuel Beckett et son sujet; une apparition évanouissante,* Paris-Montréal 1996.

source located in absolute externality, it is a mystery that becomes reversed in the figure of a chiasm, and transforms into the laughter of a mystery.

This difficult relationship between the face, laughter and death is illustrated by different names and forms ("the worst," external) that much more clearly and in an extremely laconic way can be seen in the second of the aforementioned texts. Laughter is a kind of pause in the existential cycle of suffering and constitutes a relief that is simply caused by the lack of cry. However, it also refers to a defined period of time. The question of temporality seems to be the most important in this poetic meditation because laughter eases the murderous necessity of persistence. At the same time, its vision seems to contradict the structure of events. Laughter that builds up and extends in time assumes the shape of an inhuman affect that is impossible to revoke. It is not an explosion, but a continuity. That is how Beckett achieves the effect of aporia. Laughter can possess two equal modalities: an event modality and a cyclical or continuous one. The consequences of such a state of affairs seem far-reaching and are not only concerned with the problems stemming from the necessity of undertaking an interpretative choice. Firstly, the aporia determining a structure of laughter results in a poem, the subject of which is cunningly hidden and is transformed into an ironic formula, decidedly distorting a literal interpretation of the text. Going even further, laughter in the vision outlined by Beckett has no substance and cannot be inscribed into the sphere of metaphysical oppositions of being and nothingness. Not only does it not bring relief, but one cannot be certain if it truly resounds in the space of the "external" or if that is even possible.

Outside of Presence

Laughter questions the classical form of ontology that allows for the inscription of that which exists into an order of binary oppositions. It reveals itself as a kind of experience and creates obstacles for any conceptual understanding of the problem. How does the relationship between laughter, death and the face look? What is the language one should speak in order to discuss this complex relationship?

Jean-Luc Nancy pointed his attention to similar issues and attempted an interpretation of the prose poem by Baudelaire *The Desire to Paint*. Let us recall the premise of Baudelaire's text from the *Paris Spleen*.[214] An artist who desires to paint a woman's portrait is the central figure of the poem. It is a special portrait because that which is unseen is the most important element. A dream reigns

---

214   Baudelaire Ch., "The Desire to Paint" in *Paris Spleen*, translated by Keith Waldrop, Middletown 2009.

over the entire project of infusing painterly signs with what is phenomenal and ungraspable: the darkness of the face, a flash of lips and a deadly gaze. One could interpret this text as contemplating the act of seduction or desire, as a story about the difficulties that accompany the act of representation, or as trying to understand the mystery of femininity. By treating Baudelaire's text as a poetic realization of his dream about actualizing that which escapes language as a form of an "other" presence, Nancy introduces conclusions that are concerned with laughter as one of the main categories of modernity. It is important to take a closer look at this interpretation because it will allow us to clearly see the structure and the meaning of laughter in Beckett's drama.

The first doubt that appears in the context of Nancy's conclusions refers to the strength of his interpretative formula. How is one supposed to find agreement between the order of presence (or the phantasm of actualization) with the fundamentally sensual and non-substantial character of laughter? Nancy claims that this first requires omitting the fundamental categories of representational philosophy. Thanks to such a stance, laughter cannot be recognized as a symptom of trivial empiricism, nor can it be recognized as a symptom of naïve subjectivity. Laughter is an event that – as shown by previous analysis of Beckett's text – functions simultaneously as an existential experience:

> Laughter, therefore, is neither a presence nor an absence, it is the giving of a presence in its own disappearance. Not given, but giving, and thus suspended on the edge of its own presentation. Neither face nor meaning, laughter is the giving of an infinite variety of possible faces and meanings. It is, in a word, the repetition of this offer. (The mouth does not burst permanently into laughter, but rather opens itself, and laughter occurs repeatedly, every time the woman is presented, every time the poem is read – better yet, it opens a repetition of reading within a single reading; laughter in general is perhaps repetition pure and simple.) Laughter offers presence, from behind and beyond any presence. The philosophical erotics of aesthetics suspends itself. Presentation is no longer the goal of desire, for the offer of presence has been made before and behind any desire, before any intention of any kind of representation.[215]

Laughter cannot be described in a language of categories, although – as an event – it demands explication through notions. Already the first sentence by the philosopher show the rules that guide the ontology of laughter. On the one hand it constitutes a symptom of presence, on the other – by revealing itself as more like a phenomenon than a sign of existence – it reveals a negative side or an absence. Laughter reveals itself momentarily (in which case it is stigmatized mostly by time) as non-identity (in which case it is motivated existentially). While

---

215   Nancy J-L., *Le rire, la présence*, in *Une pensée finie*, Paris 1990. In English, see "Wild Laughter in the Throat of Death," *MLN*, Vol. 102, No. 4, French Issue. (Sep., 1987), pp. 729-730.

existence is not so much something that "is," but rather announces an unnamable absence. Additionally, staying outside of oppositions, laughter is resistant to the rigors of the economy of being as well. Not only does it escape the workings of consciousness, *de facto* undermining the possibility of representation, but it also disturbs fundamental ontological assumptions about the possibility of the substitution of being and non-being. Laughter is not so much the "gift" of varying meanings, but a process of offering. Paradoxically but according to the more important logic of the gift – the object of that process is pure nothingness. That is why the destabilization of an economic model of ontology (if a being exists, nothingness has to exist) created by laughter is so radical that the centre of the event becomes unimaginable and impossible to represent.

Why then are we talking about the possibilities of its actualization? Nancy's suggestion is the following: because laughter leaves behind a trace of its presence, by changing a given facial expression, but also very simply – by being extracted and persisting for a given period of time as a sound. However, a transcendental aspect compliments this dimension. Laughter makes space available to what can appear not so much in the field of consciousness but in the field of experience, and can establish itself within the sphere of existence. By connecting ontological contradictions within itself, it is simultaneously an event and its very possibility.

The formulation of the "edge of disappearance" sounds surprisingly unclear, but it seems to be concerned with an incredibly important question. The only quality of laughter, as such, is the boundary. Laughter is a boundary in the sense that it separates two modalities of being from each other: presence and absence. One can clearly see that the temporal and not static character of laughter pertains to both its status as an event and as a boundary of what can be thought and experienced, as well as what is inexpressible and inaccessible for experience. It creates conditions for the emergence of individuality (the face and voice) but also makes discursive space accessible; a space dominated by repetition thanks to which subjectivity finds a confirmation of itself in language.

"Laughter offers presence, from behind and beyond any presence" – claims Nancy. This does not mean, however, that it is a figure of a primal event, irreducible and – as a result – mythical. This sentence shows, rather unquestionably, the mechanism of the existence of laughter that cannot freeze in just any figurative form. Its presence enables that which is placed beyond time and space; that which does not allow itself to be verified, even though it is the most perfect form of presence. At that point, the idea of an "ontology outside ontology" and, as a consequence, "presence outside of presence" reaches is apex. The existence of laughter is selfless and inexplicable, but it is not its pure form. Standing against a different, completely external sphere of that which is "differently" present, although completely enigmatic, it reveals the heteronomic and irreducible non-identity of all events. In other words, laughter illustrates a fundamental gap, and impossible to conquer through consciousness,[216] between what is potential and what is revealed as a permanent foundation of being. This ontological gap is constituted by a boundary: the material trace of that which can appear as a form of presence.

Let us observe how many points of intersection there are between Nancy's reflections and the writings of Beckett. The reality of the Mouth delineates a border on the most fundamental level – it separates the world of the mysterious interior from the external reality in which that mad monologue is supposed to resound. The Mouth is supposed to gain its status as an independent organ during speaking, although it would be wiser to say: the status of a speaking machine. That is where the suggestions from Beckett himself to Billie Whitelaw, on how she should deliver her monologue completely impassioned, came from.[217] It seems that Beckett's directions were something more than simply a technical suggestion. Rigorous in design following certain rules established in advance were supposed to secure delivered lines not only from emotional triviality but also to make the effect of laughter more vivid; by tearing the homogenous and monotonous tissue of the story being told apart, laughter places the recipient (a member of the audience rather than a reader) at the edge of experience, beyond which there hides an aseptic emptiness and enigmatic absence. Hence, it is understandable that in *Not I*, laughter does not resemble anything with which it is commonly associated. Both in reading and – even more so – on stage, laughter easily transforms into a scream without losing its properties along the way. It remains an event that erases the outlines of the existing world and does not leave any hope for the emergence of its new form.

While screaming and laughing, the Mouth remains a synonym of an unconditional and unpredictable opening. Laughter and screams constitute places of multilateral boundaries, generating many tensions. But they also become sites of death:

> It is instead laughter "in the throat of death," as something which does not belong to death (at least, if death is represented as the pure negation of presence – not if death is the ultimate possibility of presence coming in its own disappearance [...]. This laughter is nothing but the vibration, the resounding and the tightening, or the tremor of the limit itself. [...] It is laughter not as an essence, but as the bursting existence of the mouth (not an "orality," but something which comes before orality, before any distinction of steps like orality, anality, genitality – beyond or behind any represented body). It is the surprise of being at the most remote frontier of any kind of presence. It is the wilderness which happens on this frontier – destroying any art, and enjoying the destruction.[218]

---

216 That is why Nancy, when speaking about "transitive" and enigmatic character of laughter simultaneously shows how far laughter questions range or even possibilities of intentions and representation.

217 Gussow M., Op. cit., pp. 84-92.

218 Nancy J-L., Op. cit., pp. 735-736.

Nancy's reflections are clearly aimed at finding such a register of language that would allow us to grasp indivisible experience, leading a hidden existence in a sphere between laughter and death. It is on that level of speech – almost literally – where the poetic idiom resounds. In order to understand such a position, one should take a look at the strict and unbreakable connection between presence and absence as principles guiding thinking about boundaries. Firstly, even though Nancy does not want to admit it – we are concerned with a classical distinction between the event and essence. Laughter comes into being beyond all binary oppositions because it is an event of existence and as such cannot possess or reveal its own essence. Secondly, the event of laughter excludes not only the possibility of representation; it also weakens consciousness, as well as the actualization of the body. The Mouth opening is in reality a wild throat of death that orders us to forget about the rest of the body and world. Thirdly, the Mouth in the act of laughter is a synonym for the complete exposition of existence about what is unexpected and absent. That is where the fundamental paradox of laughter appears, lasing momentarily and confirming the primary state of nothingness. Laughter is a form of existence because it reveals in its own event-structure the time gap that touches both all the forms of existence as well as absence. In that sense, the Mouth explodes with an irritating, undefined, and wild laughter that – lasting for just a moment – which not only illustrates its own ethereal nature, but also, by disappearing in the space of externality, it provides a confirmation of a dream about expression that does not allow itself to be fulfilled, even in its most radical form – the form of death. The language in which the subject can depose its dream about simultaneous reflection and the experience of death is poetry.

Illumination of the Face

> rentrer
> à la nuit
> au logis
> allumer
>
> éteindre voir
> la nuit voir
> collé à la vitre
> le visage[219]
> – Samuel Beckett

Where does the wildness of laughter come from? Why is it so neurasthenic, even though it was programmed in advance by the author and later mechanically

---

219   Mi, s. 33.

activated by the performer? There are several reasons. The first three that I have mentioned before were concerned with important ontological questions: existential difference, an inability to represent the body (which is connected with the general idea of Beckett, but also that of Baudelaire and Nancy, which is an attempt to remove all context from the experience of laughter) and laughter as a figure of existence or exposition. Another element is the close relationship between the figure of the Mouth and face.

Nancy observes that in *The Desire to Paint*, the character of a woman is inscribed into a series of metaphors used to extract that which is singular, as well as that which it is impossible to represent. Only that way, in the face of a primal impossibility to reach one's goal does desire appear. However, this is also the only way in which laughter becomes a mystery. It is a key term – next to the event and laughter – in Beckett's drama. Mystery, as opposed to the secret,[220] does not suggest any model of behaviour, does not seduce and, in reality, does not hide anything. Differently than in phenomenology of a secret, there is no permanent sanction (metaphysical, religious, cognitive) standing behind it because, as such, it is the strongest figure of an individual existence. The mystery of laughter forces a return to reflections on death:

> It is the glance at tragedy as tragedy, in its tragic truth: namely, that immortality comes only with death, as death itself. Laughter is the knowledge of this truth, and therefore the highest, the consummate knowledge. That is why it is "divine," like the woman in whom "mystery dimly glistens." IT is the divine and the feminine knowledge of the mystery of art as the mystery of life – of the mystery of life as the mystery of art. And this is why laughter itself remains mysterious. It knows with a knowledge that not only remains hidden but is this very knowledge precisely in its own hiding. It shows itself as its hiddenness. Laughter reveals that it comes from the hidden place, which it keeps hidden.[221]

Despite the obvious philosophical terminology taken from Heidegger, it is worthwhile to point to the most important conclusions of Nancy. Laughter, despite the fact that it suspends the possibility of deciding about being and undermining the opposition between presence and absence, establishes and deconstructs, at the same time, yet another pair of oppositions: covertness and overtness. Both properties exist simultaneously and are – roughly speaking – other properties of the event. Let us recall the planned sites for the explosion of laughter in the text. It emerges after a moment of silence that stopped a stream of words spewed out by the Mouth. The genealogy of the laughter remains unknown, even though Beckett,

---

220   On this topic, see Derrida J., "La littérature au secret. Une filiation impossible," in Le secret: motif et moteur de la littérature. Etudes réunies et introduction par Chantal Zabus avec une préface de Jacques Derrida, Louvain-La-Neuve 1999.

221   Nancy J.-L., Op. cit., p. 724.

with his entire might, underlines that the source – even though it most certainly exists – is a beginning that is impossible to be disclosed. It is a foundation that constitutes a fictional base, because in place of certain presence nothing appears. Nothingness is a paradoxical foundation of laughter that as an event does not stop in any form of potentiality but is an incarnation of the mystery. It is a "vibrating" – as Nancy would metaphorically put it – an incorporation of that which is enigmatic.

However, the experience of laughter has a sensual and aesthetic character as well: the open Mouth, like in the painting-dream of Baudelaire; the Mouth, an organ without a body, screaming and uttering words almost in the same breath for which the pause in laughter is a form of necessity reminding us of a bodily anchoring, as well as the entire structure of the text. They constitute signs of not only the mystery of laughter but also an expression of the affirmation of existence that is unaware of one's own beginnings. Is that why the Mouth keeps laughing? If that is the case, then – I believe – we would remain within the same range of typical interpretations of Beckett's work as those that inscribe his ambiguity within homogenous anthropological formulations about the absurdity and nonsense of existence. Meanwhile, laughter is proof of the confrontation of consciousness and death, its inevitable approach but also its sublimity that comes into being based on the impossibility of subjectivity facing this clash. Consciousness is defeated when confronted with the event, but at the same time it attempts to find a place in which death could be tamed, even for the price of extra-linguistic existence. This attempt to disenchant is clearly visible in Beckett's drama, where the event of death, while dispersing all identity, remains stuck in an empty place between consciousness and its negation (just like in the title, in the emptiness contained in a narrow passage from "I" to negation); between the desire to disenchant and the rational reign over death and a contradictory desire: allowing its presence to reign.

It seems that precisely for that reason, from the point of view of the relationship between laughter and death, one could speak of a particular kind of sensuality that is partially embodied by laughter. Sensuality is a path not only to tame death but an attempt to open subjectivity to the individual and difficult to verbalize experience of the borderline situation in which death appears. Laughter is a sensual beauty thanks to which existence can focus within itself two contradictory tendencies. On the one hand, it puts death at a safe distance from aesthetic experience. On the other hand, however, in that same aesthetic experience it makes itself accessible to its destructive actions. The sensation of its undefined "vibration" that we have mentioned before refers to the tension created at the intersection of these two contradicting qualities that are incapable of finding a release and cannot be stopped. That is why the compositional strategy of Beckett seems even more understandable. He aimed for petrifying the gesture of laughter within the text of his drama but also – which is far less obvious – in his planned stage practice. The place of laughter, even though precisely marked, does not stop signalling that internal and impossible to diffuse conflict between physicality and death. This power of conflict operates in a narrow strip between these two worlds and before it can dominate the external space through sound, before the Mouth will extricate from the depth (from the "throat of death") laughter, and the audience will witness simultaneously the sensual and metaphysical surface of the face:

> The woman's laughter is clearly at the centre of her glance. Or it becomes this glance, it gives the glance its specific and final character: a tone, a light, and a colour, simultaneously. The laughing mouth is the very illumination of the face. It is its flower, it makes it a flower, the "blooming" or coming of a flower. What is the woman laughing (or coming) at? She is laughing at the dying artist as he comes in his own death, because she knows about death. All that she is and all that she knows is "nocturnal."[222]

What is the Mouth laughing about? Nancy's answer is only partial. In order to arrive at a satisfying conclusion one should say that it's laughing at nothing. A nothing – according to what has been said before – that constitutes a foundational and irremovable mystery of *Not I* and complicates the vision of existence emerging from the text. Where is the place of the face if on stage only the Mouth is visible? The image of face can be found in fragments of the story being told and the Mouth constitutes a figure of the relativity of all language. However, from that point of view, the face itself (materially not present on stage, but surfacing in the fragments of the story) becomes a figure of the desire to be liberated from the law of representational consciousness and a figure of the desired, unreal loneliness:

> ...hit on it in the end... then back... God is love... tender mercies... new every morning... back in the field... April morning... face in the grass... nothing but the larks... pick it up – [NI, s. 413]

The Mouth, being a borderline space, does not freeze in an unambiguous poetic figure – through the unfinished dialectic of speech and silence, presence and absence, it reveals the emptiness of the face. The edge of experience and language, embodied by the Mouth, leaves readers and recipients of *Not I* with an impression of an insolvability[223] that is impossible to rework. It is unknown whether, besides the Mouth and the narration it creates, there is another reality. Or if it simply constitutes an obstacle on the path to arriving at the true reality that reveals itself

---

222 Ibid., pp. 723-724.
223 Beckett would be a key figure in the kaleidoscope of different, modernist "poetics of insolvability" On this topic, see Nycz R., "Teoria interpretacji: problem pluralizmu," in *Tekstowy świat. Poststrukturalizm a wiedza o literaturze*, Kraków 2000.

only through a movement of negation, in a gesture of incontrollable laughter that shows a glimpse of the mystery of reality through defining the enigmatic and shimmering character of its identity? It seems that both possibilities are equally plausible, even though none of them lead to some stable form of synthesis that could allow for the expression of the fullness of experience. Both – similarly to the beginning of *The Unnamable* – create within the space of language hope for finding identity, as well as a degradation of the existence disappearing in silence. Poems from *Mirlitonnades* also address that very issue. In them, isolated from external influences, the unconditional will of confrontation not with death or with nothingness but with what is absolute, or absolutely undefined, leads to a complete erasure of the traces of being. It heads, through language, toward the annihilation of the most serious, concrete sign of the individuality – the face. In that way, the natural features of existence, individuality and peculiarity, become ambiguous. It feels as if Beckett wanted to leave the reader with an impression of a pure, singled out, indecisiveness – with a pure structure of the decision.

In *Not I* the face cannot, however, ultimately be discarded. Returning not only in the frame of a particular image, but also in the figure of a reflection – as often happens in Beckett's works – that turns out to simultaneously be a sign of an existential reflection (on the personal level) and a symptom of recognizing the fundamental, meta-linguistic conditioning of the subject (on the textual level). This return of the face is mediated numerous times (through language, its irreducible metaphorical character and the structure of narration) but only thanks to this mediation it is possible to transpose hope onto a real, directly experienced presence:

> so-called… no part of her moving… that she could feel… just the eyelids… presumably… on and off… shut out the light… reflex they call it… no feeling of any kind… but the lids… even best of times…. who feels them?… opening… shutting… all that moisture… [NI, p. 408].

The Explosion of the Poem

However, laughter is first and foremost tied to the voice. Although it reveals and covers the face, allowing us to observe the existential and metaphysical phenomena within it, it fundamentally appears as a pure intensity of sound, as an event resounding beyond any binary oppositions, hence also beyond the routine of naming. It undermines the rules of classical metaphysics through several mechanisms – diverting access to primal language, while providing justification for the search for individual intentions and the possibility of representation.

Laughter is the setting up of the model of the mode, or of a circularity of models – a circular mimesis. (Such a circularity is the reverse side of "modelling": the same thing as "modelling" the model, but considered from the point of view of representation.) And that is why laughter is laughing: it is laughing because painting bursts into pure sound, and because poetry bursts into this non-painting painting – and also because it does not make music. It makes a sound, the sound of a resounding voice. But this voice is not a voice: it is an absence of voice, and a voice behind any voice. It is the breath, the timbre and the material of voice, but it is not a speaking voice. It lies between the colour of voice, the modulation of voice, and the articulation of voice. Laughter is a voice without the qualities of voice. It is like the substance of voice, and even the subject of voice, which would disappear in their own coming into being.[224]

Here we encounter a different and more precise account of the structure of the event. Laughter is established and simultaneously torn apart by two counteracting forces. On one side, according to Nancy, it anchors being in a sphere of the deepest and most fundamental transcendental structure, a space of fundamental conclusions to which neither reason nor imagination have unimpeded access and which have to be accepted as a given of reality's structure. On the other side, this aspect of anchoring is undermined by sensuality understood in the simplest way: as an experience of physicality but also an empirical character of the laughter event that neutralizes not only the rule of the economy of being, but questions the very possibility of establishing language. At the intersection of these two spheres – transcendental and empirical – the event emerges.

Nancy talks about a kind of breathlessness that embodies the paradox of representation. The same happens in literature. The voice in *Not I* remains grounded – somewhat according to the dialectic of the dead letter and bracing phoneme[225] – in the centre of the text but also in the space of experience. The laughter and scream, situating themselves outside of oppositions, disable the power of conventions and the arbitrariness of language. They are located outside of language and also outside of the meaningful voice, in the sense that they do not obey the laws of meaning and representation and are not contained within the boundaries of language and the voice understood as a system or a presence (of sense) as an opportunity for "touch" – they contradict the powers of consciousness and language, assuming the necessity of direct contact and infinite mediation.[226]

However, laughter is not a realization of the pure sensuality that situates itself outside of a given network of meanings and does not constitute conditions for the possibility of what is sensible and is not a pre-initial criterion for the communicative properties of the voice. That disjunction indicates the extent to which Beckett's strategy of up keeping the poetics of ambiguity reaches, but also shows – brought

224   Nancy J.-L., Op. cit., p. 733.
225   See Derrida J., *De la grammatologie,* Paris 1967.
226   See Derrida J., *Le toucher, Jean-Luc Nancy,* Paris 2000.

to its limit – the semantic capacity of laughter as an event and as a boundary. Nancy well-understood the kind of boundary with which we are concerned. It is impossible to indicate the path of laughter because, in the moment it appears, it distorts the structure of language and creates new effects. The meanings of words that have been previously established (or even stabilized for a brief moment) become malleable and susceptible to the anarchic framework of laughter. Laughter situates itself in an unmarked sphere between the semantic potentiality of language and the reality of its actualization, or "colour," "modulation" and "articulation." It cannot be any of them without the rest but it can freely switch to any of the aforementioned positions that allows for its observation in the unobvious source of poetic language. This is how one should explain the final sentence from the quoted excerpt of Nancy's work: laughter residing outside of oppositions does not undergo conceptualization, even though – as an event – it changes the structure and semantics of the expression. Through its own, unmarked and aporetic character that is revealed simultaneously in two equal and contradictory possible forms of presence – the empirical and transcendental – it becomes a symptom of the mortality of language that marks the narration of the drama.

Laughter does not constitute a kind of liberating verbal energy that neutralizes the coming of death, but reversibly: it begins – along with its every appearance – a process of the degradation of language that is incapable of revealing anything anymore. It begins the process of erasing traces of the subjectivity as well; traces that in *Not I* gradually disappear between the folds of neurotic repetitions and in the mad rhythm of the expression. But such a radical method in which the moments of inhuman laughter constitute a turning point seem to be the only accessible way of saving the possibility of articulation. This occurs at the moment when laughter creates a false impression of beginning. This linguistic effect is – as Nancy metaphorically repeats after Baudelaire – an explosion of the poem, or the source of a freed language, a mad speech of the Mouth creating – through idiosyncratic recurring motifs – a single, believable epistemological poem about the consciousness of a singular existence.

Hence, laughter allows for the illusion of the beginning and creates the effect of an existential reality. In that context, the question of voice remains incredibly important; a voice that seemingly constitutes a foundation for all the forms of presence and in reality turns out to be a sign of its negation. Laughter, that is located somewhat on the doorstep of the voice, on the borderline of a verbal meaning and physical nonsense, results in silence and exposes the subject to the actions of the event. Let us observe, however, that despite the incredibly precise assignment of places in which laughter is supposed to appear within the structure of the drama, it is its structure that results in all the identifying traces of subjectivity becoming phantasmal. In other words, the power of narration forces the Mouth to laugh, but it remains an autonomous force, breaking up the identity of the main protagonist telling the story; a force deconstructing the coherence of the narration itself. Finally, it neutralizes the relationship between the Mouth, the heroine and the reconstructed story.

In that way, Beckett strengthens – the already multi-dimensional – paradox of the event that not only becomes a trigger for the transformation of existence but, more importantly, demonstrates the inability of exiting the given ontological and cognitive situation. Laughter – which is obvious – is not subordinated to epistemological or cognitive powers and escapes individual consciousness that remains helpless against its implosion. Looking at the event of laughter through the categories of being is no longer transparent. Situating itself at the edge of language, it forces consciousness to be silent even though, simultaneously, it seems to be a pure effect of "work" at the borderline. Laughter – according to Beckett – is not entirely spontaneous, hence sensual and random, but it likewise does not result from a precise plan designed by consciousness; a consciousness that brings speech to a moment of exhaustion only to find a new source of language, a new cause for a continuation of the efforts of articulation.

In that sense, *Not I* is a drama about the creation of poetry, about the birth of a new language in which laughter constitutes a final destination, but also a point from which another stage of consciousness's work can begin, trying to clash with that which is inexpressible. By questioning the order of representation, Beckett demonstrates the inevitable ill-timing of all speech: impure at its source, distorted, and presenting a pre-established separation of words and objects. The radical character of the event is based on the fact that it illustrates not only the insurmountable conventionality of language and the limitations of consciousness, but also the phantasmal character of every beginning, of every source of sense. For this reason, Beckett arrives at the mechanism ruling poetry understood as an energy of invention. Simultaneously, the same energy reveals the incoherence of language from which it derives its strength. This fundamental gap in the womb of identity (the heteronomy of language is a condition for that which is different, new and external to language) of poetic idiom was observed by Derrida in his reflections on Paul Valéry:

> The spontaneous can emerge as the pure initiallity of the event only on the condition that is does not present itself, on the condition of this inconceivable and irrelevable passivity in which nothing can present itself to itself. Here we are in need of a paradoxical logic of the even as a source which cannot present itself, happen to itself. The value of the event is perhaps indissociable from that of presence; it remains rigorously incompatible with that of self-presence.[227]

---

227 Derrida J., "Qual Quelle: Valéry's Sources," in *Margins of Philosophy,* Op. cit., pp. 296-297.

The phantasm of the beginning of the event is extremely important for understanding the vision of the subject in Beckett's works. First, it clearly expresses one of the fundamental paradoxes powering his writing: the contradiction grounded in the mythologized, internal imperative of representation conjoined with a prior absolutization of its impossibility. Second, as Derrida established, it is impossible to extract the essence of an event from its structure. In other words, the logic of an event suggests two, mutually exclusive possibilities: either the event itself is a substance, or – as such – it remains outside of its essence. That is why laughter is not a signal of identity, a linguistic fulfilment or an existential opening, but it constitutes an expression of a temporal spread in the linguistic system, aiming for the fullness of poetic expression. Third, due to the understanding of laughter in the categories of an event one is able to understand the slogan of "not I," suggesting the fundamental impossibility of marking the identity of the subject. In a deeper sense – through an event – an agreement cannot be reached between empirical and transcendental orders. The subject will never attain complete unity, and the moments in which the speech of the Mouth dies out under the weight of experience opens the space of death. It is not difficult to surmise that the sensation of death described in the drama turns out to be a desire for the absolute homogeneity of the subject. It is a dream that one could describe, after Derrida, as a drive to actualize an "impossible to understand and neutralize passivity" reaching the borderline state between life and death. As a consequence, the power of laughter allows for a moment to remove the existence outside its bounds delineated by the memory and trauma. Through its own, untamed and enigmatic presence, the laughter flares up the effort of searching for the beginnings of poetry, releases the movement of the subject in the direction of an impenetrable absence toward which any kind of event has no access.

The Time Syncope

The events of laughter and screams fundamentally embody the obsession of the temporal determination of the reality written down in the drama and the imbalance of different experiences: consciousness, speech and the voice. In *Not I* we read:

> ...no idea what she was saying!... till she began trying to... delude herself... it was no hers at all... not her voice at all... and no doubt would have... vital she should... was on the point.... [NI, s. 409].

One could say that the quoted excerpt reveals the mechanism used by Beckett to constitute and undermine the power of consciousness. The moment of relaxation, of rest from the overwhelming, obtrusive thoughts and unwanted memories is illusory because in the place of that neurotic logic of presence, an order of a different rank is substituted; one in which what is most important is the relationship between the subject and language. The third person singular – through which the Mouth builds its narration, as well as creates a distance between itself and the heroine of its own story – reveals more clearly than in the "plot" parts of the drama a mechanism of unending corrections of the subject's position. That is how things look from the side of the grammar of the entire text. How about from the side of meaning?

Without a doubt, the central elements of the text are time and speech. The latter is subject to the power of time almost entirely. Time's passing, on the other hand, determines the shape of language, but also forces the one speaking to continuously test speech through attempts to bring it closer to moments of silence. Language is not used for communication or marking reality, it is used to mark the passing of time. The opposite is true as well: it is time that establishes the rhythm of speech, which becomes the only accessible, existent universe.

However, in this double-binding mechanism there is yet another goal at stake, something more radical. Language is – to use one of the key terms of Nancy – a "syncope"[228] of time. This means that through time one can achieve – as the etymology of a word "syncope" suggests – an effect of "cutting off" a particular existence. This shortening – as is easy to deduce – becomes turned toward language itself as well. The Mouth is not capable of stopping the voice external to itself that freely escapes the rule of consciousness it symbolizes. Their silence is equally illusory because in those empty places, pauses to take a breath are necessary, where the degenerative effects of time are most clearly revealed. That is why the speaking Mouth – according to Beckett's suggestions – has to express itself in a great rush in order to forget about the instability of meanings that are the only form of shelter for this isolated existence; finally, in order to secure itself from a confrontation with the true, not phantasmal, end – a sphere in which any kind of a sign, even in the form of graphic suspension (a hyphen at the end of the work), has no right to appear.

A short-lived but intense laughter seems justified, in terms of both the compositional and philosophical perspective. On the one hand, the event anticipates the coming of death and becomes an attempt to tame it. On the other hand, by placing language inside its borderline form, the event incarnates that which escapes the power of meaning:

> But only something which can disappear at any moment, can also appear. Only the disappearance of presence makes up the offer and give the surprise of presence. Only death gives to existence the "inexpressible gracefulness" (better than the "loveliness" of the translation) of simply coming in(to) presence. Behind the red and white mouth, or as the very wideness of the mouth, as its indefinite and repetitive aperture, the

---

228   See Nancy J.-L., *Discours de la syncope. Logodaedalus*, Paris 1976.

throat of death bursts into laughter: coming forth from behind any presence, and going beyond any presence. The laughter of presence – which is never to be, itself, but only to be infinitely offered in its own finitude.[229]

The concern is with the same phenomenon of speaking that the moving Mouth embodies. In the stage productions of Beckett's drama, this particular theme is displayed almost entirely and in a plain sight, even though it is not unambiguous. The Mouth – as I have remarked before – constitutes a borderline separating several contradictory, albeit stubbornly persistent categories, but it is also a screen[230] that distorts the distinction between interior and exterior and the gap through which an obscure reality hidden in the depths of the face comes to the surface. Both figures used by Nancy show – using different but equally strong terms – the ambiguous character of laughter as a borderline event/experience. Laughter reveals the absence of its own source but also the absence of any base for identity; it reveals itself only as an illusion. It does not bring relief, nor does it grant any profit, as if it existed not only outside a stable essence but also outside of any kind of goal or order. It focuses the entirety of attention on itself, even though it does not undergo any form of conceptualization. It appears as an event, which means that it appears suddenly and brings results impossible to foresee. That is why the variations between different productions of *Not I* can be seen most vividly during scenes of laughter and screaming. Even though we anticipate their arrival[231] but the strength of the individual production makes it impossible to plan the final results that inform the interpretation of the entire play. This performative aspect of the laughter and scream should be understood not only through the prism of theatre, but also philosophy. They become synonyms of the temporal instability of existence, as well as a glimmering desire to express this condition fully.

---

229 Nancy J-L., "Wild Laughter in the Throat of Death," Op. cit., p.730.

230 On understanding the category of a "screen" see Buci-Glucksmann Ch., *La folie du voir. De l'esthétique baroque*, Paris 1986, Buci-Glucksmann Ch., "La paradoxe du moderne: Tristesse et Beauté," in *L'enjeu du beau. Musique et Passion*, Paris 1992, p. 41.

231 If we know the drama beforehand, of course. The situation gets complicated, however, when – even without a prior acquaintance with the text – we watch the performance and for the first time encounter a moment in which the scream, that will be later repeated, resounds. The question remains open as to whether every act of laughter and screaming that follows is a repetition of the initial event or if it is a completely different event.

Nothingness and Game

No idea. [232]

– Samuel Beckett in conversation with Tom Gussow

Let us pose a question about the goal of laughter. Is it only a means of releasing the abundant energy created from the clash between different forces that pressure the subject? According to the traditional understanding, laughter is a reaction to an amusing situation or the spontaneous answer of an individual to the comical values inherent in an object or another man. In case of modern laughter, under the patronage of Kant and Baudelaire, its rule is beyond pragmatics and – paradoxically – beyond the sanction of personal existence.

In his *Critique of Judgment*, Kant performs an analysis of laughter by moving the weight of his interpretation from the affective character of laughter to the turning point and the diffusing of tension. Laughter becomes incredibly close in its essence to music, because just as a system of sounds – harmonically and melodically structured – it does not fulfil what it pronounces. Listening to music one is rousing his or her imagination and we enter into a game with it; a game that cannot have any conclusion – the sound reverberates, leaving the listener with nothing. Even though it is subject to the mathematical rigor of structure, music is a challenge posed to the intellect. Although it allows us to recognize the mechanism behind its creation, the intellect remains helpless in direct contact with music. It surrenders before laughter, but it is a defeat that constitutes an initial condition of its emergence. These three elements of laughter are bound together permanently and according to the laws of necessity: a free play of representations, an organic range of the action of intellectual powers, and emptiness as its final goal.

> Laughter is an affect resulting from the sudden transformation of a heightened expectation into nothing. This very transformation, which is certainly nothing enjoyable for the understanding, is nevertheless indirectly enjoyable and, for a moment, very lively.[233]

Kant's conclusions could be interpreted in several ways. Each way sheds light on the phenomenon of laughter from a different angle. From our perspective, the interpretation of its inherent inability to be tamed is the most interesting. Although Kant proposes many examples of concrete situations, in the latter part of his reflection, his investigation meanders toward ever more subtle tracks, but

---

232 Gussow T., *Conversations with and about Beckett*, Op. cit., p. 43.

233 Kant I., *Critique of the Power of Judgment*, translated by James Creed Meredith, Cambridge 2001, p. 209. See also, Kant I., *Anthropology from a Pragmatic Point of View*, edited by Robert B. Louden, Manfred Kuehn, Cambridge 2006, section 79.

is unable to provide and explain the reasons for laughter, nor the possible benefits for an individual surrendering to it. This seems reasonable, if we accept the radical separation of the subjective and objective orders in his critical philosophy. Laughter does not fall under the auspices of the intellect simply because it constitutes a specific kind of affect, but mostly because the subject, with the help of the work of reason, is not able to turn it into an object. Even though Kant observed the heteronomic character of laughter, to preserve his systematic classification he moved it to the level of pure sensuality. In the meantime, such an attempt to override the problem through the procedure of delegating laughter into the realms empiricism does not bring any result. It is suggested already by the very definition formulated by Kant in which the unplanned – or so it seems – contamination of transcendental and empirical orders takes place. This confusion can be observed already in the first sentence, in which the claim about the source that is not a source is eventually expressed. We do not know what the "heightened expectation" is and in what way it could constitute a source of laughter. Kant proposes only part of a solution, somewhat unclear, and refers back to the authority of time and substance and claims that laughter is a form of violent metamorphosis. He changes the status of being through the transposition of the state ("heightened expectation" turns into "nothingness") that constitutes a transformation of substance at the same time (like in poetry).[234] It is not clear, however, how we should understand the state preceding the outburst of laughter. It suggests a physical order that excludes any form of reflection, but at the same time one cannot treat it as a symptom of sensuality because the final result it brings is nothingness.

The second sentence of Kant's definition seems only a more precise version of the thesis contained in the first. He claims that laughter as such, autonomous and affective, cannot constitute for the intellect any form of satisfaction, just so he can admit immediately that his mediation between two different dispositions of the individual appears as mediation that, in effect, could bring a kind of satisfaction that is harmless for the brain. Regardless of how subtly Kant would like to neutralize the revolutionary characteristics of laughter, one can clearly see the contradictions impossible to overcome within the discourse that – in short – allow for the description of laughter following the pattern of disjunction: it is not entirely sensual, nor completely independent from the intellect.

---

234 Brodski J., *List do Horacego* in the collection, *Pochwała nudy*, translated by Stanisław Barańczak, Kraków 1996, pp. 275-276. This is where the Russian poet interprets metamorphosis as a fundamental characteristic of poetic language. Brodsky speaks clearly about rhymes but the substitution of "one thing for another" that without a change of its existential status could take place only in poetic speech is concerned also with the rule of a condensed relationship between affect, language, and nothingness in Beckett.

In Kant's critical dictionary, laughter was supposed to be an affective result of a game between the elements from separate areas of reality. The result of the game – nothingness – is at the same time a final destination that laughter arrives at on its, meticulously described, trajectory. It is not enough, however, to say that we are dealing with a refreshing release of the tension for a person's benefit, with an expulsion of gathered energy while awaiting the event. Laughter dissolves into nothingness, which, from the perspective of aesthetics based on the project of critical philosophy has to constitute a positive solution. From the perspective of laughter as ambiguous sign of being, however, the question seems a little more complicated.

Laughter discovers its purpose in nothingness. Most fundamentally, it means that it eventually ends and that the – previously analyzed – disappearing ontological feature ceases to be a fundamental phenomenon of being. However, one could also come up with more radical consequences for what Kant claimed and conclude that the only real end to the unrestricted game of the aesthetic faculties, founded on the phantasms of pure and designed rules of contemplation turned out to be an empty, unimaginable negativity. For Kant, laughter has always been a phenomenon, the properties of which situated themselves between the mechanics of the body and the rituals of its cognitive powers. However, when he attempted to think through the radical, although not entirely disclosed, intuition of its negative goal, laughter did not simply serve as a borderline or subversive element against the stability of the critical mind. Laughter raised a question about its own expressibility in experience, not simply in writing.

This is why Kant's uncertainties seem plausible. After engaging the dual apparatus of subjective-objective metaphysics, he perhaps recognized the helplessness of his own model in the face of the event. From yet another perspective, this critical dichotomy allows for the disclosure of laughter in its relation to nothingness. As an event that is deprived of essence, it does not possess its own source, or a clear target. Its sole fate is to undermine itself, erasing the trace of its own existence. If, as Nancy claims following Baudelaire, the opened mouth, frozen in the figure of laughter is a sign of the most developed access to what is real, or the adjacency of existence to death. The shimmering existence of laughter itself materializes the insurmountable paradox of its presence. The more intensely and the longer it lasts the stronger it marks the negative aspect of being. Real laughter does not belong to concrete subjectivity but constitutes an incarnation of the movement destabilizing identity – it is always some unidentified individuality that laughs, not some "not I."

In Beckett's drama the Mouth laughs only four times, but it is precisely this scarcity of laughter that becomes important. First, one sees the grimace and then hears the spasmodic sound of an ungraspable tone, thrown into the projected space (outside of the stage and outside of the text). Although the heroine of the narrative often freezes, staring into a fixed point, the laughter, directed by the autonomous bands of sounds and not the power of gaze, creates the effect of an extreme usage of language (both on the page and stage). Distinct from the story in which there are no chances for the appearance of a meaningful gesture that could disturb the mimetic illusion of the realness[235] that accompanies the narrative, laughter marks the radical and only way possible to reach registers of a sterile emptiness that is an effect of the "end of all things": language, imagination, stage, reason and finally – life.

Reversed Theology

> The Devil's laughter has the energy of destruction within it, with crashing crockery and collapsing walls, and evil laughter above the debris. In positive ecstatic laughter, by contrast, the energy of a perplexed affirmation is at play; in spite of its wildness, it sounds contemplative, celebratory. [..] The devil's energy is the energy that laughs until the others fall silent. [236]
>
> – Peter Sloterdijk

The second of the aforementioned officials of modern laughter is Baudelaire.[237] In an indirect way, his reflection on the subject has been revealed by Nancy's analysis mentioned earlier in the text. The fullest and the most discursively

---

235 See Nycz R., "Tezy o mimetyczności," in *Tekstowy świat. Poststrukturalizm a wiedza o literaturze*, Kraków 2000 and Barthes R., "L`effet de réel," in *Le bruissement de la langue. Essais critiques IV*, Paris 1984.

236 Sloterdijk P., *Critique of Cynical Reason,* translated by Michael Eldred, Minneapolis 1988, p. 144

237 Next to, of course, Nietzsche. Without going into extremely complex issue here I would like to send the reader back to the most important book on the issue, *Beyond Good and Evil* where we read: "We are the first age to be educated *in puncto* of 'costumes,' I mean of moral, articles of faith, artistic tastes, and religions, and prepared as no age has ever been for a carnival in the grand style, for the most spiritually carnivalesque laughter and high spirits, for the transcendental heights of the highest inanity and Aristophanean world mockery. Perhaps it's that we still discover a realm of our *invention* here, a realm where we can still be original too, as parodists of world history or buffoons of God, or something like that, – perhaps it's that, when nothing else from today has a future, our *laughter* is the one thing that does!" Nietzsche F., *Beyond Good and Evil*, translated by Walter Kaufmann, Cambridge 2010, p. 114. Nietzschean line of thinking about laughter finds its conclusion in Bataille's reflection: "Man ceasing – at the limit of laughter – to want to be everything and wanting in the end to be what he is, imperfect, incomplete, good – if he can be, up to moments of cruelty; and lucid… to the point of dying blind." Bataille G., *Inner Experience,* translated by Stuart Kendall, Albany 2014, p. 32.

expressive interpretation of that category Baudelaire provided in his essay entitled "On the Essence of Laughter." In his text, Baudelaire admits that laughter remains an obsessive theme for him, which in and of itself seems important. As his goal, he recognizes not so much the necessity to grasp the rules guiding laughter within the arts, or even discovering its essence, but rather revealing irreducible attitudes. In other words, he possess a question about the pre-beginning, looks for the *arché* of laughter, which leads to questioning which representation of it would properly inscribe it in the space of aesthetic categories. Laughter is not a purely positive sensuality. It is derived from reversing the divine version of reality. It is born in the moment in which the metaphysical sanction becomes recognized as insufficient because it turns out to be an illusory and oppressive:

> In the eyes of Him who knows and can do all things, the comic does not exist. And yet the Incarnate Word did know anger; he even knew tears. [...] If we are willing to adopt the orthodox standpoint, it is certain that human laughter is intimately connected with the accident of an ancient fall, of a physical and moral degradation. Laughter and grief express themselves through the organs that have the control and the knowledge of good and evil, the eyes and mouth. [...] From the standpoint of my Christian philosopher, the laughter of his lips is a sign of as great a state of corruption as the tears in his eyes. God, who desired to multiply his own image, did not place lion's teeth in man's mouth – but man bites with his laughter; nor did He place, in man's eyes, all the fascinating duplicity of the serpent – but man seduces with his tears. And pray observe that it is also with his tears that man washes away man's sorrows, that it is with laughter that he sometimes softens man's heart, and draws it closer; for the phenomena produced by the Fall will become means of redemption.[238]

The interpretation presented by Baudelaire is almost too revealing. Laughter does not constitute an element in the hierarchy of beings because it is not at all important to ask a question about its ontological status, it is not worth investing time in investigating the ways in which it manifests itself. The forgoing of metaphysical ground turns out to be of importance. Baudelaire interprets this in openly epistemological categories. The figure of a mythical fall does not exclusively serve the purpose of generating the moral or ethical sanction that would be, theoretically, a substitute for a full life, but describes an existence immersed in a deep lack of knowledge. Baudelaire cannot situate his human abilities within the sphere of consciousness because it constitutes one more example of the total existential degradation of man. In its place, unexpectedly, the body appears; a body which justifies a singular existence – these are eyes and a mouth that turns out to be the only, dense with meanings, a space in which the ethical drama of an individual

---

238   Baudelaire Ch., "Of the Essence of Laughter, and generally of the Comic in the Plastic Arts," in *Selected Writings on Art and Artists,* translated by P. E. Charvet, Cambridge 1981, pp. 142-143.

takes place. Laughter – paradoxically – transforms from the ungraspable affect into an important element of a confrontation with God.

As an obvious figure of laughter, the Mouth illustrates yet another aspect, more important than its relation to religion. Baudelaire claims that the poet combines in one series both power and ethical knowledge, as well as the possibility of recognizing reality. Hence, the cognitive perspective is not innocent but burdened with the task of ordering the world. Laughter becomes the existential disposition of an individual not because it frees the interior from the oppression of the external world and its evils, but because it establishes a strategic relationship between cognition and the orders of the world. Laughter cannot be anything spontaneous in such a configuration, it cannot become proof of authenticity and directness, but on the contrary: it turns out to be the embodiment of an evil illusion that successfully blocks access to true reality, existing before and beyond language. In that way, epistemological and metaphysical perspectives meet. Laughter finds itself in an unending movement between the two: sometimes it is a handy cognitive tool and sometimes it reveals itself as a memory of a mythical order of unity between the word and the object; as a souvenir after the divine order in which no ethical form was necessary.

This reserved and "preliminary" diagnosis concerned the properties of laughter from the perspective of the critique of the aesthetic experience do not change the fact that Baudelaire is headed toward radical conclusions. When he claims that "the phenomena produced by the Fall will become means of redemption," he not only points to irony as a mechanism of establishing and legitimizing laughter, but shows the condition of dramatic subjectivity, torn between longing for infinity and the dream of salvation in the face of empty transcendence. Quite obviously, both these orders cannot be reconciled: divine unity and the necessity for emancipation split within the totality of an individual experience. In their respective contexts, laughter could be interpreted in two ways, as different modalities of existence. On the one hand, laughter is a symptom of losing one's balance, of the deprivation of identity and the despair resulting from the confusion of cognitive and ethical orders. On the other hand, it opens a path for escaping the limitations of one's own condition; it constitutes a "means of redemption" in a secularized, emancipatory version.[239]

---

239 Adorno writes: "In the lyric poem the subject negates both his naked, isolated opposition to society as his mere functioning within rationally organized society. But as organized society's ascendancy over the individual grows, the situation of lyric art becomes more precarious. The work of Baudelaire was the first to register this, in refusing to stop at the individual's suffering. Rather (an extreme consequence of European world-weariness), it went beyond the suffering of the individual and accused the entire modern epoch itself of being antilyrical, and by means of heroically stylized language, it hammered out of this

This is characteristic for the entire modern formation of a dynamic clash between despairing subjectivity and an absent, although continuously postulated by the subject, "divine" objectivity. Beckett seems to push this condition to its ultimate consequences. As in Baudelaire's work, the Mouth in *Not I*, as a metaphor of the boundary of presence and absence, constitutes an axis around which circulates sense and nonsense. Also, there is an exchange of values of what is individual and what is total. However, in case of Beckett there is no longer remains hope or the autonomous power of the subject, as Baudelaire sought to sustain.[240] In the figure of the Mouth, attempting to create a kind of continuous narrative, Beckett shows not only the uselessness of such modernist hope, but criticizes the very justification of the autonomy of a subject that, can identify metaphysics as a collection of representations of a restricted mind. Let us observe that in *Not I* laughter appears at moments when the Mouth is forced – through the spontaneous energy of language – to express an opinion about God. But the phrases do not create a cycle of sarcastic gestures that would prove a rejection of all metaphysical perspectives. First and foremost, Beckett demonstrates the fall of the idea of consciousness. He describes an existence, building a shelter in words, which only arrives at a dispossessing madness and chaos of nonsense; an existence which, while searching for a definite foundation for the simplest act of thought brings closer its only possible form: residing in the single image of the catastrophe of solipsism.[241] If, in the case of Baudelaire, one can speak of a reversed and negative theology, then in Beckett's writing one is confronted by a confirmation of negativity,[242] often deploying religious idiom. This affirmation is a difficult process of translating the category of absence into the language poetry, a point which is fundamental for Beckett's imagination and ontology. That is exactly what happens in the fragment in which the Mouth talks about the torment of thinking and shows its inability to ground itself in metaphysics:

> sudden flash... brought up as if she had been to believe... with other waifs... in a merciful.. [Brief laugh.]...God...[Good laugh.]... first thought was ... oh long after...

accusation the sparks of genuine poetry." Adorno T. W., "On Lyric Poetry and Society," in *Notes to Literature*, vol. 1, New York 1991.

240   This aspect receives its most incisive treatment in the work of Walter Benjamin. See Benjamin W., *Charles Baudelaire. Ein Lyriker im Zeitalter des Hochkapitalismus*, Berlin 1969.

241   As Georges Poulet proves, this is solipsism brought to the extreme. Beckett's protagonists cannot confirm their own identity inside of the illusions they create, but expose themselves to what is completely deprived of any form of representation, or rather: they desire to find themselves in the pure emptiness of representation, an absence undisturbed by any image. See G. Poulet, *Myśl nieokreślona*, Op. cit., pp. 277-278.

242   See "Samuel Beckett Today/Aujourd'hui" (*Beckett and Religion/Aesthetics /Politics*) 2000 no. 9.

sudden flash... she was being punished... for her sins... a number of which then... further proof if proof was needed... flashed through her mind... one after another... then dismissed as foolish... oh long after... this thought dismissed... as she suddenly realized... gradually realized... she was not suffering... imagine!... not suffering!... indeed could not remember... off-hand... when she suffered less... unless of course she was meant to be suffering... ha! Thought to be suffering... just as the odd time... in her life... when clearly intended to be having pleasure... she was in fact... having none... [NI, pp. 406-407].

Religious language is subjected to a categorical critique through the poetics of sarcasm in Beckett's work. Through the method of a linguistic ridicule taken from a system based on punishment and sin, he arrives at a state of insolvability on the level of consciousness, rather than on an axiological level. We do not know whether the illusory or certain character of cognition is granted primacy. It is enough to turn one's attention to highlighted formulas. Each of them points to an undefined form of priority, which in turn points to some – again not entirely clear – state of working consciousness. This aspect of a lack of definition continuously collaborates in Beckett's work with a decomposition of a clear metaphysical model that becomes compromised by its own means. This dialectical coupling shows that the actuality of reality has to be both permanently "assumed" and projected. This is so because not only it cannot find a justification for itself in experience (when the heroine mentions her failed sexual initiation) but also more importantly because it constitutes an imperative figure of what is external. There is no final sanction or permanent ground to which one could refer.

The failure of language is parallel to the intimate experience of an existential failure and laughter seems not so much a gesture of re-establishing the identity of a subject, but a symptom of its radical decomposition. It seems that such a radical questioning of religious language serves to undermine the permanent position of existence that takes form depending on where language is located: what it could possibly mean and what it could possibly communicate. Laughter not only cancels the claim to priority of all three dimensions (ontological, semantic and communicative) but also becomes the autonomous sphere of an event that – paradoxically – saves the sphere of accidental existence on its way to "annihilating" all orders of consciousness. Laughter, does not deprive us of a name (after all, we do not actually know the name of the heroine from the story of the anonymous Mouth), but constitutes the only path to its survival. How should we understand this antinomy? We should go back, once again, to Baudelaire's text.

Laughter is satanic; it is therefore profoundly human. In man it is the consequence of his idea of his own superiority; and in face, since laughter is essentially human it is essentially contradictory, that is to say it is at one and the same time a sign of infinite greatness and of infinite wretchedness, infinite wretchedness in relation to the absolute

being, of whom man has an inkling, infinite greatness in relation to the beasts. It is
from the constant clash of these two infinites that laughter flows.[243]

The anthropological vision of Baudelaire, in which laughter gains the position of
a power that determines the shape of the spiritual development of an individual,
establishes a clear direction for the interpretation of laughter – it is not external to the
man category (aesthetic, physiological) but a signal of its internal transformation.
Laughter, treated as an event of confrontation between "two infinities" allows for
the establishment of a hierarchy within the world surrounding the individual. It
can appear as far as the interiorisation of the subjective sensation created at the
point of contact that which is empirical and that which is transcendental, or that
which is material and metaphysical will take place.

None of these infinities exist in Beckett. Laughter is created mechanically,
or rather with the help of the authorial, clearly visible, interference in language.
However, a certain kind of automatisation and unintentionality reveals its one more
dimensions. If we were to follow Baudelaire's line of reasoning, then the laughter
in *Not I* would constitute the ultimate proof for the radical contradiction of the
possibility of subjectivity and would be an example of its complete annihilation
within the folds of language and perdition pronounced throughout the entire
monologue: neither the divine, which is ridiculed, nor the human, because the
heroine of the story – speaking through the Mouth – is not able to state anything
reasonable about the world. Where is the place for the dramatic dimension of an
experience and the event of laughter that is announced by the very initial phrases
of the text?

The issue – I believe – is contained within the most fundamental authorial
epistemological choice that is prior to the ontological dimension of the reality
visible in the work. The subject undergoes a cognitive reduction and becomes an
almost isolated centre of the experiment of consciousness, the purpose of which
is to purify the subject from what is accidental to the greatest extent possible.
However, instead of discovering the essence of consciousness, its only effect turns
out to be disintegration under the push of the memory of a language that cannot
be cleansed from what is accidental. In other words, the voice of consciousness,
despite pretenses about being immersed in an absolute loneliness, turns out to be
heteronomic and built of various elements extracted from memory.

In *Not I*, consciousness constitutes a centre of the world. However, it is
not consciousness that has failed, or the immersion in the power of repetition
that erases subjectivity – such that it disappears, dispersed among the traces of
language, fragments of images of unknown origin. It does not find an opportunity
for support on any side: in metaphysics or the realm of the sensual. By cancelling

---

243   Baudelaire Ch., Op. cit., p. 148.

both spheres it moves the subject – through the experience of laughter – to a more rudimentary level of confrontation with what is negative. In this movement, Beckett reveals the double property of laughter that, while being an event, can also hold within itself (just like in the reaction of the Mouth to the word of God) the echoes of a mythical clash between the two infinities about which Baudelaire wrote.

As I have mentioned before, laughter in *Not I* is connected with examining the sources of existence, as well as the birth of consciousness. The very beginning of the text touches upon that very theme. It constitutes a kind of summoning to life through language. That is also where the direct reasons for the Mouth's laughter are located. The "sudden epiphany" is concerned with recognizing the redundancy of one's own name, but it is also a testimony of a cognitive intuition. The figure of a girl, somewhat organically, justifies laughter by earning the rank of neutrality behind which there is the misery of an individual consciousness unable to recognize itself. From that point of view it is a pseudo-anonymous laughter, a supplementary and figurative laughter that constitutes the sign of the woman's projection that helplessly attempts to communicate the story of her own birth (literally, as well as the birth of her own language). On the one hand, the effort of consciousness creates an illusion of access to the lost directedness of experience, on the other – it exaggerates the phantasmal character of that project. It is hard to establish what the properties of the laughing voice really are or ought to be. It belongs to the child protagonist of the text, at the same time being a projection of the Mouth itself. Everything in *Not I* seems to serve the collapse of the myth of intentionality – the girl is not on stage in a real sense; she exists only in the space of the story. The Mouth, on the other hand, is a physical and narrative instance, but the stories become their own signs. Laughter as a longing for innocence is illusory because at the core disturbed, and tied with the persistent potentiality of the voice.

> The laughter of children is like the blossoming of a flower. It is the joy of receiving, the joy of breathing, the joy of confiding, the joy of contemplating, of living, of growing up. It is like the joy of a plant. And so, generally speaking, its manifestation is rather the smile, something analogous to the wagging tail in a dog or the purring of cats. And yet, do not forget that if the laughter of children may, after all is said and done, be distinguished from the outward signs of animal contentment, the reason is the this laughter is not entirely devoid of ambition, and that is as it should be, in mini-men or in other words Satans of early growth.[244]

In *Not I*, the vagueness of laughter is based on the irreducible, double character of its nature described by Baudelaire. On the one side, it is retrospectively assigned to a little girl, on the other – it is "performed" in a way by the Mouth that decides

---

244   Ibid., p. 151.

about the dimensions of the world available on stage and in the text. In that way, the aspect of passivity appears in the spontaneity of a bodily reaction, as well as an element of its control: a moment of realizing to oneself one's own separateness that, in the language of Baudelaire's theology, is connected with closely to the loss of the unquestionable rule of reality. That is why the child's laughter, combining naturalness and fiction, innocence and recognition of a tragic nature, leads toward the ambivalence of the very structure of an event that does not bring a final solution. It leaves a trace within language, proof of which can be found in the form of the following part of the monologue delivered by the Mouth after the act of laughter.

What is the final result of laughter? Is there any linguistic form that could bring back the hope for uniting words and object? And, what follows, would reviving that allow for the construction of a real history of existence in language? Or, on the contrary, is it the case that the Mouth that will speak, as long as there will be a gap between language and the event? It seems that the only yield foreseeable in this scenario would be consciousness of antinomy, a notional ungraspable quality of the event and of the presence of experience that – paradoxically – announces, through a recurring act of postponing, the coming of absence and the rule of "that, which is the worst." Laughter, without being contained fully in consciousness or in the empirical can reach the form of a literary absolute,[245] which means that it creates the linguistic effect, momentary and utopian, of a complete freedom of the subject. Understood in that way, the antinomian character of laughter in *Not I* situates itself closely to the general conclusions presented by Baudelaire on the example of E.T.A. Hoffmann's work:

> In order for the comic, in other words an emanation, an explosion, an emergence of the comic, to exist, there must be two beings in the presence of each other […]. I submit that when Hoffmann engenders absolute comic he is surely aware of the fact; but, equally, he knows that the essence of this type of comic is to appear to be unaware of oneself and to instil in the spectator, or rather the reader, the feeling of joy at his own superiority and the joy of man's superiority over nature. Artists create the comic; having studied and brought together the elements of the comic, they know that such and such a creature is comic, and that he is comic only on condition that he is unaware of his own nature; just as, by an inverse law, the artist is an artist only on condition that he is dual and that he is ignorant of none of the phenomena of his dual nature.[246]

Hence, it is not all about evoking a temporary effect on the borderline of language that, at the same time, is an event and its own, indefinable although present being, but rather about grasping consciousness in the moment of it losing its own

---

245 The category of a "literary absolute" I understand the same way it has been presented in the work: Lacoue-Labarthe Ph., Nancy J.-L., *L`Absolu littéraire. Théorie de la littérature du romantisme allemand*, Paris 1978.
246 Baudelaire Ch., Op. cit., pp. 160-161.

prerogatives and allowing it to become that which is incredible and unsuspected. A complete liberation of laughter, its overflowing and proliferation, are possible under the condition of the resignation of a subject from performing a meta-reflexive gesture. Individual consciousness can achieve full self-knowledge only at the price of questioning itself. The absolute comical character assumes a form that is not simply comprehensible in amusement, but of an ironic game that takes place inside subjective consciousness. It has to not only design the negation of a prior self-knowledge in order to re-enact the show for others, but more importantly, it has to lead consciousness to the absolute boundary of that which could be thought. Laughter is not a symptom of the decline of reason, nor of its victory. It is an event, or rather it is the very energy created as a result of a confrontation of working consciousness with what is inexpressible. This last element in Beckett's play takes up different forms: it can be the figure of a compromised but "merciful God," or at the same time be connected with a possibility of expressing his name; it can be a figure of the unquestionable sanction of the mind, but also a sign of its boundaries.[247] In Beckett's works, laughter constitutes a reaction of consciousness to a meeting with what is inexpressible without allowing subjectivity to stop in its constant shift between the poles of the "nonsense" of appearing thoughts and the "sudden epiphanies" that will become – possibly – epiphany-like forms of experiencing what is negative.

---

247   See Howard P., "Not Mercies/Not I", *Samuel Beckett Today/Aujourd'hui* 1990, no 2.

Chapter Three
Objective Suffering

Mad Moment

Laughter and screams constitute two modalities of the event that – as I am trying to prove – are the most important elements around which the sense of Beckett's works is organized. So far, I have been considering the ontological and epistemological character of his works. Now, it is time to look at its anthropological dimension as revealed by the event. The question seems extremely complicated because, starting with the title, Beckett effectively sabotages all forms of subjectival cohesiveness. The paradox is built on a systematic breaking of the separate character of the individual, a process which is confirmed by the poetics of the text for the sake of the impersonal form of language and accompanied by an attempt to tell a story about a particular existence. Beckett juxtaposes and confronts both conscious and existential possibilities of subjectivity. While the first is concerned with the process of constituting individuality, based on the change in the position of subjectivity when confronted with the event, the second case is about representing the experience of a particular degree of intensity. In other words, the transfer from the event to experience is equivalent to the change of perspective from the epistemological-ontological to the existential. *Not I* could be read as a recording of an experience of existence, a figure that illustrates its innate characteristics: exposition, openness and – what is my primary interest – ecstasy.[248] I am interested in its philosophical, rather than religious-mystical, interpretation. George Bataille has provided one of the most interesting modern interpretations of the concept. Let us focus on his work for just a moment, as it provides tools thanks to which this very aspect will be far more visible in Beckett's drama.

In several places in his work, Bataille grasps a number of directions that the interpretation of ecstasy might take. The most important questions are concerned with its guiding principle, which should be interpreted as a tautological definition of existence. On the level of the structure there is no difference between existence and ecstasy – both mark steps of the individual beyond their own given condition. Of course, in the formulation of this crossing the experience of ecstasy is embedded with a double aspect. On the one hand it is a figure of the existence exiting beyond its accessible sphere, on the other – an excessive gesture aimed against it, illustrating the surplus that shatters its structure. This very gesture of crossing

---

248   From Kelly K., "The Orphic Mouth in 'Not I'," *Journal of Beckett Studies* 1980, no. 6.

is not motivated, however, by the normative order of knowledge or an order of consciousness. It assumes a prior total lack of consciousness, beyond recognition, and a barrier constituted by (hinted at by the system of a symbolic imagination) the terror of a final situation. As a consequence, the borderline of the ecstasy is established by the fear of death. Simultaneously, being an embodiment of the irreducible rule of reality, the borderline established by it becomes a source of desire that lies at the bottom of the phantasm of excess (as surplus and crossing). In the "Preface to Madame Edwards" Bataille writes:

> To reach the point of ecstasy, the moment when we lose ourselves in the joys of the flesh, we must always posit an immediate limit to this joy: this limit is horror. Not only the suffering of others but also my own suffering, pushing me to the moment when my horror arouses me, can help me reach the state where joy slides into delirium; but then there is no form of revulsion whose affinity with desire I do not perceive. Not that horror is never confused with attraction; but if it cannot inhibit or destroy it, horror increases the attraction. Equally, danger typically paralyses us; but when it lacks the power to do so, danger excites our desire. We never reach ecstasy except when, however remotely, we are faced with the prospect of death, with the prospect of what destroys us.[249]

And in *Les Larmes d'Eros* [*The Tears of Eros*] he almost directly explains what the stakes in the game between the subject and death actually are:

> It is nonetheless true that the animal, the ape, whose sensuality at times becomes exacerbated, knows nothing of eroticism. And this is precisely because it lacks all knowledge of death. To the contrary, it is because we are human and live in the somber perspective of death that we know this exacerbated violence of eroticism.[250]

The fear of death, directly connected to the knowledge of mortality for Bataille, forces the individual into a constant extension of the dream of transgressing one's own condition. Ecstasy is preceded by the state of permanent tension of the will and consciousness, but it is not a deciding factor in the end. The moment of crossing seems to be impossible to pin down, unwilling to surrender to the laws of language. Differently than in transgression, where the dialectical feedback between the boundary and the system, between the normal and the pathological and, finally, between inexpressible experience and a principle of expressiveness is necessary. Existence in ecstasy grants the voice of death to itself. Somewhat voluntarily, it gives itself away to death's mercy, depriving itself from its own, self-chosen condition but also awaiting its new form. That is precisely that "mad moment" that Bataille writes about and in which the fullness of existential

---

249 Bataille G., "A Preface to 'Madame Edwards'," in *Erotism,* translated by Mary Dalwood, San Franscisco 1986.
250 Bataille G., *Les larmes d'Eros*, Paris 1971, p. 62. *The Tears of Eros*, translated by Peter Connor, San Franscisco 2001. p. 33.

ambivalence becomes revealed: death, or the necessity of disappearing, turns out to be simultaneous with the imperative of holding down individual autonomy.

This internal imperative also establishes one of the possible perspectives for reading Beckett's works. The act of speech, on the one hand, produces an effect of presence and a summons or thematises death directly. On the other hand, it constitutes only a form in which one could contain an existence that searches for the determinants of reality. In other words, the language resounding through the Mouth is independent from the experience to a certain degree, creating the general conditions in which it can take place. The events of laughter and screaming focus in themselves both these characteristics of antinomy: they are a point of particular tension, a point in which a totality is revealed, along with the indivisibility of a sense against which the individual remains helpless. Ecstasy also constitutes a moment in which its very rule is revealed, or the realization of both radically different possibilities of existence taking place: absolute identity and a complete heteronomy. Between these two existential poles, there is no room for negotiations and that is why the narrative lead by the Mouth comes closer to the one or the other, ultimately identifying with neither. The only moments of identification are the moments of laughter and screams, moments that push the existence represented by the Mouth from the space of language toward that which is unexpected and radically temporal. In such moments, Beckett's poetics of insolvability reaches its climax but also its temporary form of a solution, if only for a moment – through the coming of the event – it cancels the continuing oscillation between two different interpretations of the subject's speech (referential or autotelic). The desires that constitute a subject are extinguished: both one that orders a continuous search for references to the real, as well as desire based on the final legitimization of the act of consciousness.

The problem is not based on the real cancelation of contradictions, their ultimate synthesis, but on the gesture of going beyond these oppositions. That is why Bataille's diagnosis concerning the subject in a state of ecstasy seems understandable[251]:

> Being is given to us in an unbearable surpassing of being, no less unbearable than death. But since, in death, being is taken away from us at the same time that it is given, we must search for it in the feeling of death, in those unbearable moments when, no longer being within us except through an excess of being, it seems that we are dying, and the fullness of our horror coincides with the fullness of our joy. Even thought

---

251   In one of his seminal works, he frames the relationship between the subject and its dependence upon death: "Thus as the object of its ecstasy, time responds to the ecstatic fever of the self-that-dies: for in the same way as time, the self-that-dies is pure change and neither the one nor the other has real existence." Bataille G., *Inner Experience*, translated by Stuart Kendall, Albany 2014, p. 77.

(reflection) only ends with its own excess. What, beyond the representation of excess, does truth signify if we do not see what exceeds the possibilities of seeing, what it is unbearable to see – just as, in ecstasy, it is impossible to attain pleasure? What if we do not think that which exceeds the possibilities of thought?[252]

Thought obtains its rank of importance only when we attempt to rethink what remains beyond the process of thinking. This is not to suggest that in the act of crossing, true reality, unfiltered by language, is revealed to us, nor are we dealing with the fact that language, as an extension of working consciousness, stops at the border of what is real. Ecstasy turns on the logic of desire of the fulfilled existence that, in theory, would not require any form of mediation. However, this desire has to be expressed, its structure and sense have to be deposed in language. The contradiction that is created at the meeting point of desire and language results in a moment of ecstasy turning into a moment of madness in which language does not play its referential functions, but circulates around the emptiness of meaning, repeating itself and gravitating toward the absolute nothingness. Bataille shows per that that is the price the individual has to pay for following the logic of desire that, even while leading in a direction known at the outset (the absolute actualization of individual life), later reveals only the desperate situation of existence forced to repeat the same gestures; an existence trapped in the space of words limited by the abstract dimension of its terms.[253]

The situation is similar in *Not I*, in which the mechanism of desire is twofold. On the one hand it is related to the Mouth itself, or rather the speech with which the Mouth cannot identify and cannot reject, but thanks to which, and through which, it wants to reach the emptiness of sense, the end of language. On the other hand, Beckett presents the desire of the heroine from the Mouth's story that sees and understands emptiness in the most literal way: the "little girl" stares ahead, deadened and attempts to overthrow the stubbornness of physical existence and subject her life to the rule of what is outside – in the world. Both registers are present in *Not I* almost simultaneously, creating a difficult to untangle knot of existence, language and consciousness:

> Something begging in the brain... begging the mouth to stop... pause a moment... if only for a moment... and no response... as if it hadn't heard... or couldn't... couldn't pause a second... like maddened... all that together... straining to hear... piece it together... and the brain... raving away on its own... trying to make sense of it... or make it stop... or in the past... dragging up the past... flashes from all over... walks mostly... walking all her days... day after day... a few steps then stop... stare into space... then on... a few more... stop and stare again... so on... drifting around... day after day... or that time she cried... the one time she could remember... since she

---

252   Bataille G., "A Preface to 'Madame Edwards'," Op.cit.
253   See Kristeva J., *L'Expérience et la pratique*, in *Polylogue*, Paris 1977.

was a baby... must have cried as a baby... perhaps no... not essential to life... just the
birth cry to get her going... breathing... then no more till this... [NI, s. 410]

When the Mouth attempts to reconstruct the situation from the past of its heroine by
recalling from its memory details of the world long gone and recreating particular
likes and idiosyncrasies, language itself follows the effort, which makes all of
the elements become rhetorical instances that confirm these experiences from the
past. What has passed does not resurface as language, does not provide access to
the world that does not simply exist, but happens "here and now" – in language
and/or on stage. It is not about a simple doubt expressed by the Mouth ("perhaps
no") because the question is located far from the semantic range of words. The
past cannot be actualized in the form of the workings of memory, nor through the
strength of language that, in theory, was supposed to call being into existence –
the word turns out to be a final veil, making it impossible to access the past world
and disinheriting the one who speaks of his subjectivity. That which truly exists
and what, at the same time, makes the space available for language is a touch of a
body in a narrow band of passage between sensation and the word.

Hence, the unmotivated necessity of the scream and crying is not a simple
imperative that comes from external experience, nor a simple physiological reflex.
It seems that the ecstatic condition, as presented by Beckett, demands an entirely
different order; an order of passage between the stable ontological (being and
nothing) epistemological (consciousness and reality) oppositions. Screams and
laughter constitute the results of that passage, but they also happen in a continuing
transfer of the event between a simple reflex of a body and an appropriating,
paralyzing power of language. They are a "substance" of the very passage that
they also create. This is where the logic of ecstasy is located, one that Bataille
wrote about as thinking of something impossible to think. Screams and cries
can be understood as attempts to override the two extremities: the overpowering
strength of language and the fall into the abyss of the silent body. As a result, they
are both antinomian beginnings for establishing a new reality, pointing only to its
own, impossible to understand and enigmatic fictionality (they appear within the
field of consciousness of the subject in order to "get started"), as well as a source
of an unending process of revealing contradictions that establish the order of a
mutual negative dependency of language and experience. It means that, on the
one hand, the very progression of language not only undermines the authenticity
of experience, but also annihilates them in their own space. On the other hand, the
event weakens the power of language that cannot remain an autonomous system
that allows forces a sense on external reality.

For these particular reasons, the scream and cry generate a different
necessity; a necessity for a constant, exhausting beginning that is founded on
the clash between the physiological compulsion and language's inertia. In order

to speak, the Mouth has to catch a breath in a literal, organic, sense but also in a metaphorical sense. It is driven by language to a point where in place of the signal of the presence of the body there is emptiness that has to be filled immediately by another act of speech that constitutes a beginning. Hence, one is concerned here with articulating desire in order to achieve individual fullness: the unity of the word and body, of desire that, even though realized solely in moments of linguistic madness, moments of intense repetition, in the rhythm established by the enigmatic logic of disintegration and loss of sense, become the only forms of hope to grant sense to random existence. The drive to transgress the individual condition, in order to attain absolute fullness, coincides with disinheriting from language and the necessity of confronting nothingness. That moment of absolute identification is a moment of the madness of language but also a moment when poetry is granted a voice. It seems that this could be the ultimate goal reached by the speaking Mouth but that is also the logic of Beckett's writing understood as a practice that creates shelter for consciousness deprived of the possibility to learn about the world and create reality. Poetry is a register of disintegrating language in which a singular desire has been deposited, which is, at the same time, a desire for the singularity.

This chiasmic reversal seems incredibly important. In Beckett's text there is no faith in the possibility of a return to the primal state of the natural contact because something like a pre-established intentionality in the relationship between subjectivity and the world does not exist. The subject becomes similar to the "hermetic box" from which, with difficulty, new phantasms are able to get out; phantasms created by consciousness. Individual desires have to come into being outside of the claustrophobic space of subjectivity that – through a multiplication of signs in its own fictionality – attempts to protect itself from the risk of the disintegration of temporary autonomy. Even though it functions as the only possibility for saving the randomness of existence, this vision of existence has to lead to a point where language, even in its most neurotic form of the inert repetition is drawn into question. This crisis is connected with the risk and hope that outside this dense network created by speech and silence there is another sphere, in which the final word of poetry will be able to resound irrevocably; a word that, even though it will not be understood, will exist permanently. This dream about the final word simultaneously constitutes a longing of consciousness after the unquestionable legitimization of its own existence.

Hence, poetry is a language of ecstasy not in the sense of the fullest possibility of its representation, an interpretation within the frames of the metaphor of a symbol, but in a sense of creating the space of the "unthinkable as that which transcends the possibility of thinking." As Alain Badiou rightly observed: Beckett "compos[ed] the poem of the unbreakable [*increvable*] desire to think.[254]

The Speech of Suffering

> [...] I'll stop screaming, to listen and hear if anyone is coming, to look and see if anyone is coming, then go, close my eyes and go, screaming, to scream elsewhere [...].[255]
> – Samuel Beckett

Ecstasy has a more concrete or sensual dimension. The scream of the Mouth is not only an abstraction and a potentiality of sense inscribed in a textual sign. On the contrary, as an event[256] it becomes an embodiment of the ecstatic scream. However, the physicality of the scream does not allow for a reduction of the appurtenance of the subject and the body, as well as to existence within the framework of the irreducible reference to the Other. It illustrates an insurmountable difficulty that is connected with presenting ecstasy, a presentation in which the event appears in an antinomian form: both radically temporalized (instability, temporariness of scream) and embodied (the scream as physicality does not constitute an organic metaphor, nor a metaphor of the organic, but – as such – it is irreversibly tied with a body). In other words, the scream, when coming out of the body, reveals simultaneously its own dependence on time and death. At the same time, death does not mean the end or a horizon of existence, but a point around which the scream circulates (both growing out of it and reaching it) – a point of radical namelessness.

The scream (in all of its actualizations) has no name or essence and continuously oscillates between the poles of the body and voice. It constitutes both pure sensuality, as well as a source experience of sense. How then is its representation possible? Posing the question in that way allows us to observe the same tension in the texts by Beckett that is present at the intersection of language, the event

---

254 Badiou A., *Beckett: L`increvable désir*, Paris 1995, p. 79.
255 U, p. 377.
256 There is no large difference in whether one is concerned with the stage production or reading. In both cases, the event planned in the text has to happen, has to come into existence. Only aspects of its particular productions would look different. From the point of view that interests me here, the conviction about the directedness of the theatrical effect is equally misleading in the case of Beckett, as is the opposite belief that suggests a pure potentiality of the text. I try to show that the works of Beckett are guided by the logic of inscription (in the sense given to the term by Jacques Derrida).

and the body that has determined the work of Francis Bacon.[257] In an intriguing analysis of his painting by Gilles Deleuze, one can find the most important tropes connecting both projects. Deleuze states:

> If we scream, it is always as victims of invisible and insensible forces that scramble every spectacle, and that even lie beyond pain and feeling. This is what Bacon means when he says he wanted "to paint the scream more than the horror." If we could express this as a dilemma, it would be: either I paint the horror and I do not pain the scream, because I make a figuration of the horrible; or else I pain the scream, and I do not pain the visible horror, I will paint the visible horror less and less, since the scream captures or detects an invisible force. Alban Berg knew how to make music out of the scream in the scream of Marie, and then in the very different scream of Lulu. But in both cases, he established a relationship between the sound of the scream and inaudible forces: those of the earth in the horizontal scream of Marie, and those of heaven in the vertical scream of Lulu. Bacon creates the painting of the scream because he establishes a relationship between the visibility of the scream (the open mouth as a shadowy abyss) and invisible forces, which are nothing other than the forces of the future. [...] Innocent X screams, but he screams behind the curtain, not only as someone who can no longer be seen, but as someone who cannot see, who has nothing left to see, whose only remaining function is to render visible these invisible forces that are making him scream, these powers of the future. This is what is expressed in the phrase "to scream at" not to scream before or about, but to scream at death – which suggests this coupling of forces, the perceptible force of the scream and the imperceptible force that makes one scream.[258]

The solution proposed by Deleuze could be presented alternatively: either one cannot present the affect, the feeling, sensations, or the representation of only the structure of the event of scream is possible. However, the very rule of such representation seems unclear. On the one side – through painting, or within the act of painting itself, a sphere of visibility is activated; the sphere of that which is fundamental – of forces that shape and generate scream as an event in its pure form, one that cannot be described in any way. However, in extracting these fundamental forces and bringing them to the surface of representation (image) the genealogy of their visibility becomes blurred (one cannot say in this case that the representation of a scream in the painting is the result of some sensation, that it screams because of some reason). The impossibility of grasping its genesis is identified with the order of invisibility and the rigor of representation combined with the necessity of making the objects visible. On the other side, the possibility

---

257 From Anzieu D., *Bacon, Beckett, Bion: pour un rennouveau empiriste*, in *Francis Bacon*, edited by D. Anzieu, M. Marjorie, Paris 1993.

258 Deleuze G., *Francis Bacon. Logique de la sensation*, Paris 1984, p. 41. In English, *Francis Bacon: The Logic of Sensation*, translated by Daniel W. Smith, London-New York 2003, p. 43.

of representation, the potential permanence of the structure of sense created by the order of consciousness does not constitute its protection from the invasion of the event that strips subjectivity from the power of an establishment because it is influenced by an element of physicality, as well as the sphere of voice. The logic of representation is the logic of exclusion and separation, which means that it successfully separates the sphere of the subject from the sphere of experience. That is why, from that point of view, the scream can constitute only a metaphor of some other, more fundamental reality, or a general state of existence.

In the case of the works by Bacon, Berg and, one is concerned with the same desire to "grasp" or to "detect" the event, and not to grasp merely its cognitive-ontological conditions of possibility. In short, each of the three authors symbolizes a different path to the same conviction about the necessity to represent the event itself (scream, laughter, etc.). In the case of Bacon, it will be a concern with making visible, through painting, that which is invisible[259] and in case of Berg[260] with making it possible to hear, through music, that which is impossible to hear. In case of Beckett it will be a concern with expressing the inexpressible[261].

However, in order for the fulfilment of this artistic postulate to take place, one needs to pose a question about the character of the forces that takes a rather vague form in Deleuze's essay. He states:

> But even then, the precision of sensation, the clarity of the Figure, and the rigor of the contour continued to act beneath the colour-patch or the traits – which did not efface the former, but instead gave them a power of vibration and nonlocalization (the mouth that smiles or screams).[262]

The notion of strength is a key notion because it does not allow us to perceive the event solely through the order of a complete externality in which its undisputable

---

259 On the subject of dialectics of what is visible and invisible see:, *Devant le temps. Histoire de l`art et anachronisme des images*, Paris 2000.

260 When analyzing the compositional strategy of Alban Berg, Pierre Boulez wrote that the composer's works are concerned with keeping different relationships in power so they could be actualized at any given moment and kept in their audibility [*audibilité*]. Boulez claims that Berg wanted to continuously broaden his field. That way the act of composing according to the principles of paradox would become possible: the unformed and fluid sounds influence stronger and more directly than those that are deposited in the most stable structures and systems. See Boulez P., *Leçons de musique. Points de repère III*, edited by J- J. Nattiez, Paris 2005, pp. 589-592. Boulez's comments show (except for the strict context of the aforementioned divagations) how close a certain tradition of modern music situates itself within a particular literary tradition in which an important element is the question of "audibility" and the status of the voice.

261 See Hale J., "Framing The Unframable: Samuel Beckett and Francis Bacon," *Samuel Beckett Today/Aujourd`hui* 1990 no. 2.

262 Deleuze G., Op., cit.,. p. 71. In English, see p. 110.

autonomy would not be exposed, as either an otherness that is impossible to accept and understand, nor as solely within the order of a purely creative and subjective will of the sense. One could say that the scream is created at the intersection of the vectors of physiological power (that condition the organic character of the event of scream) and the power of voice (giving the event a semantic dimension).

The strength marks not so much the horizon of cognition or the possible of being, but breaks apart any possibility of bringing together singularity and reveals the fictionality of transcendental categories (of time and place) that could constitute an immobile and unshakable order of reality.[263] Through the work of strength, the identity of time and place becomes imbalanced and in their place there are notions of vibration and displacement that appear. The first of these has to be understood as the power of the actualization of a multi-dimensional, indivisible time that, inside of a laughing or screaming mouth, is dependent on the physiology of the body – by having its source within it, it also experiences a dissolution into it – vibration is a movement of time dependent on the laws of physicality. The second notion is concerned with a strategy of disassembling the fundamental possibility for a particular actualization. The power of the scream shatters all possibilities for the stability of consciousness but also blocks the possibility of making objects visible. The lack of place, the absence of space, is not so much an incommensurable result of a critical gesture aimed at the fictionality of order as an abstract order, or a result of the workings of the critical mind that desires to clear the field of consciousness but it involves the very event going beyond the categorical approach to understanding reality. The sense of the event is contained outside the opposition of presence and absence because the lack of place is not an effect of its work, but its very essence. In other words, "the power of nonlocalization" does not constitute simply a dispersion of sense, but it disarms the possibility of a cognitive rule over the very foundations of what could appear in the field of consciousness. From that perspective (one of painting or literature), the representation of the scream in its own autonomy cannot appear as visible or an ontological remnant. The logic of the sensation works exactly the other way around: it results in the sketch being not final, nor symbolic in any way. The outline and the figure[264] are actions of powers that replace the work of consciousness and the presence of sense.

The logic of expression remains identical with the logic of force. And force, as Deleuze states,[265] in the case of the event of a scream is a pure modulation,

---

263 In that sense, the destiny of strength is to create a different order that could be described by the name of "disfiguration," or "distortion." See E. Grossman, *La défiguration. Artaud-Beckett-Michaux*, Paris 2004.

264 Deleuze G., Op. cit., p. 48.

265 Ibid., p. 76.

hence it does not constitute an isolated articulation or a sensible act of speech, but oscillates between the pole of pure sensuality and pure meaning. That is why making the scream expressible (and, automatically, audible and visible) is radical in its reformulation of the category of the subject, based on a conviction about the necessity to search for the essence of an object outside its essence, the being of the world outside of what is definable as its permanent state. And finally, the individual outside of itself.

Such logic likewise guides the event of the scream in *Not I*; one that is not subject to any definite ontological or existential sanction. The scream, appearing in the space between words, breaks apart their structure and meanings. Without being a figure of sense, or a nonsensical string of the empirical, it is a gesture of opening to what could come from outside. The Mouth, open during laughing or screaming, does not constitute a simple symbol of a tormented existence, but rather it is a gesture of awaiting what is radically different, what could appear in the form of entirely new forces, what could once again – entirely differently – enable language and create the space for true speech; a speech that could finally constitute a sphere of the salvation of the randomness of individual existence.[266] The scream is a result of a search for a radical otherness, an effect of desire to move the absolute externality on the side of presence. The event cannot happen without a context for the words uttered by the Mouth. It cannot appear in the space of a complete silence and as a consequence it exists only "by" words. At the same time, however, the force of the event deprives it of the possibility of occupying some permanent spot. The event is not located anywhere and does not possess any permanent anchoring in being. That way the scream or the laughter reveal themselves as effects of a disintegration of temporary language, or in a form of speech in the state of reduction and on the borderline of an aphasic statement.

In the end, this is not about, as Deleuze claims, the Mouth screaming or laughing against something or because of some reason, but because by awaiting the irreducible form of presence, tired by leading the narrative, they have to release the tension created at the intersection of sensuality, or materiality and the intransitivity of language and its structure and meaning. The scream and laughter are not merely affects, or signs referring back to a true "somewhere else" but constitute a realization of the event, the logic of which has been set in motion by the discovery in the space of speech of simultaneity of these contradictory orders. The Mouth, desiring to reach through language, through the story being told to an indivisible and unquestionable identity (of language and sense, of the heroine and the Mouth, narrative and life, etc.) that could crystalise in a permanently present and central "I," becomes the hostage of speech. The latter seems to hide, with the

---

266 See H. Zeifman, "Being and Not Being: Samuel Beckett's 'Not I'," *Modern Drama* 1976, no. 19.

use of reality of representation,[267] the dreamed reality of exteriority. That is why the means and content of expression are so reliant on that fantasy. The sense of speaking is included in the infinite search for a respite from its necessities and in the possibility of coming into existence – for a moment and in a non-obvious way – of an event that would allow for an escape from existential collapse, to escape the "long hours of darkness." The character of the scream or laughter as events reveals not only the tear between sensuality and meaning, but also shows that the scream and laughter perform a double function in the drama. The scream is, at the same time, an event – an actualization – of sense, but also influences phrases that follow it that become speech-screams, shattering the continuity of the narrative.

Beckett shows that the only possibility of saving the arbitrariness of the individual is to reveal the pre-established failure of the expression of conscious identity; a failure that would lead to madness or death. It also demonstrates the stakes in the game of the subject with the world and language. These stakes do not involve the erasure of that which is negative from existence (a conflict-free transfer from "not I" to "I") but a legitimization of the order of consciousness and experience that is based on a primal absence. One is aiming to undertake the effort of searching for a final register of speech every time and despite all obstacles; an effort that would not so much establish the homology between words and objects, but that would lead to their ultimate unification:

> [...] keep on... trying... not knowing what... what she was trying... what to try... whole body gone... just the mouth... like maddened... so on... keep –[...] [NI, p. 412]

The scream, even though articulated, is at its base undermined by its own contradiction: silence, or rather – a silent terror.[268] The event that, by tearing the structure of narrative apart, allows for the revelation of the sphere of inexpressible nothingness that identity deprived of language has to confront. At the same time, however, it reveals that which is most fully present: the suffering and pain that constitute a final sanction of objectivity thanks to which the individual can find confirmation of the realness of his/her own existence. We are concerned with a form of objectivity that does not undergo any negotiations, nor is it a result of intersubjective conclusions of an idealized or speculative understanding, but a

---

267 The stage can be understood literally as a place for the theatrical representation and, metaphorically, as a stage of language on which subjectivity attempts to articulate aporetic desire for the presence of the event and the desire for the power of consciousness over that event. Moreover, the critical device used by Beckett to reach a certain and complete presence reveals the irreducibly fictional side of writing. Olga Bernal wrote interestingly about that mechanism in a chapter of her book under a telling title: "Who speaks?". Bernal, O., *Langage et fiction dans le roman de Beckett*, Paris 1969 p. 113.

268 See Janion M., "Nadmiar bólu," in *Żyjąc tracimy życie. Niepokojące tematy egzystencji*, Warszawa 2001, pp. 202-203.

constitutes an objectivity that does not substantialise itself – like in Hegel – in the subjective sovereignty of a notion, but in a haunting presence of that which is non-identical and heteronomic with itself. Beckett's drive seems understandable: to show a place in which a radical absence revealed by the event, as well an objective presence of the persistent suffering of an individual, reaches a moment of crisis that is impossible to overcome. This tension cannot be released otherwise than through another attempt to escape the "long hours of darkness," an escape that can take place only by upholding – even minimally – the possibility of speech. At the foundational level of such fear-oriented and crisis-like conditions of the subject lies a radical nominalism that appears throughout almost the entire mature body of Beckett's work,[269] accompanied by a gap between words and sense. The consequences of such a gap are not only the inability to establish a corresponding or coherent notion of truth, but also a turn toward the autonomy of linguistic mediation. That is why all images of speech in *Not I* serve to highlight the fundamental intransitiveness of words that cannot be contained in some form of an ontological generality. The linguistic moment is a moment of resistance of that which is completely singular, idiomatic and that is born in a confrontation with consciousness. This temporal aspect results in the fact that the linguistic moment of mediating is not so much a refusal of participation in the world, articulating itself through contradicting faith in the realness of a direct access to it. It also constitutes a fundamental existential disposition and not only an epistemological justification for the working of consciousness.

The irreducible historicity of language, understood as a mediation, brings the writing practices of Beckett closer to the necessity of understanding literature as – speaking metaphorically – a stage on which the attempt to express and represent that what is inexpressible – a structure of time, events and/or structures of space, or the exterior. In *Not I*, Beckett demonstrates that by trying to reveal through conventionality and the common character of language that which is an event of a heteronomic nature, consciousness has to work somewhat at the fringes of language. At the same time, it is precisely this discord of generality as a fundamental mimetic force of language that results in writing becoming an experience, which means that literature does not create a chance either for recreating any principle of reality, or for the justice for what is visible (that assumes the stable structure of reality). Writing and speaking within the range of the institution of literature is an act of resistance for Beckett, against both the transcendental-mimetic model, as well as the empirical-ideological one. If we were to use the, classic for modernity, definition of the work of art proposed by Hegel once again, than we would have to say that the art for Beckett is no longer a "sensuous manifestation of the Idea,"

---

269   See Knowlson J., Pilling J., *Frescoes of the Skull: The Later Prose and Drama of Samuel Beckett*, London 1979.

but what remains as a remnant after a total aesthetic experience. Adorno phrased this logic perfectly in writing about the poetry of Hölderlin as the beginning of modern aesthetics, which arrived at its fulfilment in the form of Beckett's project:

> Its general nouns are resultants; they attest to the difference between the name and the meaning evoked. They acquire their strangeness, which in turn incorporates them into poetry, by having been hollowed out, as it were, by names, their adversaries. They are relics, *capita mortua* of the aspect of the idea that cannot be made present: they are marks of a process, even in their seemingly atemporal generality. [...] They have their own life, precisely by virtue of having divested themselves of immediacy.[270]

The scream and the explosion of the poem, laughter and absence, the sensuality of the body and ascetic language – all of these elements are focused in *Not I*, this "text-representation" that is both a recording and a stage production of speech as a boundary and as an expression of singular suffering.

---

270   Adorno, T. "Parataxis: On Hölderlin's Late Poetry," in *Notes to Literature*, vol. 2, New York 1992, p. 123.

PART FOUR
DREAMS OF STABILITY

Chapter one
Poetry of absence

> imagine si ceci
> un jour ceci
> un beau jour
> imagine
> si un jour
> un beau jour ceci
> cessait
> imagine [271]
>
> – Samuel Beckett

Let us return to the interpretative trail established by Maurice Blanchot in writing about Beckett's "trilogy." The interpretation proposed by Blanchot is based a conviction about the necessity of discovering an order of description beyond metaphysics – not so much of the work (its structure and poetics), but of the experience of an encounter with the authorial idiom, with a singular imagination. The reading of Blanchot allows us to see the variety of Beckett's writing strategies that are subordinated to one, fundamental gesture of writing. And writing, similar to thinking, begins with imagination.

Sense as a Fable

Imagination Dead Imagine is a work in which the concept of the imagination functions on three levels: the figurative, ontological and cognitive.[272] None of them

---

271 Mi, p. 35.
272 One has to remark that this is not the only work in which the imagination appears at the centre of the text. A previous version of the text in question was entitled *All Strange Way* in which the phrase "imagination dead imagine" opened the text.

appear separately and Beckett is concerned more with the coexistence and mutual saturation of each of these registers. The first is about the position, structure and meaning of the metaphor. The second works with the modal frameworks in which presence and sense can appear and be actualized. Finally, the third is focused on the foundations of consciousness.

The most obvious is the first, as it is easily observable in the form of an image of a white rotunda. The anonymous narrator of the piece (as often happens in Beckett's writing) begins by establishing the position of the imagination by clearing the external sphere of reference: outside of "I" there is nothing, or rather everything that could spring into existence is in fact left in the world after a disaster.[273] But this movement of a radical internalization is counterpointed by a signal to the force of expression, an imperative of speech that appears as the voice of a storyteller that delineates the boundaries of reality.

"White rotunda on white" – this elliptical term perfectly shows the character of the experience of imagination that functions not so much according to the rules of fiction supplanted in place of that which is real, but rather as the only reality: autonomous and unquestionable, but also mysterious. Despite being seemingly perfect in geometrical organization, it remains marked by the enigmatic fatalism of the deadly fall:

> Lying on the ground two white bodies, each in its semi-circle. White too the vault and the round wall eighteen inches high from which it springs. Go back out, a plain rotunda, all white in the whiteness, go back in, rap, solid throughout, a ring as in the imagination the ring of bone. [IDI, s. 361]

What might surprise us in the image of the rotunda presented by Beckett is the drive to erase the possibility of establishing the relationship between the interior and exterior. All the elements composing the figure of the "white rotunda" (the smoothness of the walls, the depth, or the precise parameters of the space) serve that purpose. The acoustic reference seems mysterious as well, because what does the comparison of the sound filling the interior of the rotunda (or the interior of its interior) to the sound of bones in the imagination mean? It seems that Beckett, while aiming at an ontological reduction and reducing the possibility of cognition to delineating a field in which the presence is a borderline modality of being and, at the same time, provides the only plausible justification of reality. It consequently destroys the motives and possibilities for authentic experience – its essence seems to be beyond any being. First, the realness of the rotunda's space is erased – even though it exists, it is not in an obvious way, situating itself outside spectrum of visibility. The figure of a doubled and contaminated whiteness is confronted with

---

273   See Hansford J., "'Imagination Dead Imagine': The Imagination and Its Context," *Journal of Beckett Studies*, 1982 no. 7, pp. 49-70.

the sphere of sounds that creates a reduced, irreplaceable principle of imagination. Both spheres, those of visibility and audibility, remain in their final abilities, somewhat at the edge of disintegration and at the moment right before definite disappearance.

However, the very moment of disappearing is crucial. Beckett wants neither to remove it by introducing the metaphor of some concrete object (that would be constituted by an actual existing white rotunda against the white background), nor to skip through the visual suggestion that opens the state of palpable transcendental tension. Instead, he wishes to sustain this movement by creating a space, in which language could reconcile itself with a direct experience. That space is enigmatic to the same degree as the "white rotunda" and the imagination, in which everything that is potential could appear, announcing simultaneously its own absence. That is why the reign of sight becomes replaced in the discussed excerpt by the reign of sound. Beginning with the inhuman, whiteness is forced out by knocking on the walls of rotunda and listening to the sounds coming from inside. Similarly to the reign of vision and sight, the reign of sound is surrendered to annihilation – the only possible sound turns out to be the vibration of bones, an ironic metaphor of death that marks the experience at its base but also its very possibility. What is more, by bringing the gesture of annihilation to its ultimate foundations, with the extreme distortion of all forms of presence and all sources of existence, Beckett breaks up the static character of an image constructed by himself. It is not purely about the dynamics resulting directly from the imperative mode of speaking, but about bringing the ideal of "erasing" the forms of presence to a point where the contradictions of movement and stillness remain as figures of ambiguity, as energy of the very enabled progression of writing, or – speaking metaphorically – progressing into the depths of the rotunda and, at the same time, into the depths of the imagination without a clearly marked goal:

> The light that makes all so white no visible source, all shines with the same white shine, ground wall, vault, bodies, no shadow. Strong heat, surfaces hot but not burning to the touch, bodies sweating. Go back out, move back, the little fabric vanishes, ascend, it vanishes, all white in the whiteness. Emptiness, silence, heat, whiteness, wait, the light goes down, all grows dark together, ground, wall, vault, bodies, say twenty seconds, all the greys, the light goes out, all vanishes. [IMI, s. 361]

The image of light serves Beckett as an inciting tool for the paradoxical effect of presence that is based on the fact that its every form is entirely separated from the sphere of consciousness and, as a result, cancels itself. Presence is so tight and so full that it does not allow for any possibility of an external intervention. That which exists allows itself to be recognized solely as an outline, a line that specifies and orders the internal world. The light of an unknown source and an unknown fate is a signal of the unbearable surplus of presence and, in a way, "x-rays" every being, removing the possibility of its visibility. In the reality sketched out by Beckett, the gaze therefore no longer plays any role, and the simplest form of contact, the touch of a body or a surface, takes its place. Only the establishment of distance creates the possibility of observing something, allowing for the construction of a perspective in which sight could play any role at all. These two spheres: sight and the blurring of sight saturate one another in the entire text and reveal the logic of an imagination that, on the one hand, delegates the sphere of sensuality to a safe distance created by the reign of sight and on the other – degrades the possibility of mastering empirical reality through the power of the gaze completely. It distances itself within its proper space that is best described by the final phrases of the excerpt cited above: "all vanishes." Reality, reduced to its fundamental elements, moves gradually into nothingness on at least two levels.

First, one can clearly observe the desire to grasp reality in a pure state, not disturbed by any form of mediation. The textual effect of that desire turns out to be a string of calculations, almost abstract interpretations of immobile being. However, the desire for a state of the complete abstraction of language, which would constitute an attempt to stop the variability of the external world in the generalness of the notion, becomes merely a sign of attempts to mark points of reference, expressing some minimally certain, ontological situation. Second, reality as presented by Beckett is not only a projection of the imagination, but also an effect of contact between the space it designated and the sphere of the empirical world. The gradual expiration of light is a double movement, both literal (in the sense of change happening) as well as conscious character (happening in and through language). Both spheres, the sensual and linguistic, overlap and create an effect of realness in which that which is expressed becomes bound with which was thought and imagined. The entanglement of these two possibilities does not allow itself to be untangled and remains, throughout the entire text, in a state of a dynamic insolubility. Both Beckett's imagination and consciousness suggesting the fullness of its own autonomy, shows irremovable heteronomies, the irreducible mediation in language that, by obscuring individual consciousness and imagination the world *in crudo* constitutes an announcement of the catastrophe of experience. At the same time, however, the foreseen failure that accompanies faith in direct insight into the essence of things enables a space for writing and constitutes an ignition point for an incredibly creative conflict between the sphere of the presence of sense and the sphere of radical absence toward which the language of Beckett is constantly headed, principally through its obsessive thematising of that very tension.

Let us observe that even that which could be described, hence that which could be deposited in the text in the form of presence, is immediately undermined by the movement of language and transposed in its own phantasm. In a quoted excerpt, the seemingly indifferent terms suggesting the description of the "state of things" are an announcement cancelling the stability of the world, whose importance they have previously confirmed. The radical character of Beckett's gesture is based on the fact that any form of affirmation of the ontological stability of the world reveals simultaneously its own, pre-established negativity that cannot be included in the image, or completed in the most vivid figure. The "disappearance" of the world is total and involves both the sense of perception, as well as touch, but also annihilates the work of imagination. Pure absence becomes viable not only in the negative categories of description, but as an affirmation of what is negative, what transgresses the horizon of the presence of sense and that which is contained outside of the range of notions or ideas. That is how one could understand the title of the text – the imagination is dead, but there exists an independent and enigmatic necessity to imagine. From the point of view of the genesis of representation, this imperative is not concrete but appears as the very challenge for the imagination. As far as the goal of this work is concerned, the actions of the imagination are not directed and the goal is the exposure of the very mechanisms of decomposition. Absence turns out to be not so much a condition for the sense of all the efforts of the individual imagination and consciousness, but a paradoxical warranty of the word's existence that becomes validated only after the entire – even the most phantasmal – perspective of establishing external reality disappears. The word attains its legitimization only after it appears in its own disappearance, when it appears as its own absence. The imagination can become resurrected only after the subject creates distance between itself and its primal state – death.

The radical character of such a gesture is based, primarily, on the refusal of reality to all the elements of human experience that point to the possibility of direct access to the sphere of real mediation, undisturbed by forms. Beckett is not interested in discovering the "principle of reality"[274] but rather in extracting the insurmountable contradictions that are hidden at the heart of thinking, speaking and imagining. The goal is to undertake the effort of thinking, speaking and imagination, and thereby cancelling the previously unquestionable existence of the word while forgetting about the possible meanings it carries with it. Only in that movement of purification and minimizing the extraction of the contradictions to the surface of the text does his project become possible. We thereby encounter a contradiction that establishes the work of writing as a search for the presence of sense outside of its presence, outside of its meaning and outside of its semiotic economy. Thanks to the continuously executed gesture of transgressing conflicts, at the meeting point of the clarity of meaning behind which there is the work of consciousness and the dark materiality of the word for which the sphere of

---

274   See, Anzieu D., *Beckett,* Paris 1992.

sensuality is responsible, the poetic idiom is born; an idiom that allows for the resurrection of the dead imagination. While commenting on the work of Maurice Blanchot, Levinas once stated the following:

> To seek – beyond the poetic discourse that expresses, dispersedly, the impossible escape from discourse – the *logos* that gathers, is to block the opening through which the circularity of coherent discourse announces (but also denounces, and in so doing transcends) itself. [...] And perhaps we are wrong in using the designation art and poetry for that exceptional event, that sovereign forgetting, that liberates language from its servitude with respect to the structures in which the said maintains itself. Perhaps Hegel was right as far as art is concerned. What counts – whether it be called poetry or what you will – is that a meaning is able to proffer itself beyond the closed discourse of Hegel; that a meaning that forgets the presuppositions of that discourse becomes fable.[275]

What is essential in Levinas's observations referring to two questions connected with the ontological and epistemological possibilities of language? It can actualize being in so far as it can express its essence. That is how he interprets Hegel's dialectical implication that is based on the fundamental belief that that there exists only that which is real, or that which is expressed, as well as the fact that the real can be only that which allows itself to expressed (uttered). Language is tied with rationality also in that way, or – according to Levinas – tied with a certain unquestionable presence, a logos, securing the sense of all linguistic strategies.

Actualized consciousness plays an extremely important part in those questions, seeking to achieve, through the work of removing contradictions, a point of absolute singular identity in which language and the body, senses and the spirit, meaning and the figure could all become perfectly aligned. Precisely that consciousness triggers a mediating plane of speech on which the "representation experiment" takes place. Its final goal would be to gain the optimal point from which every possibility of being would be not only plausible, but also legitimate. Beckett is not a phenomenologist and does not believe in the effectiveness of the experiment conducted on the self during and through the practice of writing. The experiment of writing opens the path to experience and is a way to open language to what is unexpected, to discord, as language is precisely and meticulously purified by Beckett. Finally, it is a procedure of acting with a limited scope, with the necessary structural and semantic support enforcing a temporary order on what is chaotic. This rigor becomes ironically countersigned by the irreducible irrationality of what – in a sense outlined by Hegel or Levinas – remains in a state of infinite and mindless chaos. This is how the aforementioned vivid and recurring orders could be interpreted; orders of extreme brightness and complete darkness, excessive

---

275   Levinas E., "The Servant and Her Master," in *Proper Names,* translated by Michael B. Smith, Stanford 1996, p. 143.

presence that is somewhat saturated with light and completely extinguished by "deadening" existence. Beckett constantly keeps juxtaposing them with one another in order to see what result he will achieve in terms of symbolic invention. However, while examining the different versions of language and examining what could happen to it in a concrete course of action (from unimaginable brightness to unimaginable darkness), he simultaneously reveals a crack between these orders, a split that becomes a place of an important experience; an experience for which there is a lack of any kind of name but which continuously demands a concrete definition.

The "geometrical" poetics of the text that are so often and willingly used by Beckett[276] were based on the crossing of both orders described above: the experiment and experience. The first pertains to a continuous examination, a testing of the possibilities and particular dispositions of an individual but also to supporting oneself on the foundations of an accumulated knowledge. The second opens precisely where consciousness and language become exhausted, where they surrender before the enigmatic space spanning "between" the two fundamental dimensions of Beckett's reality: silence and the darkness. This gap refers not to the lack of coincidence between the separate spaces, but to the time in which the drama of the disappearing world of the subject takes place. This gap is not the result of a difference that emerges from a clash between distinct structures of space, but is connected with a place that is entirely empty, one that escapes all forms. It is there, in the sphere designated by the signal lasting "20 seconds" that the drama of consciousness left in a state of total suspension takes place. But that is also where sense has an opportunity to arise; a sense that not only constitutes a source or the crowning of language, but a sense that is perceptible as a trace of its shift, as a rhetorical trace of the metamorphosis that results in the change of the seemingly stabilized parameters of reality. That which is real does not situate itself definitely and fully on any of the sides of the available incarnations of subjectivity (imagination, consciousness, language or body), and it does not send one back to the particular source of sense, nor does it announce a final synthesis. It is contained in, even the smallest and barely noticeable, the change of state in which we encounter the ones summoned to life, the ones killed by the deteriorating and re-emerging imagination. In Beckett, the change takes place in the smallest of possible spaces:

> Wait, more or less long, light and heat come back, all grows white and hot together, ground, wall, vault, bodies, say twenty seconds, all the greys, till the initial level is reached whence the fall began. More or less long, for there may intervene, experience

---

276 The most telling example is the short story *The Lost Ones*, in which the construction of the text, as well as the main metaphor of closed space (the rotunda) remain subjected to the rigorous vision of the "geometric" world.

shows, between end of fall and beginning of rise, pauses of varying length, from the fraction of the second to what would have seemed, in other times, other places an eternity. Same remark for the other pause between end of rise and beginning of fall. The extremes, as long as they last, are perfectly stable, which in the case of the temperature may seem strange, in the beginning. [IMI, s. 361-362]

Let us observe that the moment of distortion in the unbreakable chain of events (aside from falling and rising, there are also memories of previously created pairs: light and darkness, silence and sound, emptiness and fullness, etc.) is not simply understood as an irrational element that is meaningless and impossible to grasp in the net of language. It constitutes a point in which sense finds its place. It is located – as Beckett observes – where the "vibrating greyness" takes its effect as well – this sole form of a metaphorically represented reality. First, the place in which sense reveals itself, while being outside of discourse, and hence outside of the logos and the rigor of rationality, constitutes an undefined space but also an irreducible one that is not susceptible to the external work of a notion or category. It means also that language, with help of which sense could be tracked, is located in a critical state and reveals its own material side by presenting itself more as a sphere of intransitivity than as a branding or naming. Second, the vehement resistance of language is only an effect of the unobvious, unstable existence of sense. In other words, sense exists only in impurity and at its base has a distorted form. Its gains its transparency through a presence that is impossible to verbalize or conceptualize.

This is where the second part of the metaphor is revealed that suggests a possibility of existing outside of metaphysical oppositions (or rather between them) and explains the rigor of the existence of the sense. However, it is no longer as a form full of presence but as an irreducible discord between the identity of being, a discord and distortion that results in the subject being unable to support itself either on the totality, homogeneity or static character of the imagined world ("unchanging, white or black") or forcing the chaos of the external, empirical reality onto the subject. "Grey" is a colour that often appears in Beckett's[277] texts, precisely because it corresponds the fragile, unstable singular condition of consciousness

---

277 This is connected with an important trope in Beckett's work, mainly an inspiration from the *Divine Comedy* by Dante. In particular, we are interested in one character, a craftsmen named Belacqua who, sentenced for the sin of sloth (lack of will), remains in purgatory. Belacqua became an important figure for the young Beckett who created a character of the same name (with a meaningful last name as well – Shuah) in his stories from the volume *More Pricks Than Kicks*. The "purgatory" of the character translated into a fascination with the state of existential half-presence, a suspension "between" being and nothingness, condemnation and salvation, flash and darkness. See Lamont R., *Beckett's Metaphysics of Choiceless Awareness*, in *Samuel Beckett Now*, ed. and introduction by Melvin J. Friedman, Chicago and London 1970, p. 199.

that cannot stop the course of things and cannot rule over the movement caused by changes, nor can it confront the horror of the external, chaotic world of sensuality. It is not difficult to understand that the described state of an ideal balance secures itself against the threat of the external interference, as well as against the excessive submersion in introjection. It is even easier to understand the strategy of Beckett, filled with difficulty, who wanted to grant the act of consciousness existential weight and use the epistemological potential found in writing that, in principle, were supposed to transform into an expanding exercise of the mind; not so much creating the conditions of possibility of experience, but tying experience with the existence in such a way as to gain unquestionable autonomy. The ideal of consciousness would not only design the current, universal representation of reality, but – in the act of reflection – it would justify itself a singular being. This utopian feature, within vision of the subject sketched in the text, based on the independence of consciousness, would gradually transform into the madness of immanence. This is all weakened by the character of the sense as radically other, that is not only not given forever and deposited in language or the world and ready to be discovered, thereby revealing itself as the inevitability of heteronomy and a possibility for a transformation of the seemingly steadily present.

One could say that the mature and late work of Beckett, more than his previous achievements, shows a fundamental and irremovable gap between the principle of identity and non-contradiction. The first is ontological because it is concerned with the reality of beings that can be identified, which means one could attain actual knowledge about them. The principle of identity creates a path through recognition to self-knowledge. The second is concerned with language and its logical syntax – that which is unquestionably expressed in language is at the same time obvious and does not demand commentary. At its base, it does not assume any difference. In Beckett's work, both of these rules not only – as one could say – reach their critical point, in which reality understood ontologically and the reality of language end on separate tracks, but also become subdued to the fundamental phantasm of the so called "meta-aporia" that could constitute a final modal framework for every expression, for language that allows for the description of every experience. One can see this perfectly well through the example of the analyzed figure of imagination that is outside of time but, simultaneously, through its inscribed deadly "tone," it constitutes its most perfect incarnation. Beckett would like to simultaneously express and contradict the expression of this aporia. At the same time, this rhetoric headed toward the search for a "perfect language" allows the literary gesture to break free, questioning the principle of identity, as well as the principle of non-contradiction. In that sense, Beckett's writing presents the primary problem of modernity in the form of negativity that, within the modernity, is connected with retreating from idealism.

For Beckett, sense is a fable. As in Levinas and Blanchot, it can exist outside of any being or defined form. It is neither an epiphany nor a construct of an insightful mind. Sense remains a fable; it mean that it is unclear, constantly escaping the laws of consciousness and language. But sense – according to Beckett – is a fable also because it can become the perfect possibility in which to search for a poetic idiom, a final register of language that will never and under no circumstances undergo any changes, hiding entirely in the fullness of its own immanence. "Further translations are infinitely variable" – we read in Beckett's work. He tells his story about the eternal shifting of the position of consciousness and language that for themselves become sense, held in motion by the dream of an absolute individuality of existence, that would be followed by a complete and paradoxical – meaning impossible to resurrect by the imagination – identification of the word and existence. The true death of the imagination would be the removal of distance and realization of the fable that would change from the figure of a "vibrating" passage between presence and absence, into a mark of an irreversible end that cannot be transformed into a beginning of another story, a true end – meaning one that would ultimately block the possibility of any invention, in which language would become a signal of a ultimate "falling silent for eternity."

The Place of the Imagination

In Beckett, everything starts with the imagination. But where exactly? More importantly, we should say that the imagination is a place, a specific emptiness that demands to be filled. At the same time, it seduces into false understanding based on its structure. In such an interpretation of the imagination – without fearing exaggeration[278] – we could look for the ambivalent attachment (both fascination and rejection) of Beckett to the idealistic tradition of thinking about consciousness and the subject. For Kant, whose philosophy remains the key point of reference for this particular tradition, the concept of "I" is completely separated from observational data, which, in turn, means that establishing the subject can take place only outside of the world of empirical sensation. In other words, "I" is an empty space, deprived of any visible content.[279] The subject can establish

---

278 Here, I am referring to a very close and inventive reading of Shoppenhauer, but also Kant. See Szafraniec A., *Beckett, Derrida, and the Event of Literature*, Standford 2007; Myskja B. K., *The Sublime in Kant and Beckett. Ethics and Literature*, New York 2002; "Beckett and Philosophy," in *Samuel Beckett – One Hundred Years*, ed. Ch. Murray, Dublin 2006, pp. 93-110.

279 See Kant I., *Critique of Pure Reason,* translated by Paul Guyer, Allen Wood Cambridge 1999, A 345, 366.

and legitimize itself only through a radical separation of the sphere of senses, establishing a level from which the concretization of the object will be possible. On the other hand, we must remember that cognition without experience is empty. What is the role of the imagination in Kant's critical system?

Martin Heidegger, in his daring but extremely controversial interpretation of the transcendental critique of Kant, claims that the imagination is a general possibility of all particular potentialities of being and that it constitutes a foundation for all existence and a source of all possible cognition. In my estimation, only several of the themes from that interpretation will be important, some of which will allow for a more comprehensive discussion of the imagination in Beckett's works as a figure of consciousness's struggle for self-legitimation and for establishing the relationship between the subject and the object.

Heidegger interpreted the *Critique of Pure Reason* from an ontologically dominant perspective.[280] For Kant, the range of consciousness is dominated by the differentiation between empirical cognition that has its own concrete object and transcendental cognition in which it has reached its paramount and became a pure cognition. In such an interpretation, consciousness is not directed at any specific object but towards the ideal "something" that Kant describes as the transcendental object = X. For Heidegger, the most important element seems to be not the primacy of the ideal dimension but the topology of that transcendental object and the conjoined topology of the transcendental imagination. He states:

> The X is a "Something" of which in general we can know nothing at all. But it is not therefore not knowable, because as a being this X lies hidden "behind" a layer of appearances. Rather, it is not knowable because it simply cannot become a possible object of knowing, i.e., the possession of a knowledge of beings. It can never become such because it is a Nothing.[281]

This means:

> The X is an "object in general," but this does not mean that it is a universal indeterminate essence which presents itself in the form of an ob-ject. On the contrary, this expression refers to that which in advance constitutes the passing over of all possible objects qua ob-jective, the horizon of an ob-jectification. If by "object" we mean an essent thematically apprehended, this horizon is not an object but a Nothing. And if by "knowledge" we mean the apprehension of an essent, ontological knowledge is not knowledge. [...] Ontological knowledge "forms" transcendence, and this formation

---

280 Heidegger does so with many texts. Perhaps the strongest variant of this (which is a significant case) is the misinterpretation present in his reading of Hölderlin's poetry. See M. Heidegger, *Elucidation of Hölderlin's Poetry,* translated by Keith Hoeller, Amherst 2000.

281 Heidegger M., *Kant and the Problem of Metaphysics,* translated by Richard Taft, Indianapolis 1997, p. 86.

is nothing other than the holding open of the horizon within which the Being of the essent is perceptible in advance.[282]

The object of pure cognition is located outside the sphere of knowledge that accumulates in the form of experience that confirms reality faith in identity inscribed into the repetition of "the same" (in the case of Beckett, this applies to almost all "technical," information serving to describe the world inside of the "white rotunda"). The object = X cannot be described as the fullness of knowledge that the critical mind could gradually discover but should be treated as a pre-established emptiness that situates itself outside of the logic of representation and the creative power of the subject.

Heidegger finds this particular nothing at the foundation of all cognition not because it creates the conditions of certain knowledge, but because it becomes a gesture of the fundamental opening for the essence of existence. Heidegger states that nothing, that is the imagination, establishes a horizon in which the opening to the being proper takes place; proper meaning that it cannot be thematised or defined within the rigor of the categories. Transcendence, being the very possibility of existence, contains itself within the gesture of opening, in the movement (in "shaping" as Heidegger states) of an unmarked, mythical being.

Even though Heidegger's conclusions about the structure of the transcendental imagination are incredibly insightful (it allows us to treat it not as an operational epistemological category, but as a dimension of consciousness that problematizes itself and shows its own existential foundations), the result of the investigation subjected to the interpretation of fundamental ontology seems to be disappointment in the end. The imagination becomes a foundation, a base for all possible cognition and experience but only seemingly. The horizon it marks is not a boundary of possible and certain knowledge about the world, nor an "unspecified directness given in the form of pure clarity" (like in Hegel),[283] but a sign of the finite subject confronted with the infinity of the enigmatic sphere of being. That is why Heidegger's conclusion stops at the "sight-centred" metaphor – true being could be observed in the movement of the opening of the ontological horizon. Only in that way is the subject able to be saved by surrendering to being, as well as nothingness with which it remains in a tight relationship. In such a case, the emptiness of the transcendental object is treated technically, as a necessary stage on the road of liberating the subject from the blindness of an over-critical mind.

In the meantime, treating the imagination as a basic dimension of irreducible absence that escapes intentions and language seems much more interesting. In

---

282   Ibid., pp. 127-128.
283   See Hegel G. W. F., *The Science of Logic*, translated by George Di Giovanni, Cambridge 2010.

Beckett's text the object X takes the form of "white rotunda on white,"[284] the result of an intensified effort of the dying imagination that works in two directions. On the one side, it attempts to uphold its own existence through problematizing its own "mortal" status, on the other – it summons to life the ideal objects that would make a return to the state of absence possible; a return of namelessness proper to its primary position. That is how we could explain doubts about the status of the imagination visible from the very title page. The imagination is dead in the sense that it has no connection to the subject that establishes it, with the consciousness that corrects it, or that directs its actions intentionally. Consciousness and intention undergo degradation and become isolated from experience (body and the senses) and turn into – according to the commentators of Beckett's text – a bitter parody of philosophical efforts headed toward establishing the final sanction of the critical mind. What is more, pure consciousness becomes an empty language and a sign of helplessness that is untainted by any signs of contingency or personal procedures of the mind that in all of its closed actions turns against itself. However, the imagination understood in that way remains in a state of an intense exertion, not only in the sense that it constitutes a source of perfect representations that the consciousness can feed on but also in the sense that it makes the exit or liberation outside from the rigor of consciousness possible – even if for a brief moment – and allows for an exposure to the actions of the exterior. The emptiness of the imagination in Beckett's writing works in two additional ways: first, as a call of death or a total annihilation of experience; second, as the totality of every possibility of existence. Between these two radical poles that absolutise the imagination there is the space of the real; a space – as the text hints itself – of "vibrating greyness."

Outlined in such a way, the topology in Beckett's text allows us to see a different aspect of subjectivity. The imagination is combined with the accidental that not only rules the perception, but is also the only term for the forms of presence that appear on the horizon delineated by the work of the imagination:

> Rediscovered miraculously after what absence in perfect voids it is no longer quite the same, from this point of view, but there is no other. Externally all is as before and the sighting of the little fabric quite as much a matter of chance, its whiteness merging in the surrounding whiteness. But go in and now briefer lulls and never twice the same

---

284 In the schematic, subdued take of Ludovic Janvier, who divides the prose of Beckett between the "place of the story" and the "story about the place." In *Imagination Dead Imagine* the place of narration remains outside of the text (just like the narrator remains outside of the textual game) and the described place is, of course, the "white rotunda." The subject of "transfer" does not exist (and it is the only case in the entire comparative study done by the French scholar). This shows that even on the level of the grammar of the text, Beckett brought the position of the imagination to the edge of possibility. Janvier L., "*Lieu dire*," in *Samuel Beckett*, Cahier de L'Herne, Op. cit., p. 170.

storm. Light and heat remain linked as though supplied by the same source of which
still no trace. [IMI, p. 362]

This is an incredibly important piece of the work, because the division of the
subject (on the grammatical level, the imperative remains; but before that, the
statement highlighting neutrality appears in the third person singular) takes place
based on this assumed perspective. Externality is – so to speak – a space in a pure
state, a space liberated from the rule of time, even though the effects of its work are
observable. It is there that the "accident" and "miracle" reign and only thanks to
them that one is capable of seeing the rotunda. But also thanks exclusively to them
anyone can find themselves in the "middle of nowhere." This sphere of externality,
so complex in its description, is guided only by natural language, as if all has been
subject to the law of a technical, scrupulous and impersonal imagination. Only the
voice of the imperative (which can be treated as the voice of the narrator or as a
"whisper" of the imagination) grants language the concreteness and that language
become a message but also a manual for how to act.

In this context, what is most important is the juxtaposition of the order of
perceiving and the order of imagination. The first is based on the primacy of
individuality. Only "that" – and not the "other" – point of view is acceptable. It
is not about its unique character but about the determinism and the imperative
to observe the object that comes from an unknown, impossible to locate, source.
Only the simplest sensations and possibilities can constitute symptoms: looking
and the sensation of warmth. Random accidents, on the other hand, can cause
the transparent reality of rotunda to finally come in to focus. Here, the power of
the imagination is revealed; an imagination that by invoking particular beings
into existence, simultaneously makes their full presence impossible. That is its
paradoxical status – not because it withholds a place within consciousness or
fulfils the function of creation – meaning summoning new worlds into existence.
It is paradoxical as a place in which consciousness reaches its own limit, in which
its two modalities are being simultaneously and inter-connectedly revealed: one
of establishing and erasing reality and, simultaneously, of reviving bringing itself
back to life and dying. It is an access point that is, at the same time, a place of
emptiness (in the ontological sense), as well as of impossibility (in the cognitive
sense). Both the commonness of the imagination as well as its singularity is
brought to the foreground. From the perspective of the text, this would mean that
this singular point of view is both the only one possible (its commonness) and
autonomous and unique (its individuality).

In the tension between these two modalities poetry is born and its language
becomes activated in order to display this site of emptiness, to find the trace of the
impossible, the absolute beginning. As Levinas observes:

> From the depths of sedentary existence a nomadic memory arises. Nomadism is not
> an approach to the sedentary state. It is an irreducible relation to the earth: a sojourn
> devoid of place. Before the darkness to which art recalls us, as before death, the "I,"
> mainstay of our powers, dissolves into an anonymous "one" in a land of peregrination.
> It is the I of the Eternal Wanderer, identified by gait rather than location, along the
> border of non-truth, a realm extending farther than the true. Truth conditioned by
> errancy, errancy conditioned by truth: a distinction without difference? I think not.[285]

In the meaning outlined by Levinas, the addressee of Beckett's prose (its appropriate subject) is always and somehow inevitably (through the structure of the order coming from the voice of narrator) relational and shifted. He/she exists only in so far as the perspective shifts and the external reality becomes "disturbed." The nomadism of the subject in *Imagination Dead Imagine* is based on the fact that all of its possibilities of participation in the world, its hopes to escape the world of radical subjectivity are undermined by the oppression and hostility of the external world. Every such attempt of breaking out of the prison of immanence is undermined by the anonymity of that which is real. The nameless "oneself" is real, "oneself" that – like in Blanchot, or Levinas – is an existential principle which is impossible to be grasped linguistically. What is more, for Beckett, that namelessness of the world is a cause of possible presence of that which is singular and external to the language. That is why the figures of physical presence like heat generated by the body, its movements or breathing play such an important role throughout the course of the entire text. Sensuality thereby stops functioning solely as a necessary element in the experience of the subject establishing its own rationality through negative reference to the sphere of undifferentiated empiricism, but constitutes the embodiment of the materiality of being. The body is not only the necessary avers of consciousness and the transcendental imagination, it does not constitute only a self-designed site to fill, but also it becomes a trace of a different presence against which consciousness remains helpless. This is so because it is not able – according to Heidegger – to "grasp it thematically."

Beckett combines within his language two extreme dispositions of subjectivity. On the one side, the subjectivity enables the entire, complex and subtle mechanism of the work done by consciousness that arrives at its own boundaries, or a place of emptiness, in which all possibilities of cognition and experience are deposited. Subjectivity summons to life a potential range of its own constitution and the universality of the results of its own work. On the other side, the subject becomes uprooted from the place in which it discovers a potential, absolute identity; where, confronting the material and physical forms of presence, it establishes itself only

---

285   Levinas E., "The Poets Vision," in *Proper Names,* translated by Michael B. Smith, Stanford 1996, p. 136.

in relation to what is sensual and what is, as such, the very sign of relocation, of moving from one position onto another.

It is from that duality that the problem – so common and ambiguous in Beckett's work – that could be described as the paradox of movement is born.[286] It results no so much from the philosophical erudition of the author, skilfully used in particular works, but from problematizing one of the most fundamental aporias of Beckett's practice of writing. This particular aporia is based on the simultaneous appearance of the two equal opportunities that, while deposited in language, construct it and question it at the same time by breaking up its structure. The aporia is tied inseparably to the two phantasms that establish the structure of Beckett's subject. The first involves a tendency toward cognitive and ontological universality, a dream about reaching the foundations of all foundations. The second is connected to the necessity of breaking through the dictate of immanence and confronting consciousness with what is sensual and unmediated through the work of the critical mind. Between these two contradicting phantasms there is the language of Beckett's prose, barring both of them from becoming an ultimate point of reference. What is more, language legitimizes the aporetic tension that is created at the boundary between a dream for the pure fullness of being and a certain ground of cognition and a dream about the direct contact of consciousness with what is different.

The rhetoric of aporia used by Becket breaks the monotonous rhythm marked by both phantasms and engages language as a poetic intensity of the central image that disarms the stability of both extreme possibilities. It is – again using Beckett's term – a "vibrating greyness" that allows us to perceive both the space of the real, as well as the reality of consciousness.

Beyond the Power of Sight, or the Presence of Absence

"Panoptikum" a manifestation of the total work of art. ... Panopticon: not only does one see everything, but one sees it in all ways.[287]

– Walter Benjamin

The questions of the imagination and consciousness, sensuality and the body, constitute a borderline point in the world created by Beckett. "Ontology outside ontology" is possible only because it supports itself on the aporetic doubt that

---

286 See Brienza S., "Imagination Dead Imagine: The Microcosm of the Mind," *Journal of Beckett Studies,* 1982 no. 8, pp. 59-74.

287 Benjamin W., *The Arcades Project,* translated by Howard Eiland and Kevin McLaughlin, Cambridge 2002, p. 531.

could be otherwise described as a vibration of the language; a language that is possible to be grasped only in the motion between the terms and images in the relocation of senses between figures. The ambivalence of the practice of writing understood as both the experiment, as well as the experience (in the sense we talked about earlier) result in the subject being unable to achieve the full legitimization without the ability to base itself either on the mechanism of self-determination and verification of oneself, or with reference to external reality. That is the manner in which Beckett draws the subject, as a full form of consciousness, into question. Auto-reflection and self-knowledge of the subject can appear only in the critical phase, right before a complete surrender to the power of affects. This nevertheless means that the subject is located in a state of double impossibility. It cannot achieve any autonomy (through speculation, the scholastic division of language,[288] or through pure, unbiased opinion). It also does not find its sanction in rational reference to the object (it cannot create or establish a path of reference). In surrendering to the mercy of the materiality of the body and madness as a point of access to the working consciousness, the subject reveals itself as an enigmatic, impossible to problematise, gap visible in its structure that simultaneously creates and grants the subject existential weight. The path of critical analysis through which the subject doubts every possibility of existence, leads to the affirmation of absence.

This attitude is clearly visible in the second part of the text. Upon closer observation, concrete shapes as well as the bodies can be seen in the rotunda. In that image, the double narrative gesture achieves its high point: both the realness of the bodies and the range of consciousness's potential are questioned. There is no use for the precise, mathematical descriptions of the space in which the man and the woman are in if their persistence is transformed into a meaningless element of the internal world of the rotunda. In the end, their bodies merge with the "over exposed" background that saturates reality:

> On their right sides therefore both and back to back head to arse. Hold a mirror to their lips, it mists. With their left hands they hold their left legs a little below the knee, with their right hands their left arms a little above the elbow. In this agitated light, its great white calm now so rare and brief, inspection is not easy. Sweat and mirror notwithstanding they might well pass for inanimate but for the left eyes which at incalculable intervals suddenly open wide and gaze in unblinking exposure long beyond what is humanly possible. Piercing pale blue the effect is striking, in the beginning. Never the two gazes together except once, when the beginning of one overlapped the end of the other, for about ten seconds. Neither fat nor thin, big nor

---

288 The parody of that kind of discourse, brought to the extreme, can be found in many texts. Pointing to the most obvious examples: the "screamed" monologue of Lucky in *Waiting for Godot* and the permutational structures in the novel *Watt*.

small, the bodies seem whole and in fairly good condition, to judge by the surfaces exposed to view. The faces too, assuming the two sides of a piece, seem to want nothing essential. Between their absolute stillness and the convulsive light the contrast is striking, in the beginning, for one who still remembers having been struck by the contrary. It is clear however, from a thousand little signs too long to imagine, that they are not sleeping. [IMI, s. 363]

Once again, Beckett introduces the principle of symmetry which he enjoyed so much; one that in the case of that particular text served him not only as a principle ordering the text itself but also referring to existence itself. It creates – so to speak – a generalized structure of existence. The figures of a woman and a man are more than merely specified types of particular physicality. In the logic of the text they become figures of existence, which means that they connect within themselves both the level of physicality, as well as a sphere of extra-sensual experience. On the one hand, a precise description of the assembling of the bodies in the rotunda are brought to their extreme and marked by irony, as well as a meticulous examination of life as a biological activity and on the other side – a "superhuman" reign of the eye. The gaze of the first type is an emotionless observation in which bodies – from the perspective of the distanced consciousness – turn out to be objects. But it is precisely from that perspective that one can clearly see how limited the range of subjectivity's power is that is unable to design ("imagine") the object of its own actions, nor analyze it with detachment, turning it into an object of knowledge. Bodies in the rotunda cannot be recognized because they escape the power of representation. Consciousness, heading toward revealing the entirety of reality, toward grasping it in its essence, in the fullness of its presence and directedness, enables a system of representations, out of necessity, with which the goal can be achieved.

The empirical sphere turns out to be a giant trap as well. What could be tested with touch, or by performing a simple experiment, merely highlights former doubts. We read in the text that the man and woman inside the rotunda fail to become more real. The body, a sensual sphere, appears more like an, impossible to agree with the mind, irreducible sphere of heavy matter that, more than meaningful confirmations of the individual existence, constitutes an obstacle in the complex process of recognizing and establishing reality.

For those particular reasons, the figure of the eye seems so important. It functions (similarly to the Mouth in *Not I*) as a separate, autonomous part. Even though it belongs in a natural way to the body, being a part of it, its organic character is questioned through being placed outside of the physiological context or, more broadly, a bodily context. Paradoxically, the eye is the sign that confirms the existential consciousness of the two figures placed in the rotunda, even though its status goes beyond existential description. Its specificity is based on its disposition: it can make objects visible, creating a space of visibility and becoming a warranty of all that can come into existence.

It seems that in this way Beckett attempts to escape the cognitive and ontological impasse thus far presented. In the figure of the eye, the body and consciousness, presence and absence would be focused into one. However, that would merely be an illusion. "Pale blue" and "piercing" turns out to be the final sanction confirming the fictionality of all the orders of that which is real. The eye, even though it creates the space of the visible,[289] it is a visibility – as the previous phrase claims – "superhuman," which cannot be justified through consciousness or through the sensation of the body. It is not through the light of reason or the flash of the body; it is not physicality that remains sanctified through the celebration of its materiality and intransitiveness as a permanent form of existence – as a visibility of that which is invisible. What is at stake is also the problematizing of the very act of looking. Beckett's strategy recalls the effects described by Georges Didi-Huberman:

> (…) we must close our eyes to see how act of seeing comes back to us, how it opens us to a void which looks at us, concentrate us and – in a sense – create us.[290]

Beckett extracts the final consequences from the desire to grasp and express the foundations of reality and not only contradicts the possibility of finding such a foundation but also opens the only possibility in which the individual existence can become justified. The effort of realizing absence constitutes that opportunity.

In *Imagination Dead Imagine*, the effort can be spotted most clearly in two instances. The first one, already mentioned, is the eye that could be read as – by referring to the analysis of Jacque Derrida concerned with the question of self-portraits – a figure of the "narcissistic Cyclops" whose gaze does not refer to any object but alone becomes an object of fixation or obsession, or becomes directed

---

289 Two of the contemporary interpretations of the term "visibility" seem to be the most interesting. In the first place, the phenomenological interpretation of Maurice Merleau-Ponty presents that which is visible and rips open the horizon of possible presence while escaping both the sphere of sense (not allowing itself to be thought or undergo reflection) and the sphere of being. "That which is visible" in that perspective would be a sign of mystery that should be experienced in the process of perception. See Merleau-Ponty M., *L'Œil et L'Esprit*, Paris 1964; also *The Visible and Invisible,* translated by Alphonso Lingis, Evanston 1969. For the second approach, that could be described as deconstructive (both Jacques Derrida and Georges Didi-Huberman would fit that category), the most important is – firstly – problematizing the opposition between the visible and invisible, and – secondly – turning attention to the fact of the irreducible materiality of reality (through that which is visible), which rips the dialectic of the visible-invisible apart. See especially, Didi-Huberman G., *Devant l'image,* Op. cit.

290 Didi-Huberman G., *Ce qui nous voyons, ce qui nous regarde*, Paris 1992, p. 11.

into the emptiness of the objectival world. In other words, the "narcissistic Cyclops" does not pay attention to what he sees because his gaze does not display a referential aspect.[291]

In the first case, what is most important remains the gesture of the fundamentally autotelic character of sight, but also its internalization. Derrida, while analyzing examples from painting, states that it is the eye of a blind man, or an eye of death. This means that the radically understood internalization of the gaze is not – as the interpretative tradition states – a discovery of a true, timeless wisdom that does not fall for the temptations of the external world of illusions. Rather, it constitutes a gesture of a radical contradiction aimed at the possibility of discovering a stable ontological ground and a final cognitive space. The Cyclops gazes because it is the only sphere in which he can acquire an identity, as if gazing was his only and finally activity, as well as the sanction that protects him from falling into the abyss. From that perspective, the eye in Beckett's text is non-human, not in the sense of a divine all-knowing total presence, however, but rather in the sense of the horror that is inscribed in its design and mechanics. The only reason for its existence, and the only function that it serves, is the necessity of looking, the imperative of "producing" gazes that, by celebrating their own limitations and capabilities, devour themselves. The eye seems to find fullfillment in the very act of opening, in the very potentiality of looking and not in the actual observing of reality. Such an interpretation is almost literally following the text word for word – the eye remains open unnaturally long and its only projection is the emptiness of representation. It does not make anything visible, on the contrary: it negates entirely the need for the visibility of objects ("reality") operating in the consecutive openings for the sake of its own instability, being a sign of mourning after the catastrophe which it announced; a catastrophe that would take the form of a disappearance of all signs of life, extinguishing the imagination, consciousness and resulting in the disintegration of the body.[292]

The second possibility refers to the essence of a "Cyclopes'" gaze. It is the opposite of both deep insight and a distanced, theoretical examination. According to Derrida, one is concerned with a gaze for which nothing is a singular point, place or experience that should be exposed, described or lived through. The eye that sees nothing has no ability to grant visibility, hence presence. On the other

---

291 See Derrida J., *Mémoires d'aveugle. L'autoportrait et autres ruines*, Réunion des musées nationaux, Paris 1999, p. 61. See Connor S., "Between theatre and Theory. „Long Observation of the Ray," in *Samuel Beckett Vision and Mouvement*, ed. K. Kondo, Tokyo 2006. See also Arsic B, *The Passive Eye. Gaze and Subjectivity in Berkeley (via Beckett)*, Stanford 2003.

292 See Hill L., "Late Text: Writing the Work of Mourning," *Samuel Beckett Today/Aujourd'hui* 1992, pp. 10-25.

hand, the proper gaze becomes immersed in absence and invisibility. In that last case, it is not about the abyss of invisibility that is deprived of meaning (what Heidegger defined as *Ab-grund*)[293] but about the impossibility of making being present, defining it as an object of cognition or experience. The invisibility (or rather the impossibility of visibility) that marks the narcissistic gaze of the eye in Beckett's text also means that it constitutes a veil that it is impossible to remove, behind which – paradoxically – there is no mystery in the sense of the source of all sense that does not allow itself to be discovered. It is the very gaze that becomes a mystery that focuses the attention of the subject-observer on itself.

But the eye is also a figure of delay in the sense that in its opening, that is full of tension and is immobile, it shows that time is feigned, hence not only immaterial but also almost completely deprived of traces of the real. The eye persists in its opening that is impossible to tame and breaks the order of the world available to the subject. That moment constitutes both the existential argument that confirms the factuality of the existence of particular figures in the rotunda, as well as the argument for the impossibility of experiencing time that is more like an "emptiness of difference" of the passing moments than the deepest, linguistically ungraspable rule of the individual existence. It is not about any form of epiphany, or a flicker of the eye [*Augenblick*], [294] or even the stable ontological dimension of a foundation

---

293 Heidegger states the following: "In trying to lay the ground for Metaphysics, Kant was pressed in a way that makes the proper foundation into an abyss." M. Heidegger, Op. cit., 202.

294 I am making an allusion here to Heidegger's analysis from *Being and Time* in which the metaphor of "eyesight" becomes included in the more general rhetoric of temporalising the being. The "flicker of the eye" – through the reference to the historicity of being – points to connections with other crucial terms from Heidegger's dictionary (*Wiederholung* – "repetition or retrieval" or *Entschlossenheit* – "resoluteness" as well as "disclosedness"). This is the case because the majority of his concrete research remained devoted to the search for connections between the being and time. In the case of Beckett's practice – with which I am working –temporality allows for the establishment, legitimation and decomposure of subjectivity interchangeably, at the same time creating an inventive poetic language. Beckett does not leave any hope for saving individuality through giving oneself away into the power of "being" that, at its base, is an authentic experience of time. Alternatively, it suggests a path of unending critique, a work of consciousness and undermining language; one that could prolong the phantasm of finding reconciliation for individual consciousness with the sphere of reality, access to which is possible only through the effort of reworking what is borrowed. See Melberg A., *Teorie mimesis. Repetycja*, Op. cit., pp. 194-202. In that sense the "utopia of negative aesthetics" proposed by Bohrer seems to be an interesting context for thought; Borher for whom Beckett's texts could constitute an expression of radical objection against the epiphany of the master-author: Joyce (but also Proust or Musil). The "constellation of the eye" established by Beckett with an almost obsessive insight and repetitiveness would be an attempt to acquire access

external to time. Beckett shows in the figure of the perceiving eye not only the dramatic dispersion of time that deprives itself of a human constitution and does not grant it existential sense, but also makes itself aware of the irreversible logic of the deformation of the reality – it changes not so much under the pressure of passing time, but under the influence of the changing, imperfect apparatus of perception. When we read that the motionlessness of the figure is a surprise for the subject from Beckett's story, the most important element is not the object of that change, but change itself. Both the enigmatic character of the transfer (for example, from one state into another), as well as the amazement of the fact that something completely different is seen, or that something else can become an object of seeing; an object that emerges from what seemingly looks like a permanently grounded and unconditionally identical object. The eye is a figure of difference and distance (inscribed in the very structure of perceiving) that does not bring with it, nor does it expect, any concrete meaning. In other words, persistence in a "superhuman" state of being open, the eye becomes a figure of absence that, even though felt in the deepest sense, escapes the power of representation. That is how one can understand the emphatic last sentence from the cited excerpt. The power of repressing and limiting expanding reality belongs to the eye – even the slightest "tremor" has to be "contained." From that perspective, every form of existence caught in the frame of the "human gaze" is killed and disappears in the silence of an increasingly expunged reality.

The effort (but also the desire) to realize absence refers to not only the faculties of perception but also to language. Speech does not serve communication, nor is it a transparent vehicle for sense but it does not constitute a handy tool or a habitat, in which the lone life could take shelter. For Beckett, the question concerns mostly the range of consciousness, the examination of that which appears in its field – language is a space of not only meaning and stories but of an event and of acquiring the voice by which it becomes impossible. The relationship between consciousness and language is extremely important here but it does not lead toward a clear judgment or the complete presence of objects. Rather, it legitimizes the work of searching without a clear goal. The subject, according to the rules of negative dialectics, reveals the following mediations that it attempts to check as meticulously as possible. And it does so for the price of cognitive scepticism.

---

to the "immanence of experience" once again; the same mentioned by Adorno in his *Aesthetic Theory* and repeated by Borher. It would be an attempt, however, in which the poetic idiom becomes inscribed in the game with the enigmatic infinity of the very negativity, every time escaping the act of consciousness, but only imaginable through it. From that perspective, all images of the world and lightness are not signs on a Manichean set of reality, but the only moments that release consciousness from the terrifying boredom of persisting in "the same." See Bohrer K. H., *Ästhetische Negativität*, München 2002.

This logic of the "wall of words"[295] leads Beckett in two opposite directions. The first is connected with a fundamental, epistemological scepticism based on the affirmation (leading, as a consequence, to cognitive sarcasm) of the very mechanism of questioning that, which exists. The strategy of questioning rationality (understood in the sense of a source or strong presence) using its own devices is connected with the second direction in which Beckett is headed – the search for a place for poetic idiom to appear, for the work of language outside the neurotic reign of consciousness, outside of the metaphysical oppositions of truth and falsity, being and nothingness. However, this movement of searching for the place that I have attempted to show earlier has no end and does not close at a one particular place (the imagination). It does not fulfil itself in a final synthesis combining presence and sense into one (the sphere of visibility of which the eye was supposed to be the working metaphor). Beckett works particularly hard to sustain both of these directions in a state of mutual tension. Even though they make the figures of aporia and the gap the only plausible versions of subjectivity, they open the space of experience of that which is different through the consciousness and not through assimilation. In that sense, the subject becomes a postponing of identity and presence or, in other words, becomes legitimate for the price of allowing itself close to that which does not obey the law of presence. It is not about constructing a new metaphysical model in which poetry would become merely a linguistic effect stemming from previous assumptions (philosophical, ideological or artistic), but about a gesture about the fundamental opening and sustaining of hope for existing outside the available ways of grasping or projecting reality – outside of consciousness, imagination and language.

> Presence of absence, fullness of emptiness, "unfurling" of that which nevertheless hides and remains closed – a light shining on the dark, a light bright from the clarity of this darkness, which abducts and ravishes the dark in the first light of the unfurling, but also disappears into the absolutely obscure whose essence is to close in upon whatever would reveal it, to attract this disclosure into itself and swallow it up.[296]

Are Levinas, Blanchot and Beckett concerned with the possibility of moving from the distinctions of reason to experience, from the category of consciousness to the world of the senses? Or perhaps their concern is with the possibility for the explication of that which is absent through the representational power of language? It seems that the positive answer to both of these questions shows only half of the complexity of the issue. The impenetrable darkness in Beckett's

---

295 I refer to Adorno's formulations from his essay introducing the works of Benjamin. Adorno states: "He immersed himself in reality as in a palimpsest." To paraphrase, "a wall of words provided his homeless thought authority and shelter."

296 Levinas E., Op. cit., p. 133. Levinas cites Blanchot from *L'espace littéraire*, Op. cit., pp. 235-236.

work is a metonymy of absence for which one cannot find a foundation or any grounds. That is why, when confronted by it, the poetic gesture does not exhaust itself during a questioning of the assumptions of the potential of consciousness (concerned with the possibility of representation, imagination and expression) but reaches much further. It is an affirmation of that which is negative that becomes a way of arriving at the source of absence; at the impossible beginning of the reality that has been always been contaminated with an empty band of time, up until the point where the lack of an identity is revealed; a lack that cannot be overcome. The subject in Beckett's work is impossible to conceive of without the negativity that is, at the same time, a category of consciousness and a fundamental dimension of poetic language.

When Levinas and Blanchot speak about darkness, the existence of which cannot be reduced to any order of the source of presence they use rhetoric in which the loss of being is the only chance for saving the experience of the accidental quality of existence: the only possibility for withdrawing beyond the objectification of a singular existence and escaping the law of historicity that becomes a nihilistic rule, in so far as it immobilizes that which is entirely un-identifiable within a false identity. In both cases, lightness is associated with the violence of metaphysics,[297] the light of day with the necessity for existence.[298] According to Beckett, full rationality as a warranty of the liberation of the subject from its contingency does not establish an order of universal presence but becomes a sphere of the impossibility of experience. The performance of that gesture that is contained in a paradoxical order of revealing darkness is possible only through referring to the language that will constantly oscillate between the strictness of the view and the precision of the category and invention and semantic density of the poetic figure. Between these two poles the idiom of Beckett's poetry vibrates. It means that it exists in the movement from absence to presence, from absolute darkness to "raging" light. Through the poetry of absence one can look both into

---

297   See Levinas E., *Totality and* Infinity, translated by Alphonso Lingis, Pittsburgh 2007. In Blanchot's things are similar. The language of metaphysics is based on violence as much as it refers to the authority of a subjectival-objectival knowledge and identity. The opening to what is "outside" of language, the subject, the visible world and the goal, the utterance of silence and the event of death: "Is it this, to die, is it this, fear? The silent dread, and this silence, like a cry without words: mute." M. Blanchot, *Le pas au-delà*, Paris 1973, p. 87. In English edition, see p. 61. Beckett – even though similar from the perspective of searching for a new language and the "speech of the other" – is focused on the very fact of cognition and the necessity of picking up the thread of its mediation through various forms of language. It mediates, hence attempts to embody, the inevitable historicity of a singular consciousness and grant it concrete existential verification.

298   This happens in one of the prose works of Blanchot. See Blanchot M., *Thomas the Obscure,* translated by Robert Lamberton, Barrytown 1995.

the empty place of the imagination, as well as observe the stillness of figures whose outlines die and become reborn, existing independently of the analogically running cycles of enigmatic light that die out and reveals itself in an unexpected way – differently every time.

In the Rhythm of Death

In Beckett's text, when we read about the surprise created by the change of the state of reality for the subject, we touch upon the principle of empty temporality but also find ourselves at the point in our reading that announces the coming of the end of the difficult process of imagining and talking:

> Leave them there, sweating and icy, there is better elsewhere. No, life ends and no, there is nothing elsewhere, and no question now of ever finding again that white speck lost in whiteness, to see if they still lie in the stress of that storm, or of a worse storm, or in the black dark for good, or the great whiteness unchanging, and if not what they are doing. [IMI, s. 363]

One could say that the end of the work is parallel to the extreme effort of the imagination that wishes to find the final point of reference. It seems that the stigma of mortality is inscribed into the body of the man and woman sitting in the rotunda. It marked the ones sitting inside of the rotunda with working consciousness, imagination and language. At the same time, it is merely another point of existence, one more necessary turn after a tiring process of analyzing one's own projections and after the completed search for a final sanction of reality that cannot be questioned in any other way. According to Beckett, the end is headed toward an impossible ending, toward the inert but also necessary work of the consciousness aimed at the space in which "there is nothing." How different is that emptiness from the emptiness belonging to the imagination! Dying and resurrecting the imagination turned out to be the only legitimate way of justifying consciousness as existence and also constituted a final consequence of a desperate subjectivity for which emancipation is no longer a transgression beyond its own condition, or a complete surrender to the neutral voice of the exterior, but submitting itself to negativity. The ending of Beckett's work seems to be a final, but also the natural consequence of sustaining the expiration of consciousness as the price for life.

Death is accompanied by the paralysis of language and the fall, a construct of the imagination that constitutes the reality of the reign of sight. There remains only one repetition that not only intensifies the previous sensations, conclusions, observations, and desires but – most of all – it constitutes a way of saving the subject from the death of the imagination and its complete withdrawal. But the repetition of the entirety of experience is an equally as radical as it is impossible, behind which is hidden the dream of extracting a textual sign of what is absent. The rhythm of repetition, registered by Beckett with the same strength in the last phrases of the work, is a rhythm of death with which the subject in *Imagination Dead Imagine* constantly experiments, which it wants to express but, most importantly, which he wants to experience. In that sense, the ending of the work is most certainly one of the bravest realizations of the modern ideal of "writing as a deathwork"[299]:

> The literary work brings us closer to death, because death is that endless rustle of being that the work causes to murmur. In death as in the work of art, the regular order is reversed, since, in it, power leads to what is unassumable. Thus the distance between life and death is infinite. Also infinite is the poet's work before the inexhaustible language that is the unfolding or more precisely the rolling or even the commotion of being. Death is not the end, it is the never-ending ending.[300]

Writing is ruled by the principle of *metastasis* of the representation of being that is not found under the rule of presence, hence escaping the metaphysics, but remains extracted to the surface of the linguistic sign on the basis of an objection against the stable forms of existence. Despite the Heidegger's linguistic staffage, Blanchot's statements could be referred to Beckett's work with the full force (as well as to its rule of "ending") in the sense that they combine the experience of writing strictly with the ripping of subject that is never independently capable of establishing itself, nor can it free itself from the pressure of consciousness and expose itself fully to be influenced by the exterior[301]. Levinas, in an effective metaphor of "the sway of being," says almost exactly the same thing as Beckett who, as previously mentioned in several places, reaches the edge of language and attempts to use the term "vibrating greyness," the image of which seems to be the last stage in the approximate[302] journey of consciousness against death. The entire affair could be treated as longing for finding the definite, irreducible level of reality (in no way

---

299   It is present both in the texts from the tradition represented by Blanchot, as well as in the texts by Adorno who, ending his essay about Beckett's *Endgame* stated the following concerning the protagonists of the work: "Consciousness begins to look its own demise in the eye, as if it wanted to survive the demise, as these two want to survive the destruction of their world". Adorno T. W., "Trying to Understand Beckett's Endgame," in *Notes to Literature,* vol. 1, New York 1991.
300   Levinas E., Op. cit.
301   In that sense, Blanchot, just as Levinas, tries to express resistance against the system of Hegel in which the "external" has been subdued to the dialectics of the whole, which constitutes the fullness of what is real. At the same time, however, without that particular reference the thought of these authors would never carry a proper weight.
302   The approximation should be understood here etymologically as, simultaneously, "approaching" and "explaining and clearing up." Both dimensions appear inseparable

mediated symbolically), the pseudonym of which might be "white speck lost in whiteness," but the course of the entire text and the ending seem to be much more complex.

In the final part of the text there are still images that highlight the possibility of the world existing after the catastrophe of death. These rudimentary representations illustrate, however, the stubborn imperative of the will stuck in the subject – undertaking the efforts of consciousness. That is what the tautological highlighting of the contradictions that build the framework of this world are for; frameworks that highlight its lack of transparency. At that moment in the text, in a very contracted and condensed way, the aporetic structure of the subject is revealed. Simultaneously, it is working to stabilize its own position again (to grasp the "white point" with the gaze) and to confront itself with the obstacle of mediations that become increasingly monstrous ("great whiteness unchanging.")

What then is the movement of the subject? Certainly it is not a movement of unification, of constructing identity. On the contrary, it constitutes a search for empty spaces that neither speech, nor consciousness will reach. These empty spaces are spaces absolutely free from the necessity of sense, unrelated to any language and constituting a pure potentiality; they become places for the subject to await what can emerge from the gesture of retraction. The subject founded on the imagination attempts to steer clear of the two versions of totality besetting it: the silent reality against which the means of taming it is a transformation of that which is perceived in a literary image ("white speck lost in whiteness") and a mediation that is impossible to represent (hence to make it a subject of consciousness) ("great whiteness unchanging"). The subject "after death" repeats and attempts once more to go back to the source of all possible speech.

Blanchot wrote very insightfully about the necessity of such a return that is a final result of the practice of writing as an exercise of consciousness, but also – in the deepest sense – about the beginning of a new language:

> The Open is the poem. The space where everything returns to deep being, where there is infinite passage between the two domains, where everything dies but where death is the learned companion of life, where horror is ravishing joy, where celebration laments and lamentation praises – the very space toward which "all worlds hasten as toward their nearest and truest reality," the space of the mightiest circulation and of ceaseless metamorphosis – this is the poem's space. This is the Orphic space to which the poet doubtless has no access, where he can penetrate only to disappear, which he attains only when he is united with the intimacy of the breach that makes him a mouth

---

in Beckett's work, behind which there is a tendency to search for that which is real, accompanying work of consciousness and language.

unheard, just as it makes him who hears into the weight of silence. The Open is the work, but the work as origin.[303]

For Blanchot, the language of poetry (and the intense form of poetry) is the most appropriate register in which the "murmur of being" can resound. His thinking shows that neither the explication of the text, nor its understanding can constitute a final sanction justifying the existence of poetry. Its language is assembled not according to the rigor of reference, but through an instance of experience. It is a gesture of opening to what cannot be represented, shown as a theme, problem or category. In that way, the space of literature is described with the language of utopia. It assumes the hope that there can be an important experience coming into existence in the sphere of speech; one that by omitting the level of expression and representation simultaneously liberates the subject from the necessity of its authority. This utopian dream is shattered by the return to a reference in the form of metaphysics. Even though this reference is highly critical, it does not change the fact that the basic vision of Blanchot is the same: there is no expressed absence that would situate itself outside of a metaphysical sanction. Any word cannot simultaneously exist as an element of language and be its "neutralized" form or its absence. And yet, at the end of Beckett's work the focus is on the gesture of invention that serves "inventing" an entirely different, incomparable with any other; language[304] that would not only communicate absence but would also become an absence. It would be an entirely "new" language in the sense that it would be created after the "death" of language understood as a system of differences and communications thanks to which it would be possible, at least to a much reduced degree, to express.

What is it then that this – uniquely understood – concept of poetry brings in exchange for the "old" language? According to Blanchot, poetry is a movement of language toward silence that does not mean simply imply the impossibility of speech, but is a means of locating the primal sphere of language. However, this aim is far from the naïve affirmation of "that which is real" and far from the technical procedure allowing for the production of clear and transparent meanings and reveals a logic that rules the creation and shaping of language outside of metaphysical oppositions. The poetic movement of language reveals the order of the source of speech that is not an aseptic, an untainted emptiness and a transcendental condition of possibility, but a paradoxical emptiness due to the law of a continuous metamorphosis of meanings and shifts of linguistic figures. The experience of the source is also a confrontation of the writing subject with the

---

303 Blanchot M., *The Space of Literature,* Op. cit., p. 142.
304 See a brilliant study of the quoted above in the direct Beckettian context: Clément B., *L'invention du commentaire: Augustin, Jacques Derrida*, Paris 2000.

sphere of externality that questions the possibility of understanding through the pressure of the system of language and through a clash between two intimacies: one created by the literary space and one that is constituted by the desperate silence of the subject. That is why it is not hard to understand that Blanchot uses the term "disappearance." But who or what is indeed disappearing?

First, the traditionally understood capability of literature to gain access to the reality through a linguistic reference disappears. Instead of being a confirmation of an existing reality, writing becomes a continuous process of questioning that, which appears as present. The opportunity of literature is the abandonment by the writer of dreams about a stable identity. The revelation and extraction of the individuality of existence is, according to Blanchot, a "madness of the day." The task of literature is to make the search for the lack of coherence in what is seemingly established and unquestionably existing. That is why Blanchot reverses the classical ontology, posing a requirement on poetic speech; one of discovering places in which langue questions itself.

Secondly, the subject disappears. However, the notion of "disappearing" in this context has to be understood in two ways in this context. On the one hand, the act of questioning the process of subjectival emancipation hides behind it; one that takes place through cracking the singular cohesiveness and establishing the horizon of death in which that singularity exists. On the other (much more important) side, "disappearing" is concerned with the experience of that which is absent and pertains to the disintegration of the structure of the subject; a disintegration that happens through a gesture of opening toward the workings of a nothingness external to language.

In *Imagination Dead Imagine* all the elements of the world undergo gradual annihilation. First, the status of the imagination as a creative force turns out to be uncertain. Next, the fragmentary and temporary representations of the world undergo annihilation while being supported by the power of gaze. This disappearance includes the attentive self that works paradoxically – the more it tries to sustain the certainty of its own constitution, the more its position becomes unstable. The more language it uses headed toward the precision, the more it reveals of its uncoordinated efforts. Consciousness, similar to imagination that it constitutes – as is common belief – reveals its own emptiness; that on which it is founded. Reality dies down completely under the influence of a thetic consciousness, the desire of which is not only that which has been almost directly expressed in the text – the arrival at the irreducible point of absolute identity, in which what was real would no longer require any form of language, but also – or perhaps especially – would make the simultaneous representation and the experience of death possible.

Hence, consciousness is alone in two ways. First, one is concerned with a menacing loneliness; loneliness as isolation. This surfaces when subjectivity, desiring to legitimize its own efforts, has not so much as to try to continuously actualize the power of language (use it) but rather refer to its potentiality and universality. Striving for that state in which the experience would become a possibility, it loses the sanction of rationality and, as a consequence, it "faints" under the pressure of the exterior from it attempts to defend itself (which Beckett contains within recurring rhythmically "phrase-moments" in which a "barely perceptible quiver" takes place). Second, we are talking about significant loneliness. In Beckett's prose (it this particular work, but also in many others[305]) loneliness understood that way becomes a way for a continuous inciting of the rhythm of speech that becomes a promise of both itself and the torn subject. Beckett leads the individual in two equally radical and equally important, for the understanding of his writing, directions: toward the loneliness of solipsism, the inertia of a cognitive language and a neurotic consciousness, as well as in the direction of the confession that comes from natural language. Between these two extreme possibilities there is a language of event, hence the language of poetry and opening.

Ruby Cohn, one of the most distinguished interpreters of Beckett's work, is most certainly right when she states that most of his short texts focuses on the 'movement from death or the non-existence of life.'[306] The last word of the work is "doing." It seems that it is not only a confirmation of the researcher's words but also – or maybe especially – the next opening after another "last" and "impossible" phrase, proper to a language that is beyond essence; a phrase that belongs to the voice of poetry that in *Imagination Dead Imagine* constitutes the fullest expression of the affirmation of absence of the unreal, constantly hypostatized beginnings and ends.

In Beckett's view, writing is an action somewhat without the ability to rest, organically necessary but also lonely and unconfirmed, without hope for fulfilment through the revelation of sense. Both of these circulations create one experience of poetry that should be understood in this case not so much through the prism of a genre, but functionally as a space of language itself, in which multiple voices compete with one another. As Derrida stated, it is all about 'the birth of rhythm beyond oppositions or exteriority, conscious imagination and an abandoned archive' or the answer coming from language. It is all the fable that becomes

---

305   It seems that the loneliness understood in that way, as a fundamental dimension of existence and being, was already fully formed in *Molloy*. See Hill L., *Beckett's Fiction: In Different Words*, Cambridge 1990.

306   Cohn R., *Back to Beckett*, Princeton 1973, p. 256. See also Davies P., *The Ideal Real. Fiction and Imagination*, London – Toronto 1994, pp. 131 – 153.

an emblem of all history, all literature's possible experience; literature that is an *exemplum* of every presented situation, one that "writes you, to you, about you"[307] This is the final word in Beckett's work: an agreement of the lone consciousness to allow into the sphere of its own language that, which is impossible. What is more, it is a detonation of the potential of negativity that is stored in language, a movement according to the project of disinheriting the subject from a language that allows to speak only about what exists, what is revealed as the fullness of presence and is hidden in appearances and representation. After such a lesson in negativity, literature's speech can become another beginning of another language that will shield, with its dense network of repetitions, the dominating absence of the singular, exceptional existence. It may become the promise of an ideal idiom that, from the language of affirmation of the visible reality will become transformed[308] in another figure of the poetry of absence. [309]

---

307 Derrida J., *Che cos'é la poesia ?*, przeł. M. P. Markowski, „Literatura na Świecie" 1998 no. 11-12, pp. 159, 157.

308 See Knottenbelt E. M., "Samuel Beckett: Poetry As Performative Art," *Samuel Beckett Today/ Aujourd'hui* 1990 no. 2.

309 This textual mechanism of the aporia of a simultaneous starting and ending is interpreter in a different spirit by Harold Bloom who juxtaposes mind's self-control and the bearing capacity of an individual project with a rhetorical power of the poetic language. However, only from the conflict between these two powers (project and language) a writerly idiom can come into existence that will get it energy, paradoxically, from designing its own finality. Bloom states while using ambiguity of one of Beckett's short prose pieces: "Hope is alien to Beckett's mature fiction, so that we can say its images are Gnostic but not its program, since it lacks all program. A Gnosticism without potential transcendence is the most negative of all possible negative stances, and doubles accounts for the sympathetic reader's sense that every crucial work by Beckett necessarily must be his last. Yet the grand paradox is that lessness never ends in Beckett." Bloom, H. "Freud and Beyond," in *Ruin the Sacred Truths*, Cambridge, 1991, p. 201.

Chapter Two
Existence as Correction

> Two possibilities: making oneself infinitely small or being so. The second is perfection,
> that is to say, inactivity, the first is beginning, that is to say, action.[310]
> – Franz Kafka

Still holds a special place in Beckett's work.[311] In no other piece of his short prose
(perhaps with the exception of *Ping*) did he reach such a level of intensity, with
such a strong effect of language resounding in such an incredibly limited form
of expression. For that reason, the work is not only mysterious but also realizes
the previously described strategy of searching for the total idiom of writing in
which linguistic invention undergoes the work of consciousness that pertains
to the pure potentiality of sense. The image of subjectivity is incredibly strong
there – its importance becomes, almost entirely, contained within the process of
searching for an ultimately certain condition of the possibility of expression. A
work read from that perspective turns out to be a poetic reflection on entrapment
in the antinomies of language that determine an order of expression and establish
the rules in which reality abides.

The title is ambiguous. It connotes both stillness, calmness, but also persistence
(in the sense of "still on") which in Beckett's dictionary means mortality and
darkness. One should add that this double meaning gains within the text a dynamic
actualization and, as a consequence, allows the author to sustain the mechanism
of establishing and destabilizing potential ontological conditions: presence and
absence, action and inaction. In that way the opening of the text heads toward an
absolute contradiction that cannot be, in the end, diffused or reworked in any available
orders: being, existential or cognitive. However, it is that ideal of the irreducible
contradiction that constitutes a starting point for constructing the textual whole.

The Real – Between Light and Darkness

A fundamental conviction about the contradictory character of language leads
Beckett to thematising contradictions that are born in the act of speech. It starts at

---

310   Kafka F., "Reflections on Sin, Suffering, Hope, and the True Way," *in The Great Wall of
      China: Stories and Reflections,* translated by Willa and Edwin Muir, New York 1946.
311   See Pilling J., *The Significance of Beckett's "Still",* "Essays in Criticism: A Quarterly
      Journal of Literary Criticism" 1978, no. 28.

the very beginning, when the dialectic connection – known under many different forms from Beckett's works – between light and darkness is introduced. At the same time, however, this dialectic should be understood in a negative way, which means that light and darkness do not constitute any permanent, symbolic references and are not easily graspable, or even an observable moment that would announce a different, fuller form of reality. Finally, it does not allow any notional, graspable or categorical sense to be reworked, abolished or sublated (in the sense of *Aufhebung*) in a concrete manner. Both forms of this conjugation often coalesce into one, indifferent and extremely difficult to describe, although strongly influential, sphere of being or reveal themselves in the text in the form of a definite cut, an ontological whole in the reality both grasped and constructed linguistically.

At the beginning, however, one faces one of the most fundamental and difficult to understand gestures that condition one's participation in the world. We are concerned with placing the subject that attempts to display its own position in relation to what is external:

> Bright at last close of a dark day the sun shines out at last and goes down. Sitting quite still at valley window normally turn head now and see it the sun low in the southwest sinking. [S, p. 415]

It is not, however, a primary situation but rather an ungraspable moment of the birth of inactive consciousness, or a version of it for which there cannot be a beginning or the end. In that way the elementary starting point is already undermined at the beginning and consequently disintegrates the possibility of a legitimate telling of the story or constructing a description. It is worthwhile to observe that Beckett builds an impression of insolvability in a very simple way, based on the principle of reversing the poles in a natural order of things. One cannot even decide if lightness belongs to the sphere of day, or if it is a temporary resting moment after darkness (the same way it is presented in the text), or if it is the other way around: a momentary, but painful, flash of the sun turns out to be an other worldly element of the night. Beckett does not construct any metaphor of the human condition but rather points to the innate consequences that result from searching for the absolute subjectival stability in the confrontation with the pre-established, paradoxical constitution of the perceived world. Day and lightness are inevitably contaminated with darkness, similar to the way night is conditioned by the light of the setting sun. The process of subject's constitution runs parallel. The simplest gesture confirming a single being (in the work: within the image of turning the head) transforms not only into an act of deconstruction of the world in place, but also destroys all dreams about the absolute existential fulfilment. That is how one could explain the title in the first place: as a figure of radical separation and an image of exclusion from the consciousness of a seemingly natural and undisputable rigor of the empirical reality. Meanwhile, it is precisely that dream that becomes a primary phantasm that, one the one hand, grants access to an individual to a space of what is unexpected and, on the other hand, almost entirely undermines the weight of that which exists.

The initiated negative dialectic of light and darkness from the very beginning leads not only toward the phantasmal character of the subject but also allows for the dominance of the epistemological within the text. This is not about anthropocentrism in the hard sense, from the perspective of which the subject, regardless of its fictionality, establishes consciously and linguistically the inalienable element of reality. Once again, Beckett goes for the primary disposition of the individual that not only observes its elements but also creates its representations while thrown into the world but, most importantly, engages in the work of its own, individual consciousness. It is that consciousness that undermines the illusions under which the essence of the world is presented and its focus is very much directed toward the fact of observation. Consciousness does not bring together scattered sensations and thoughts into one sphere of a reasonable word – *logos* – but works in a revolutionary way, revealing the emptiness of sense. On the one hand, it establishes the subject as such, on the other – it constantly deconstructs it. That dynamic of consciousness does not allow itself to be removed and is kept in an unsteady contemporariness over which reigns the principle of negation.

In *Still* the logic of perception is contaminated throughout the entire course of the text with the logic of consciousness. To understand the latter, figures of looking are the most important:

> Eyes stare out unseeing till first movement some time past close through unseeing still while still light.
> Or anywhere any open staring out at nothing just failing light quite still till quite dark though of course no such thing just less light still when less did not seem possible. [S, pp. 415, 416].

The immediately imposed symbolic key seems to be insufficient. Even though the authority of sight is extremely important throughout the text, it does not pertain to some permanent metaphysical order that exists outside of the space delineated by the written word. The course of *Still*[312] proves how far away its structure is placed outside the principle of a symbol or metaphor. The gaze is not an emblem of light and lasting reason or a possibility and range of perception, but rather the only element of a metonymic line allowing to show the aporetic situation of the subjectivity. Looking initiates the logic of the chain of corrections of the position

---

312 One is concerned with a particular progression of language that is based on subduing its fundamental structures to the rigor of permutations and repetitions, alliterations and internal rhymes, or to the similar – just like in *Ping*, *Ill seen Ill said* or *Not I* – principle of textual construction.

of the working consciousness, which desire to be entirely liberated from itself and from the necessity of observing – all at the same time – becomes the only goal. However, more importantly, it becomes the only means of legitimizing its own, far from obvious and disturbing autonomy. But even that gaze remains employed by the author within the constructed image of the body: repressed, surrendered to the dictate of a deadly oversight of consciousness, mute and – even though completely alien – entirely impossible to describe. It is difficult to decide if the body remains entirely degraded because Beckett had almost entirely abolished the hierarchy inside the world he constructed. One does not know on which side there is a dominating presence of meaning, which of the sides of the traditional metaphysical set up is granted the status of an unquestionable presence. On the side, it is the body (one of the forms of actualization, which is physiologically understood as the body) that constitutes the only warranty of that which is real. On the other side, this empirical and perceptional aspect of reality remains completed (but also undermined) by the transcendental aspect in which that which is ungraspable for the senses comes forward.

This paradox, based largely on breaking through the opposition of nature and consciousness, is perfectly visible in the first of the above-mentioned phrases. Beckett, using the optical mechanisms guiding the gaze, breaks the seeming objectivism of the description and introduces the dialectic of light and darkness once again. Closing and opening one's eyes seems to be a physiological act, but in the space of the text guided by a fundamental logic of poetic repetition it becomes a desire to find a completely different sphere of being, enigmatic and not following any rules: of consciousness, language or body. We are concerned with a logic that would exclude any form of dialectics, reasonability, hierarchy and discursiveness, and one that would hence be inhuman.

This striving toward what is inhuman is most noticeable in the second quoted excerpt, a key moment for the entire text. The gaze (that is a symptom of physicality, sometimes illustrates the movement of de-physicalisation) turned toward pure nothingness. First, however, it arrives at a very concrete sphere of darkness and disappearing light. The line of the gaze, even though based on impossibility and its ungraspable character seems to be understandable. Looking becomes a search for that which is impossible and – as a consequence – contradicts its own essence and its own status: it does not confirm physical presence, nor does it strengthen authoritarian, sweeping reality. In exchange, it continuously oscillates around the boundary of that which could be observed, but also that which could be designed. In effect, such a borderline perspective blurs the unanimous status of reality. There is no more significant difference between the reality that physically exists and one which is established by the conditions of the possibility of cognition.

It is difficult to say that Beckett's text is a poetic realization of the phenomenological dream of direct insight into the essence of things themselves. In *Still* one does not confront any suspension of the empirically existing world. Both spheres, empirical and transcendental, overlap one another constantly and lead to a radical undermining of the unity of a singular existence. It also seems, however, that the problem of the status of consciousness is secondary with respect to the possibility of explicating experience as such. The figure of the searching gaze, illustrating the power of logocentricism, refers to the problem of examining the consciousness that attempts to express that which does not undergo the laws of discourse, hence does not exist as such.

In that context – Hegelian at its heart – the light seems to be the paradox that has been grasped in a sober conclusion: "still till quite dark though of course no such thing just less light still when less did not seem possible". Epistemology precedes ontology here, and what is more both orders do not allow for coordination. That is also how the logic of the text looks: a question about what is unknown and what still exists, or what changes according to a varying of perspective (literally physical or treated as a metaphor of distance, conditioning the theoretical gaze) is secondary to the question of the status of the reality. That is why it is so important to leave the understanding of the situation of "staring at nothing" as the necessity to express that which cannot be expressed. This particular imperative of searching, however, is not directed towards the justification of the being in general, does not pretend to be searching for the foundation,[313] but rather exposes the one who remains in the power of the gaze for the sake of the event. The constant movement of language seemingly headed toward establishing the final, inevitable position of the undefined subject, in reality turns out to be an effort of rethinking – in the form of the practice of writing – the contradictions that constitute an event. The event removes the solid foundation of cognition and existence, even though simultaneously – from the perspective of the subject – it can appear only through language. "Nothing" does not constitute a final horizon for the peregrination of the gaze and reason, but is a description of a paradoxical situation of awaiting an event for which one cannot truly prepare. The stillness from the title can be understood only through the ontological order and existential hypostasis established in order

---

313	It seems that Beckett's strategy is completely different from Heidegger's, the most important proponent of the necessity to find "the grounds of Being." Heidegger states that the true reality (which in his idiom stands for "authenticity") of existence is reached by virtue of loosing the subject that happens through a fundamental opening to what is different and what cannot be finally absorb. See M. Heidegger, "On the Essence of Ground," in *Pathmarks*, translated by William McNeil, Cambridge 1998. Beckett shows the impossibility of all the attempts to reach the "source" of existence and explicate that experience in language.

for the gesture of discovering the event to be possible at all. It is not, however, any kind of form of cognitive assurance but an attempt to create the possibility of an insight that does not constitute a version of an epiphany but possesses a processual character. It is thanks to hypostasis that the gaze is possible "through any kind of gap."

That is how consciousness seems to be working, while being torn apart by simultaneously actualizing powers of perception (physiology, nature, and the body) and sensibility (reflections recorded in the form of a meta-language). This dialectic that – so to speak – remains terrifying because it does not leave any possibility of abolishing or reworking itself, at the same time constitutes a gesture of permanent opening. Once again, that which is negative paradoxically becomes a warranty of the very practice of consciousness that neither surrenders completely to what is affective, nor becomes inscribed in an unconditional primacy of reason. That which glues together these extremes is language that in *Still* reveals itself not so much in some crystal forms of symbols but in a constant movement of endless progression, as well as in its own intransitiveness. It means that in *Still* we are dealing with not only a vision of antonymic consciousness, but with questioning its personal, individual status. Already at the simplest level of grammar, the complete disintegration of subjectivity takes place in the text; a subjectivity that seems to be disappearing under the weight of repetition and the scrupulous corrections of the description of the location of the one who in speaking attempts to establish himself/herself as an impersonal centre of self-knowledge.

The Crisis of Self-Representation – From Intention to Description

Neutralized and deprived of a meaning or centre, language questions the legitimacy of the very notion of the subject and not simply its presence in the text. It is not only about the inability to identify particular figures in the text that defines its dimensions, but also about the much more serious consequences of ontological doubt. In *Still* one is confronted with two equal and competing visions of subjectivity. The first pertains to the self as a function of the developing text, as a local effect of repetition in language. The second precisely illustrates the contradictory possibility of achieving full individuality. At the base of this dream of fullness lies a desire (appearing as neurosis or a lack of originality) to merge into a mythical wholeness of all available spheres of activity: bodily sensations, mechanisms of consciousness and linguistic control that – from that perspective – seems to be the highest level of revelation and insight. In that way, the aporia of consciousness meets with the aporia of language. However, that leads us back to the impossibility explicating the very title of the work. *Still* becomes a figure of pure antinomy: it embodies within a textual sign both a dream about a pure, dematerialized and – what is most important – ascetic existence, and the phantasm of the imperative of working with an unknown source and an unforeseeable goal. Striving toward the state of absolute stillness is indeed a search for a final sanction, justifying not so much the existence of the world, but the presence of reality reworked by the subject. This internal striving comes from its very structural properties. In other words, the figure which is symbolized by the title is an irreducible, double phantasm that engulfs both the sphere of consciousness, as well as the linguistic representation that no so much as enables the emergence of the relationship between the subject and the reality, but successfully abolishes it. As a result, the dream of stillness does not fully become a foundation of neither the mythical story, nor – even more so – a metaphorical description of the ascetic ideal. It does not legitimize the search performed by the self, but on the contrary: dodging consciousness and the linguistic state of stillness, it constitutes an unreachable, although fundamental point of inexpressiveness.

It is important to observe that understanding the title as an immanent category allows us to observe how problematic and only apparent the cohesiveness of the text turns out to be. The text is not only about the disruption of the relationship between the function of language in communication and its rhetorical power, or – speaking more generally – an impossible to enslave, internal order of rhetoric,[314] but also a questioning of the transparent metaphysical division between the interior and exterior and its corresponding distinction between depth and surface.

Beckett insightfully and successfully abolishes the division between what is essential and meaningful and that which is accidental and unmarked. The internal and external spheres fluently move between one another and there is no way to grant any of them any final semantic sanction. This rhetorical mechanism of blurring divisions is perfectly visible in different attempts at an unbiased description (almost a vivisection) of the position of the body that attempts to, simultaneously, persist in the state on stillness and design the future shape of reality:

---

314 Rhetoric as a property of writing is essential for Beckett. On the one side, it fulfils the function of merging the unrevealed, perceived "I" in the pre-linguistic moment of consciousness. On the other side, in that very writing the mechanism of writing deprives – through disrupting the surface of language: its grammar and logic – us of the category of identity. Beckett's works, in that sense, focus on both these tendencies and make observing the gap between them possible. The same way, somewhat at the cross section of these traditions – anthropological and sophist/deconstructionist – Beckett constructs his own rhetoric. Bruno Clément writes about this in his monumental study. See also *Samuel Beckett and the art of rhetoric*, Chapel Hill, 1976.

Legs side by side broken right angles at the knees as in that old statue some old god twanged at sunrise and again at sunset. Trunk likewise dead plumb right up to top of skull seen from behind including nape clear of chairback. Arms likewise broken right angles at the elbows forearms along armrests just right length forearms and rests for hands clenched lightly to rest on ends. So quite still again then all quite quiet apparently eyes closed which to anticipate when they open again if they do in time then dark or some degree of starlight or moonlight or both. Normally watch night fall however long from this narrow chair or standing by western window quite still either case. Quite still namely staring at some one thing alone such as tree or bush a detail alone if near if far the whole if far enough till it goes. [I, s. 415-416]

The body that does not allow itself to be represented or expressed becomes – paradoxically – the main subject of the description. At the same time, the tendency to provide an exact record of its movements is headed in a somewhat contrary direction – toward disrupting the simple division between what is physical (physiological) and conventional and arbitrary in the sphere of expression. The language there is not so much submissive to one of the spheres of experience (only to the body or the world) but functions according to the laws of a performative energy. The very gesture of the description that immobilizes bodies opens up a space for another gesture, one distorting a seemingly transparent relationship between the subject and the world. Even more so, it is a gesture of describing (that marks itself in the text in the form of a visible intention to faithfully render the body's placement) that becomes the very site of transformation. That is why it is not enough to say that we are dealing with a dynamic treatment of the text that – with an apparent structure of "mathematical" severity – develops in a way that is impossible to foresee. One has to add that the shifting logic and semantics of the text, by disrupting the division between the interior (consciousness) and exterior (inaccessible and mute world), sets in motion the logic of the event and project.

Writing that takes place in front of the reader is headed in an enigmatic direction. One cannot establish precisely that it is constituted by a literal definition of the possibility of "being immobile" or the poetic divagations with variations on the paradox of the representation of a permanently existing being. In the end, what is most important remains the progression of language that develops the phantasm of a unity of sounds and sense. Of course, the dream of a complete word is not mythical; a myth with the help of which one could explain the fullness of reality. It is more about the phantasm constituting a negative foundation of the work of language that, with irony, derails all gestures aiming at semantic coherence, poetic rigor, the schematic character of representations and, finally, at the expression of the true "I." The irony is inscribed in the concept of immobility that, during the reading, creates the effect of ambivalent meaning and undergoes decomposition through the impossibility of fulfilling the project included in the title.[315] The process of describing the body is, on the one hand, an indifferent action serving to separate oneself from the world and, on the other hand, a result of almost pure affect and an effect of the failure of the consciousness that cannot become present for itself because, from the very beginning, it is mediated in a structured system of language.

That is how the aporia of the event works. It is impossible to create conditions that would allow for preparations for its arrival and its presence, because all the efforts aimed at that goal (like repeated attempts at a vivisection of the body and space) remain inscribed in a string of immobile mediations that appear under the guise of a general rule of repetition. The apparent transparency of language is due to the rigor of repetition and the formula of expression is identified (as in many of Beckett's texts) with the power of the potential sound of the text. This is mostly about the particular "acoustics" of the text, the possibility of its appearance in sound, as an event that might abolish the distance between various oppositions: body-language, consciousness-world and voice-writing. On the other side (and here, the vision of Beckett seems to be extremely radical) the event can appear and take place not so much in the space of speech but in the sphere of recording. This means that that any efforts serving the purpose of recording the experience become indispensable. It is important to observe that this is not about a metaphysical understanding of the category of expression, of the internal imperative ordering the author to write, but about the more complex question of the confrontation of the unspeakable experience of consciousness that cannot establish itself within reflection with a system of language that, from the perspective of the concept of an event, inevitably becomes a space of the resistance of the very materiality of writing – an inscription.

That is what happens in the quoted excerpt from the text: the meticulous description of the body takes place according to the rules of a distanced observation. The order of a full representation is, however, broken by the irony of the language that is enclosed within the meta-reflexive observation that highlights the illusory status of both the intentions of the ideal depiction of the body as an immobile but living object, as well as simultaneously recorded, dead textual sign. The subject remains torn between the intention (of the description, representation) that upholds it in the world of consciousness and the body. What is more, all three (body, consciousness and intention) constitute a modality of the existence of the subject

---

315 It seems reasonable to agree with Bataille who, attempting to criticize the "system" that the philosophy of Hegel constituted, stated that 'the project is the accumulation of life for later.' And indeed, the event rips apart the potential reworking of contradictions because it allows us to see that not everything has to (or can) be realized; meaning that not everything has to (or can) be framed as a discourse. See Bataille G., *Inner Experience,* Op. cit.

and remain in an unbreakable relationship. All of them are also co-dependent and – so to speak – subject to mutual control in a way that prohibits any side from gaining a dominant status around which the constellation of the senses dispersed in the text would be established.

The concept of appearance does not pertain only to the order of representation in the sense of a doubled incarnation of that which initially was alien. It seems that the second part of the cited excerpt invokes the process of description as something awakening consciousness from its tedious lethargy and driving it toward the future. From that perspective, one can see more clearly that the illusion of a faithful representation of the body was also an element of the concepts of intention and consciousness. However, when there is a temporal mark appearing in the text to "run ahead" it seems like one is dealing with a project *par excellence*. One has to admit that it is a peculiar vision of a project, one in which few objectives have been planned and those presented are subject to severe questioning. One does not know if the eyes will open in the future and if they will see anything at all. If that will happen, observing the world might be possible or not. The order of the project becomes reversed and compromised not only on the existential level, but also on the level of explication: the world that can be observed can be almost any one of the elements listed (the dark sky, the light of the stars, the gleaming of the moon). The world, which potentially, in the future, could come into existence before our eyes, becomes an element of individual perspective, a singular "power of sight," or in other words: transforms into a singular reality.

In the end, that is how I would suggest understanding the meditation that – in the form of a consciousness experiment – Beckett undertakes in his work. There is not stable interior of the individual, nor an unquestionably existing world, nor even its plausible representation. Questions about the legitimacy of existence and the rules guiding it are abolished in *Still*, just like questions of the boundary between the speaking subject and language, or between the being of speech and the nothingness of the world, all turn out to be irrelevant. That which remains is a celebration of the passage[316] itself – a poetic acceptance of the process of blurring differentiations, this search for a register of language that could transmit the totality of experience. Even the body, which seemed to be the only existential certainty, turns out to be – from the perspective of consciousness (and there cannot be a different perspective in Beckett's text!) – another phantasm resulting from

---

316 One of the most interesting concepts of the idea of "passage" was provided by Jacques Rancière in his work dedicated to the modern ideas of "pure art." The passage is "the infinite crossing between two borders, from life to work and work to life, from the work to discourse about it and from discourse about the work to the work itself, an unceasing crossing that can only occur insofar as it leaves the tear visible." Rancière J., *Literature, Critical Theory, and Politics*, translated by James Swenson, New York 2011.

the pretense of subjectivity aiming for solidity. We do not know where the place of the body is, if it possesses any form of presence or if all the elements of the world have been subdued to the passionate gaze. But even the gaze remains disqualified in the timeless and empty band of the disappearing world, the image of which is spread between entrapment in a projecting consciousness and an observed illusion, a perpetually alien mediation.

Still as Neutrality

What exactly does the title of "still" mean? Similar to many other works, Beckett sabotages classical ontological questions. We are not dealing simply with poetic activity, but rather the radical dimensions of an authorial search. The structure of the work, based on the principle of inciting immanent contradictions, allows us to observe that the final point of access to understanding becomes the multiplication of the names of impossibility at all levels (semantic, ontological, and cognitive). *Still* is not only a point of access, toward which the subject is headed, but an inexplicable contradiction that is created at the crossing of the relationship of the consciousness of language and reality. On the one hand, the subjectivity reveals its own positive side; a side of searching for the level of absolute absence, of quiet, of almost ataraxic quality. On the other hand, it reveals the complete fictionality of such gesture. In that contradiction the fundamental impossibility of grasping the boundary between the motions of stillness are revealed; an impossibility that simultaneously makes a statement about the legitimacy of the entire image constructed in the text and its message. It seems that the further away from the postulated state of stillness we travel, the stronger the forces of rhetorical confirmations and the more powerful a conviction about the necessity of a continuous beginning really are:

> Quite still again then at open window facing south over the valley in this wicker chair though actually close inspection not still at all but trembling all over. Close inspection namely detail by detail all over to add up finally to this whole not still at all but trembling all over. But casually in this failing light impression dead still even the hands clearly trembling and the breast faint rise and fall. [I, p.415]

At first glance, one can observe that the meaningful change of perspective took place several times: from the close gaze to attempting to grasp the whole and finally a return back to observation at a close distance. The literal meaning of that excerpt that could stand for an examination of the physiological and psychological reflexes if the unspecified individual is not sufficient. In the quoted excerpt, similar to the rest of the text, the non-existence of two competing orders is revealed simultaneously: the orders of consciousness and the world. On the side of consciousness there is an entire set of signs that are meant to correct the actual position of the body, but also a critical power that allows us to locate points of error between postulated and desired states and their actual realization. On the side of the world there is, almost according to the logic of the "eye of the camera," the image of the body searching for absolute peace and later on the entire system of a subversive language. Its structure, built on the principle of a supplement[317] that can constitute in a positive aspect a definition, while in the negative aspect its very negation, breaking the established reality. We are not concerned here with the transparent terms that change the modality of the text ("first glance", "apparently") but with introducing the new, other kinds of elements that shatter the order of a rigorous representation ("close inspection namely detail by detail", "in this failing light"). By contaminating both orders, Beckett achieves the effect of lacing definitions (within the sphere of language) and phantasmal characters (in the context of the reality's status). *Still* is not a state of untouchable being outside of time, nor a mystical imperative of the nameless positing of the existence in the world. It hides within itself a burden of contradiction (both in meaning and ontology) that is impossible to overcome. In the movement of language, on the other hand, this contradiction is revealed and undergoes a process of testing in the form of different variations.

Hence, what is most important is not the perspective established by the speaker that constitutes the immanent rule regulating the text, but the problem of the temporal conditioning of the subject. It is not about the fact that as the narration progresses a gradual sedimentation of the subject takes place, but about the irreducible fact of its immersion into the stream of time. Beckett, however, reverses the entire eternal philosophical problem and poses the question of the historicity of existence in existential, rather than ontological categories, or even in the rigor of expression itself. *Still* is – as suggested by its grammar – an empty space of language; a space in which the power of defining and naming becomes useless. At the same time, however, the subject on the base of a performative contradiction becomes entangled in a trap of consciousness that controls it. By attempting to reach that sphere of experience with the help of language, it sentences itself to a discovery of unsolvable contradictions concerning the very representation of that effort. Empty ideality, outside of time and space, turns out to be a recurring and endlessly thematised phantasm that cannot be ascribed to the sphere of carnal sensation, nor to the dimension of consciousness. It situates itself somewhere between these spaces, in a poetic sign, in the sound of the phrase that allows for the diffusing of tensions between apparent oppositions.

---

317   I refer here to a classic text by Jacques Derrida, "The Supplement of Copula: Philosophy before Linguistics," in *Margins of Philosophy,* Op. cit.

Once again, Beckett approaches writing understood as neutrality. This time, however, he reveals the force of a paradox that is impossible to overcome and that lies at the foundation of the literature it supports. On the one side, stillness is a postulated state outside of language, and on the other – it constitutes an illustration of the extent to which language remains inconsistent with the event, in its inability to express it. The phrases of the text circulate around the enigmatic meaning of the title the same way they circulate around the suggested centre of being or the most important existential disposition. As Michael Foucault shows, while commenting on the work of Gilles Deleuze, the problem of the event connects with the question of sense already at the level of grammar:

> Finally, this meaning-event requires a grammar with a different form of organization, since it cannot be situated in a proposition as an attribute (to be dead, to be alive, to be red) but is fastened to the verb (to die, to live, to redden). The verb, conceived in this fashion, has two principal forms around which the others are distributed: the present tense, which positions an event, and the infinitive, which introduces meaning into language and allows it to circulate as the neutral element to which we refer in discourse. [...] The meaning-event is always both the displacement of the present and the eternal repetition of the infinitive. To die is never localized in the density of a given moment, but from its flux it infinitely divides the shortest moment. To die is even smaller than the moment it takes to think it, and yet dying is indefinitely repeated on either side of this widthless crack. The eternal present? Only on the condition that we conceive the present as lacking plenitude and the eternal as lacking unity: the (multiple) eternity of the (displaced) present.[318]

Foucault performs the heuristic of breaking up inseparable orders (sense and event) in order to visualize the particularity of the dynamic of thought that constitutes an expression of a rebellion against dualistic thought. From that perspective, that which is neutral is the infinitive that – in a rhetorically saturated reasoning of Foucault – becomes an almost mythical centre of discourse which, nevertheless, does not constitute a stable transcendental rule. At the moment of establishing meaning, it reveals its own, indispensable contradiction, or verb, that breaks a well-founded, somewhat pre-established, position of sense. In essence, Foucault shows that the expression of the experience of time is equal with constituting sense. However, it is also the contrary: the grounding of the sense turns out to be a discovery of the temporal character of language. The event-sense is a notion that allows for the analysis of the paradox of expression and, at the same time, of the paradox of the event. It is also necessary to understand the most complete event – death.

Death – which for Foucault reveals itself in the form of the logic of the sense-event (in the form of the verb "to die") – constitutes a final point in language's

---

318   Foucault M., "Theatrum philosophicum," Op. cit., p. 350.

insurmountable aporia. At the same time, it reveals within its structure and within its semantics a double impossibility. On the one hand speaking and writing are nothing other than postponing *ad infinitum* the actualization of the moment. On the other hand, somewhat through inertia, without complete control over revealed meaning, language prolongs dreams about expressing that which does not fall under its authority, hence that which is neutral.

In his poetic realization, Beckett radicalizes Foucault's thought. It is no longer the verb in the form of the infinitive[319] that constitutes a central point of sense, but the anonymous *still* of the title constitutes the neutrality around which the poetic discourse circulates. Although endlessly thematised reworked and repeated – according to the logic of namelessness – this neutrality remained not only unreached but also inexhaustible, illustrating the fundamental lack of continuity of language with that which it attempts to express. The word of the event – the word of death – and the word of the real, always come too late. "To die" in Beckett appears in an unmarked moment of the helplessness of individual perception and consciousness situated against that which remains immersed in absolute stillness. Not only does it undermine the principle of a linear expression and decompose the sphere of the possibility of the interpretation of time, but also it changes the status of the event-sense. In *Still* both these modalities of time are brought to their limit and become conditions of the impossibility of cognition and – longer-term – contradictions of the reality of any form of existence.

Similarly, movement and stillness do not constitute an oppositional pair in the text; they do not allow themselves to be inscribed in any structure of language. They saturate one another and reveal themselves as elements of the world outside of its essence – the word kept in a frame becomes a dead sign. This double gesture of establishing and degrading that which transpires or moves, as well as that which is still, seems to be without end. And similar to the tormenting work of perception and consciousness, it becomes infinite:

> Quite still then all this time eyes open when discovered then closed then opened and closed again no other movement any kind though of course not still at all when suddenly or so it looks this movement impossible to follow let alone describe. [I, s. 416]

From the perspective of the described relationship between the subject and the event of death, the excerpt above says nearly everything. If stillness is an unreachable but necessary "empty ideal" enclosed in the writer's idiom, it is a movement that turns out to be the modality of all existence that is impossible to traverse, of all being as such. They constitute boundaries between which the subject, which establishes and degrades itself, constantly tries to find itself. Language, with the

---

319 Infinitives, so widely utilized in the text, constitute a kind of semantic interlude to the proper object of the statement, or neutrality, to which the title refers.

help of which subjectivity attempts to escape from the imprisonment in a singular image, is only one constellation of meanings and becomes a kind of sentence to repetition which is nevertheless the only opportunity for a seeming stability, behind which there is only the chaos of an unrecognized world. Against these two dimensions of what is inexpressible, the direction of the action of subjectivity no longer reaches full autonomy, but tests its own conditions against the enigmatic space of that which is "impossible to follow let alone describe."

The Sound to Come

The change – once again unclear if true or illusory – is brought by the last phrases of the work:

> As if even in the dark eyes closed not enough and perhaps even more than ever necessary against that no such thing the further shelter of the hand. Leave it so all quite still or try listening to the sounds all quite still head in hand listening for a sound. [I, p. 417]

Everything that Beckett records in the end falls under the poetics of a lack of specificity and abstraction.[320] On the one side, the eye is "as if" not entirely closed, on the other – time and reality remain inscribed into the rigor of generality ("whenever, whatever"). The force of sight becomes weakened and the efforts of constructing or representing reality are abandoned for the sake of a complete opening and passive awaiting of sound. The gesture of opening is not, however, a simple change within the range of cognitive powers but constitutes a radical metamorphosis of the subject that, from attempting to neurotically cancel established conditions became a pure passivity supporting itself on coincidence and resigning from the power of constituting reality. Of course, this shift stems from the difference of perspective between sound, the gaze and listening. This shift suggests solutions, which Beckett, fully conscious of his own poetic gesture, left half-spoken. One can only speculate about what could constitute "listening for a sound:" an opposition against the primacy of presence that was carried by the gaze, an escape from the metaphysical oppositions that appear inevitably when one wants to record what escapes naming, or the travesty of the biblical calls from God?

This unexpected finale is more of a proof of the impossibility of ending the meditation over the complexity of stillness that is, at the same time, a mysterious trace or a "challenge" that comes from the side of what is real, as well as desired

---

320   See Perloff M., "'The Space of a door.' Beckett and Poetry of Absence," in *The Poetics of Indeterminacy: Rimbaud to Cage*, Princeton 1983.

by subjectivity – an enigmatic state of impersonal stability. However, perhaps it is about stillness being a seal of language that kills in the gesture of repetition any potential sense, bringing closer the subjectivity uncertain of itself into a confrontation with the event. At the same time, the logic of repetition becomes radicalized: the only sanction remains not so much the written word, but an empty echo of the first gesture of consciousness that resounds on the stage of memory from which the subject can extract the passing voices. In that way, the shift in what is an ontologically dominant turn out to be a change in the constitution of the subject that becomes even more ungraspable, ever more present in the text. The voice (and it is a voice that is about to come) forces on the subject a return to the foundations of existence.[321] It is not a movement, however, of a pure ontological regression because it is not concerned with a co-existence with the sphere of being that encompasses the entirety of experience, but about a different, far more fundamental treatment of the category of event.

The subject understood in that way does not remind of a stable modern subject. By questioning its own foundations, it attempts to, once again, undertake the effort of justifying the existence of itself as consciousness, but in a context that excludes any form of transparent reflection that legitimizes self-presence. The only task of subjectivity is a hierarchical establishment of the objective sphere and submission of the exterior to the interior sphere of the homogenous and indivisible sense of which metaphor is the voice. The act of hearing, or rather vigilant listening, would become a "morphology of the metamorphosis"[322] of the subject. I refer to the observations by Roland Barthes concerning listening/hearing, thanks to which we are able to return to the problems we have mentioned in the introduction and first part of this book. Barthes distinguishes between three types of listening. The first includes both animals and people and is a kind of "alarm." The second is based on a "decoding" of audible sounds and using the "code" that enables such a procedure. The third or modern form is not built on the concept of the passive reception of sounds, nor decoding their meaning, but on asking about the source and sense of the statement. Listening is inscribed into the intra-subjective space. According to Barthes, the ascertainment of "I'm listening" means in this case also "listen to me." The last phrases of *Still* describe (or rather design) the first mode of listening that remains at the border of what is audible and what is heard. The desire to come back to what is entirely "still" would be the most radical attempt of finding the most primal level of thinking that would be simultaneously a "consciousness of something."

---

321 See Anzieu D., "Le théâtre d'Echo dans les récits de Beckett," *Revue d'Esthétique* 1990, p. 41.

322 Barthes R., "Écoute," in *L'obvie et l'obtus. Essais critiques III*, Paris 1982, pp. 219-220.

The subject, wanting to deny its own status, which is always a status of presence, attempts to simultaneously gain access to what is real and what would release it from the torment of thinking. The unreality of that project becomes a final warranty of writing that, in case of *Still*, takes on the form of exercises of the isolated consciousness dreaming of ultimate absence and becomes a series of seemingly endless confrontations with the inhuman world.

However, in this way one has to go back to the question with which we have started these reflections: who is speaking? The author? A singular consciousness? The logos appearing in the space of a static text? The text itself, which would be a possible variant of Blanchot's "empty speech" or the "torture of language?" Or maybe it is a voice of the exterior, transpiring and constituting subjectivity? Finally, could it be a concrete existence, tormented by phantasms, surrendered to the rule of neurotic repetitions and unending corrections of what has been said and later recorded? Blanchot states:

> But what can this title designate, if in any case the one writing is already no longer Beckett but the demand that led him outside of himself, dispossessed him and let go of him, gave him over to the outside, making him a nameless being, the Unnamable, a being without being who can neither live nor die, cannot cease or begin, the empty place in which the listlessness of an empty speech speaks, one that with great difficulty regains a porous and agonizing I.[323]

Beckett does not give an answer to any of the above questions, but also reaches much further. Through the annihilating force of the metaphor he leads his imagination and his language, that both describes and establishes these processes of disintegration, to a point in which it is extremely difficult to generally pose such questions. It leads to a place of absolute beginning and of the source identity that – filtered through the experience of consciousness – becomes the same hypostasis as the designed and continuously summoned, inevitable end. Thanks to that, the text is extremely close to its own anxious autonomy to which the reader can hardly find access. However, thanks to that very turn toward its own immanence the text proves even more fascinating.

"How to Say It?"

Right before he died, Samuel Beckett wrote a poetic text dedicated to his American friend, Joe Chaikin, both an actor and director. For at least several reasons, this work is truly amazing. It is worthwhile to begin with the most basic of reasons. In

---

323   Blanchot M., *Le livre à venir*, Op. cit., p. 290. In English, see *The Book to Come*, p. 213.

the last period of his work, Beckett[324] performed yet another linguistic turn, once again complicating the lives of his critics. In practice, it stands for the attempt to go back to English. As he himself stated, after the many years of writing in French that he imposed on himself, English became a salvation, widening the scope of his abilities as a writer. Of course, in the case of Beckett this broadening was nothing other than a new or refreshed mode of expression, another form of linguistic buffer and a new striving for maximum precision. In addition, this was a sign of a process of finding the optimal register of speech in which speech would cease to simply be an object of the author's hand and begin to function as a subject or, speaking more carefully, as an autonomous centre of literary expression. In that way, once again, Beckett left us with two legitimate versions (and not translations) of the same text. *Comment dire*, the first title, is equally idiomatic (hence almost as untranslatable) as *What Is the Word*:

> folly -
> folly for to -
> for to -
> what is the word -
> folly from this -
> all this -
> folly from all this -
> given -
> folly given all this -
> seeing -
> folly seeing all this -
> this -
> what is the word -
> this this -
> this this here -
> all this this here -
> folly given all this -
> seeing -
> folly seeing all this this here -
> for to -
> what is the word -
> see -

---

324 I recognize this period as the time from the creation of the last part of the "Trilogy" (1979) to *Company*, including the following: *Mal vu, mal dit/Ill seen, Ill said* and *Worstward Ho*. It is important to mention that Beckett was not faithful in his turn toward the English language in that period, as proven not only by writing *Comment dire* first in French but also by his comments in that book on *Ill seen, Ill said*. The situation with respect to his last work has been clarified elsewhere. See Knowlson J., *Damned to fame*, Op. cit., p. 703, Cronin A., *Samuel Beckett. The Last Modernist*, Op. cit., pp. 587-588.

glimpse -
seem to glimpse -
need to seem to glimpse -
folly for to need to seem to glimpse -
what -
what is the word -
and where -
folly for to need to seem to glimpse what where -
where
what is the word -
there -
over there -
away over there -
afar -
afar away over there -
afaint -
afaint afar away over there what -
what -
what is the word -
seeing all this -
all this this -
all this this here -
folly for to see what -
glimpse -
seem to glimpse -
need to seem to glimpse -
afaint afar away over there what -
folly for to need to seem

to glimpse afaint afar away over there what -
what -
what is the word -

what is the word[325]

I would not like to interpret this text, but merely to indicate – in the form of a summary – several themes that I find particularly important and that, in the form of this dense textual-mediation, appear extremely vivid. The poem – as is commonly believed – carries the dedication "for Joe Chaikin" and this is an incredibly important fact because this American actor was a somewhat empathetic *alter ego* for Beckett. Before he staged and performed Beckett's works, the illness he suffered from brought him incredibly close to their sensitivity and imaginative

---

325   I provide information on both editions: S. Beckett, *What Is the Word* in *CE*, vol. 4, pp. 50-51; S. Beckett, *Comment dire*, Paris 1989.

scope.[326] After becoming paralyzed, Chaikin lost his ability to articulate and became aphasic. Despite that, he continued his theatre work. With dramatic irony and an almost existential absurdity, he literally embodied being almost entirely mute. This contradiction, having its source in physiological pain, constituted for Beckett – extremely sensitive to all forms of suffering – a guaranty and encouragement to thematise one of his main obsessions: how is it possible to express anything if language does not mean anything and no longer serves the purposes of communication? In what way should one express the fact that there is absolutely nothing left to be said? In other words, how could we establish the speaking subject against these two extremes? How should one, on the one hand, situate the subject against the silence and chaos of reality and, on the other hand, escape the madness of what is inexpressible and what is continuously seeking expression?

In suggesting that there is no escape from that impasse, Beckett returns to the source of his own project of writing that he established in his first essays and works and which he crystalised in the form of achievements such as *The Unnamable* and *Not I*. It seems that Beckett was not interested in mere fidelity to his own practice, but in the search for the possibilities of finding a unique voice, an unquestionable idiom that could abolish the institution of literature. The description of the state and the possibilities of literature have a single end – writing is credible only as a testimony to the epistemological failure of subjectivity. As we read in the text, madness is the very possibility of looking, the very act of imagining the gaze that could encompass a concrete sphere of reality. In that sense, the act of cognition is undermined by its own lack of reality, opening up a space for poetry and the rhythm of language, thanks to which the madness accompanying the observed consciousness can be expressed. In *Comment dire/What Is the Word* the mathematical precision of his form is combined with the precision of a euphonic order. On the one hand, the poem is a text of a particular kind, a *carmen figuratum*,[327] for which the deadly work of mind, the process taking place "inside the skull" – to use one of Beckett's favourite images – is the objective. On the other hand, only during verbal recitation does the text acquire its organic strength, combining the words that follow into a single rhythmical chain.

The text is guided by the logic of *epanorthosis* and catachresis – dependency and arbitrarily understood as structural rigor but also as an order of thought. In this particular case, madness "develops" during the process of writing, just like it functions according to the laws of a figure from the beginning of its opening;

---

326 See. Salisbury L., "'What is the Word': Beckett's Aphasic Modernism": *Journal of Beckett Studies*, Volume 17, Issue 1-2, Page 78-126.

327 In order to see that this is the case, it is enough to turn the text along the vertical axis of the page to see it – rather than read it.

a figure constituting an object of continuous repetition that is the main force of the poem. From such a perspective, that which is closed, ended and silently rests among the signs of the text is resurrected by the difference of continuous repetition. These repetitions, respectively, trigger both accidental and planned shifts, substitutions, and interchangeable effects of verbal combinations aimed at revealing the unspecified and utterly "other" face of reality. Madness is not based on the direct dependency of the internal world of intimate experiences of the subject, nor on a representative homology that was supposed to be guaranteed by a linguistic system of references, but on a potential fulfilment of the word and body, on the figure of their absolute identity that is impossible to implement in artistic practice, or a dependency that stretches so far that whatever is merged within it cannot again be separated. A language that leads from what is identical to what is other can be thought of in reality only as an attempt to actualize death, or as a sign of a madness that proclaims – as Émile Cioran, close to Beckett on many levels, would put it – the presence of "time's demonism."[328] In that clasp of hypothetical integrity in which one side is constituted by the postulated (or imagined) unity of words and objects, and the second side – the poetic effect of the decomposition of the temporary language is where the strength of *Comment dire/What is the word* is located. From such a perspective, established by *epanorthosis* and catachresis (and not the metaphor or a symbol), the poem presents itself as a trajectory of working consciousness the elements of which are the points of focus and dispersion of words and signs in the space of the text (understood most literally as typographical insight). The figurativeness of language does not allow the subject to reconstruct its object by delineating only the space of the worrying autonomy of the poem, hermetically sealed in several neurotically persistent phrases. Jacques Derrida describes this dependency accurately when he comments on the concept of the "echo of the subject" by Philippe Lacoue-Labarthe:

> Another way of marking the fact that there is no simple beginning; no rhythm without repetition, spacing, caesura, the "repeated difference-from-itself of the Same," says Lacoue-Labarthe – and thus repercussion, resonance, echo, reverberation. We are constituted by this rhythm, in other words (de-)constituted by the marks of this "caesuraed" stamp, by this rhythmo-typy which is nothing other than the divided

---

328 Émile M. Cioran says: "The feeling of the irrevocable, which appears as an ineluctable necessity going against the grain of our innermost tendencies, is conceivable only because of time's demonism. The conviction that you cannot escape an implacable fate and that time will do nothing but unfold the dramatic process of destruction is an expression of irrevocable agony." Cioran É. M., *On the Heights of Despair*, translation by Ilinca Zrifopol-Johnston, Chicago 1992.

idiom in us of desistance. There is no subject without the signature of this rhythm, in us and before us, before any image, any discourse, before music itself.[329]

The logic of the poetry of absence that Beckett used so persistently is based on the attempt to recreate the work of consciousness and discovering the final word after which literature would never be necessary again. Consciousness and language, undergoing the endless process of a dialectical negotiation, illustrates both the nameless and the unnamable emptiness that is placed on the side of what is real. The very negotiation, undermined by the impossibility of merging, synthesizing, or of actualizing turns into a poetic rhythm and a passionate search for the proper word that would in the end abolish the necessity of repetition contained in the perpetual question: *"comment dire/what is the word"*? On the one hand, consciousness uses language in order to name a reality and establish itself, on the other hand – language itself acquires autonomy to which subjectivity has no access. To express this absence and to grant a voice to the silence situating itself before and outside of language, as well as before and outside of consciousness – that is a mad task, but also – what Beckett's texts convinces us of – one of the most important tasks of literature.

---

329 Derrida J., *Désistance*, Op. cit., pp. 626-627. In English, see *Psyche*, translated by Peggy Kamuf, vol. 2, p. 222.

Bibliography

All citations of Beckett in English are taken from the following four volume edition: S. Beckett, *The Grove Centenary Edition*, series edited by Paul Auster, New York: Grove Press, 2006 (abbreviated CE).

Abbreviations

NI – "Not I"
Mi – "Mirlitonnades"
U – "The Unnamable"
ISIS – "Ill seen Ill said"
S – "Still"
IDI – "Imagination Dead Imagine"
B – "Bing"
P – "Proust"

Texts by Samuel Beckett

Breath, in *CE*, vol. 3
Dante, Vico...Bruno,...Joyce, in *CE*, vol. 4.
Ghosts Trio, in *CE*, vol. 3,
Imagination Dead Imagine, in *CE*, vol. 4,
Ill seen Ill said, in CE, vol. 4 oraz *S. Beckett`s Mal vu mal dit/Ill seen Ill said. A bilingual, Evolutionary, and Synoptic Edition,* ed. by Ch. Krance, Routledge 1996.
Molloy, Malone dies, The Unnamable, How It Is in *CE*, vol. 2.
neither, in *CE*, vol. 4
Not I, in *CE*. vol. 3.
Bing, in *CE*, vol. 4.
Poèmes suivi Mirlitonnades, Paris 1978; *Poems in English,* London 1961 in *CE*, vol. 4.
what is the word, in *CE*, vol. 4,. Beckett, *Comment dire,* Librarie Compagnie, Paris 1989.
Proust, in *CE*, vol. 4.
Three Dialogues, in *CE*, vol. 4.

Se voir in *Pour finir encore et autres foirades.*
Still, in *CE*, vol.4.
The Piece of Monolgue, in *CE*, vol. 3.
Whoroscope, in *CE*, vol. 4.
Worstward Ho, in *CE*, vol. 4.

References on Beckett

Samuel Beckett Today / Aujourd'hui (*Beckett and Religion / Estethics / Politics*) 2000, nr 9.
Ackerley C., "The Unnamable"'s First Voice?," *Journal of Beckett Studies* 1993, no 2.
———., "The Uncertanity of Self: Samuel Beckett and Position of the Voice," *Samuel Beckett Today / Aujourd'hui* (*After Beckett/ D'aprés Beckett*) 2004, no 14.
Adorno T. W., "Trying to Understand Endgame," *New German Critique* 1982, no. 26.
Amiran E., *Wandering and Home. Beckett's Metaphysical Narrative*, Philadelphia 1993.
Anzieu D., "Le théâtre d'Echo dans les récits de Beckett," *Revue d'Esthétique* 1990.
———., *Beckett*, Paris 1992.
———., *Bacon, Beckett, Bion: pour un rennouveau empiriste*, in *Francis Bacon*, éd. par D. Anzieu, M. Monjauze, Paris 1993.
Arsic B, *The Passive Eye. Gaze and Subjectivity in Berkeley (via Beckett)*, Stanford 2003.
Badiou A., *Beckett: L'increvable désir*, Paris 1995. In English, see *On Beckett*, translated by Nina Power, Manchester 2002.
Beckett avant Beckett. Essais sur les premières oeuvres, éd. par J.-M. Rabaté, Paris 1984.
Began R., *Samuel Beckett and the End of Modernity*, Standford 1996.
Bernal O., *Langage et fiction dans le roman de Beckett*, Paris 1969.
Bernard M., *Samuel Beckett et son sujet; une apparition évanouissante*, Paris–Montréal 1996.
Blanchot M., "Où maintenant? Qui maintenant?," in *Le livre à venir*, Paris 1959. In English, see *The Book to Come*, translated by Charlotte Mandell, Stanford 2002.
Brienza S., "Imagination Dead Imagine: The Microcosm of the Mind," *Journal of Beckett Studies* 1982, no. 8.

Bryden M., "Beckett, Deleuze, and 'L'Épuisé'," *Samuel Beckett Today/Aujourd'hui* (*Beckett et La Psychanalyse / Beckett and Psychoanalisys*) 1996, no. 5.

Catanzaro M., *Recontextualizing the Self: The Voice as Subject in Beckett's „Not I"*, „South Central Review: The Journal of the South Central Modern Language Association (College Station)" 1990, nr 7.

Clément B., *L'oeuvre sans qualités. Rhétorique de Samuel Beckett*, Paris 1994.

————., "Mais quelle est cette voix?," *Samuel Beckett Today / Aujourd'hui* (*Bordless Beckett/ Beckett sans frontièrs*) 2008, nr 19.

Coetzee J. M., "Eight ways of looking at Samuel Beckett," *Samuel Beckett Today / Aujourd'hui* (*Bordless Beckett / Beckett sans frontièrs*) 2008, nr 19.

Cohn R., *Back to Beckett*, Princeton 1973.

Connor S., *Samuel Beckett. Repetition, Theory and Text*, Aurora Colorado 2006.

————., "Between Theatre and Theory. Long Observation of the Ray," in *Samuel Beckett Vision and Mouvement*, ed. by K. Kondo, Tokyo 2006.

Cronin A., *Samuel Beckett. The Last Modernist*, London 1996.

Davies P., *The Ideal Real. Fiction and Imagination*, London–Toronto 1994.

Deleuze G., "L'Épuisé," in S. Beckett, *Quad et autres pièces pour la télévision*, Paris 1992.

Esslin M., "Głosy i glosy," translated by M. Kędzierski, *Kwartalnik Artystyczny* 1996, no. 4.

————., "Beckett i współczesny dramat," translated by M. Sugiera, *Didaskalia* 1997, no. 19–20.

Grossman E., *La défiguration. Artaud – Beckett – Michaux*, Paris 2004.

Gussow M., *Conversation with and about Beckett*, New York 1996.

Hale J., "Framing The Unframable: Samuel Beckett and Francis Bacon," *Samuel Beckett Today / Aujourd'hui* 1990, nr 2.

Hansford J., "Imagination Dead Imagine": The Imagination and Its Context," *Journal of Beckett Studies* 1982, no. 7.

Harvey L., *Samuel Beckett: Poet and Critic*, Princeton 1970.

Hill L., *Beckett's Fiction: In Different Words*, Cambrigde 1990.

————., "Late Text: Writing the Work of Mourning," *Samuel Beckett Today / Aujourd'hui* 1992, no. 1.

Hunkeler T., *Echos de l'ego dans l'oeuvre de Samuel Beckett*, Paris–Montreal 1997.

Iser W., *Der implizite Leser. Kommunikationsformen des Romans von Bunyan bis Beckett*, München 1972. In English, see *The Implied Reader: Patterns of Communication in Prose Fiction from Bunyan to Beckett*, Baltimore 1978.

Janvier L., "Lieu dire," in *Samuel Beckett, Cahier de L'Herne* 1976, dir. Par T. Bishop et R. Federman.

Katz D., *Saying I No More. Subjectivity and Consciousness in the Prose of Samuel Beckett*, Evanston 1999.

Kelly K., "The Orphic Mouth in 'Not I'," *Journal of Beckett Studies* 1980, no. 6.

Kenner H., *Samuel Beckett. A Critical Study*, New York 1962.

Knottenbelt E. M., "Samuel Beckett: Poetry As Performative Art," *Samuel Beckett Today / Aujourd'hui* 1990, no. 2.

Knowlson J., *Light and Darkness in the Theatre of Samuel Beckett*, London 1972.

————., Pilling J., *Frescoes of the Skull: The Later Prose and Drama of Samuel Beckett*, London 1979.

————., *Damned to Fame. The Life of Samuel Beckett*, London 1997.

Kristeva J., "Le père, l'amour, l'exil," *Cahier de L'Herne* 1976, dir. par T. Bishop et R. Federman.

Lamont R., "Beckett's Metaphysics of Choiceless Awareness," in *Samuel Beckett Now*, edited and introduced by Melvin J. Friedman, Chicago–London 1970.

Libera A., "Jak zbudowane jest 'Dzyń' Becketta?," *Literatura na Świecie* 1975, nr 5.

————., "Jak przełożyć 'wyrażenie bezpośrednie'? Wokół jednego zdania Samuela Becketta," *Kwartalnik Artystyczny* 2002, nr 4.

Louette J.-F., "*De la littérature en général, et de Beckett en particulier, selon Deleuze*," in *Deleuze et écrivans. Littérature et philosophie*, éd. par B. Gelas et H. Micolet, Paris 2007.

Marculescu I., "Beckett and the Temptation of Solipsism," *Journal of Beckett Studies* (Special Double Issue) 1989, no. 11–12.

Myskja B. K., *The Sublime in Kant and Beckett. Ethics and Literature*, New York 2002.

Perloff M., "The Space of a door. Beckett and Poetry of Absence," in *The Poetics of Indeterminacy: Rimbaud to Cage*, Princeton 1983.

Philips J., "Beckett's Boredom and Spirit of Adorno," *Samuel Beckett Today / Aujourd'hui* (*After Beckett / D'après Beckett*) 2004, no. 14.

Pilling J., "Beckett's Proust," *Journal of Beckett Studies*, Winter 1976.

————., "The Significance of Beckett's 'Still'," *Essays in Criticism: A Quarerly Journal of Literary Criticism* 1978, no. 28.

Pothast U., *Die eigentliche metaphysische Tätigkeit. Über Schopenhauers Ästhetik und Anwendung durch Samuel Beckett*, Frankfurt/M. 1982.

Samuel Beckett and Music, edited by M. Bryden, Oxford 1998.

Samuel Beckett and the art of rhetoric, edited by E. Morot-Sir, H. Harper, D. McMillan, Chapel Hill 1976.

Szafraniec A, *Beckett, Derrida, and the Event of Literature*, Standford 2007.

Stasiuk A., "Twarz Samuela Becketta," *Kwartalnik Artystyczny* 1996, no. 4.

Trezise T., *Into the Breach: Samuel Beckett and the Ends of Literature*, Princeton 1990.

Tsushima M., *The Space of Vacillation: The Experience of Language in Beckett, Blanchot and Heidegger*, Bern 2003.

Willits C. G., "Le lecteur blanchotien. L'écrivain in situ," *Europe* 2007, no. 940–941.

Women in Beckett: Performance and Critical Perspectives, edited by L. Ben Zvi, Chicago 1990 (included in the volume: Ben Zvi L., "'Not I': Through a Tube Starkly"; Diamond E., "Speaking Parisian: Beckett and French Feminism"; Oppenheim L., "Female Subjectivity in 'Not I' and 'Rockaby'"; Scherzer D., "Portrait of Woman: The Experience of Marginality in 'Not I'"; Wilson A., "Her lips Moving: The Castrated Voice in 'Not I'").

Wynands S., *Iconic Spaces. The Dark Theology of Samuel Beckett's Drama*, Notre Dame, Indiana 2007.

Additional References

Adorno T., *The Jargon of Authenticity*, translated by Knut Tarnowski and Frederic Will, Evanston 1973.

———., *Negative Dialectics*, translated by E.B. Ashton, New York 1973.

———., "On Lyric Poetry and Society," in *Notes to Literature,* vol. 1, translated by Shierry Weber Nicholsen, New York 1991.

———., "Trying to Understand Beckett's Endgame," in *Notes to Literature,* vol. 1, translated by Sherry Weber Nicholsen, New York 1991.

———., "Parataxis: On Hölderlin's Late Poetry," in *Notes to Literature,* vol. 2, translated by Sherry Weber Nicholsen, New York 1992.

———., *Aesthetic Theory*, translated by Robert Hullot-Kentor, Minneapolis 1997.

———., *Prisms,* translated by Samuel and Shierry Weber, Boston 1982.

———., *Metaphysics. Concept and Problems*, edited by R. Tiedemann, translated by by Edmund Jephcott, Standford California 2001.

———., *Minima Moralia. Reflections on a Damaged Life*, translated by Edmund Jephcott, New York 2005.

Agamben G., *The Language and Death: The Place of Negativity*, translated by K. E. Pinkus, M. Hardt, Minnesota–Oxford 2006.

———. , "The Author as Gesture," in *Profanations,* translated by Jeff Fort, New York 2007.

Barthes R., *Écoute*, in *L'obvie et l'obtus. Essais critiques III*, Paris 1982.

———., *L'effet de réel*, in *Le bruissement de la langue. Essais critiques IV*, Paris 1984. In English, see "The Reality Effect," in *The Rustle of Language*, translated by Richard Howard, New York 1989.

————., "Pomysł na 'Poszukiwanie'," translated by M. P. Markowski, in *Lektury*, selected, edited with an afterword by Michał Paweł Markowski, Warsaw 2001.

Bataille G., "A Preface to 'Madame Edwards'," in *Erotism*, translated by Mary Dalwood, San Franscisco 1986.

————., *Les larmes d'Eros*, Paris 1971. In English, see *The Tears of Eros*, translated by Peter Connor, San Franscisco 2001.

————., *Inner Experience,* translated by Stuart Kendall, Albany 2014.

Baudelaire Ch., "Of the Essence of Laughter, and generally of the Comic in the Plastic Arts," in *Selected Writings on Art and Artists,* translated by P.E. Charvet, Cambridge 1981.

Benjamin W., *Charles Baudelaire. Ein Lyriker im Zeitalter des Hochkapitalismus*, Berlin 1969. In English, see *The Writer of Modern Life: Essays on Charles Baudelaire*, translated by Howard Eiland, Cambridge 2006.

————., *Zwei Gedichte von Friedrich Hölderlin*, in *Gesammelte Schriften*, Frankfurt/M. 1974–1989, t. II (1). In English, see "Two Poems by Friedrich Hölderlin" in *Selected Writings*, edited by Marcus Bullock and Michael W. Jennings, Cambridge 2004.

————., *The Arcades Project,* translated by Howard Eiland and Kevin McLaughlin, Cambridge 2002.

Bielik-Robson A., *Duch powierzchni. Rewizja romantyczna i filozofia*, Kraków 2004.

Blanchot M., *La Part du feu*, Paris 1949. In English, see *The Work of Fire*, translated by Charlotte Mandell, Stanford 1995.

————., *L'espace littéraire*, Paris 1955. In English, see *The Space of Literature*, translated by Ann Smock, Lincoln 1989.

————., *Le livre à venir*, Paris 1959. In English, see *The Book to Come*, translated by Charlotte Mandell, Stanford 2002.

————., *L'attente l'oubli*, Paris 1962. In English, see *Awaiting Oblivion*, translated by John Gregg, Omaha 1999.

————., *L'Entretien infini*, Paris 1969. In English, see *Infinite Conversation*, translated by Susan Hanson, Minneapolis 1992.

————., *L'Amitié*, Paris 1971. In English, see *Friendship*, translated by Elizabeth Rottenberg, Stanford 1997.

————., *Le Pas au-delà*, Paris 1973. In English, see *The Step Not Beyond*, translated by Lycette Nelson, Albany 1992.

————., *L'écriture du désastre*, Paris 1980. In English, see *The Writing of the Disaster*, translated by Ann Smock, Omaha 1995.

————., *Madness of the Day,* translated by Lydia Davies, Barrytown 1995.

————., *Thomas the Obscure,* translated by Robert Lamberton, Barrytown 1995.

Bloom, H. "Freud and Beyond," in *Ruin the Sacred Truths*, Cambridge 1991.

————., *The Anxiety of Influence*, Oxford 1997.

Bohrer K.-H., *Ästhetische Negativität*, München 2002.

Boulez P., *Leçons de musique. Points de Repère III*, textes réunis et établis par J-J. Nattiez, présentations de J.-J. Nattiez et J. Goldman, préface posthume de Michel Foucault, Paris 2005.

Buci-Glucksmann Ch., *La folie du voir. De l'esthétique baroque*, Paris 1986.

————., "La paradoxe du moderne: Tristesse et Beauté," in *L'enjeu du beau. Musique et Passion*, Paris 1992.

Buczyńska-Garewicz H., *Metafizyczne rozważania o czasie*, Kraków 2003.

Bürger P., *The Decline of Modernism*, trans. Nicholas Walker, Cambridge 1992.

Ceronetti G., *Milczenie ciała*, translated by Maryna Ochab, Gdańsk 2004.

Cichowicz S., "Wyraz, zdarzenie, siła," introduction to G. W. Leibniz, *Korespondencja z Antoine'em Arnauldem*, translated by Stanisław Cichowicz i Jerzy Kopania, Warszawa 1998.

————., "Siła. Zarys pojęcia," Twórczość 2001, no. 8.

Cioran É. M., *On the Heights of Despair*, translated by Ilinca Zrifopol-Johnston, Chicago 1992.

————., *Brewiarz zwyciężonych*, translated by A. Dwulit i M. Kowalska, Warsaw 2004.

————., *Drawn and Quartered*, translated by Richard Howard, New York 2012.

Clément B., *L'invention du commentaire: Augustin, Jacques Derrida*, Paris 2000.

Coetzee J. M., *In the Heart of the Country*, New York 1982.

Collin F., *Maurice Blanchot et la question de l'écriture*, Paris 1986.

de Man P., *Allegories of Reading: Figural Language in Rousseau, Nietzsche, Rilke and Proust*, New Haven 1982.

de Man P., "Hegel on the Sublime," in *Aesthetic Ideology*, edited by Andrzej Warminski, Minneapolis 1996.

de Man P., "The Rhetoric of Temporality" in *Blindness and Insight*, New York 1996.

Deleuze G., *Francis Bacon. Logique de la senasation*, Paris 1984. In English, see *Francis Bacon: The Logic of Sensation*, translated by Daniel W. Smith, London-New York 2003.

————., *Logique du sens*, Paris 1968. In English, see *The Logic of Sense*, translated by Mark Lester, Charles Stivale, New York 1990.

————., *Le pli. Leibniz et le baroque*, Paris 1988. In English, see *Fold: Leibniz and the Baroque*, translated by Tom Conley, Minneapolis 1992.

————., *Difference and Repetition*, translated by Paul Patton, New York 1995.

————., *Proust and Signs*, translated by Richard Howard, Minneapolis 2004.

Derrida J., *De la grammatologie*, Paris 1966. In English, see *Of Grammatology*, translated by Gayatri Chakravorty Spivak, Baltimore 1998.

————., "De l'économie restreinte à l'économie générale. Un hegelianisme sans réserve," in *L'écriture et la différence*, Paris 1967. In English, see "From Restricted to General Economy: A Hegelianism without Reserve," in *Writing and Difference*, translated by Alan Bass, Chicago 1978.

————., *Glas*, Paris 1974. In English, see *Glas*, translated by John P. Leavey Jr., Richard Rand, Omaha 1986.

————., *La loi du genre*, in *Parages*, Paris 1986. In English, see "The Law of Genre," *Critical Inquiry*, vol. 7, no. 1, 1980.

————., *Désistance*, in *Psyché: Inventions de l'autre*, Paris 1987. In English, see *Psyche: Interventions of the Other*, vol. 2, translated by Peggy Kamuf, Stanford 2008.

————., *Ulysse Gramophone: Deux mots pour Joyce*, Paris 1987.

————., *Demeure. Maurice Blanchot*, Paris 1998. In English, see *Demeure: Fiction and Testimony*, translated by Elizabeth Rottenber, Stanford 2000.

————., *La littérature au secret. Une filiation impossible*, in *Le secret: motif et moteur de la littérature. Etudes réunies et introduction par Chantal Zabus avec une préface de Jacques Derrida*, Louvain-La-Neuve 1999. In English, see *The Gift of Death and Literature in Secret*, translated by David Wills, Chicago 2008.

————., *Mémoires d'aveugle. L'autoportrait et autres ruines*, Paris 1999. In English, see *Memoirs of the Blind: The Self-Portrait and Other Ruins*, translated by Pascale-Ann Brault, Michael Nass, Chicago 1993.

————., *Le toucher. Jean-Luc Nancy*, Paris 2000. In English, see *On Touching: Jean-Luc Nancy*, translated by Christine Irizzary, Stanford 2005.

————., "Cogito and the History of Madness," in *Writing and Difference*, translated by Alan Bass, Chicago 1978.

————., "The Theatre of Cruelty and the Closure of Representation," in *Writing and Difference*, translated by Alan Bass, Chicago 1978.

————., "The Pit and the Pyramid: Introduction to Hegel's Semiology," in *Margins of Philosophy,* translated by Alan Bass, Chicago 1982.

————., "Signature Event Context," in *Margins of Philosophy,* translated by Alan Bass, Chicago 1982.

————., "The Supplement of Copula: Philosophy before Linguistics," in *Margins of Philosophy,* translated by Alan Bass, Chicago 1982.

————., "Qual Quelle: Valéry's Sources," in *Margins of Philosophy,* translated Alan Bass Chicago 1982.

————., "Before the Law," in *Acts of Literature,* edited by Derek Attridge, New York: Routledge, 1992.

————., "This Strange Institution Called Literature": An Interview with Jacques Derrida, in *Acts of Literature*, New York 1992.

————., "Che cos'é la poesia?," translated by M. P. Markowski, *Literatura na Świecie* 1998, nr 11–12.

————., *Monolingualism of the Other: The Prosthesis of Origin*, translated by Patrick Mensah Stanford 1998.

————., *Voice and Phenomenon: Introduction to the Problem of the Sign in Husserl's Phenomenology*, translated by Leonard Lawlor, Evanston 2010.

Descartes, R. *Meditations on First Philosophy*, translated by Michael Moriarty, Oxford 2008.

Didi-Huberman G., *Devant l'image. Question posée aux fins d'une historie de l'art*, Paris 1990. In English, see *Confronting Images: Questioning the Ends of a Certain History of Art*, translated by John Goodman, University Park 2009.

————., *Ce qui nous voyons, ce qui nous regarde*, Paris 1992.

Dolar M., *A Voice and Nothing More*, Cambridge–London 2006.

Fischer-Lichte E., *Estetyka perfomatywności*, przeł. Mateusz Borowski, Małgorzata Sugiera, Kraków 2008.

Foucault M., "The Order of Discourse," in *Untying the Text: A Post-Structuralist Reader*, edited by Robert J. C. Young, Boston 1981.

————., "Language to Infinity" in *The Essential Works of Michel Foucault: Aesthetics, Method, and Epistemology*, edited by James D. Faubion. New York 1998.

————., "Theatrum Philosophicum" in *The Essential Works of Michel Foucault: Aesthetics, Method, and Epistemology*, edited by James D. Faubion. New York 1998.

————., "What is an Author?" in *Aesthetics, Method, and Epistemology*, edited by James D. Faubion, New York 1999.

Gasché R., *The Wild Card of Reading: On Paul de Man*, Cambridge 1998.

Geier M., *Gra językowa filozofów. Od Parmenidesa do Wittgensteina*, translated by Janusz Sidorek, Warsaw 2000.

Habermas J., *The Philosophical Discourse of Modernity: Twelve Lectures Studies in Contemporary German Social Thought*, translated by Frederick Lawrence, Cambridge 2000.

Hegel G. W. F., *Phenomenology of Spirit*, translated by A.V. Miller, Oxford 1976.

————., *Hegel's Aesthetics: Lectures on Fine Art, 2 vols.*, translated by T. M. Knox, Oxford 1998.

————., *Encyclopaedia of the Philosophical Sciences, 3 vols.*, translated by A. V. Miller, J. N. Findlay, Oxford 2004.

————., *The Science of Logic*, translated by George Di Giovanni, Cambridge 2010.

Heidegger M., "The Nature of Language," in *On the Way to Language*, translated by Peter D. Hertz, Joan Stambaugh, New York 1982.

————., *Kant and the Problem of Metaphysics*, translated by Richard Taft, Idianapolis 1997.

————., "On the Essence of Ground," in *Pathmarks*, translated by William McNeil, Cambridge 1998.

————., *Elucidation of Hölderlin's Poetry*, translated by Keith Hoeller, Amherst 2000.

————., *Being and Time*, translated by Joan Stambaugh and Denis J. Schmidt, Albany 2010.

Hill L., *Blanchot: Extreme Contemporary*, London–New York 1997.

Horkheimer, M. T. W. Adorno, *Dialectic of Enlightenment: Philosophical Fragments*, translated by Edmund Jephcott. Stanford 2002.

Husserl, E. *Cartesian Meditations*, translated by Dorion Cairns, The Hague 1982.

Iser W., *Apelacyjna struktura tekstów. Niedookreślenie jako warunek oddziaływania prozy literackiej*, przeł. W. Bialik, w: *Teorie literatury XX wieku. Antologia*, pod red. A. Burzyńskiej, M. P. Markowskiego, Kraków 2007.

Janion M., "Nadmiar bólu," in *Żyjąc tracimy życie. Niepokojące tematy egzystencji*, Warszawa 2001.

Jay M., *Adorno*, Cambridge 1984.

————., *Songs of Experience: Modern American and European Variations on a Universal Theme*, Berkeley 2006.

Kafka F., "Reflections on Sin, Suffering, Hope, and the True Way," *in The Great Wall of China: Stories and Reflections*, translated by Willa and Edwin Muir, New York 1946.

————., *The Blue Octavo Notebooks*, translated by Ernst Kaiser, Eithne Wilkins, Cambridge 2004.

————., "The Silence of the Sirens," *in The Complete Stories*, edited by Nahum. N. Glatzer, New York 2012.

Kant I., *Critique of Pure Reason*, translated by Paul Guyer, Allen Wood, Cambridge 1999.

————., *Critique of the Power of Judgment*, translated by James Creed Meredith, Cambridge 2001.

————., *Anthropology from a Pragmatic Point of View*, edited by Robert B. Louden, Manfred Kuehn, Cambridge 2006.

Kierkeggard S., *Fear and Trembling / Repetition*, translated by Edna H. Hong, Howard V. Hong Princeton 2013.

Komendant T., *Władze dyskursu. Michel Foucault w poszukiwaniu siebie*, Warsaw 1994.

Kristeva J., *L'Expérience et la pratique*, in *Polylogue*, Paris 1977.

Lacoue-Labarthe Ph., *L'Echo du sujet*, in *Le sujet de la philosophie. Typographies 1*, Paris 1979. In English, see *The Subject of Philosophy*, edited by Thomas Trezise, Minneapolis 1993.

Lacoue-Labarthe Ph., Nancy J.-L., *L'Absolu littéraire. Théorie de la littérature du romantisme allemand*, Paris 1978. In English, see *The Literary Absolute: The Theory of Literature in German Romanticism*, translated by Philip Barnard, Cheryl Lester, Albany 1988.

Levinas E., *Time and the Other*, translated by Richard A. Cohen, Pittsburgh 1990.

————., "The Poets Vision," in *Proper Names*, translated by Michael B. Smith, Stanford 1996.

————., "The Servant and Her Master," in *Proper Names*, translated by Michael B. Smith, Stanford 1996.

————., "Exercises on 'The Madness of the Day'," in *Proper Names*, translated by Michael B. Smith, Stanford 1997.

————., *Existence and Existents*, translated by Alphonso Lingis, Pittsburgh 2001.

————., *Totality and Infinity*, translated by Alphonso Lingis, Pittsburgh 2007.

Melberg A., *Theories of Mimesis*, Cambridge 1995.

Merleau-Ponty M., *L'Oeil et L'Esprit*, Paris 1964.

————., *The Visible and Invisible*, translated by Alphonso Lingis, Evanston 1969.

Michalski K., *Logika i czas. Próba analizy Husserlowskiej teorii sensu*, Warszawa 1988.

Morawski S., *Czytanie Adorna*, w: tegoż, *Na zakręcie: od sztuki do po-sztuki*, Kraków 1985.

Nancy J.-L., *Discours de la syncope. Logodedalus*, Paris 1976. In English, see *The Discourse of the Syncope: Logodaedalus*, translated by Saul Anton, Stanford 2008.

————., *Ego sum*, Paris 1979.

————., "Le rire, la presence", in *Une pensée finie*, Paris 1990. In English, see "Wild Laughter in the Throat of Death," *MLN*, Vol. 102, No. 4, French Issue. (Sep., 1987), pp. 719-736.

————., *À l'écoute*, Paris 2002. In English, see *Listening*, translated by Charlotte Mandell, New York 2007.

Nietzsche F., *Unfashionable Observations*, translated by Richard T. Grey, Stanford 1999.

————., *Beyond Good and Evil*, translated by Walter Kaufmann, Cambridge 2002.

Nycz R., *Język modernizmu. Prolegomena historycznoliterackie*, Wrocław 1997.

————., "Tropy 'ja'. Koncepcje podmiotowości w literaturze polskiej ostatniego stulecia," in *Język modernizmu*, Wrocław 1997.

————., "Gest śmiechu. Z przemian świadomości literackiej początku wieku XX (do pierwszej wojny światowej)," in *Język modernizmu*, Wrocław 1997.

————., "Tezy o mimetyczności," in *Tekstowy świat. Poststrukturalizm a wiedza o literaturze*, Kraków 2000.

Quattara B., *Adorno et Heidegger: une controverse philosophique*, Paris–Montréal 1999.

Politzer H., "Milczenie syren," in *Milczenie syren. Studia z literatury niemieckiej i austriackiej*, przeł. J. Hummel, Warszawa 1973.

Poulet G., *L'espace proustien*, Paris 1963.

————., "Mallarmé," translated by D. Eska, in *Metamorfozy czasu. Szkice krytyczne*, edited by J. Błoński and M. Głowiński, Warsaw 1977.

————., "Sen Kartezjusza," translated by D. Eska, in *Metamorfozy czasu. Szkice krytyczne*, edited by J. Błoński i M. Głowiński, Warsaw 1977.

————., "Czas i przestrzeń Prousta," translated by J. Błoński, in *Proust w oczach krytyki światowej*, edited by J. Błoński, Warsaw 1990.

————., *Myśl nieokreślona*, translated by T. Swoboda, Warsaw 2004.

Proust M., *W poszukiwaniu straconego czasu*, translated by T. Żeleński (Boy), Warsaw 1992.

Przybylski R., *Pustelnicy i demony*, Kraków 1994.

Rancière J., *La parole muette. Essai sur les contradictions de la littérature*, Paris 1998. In English, see *Mute Speech: Literature, Critical Theory, and Politics*, translated by James Swenson, New York 2011.

Ravel E., *Maurice Blanchot et l'art au XXème siècle: une esthétique du désoeuvrement*, Amsterdam–New York 2007.

Rouger F., *Existence – Monde – Origine. Essai sur le sens d'être de la finitude*, préface Jean-Luc Nancy, Paris–Montreuil 1994.

Schopenhauer, A. "Additional Remarks on the Docrine of the Suffering of the World," in *Philosophical Writings*, edited by Wolfgang Schirmacher, New York Continuum, 1998.

————., *The World as Will and Representation*, Vol. 1, Cambridge 2010.

Siemek M. J., *Heglowskie pojęcie podmiotowości*, in *Hegel i filozofia*, Warsaw 1998.

Sloterdijk P., *Critique of Cynical Reason*, translated by Michael Eldred, Minneapolis 1988.

Wittgenstein L., *Philosophical Investigations*, London 2009.

Žižek S., *On Belief*, New York 2003.

Cross-Roads
Polish Studies in Culture, Literary Theory, and History

Edited by Ryszard Nycz and Teresa Walas

www.peterlang.com